# A SHOCK TO THOUGHT

'For those interested in new developments in aesthetics, literature and cultural theory, this will prove an indispensable volume and an inspiring collection.'

Keith Ansell Pearson, *University of Warwick*

'This volume will have a prominent, indeed privileged, place at the interface between philosophical and aesthetic reflections within the burgeoning field of Deleuze–Guattari studies.'

Charles Stivale, *Wayne State University*

*A Shock to Thought* brings together a collection of outstanding essays that explore the implications of Deleuze and Guattari's philosophy of expression in a number of contemporary contexts: beauty vs. the sublime in post-modernism, sensation and politics, the conditions of cultural emergence, and the virtual in politics, poetry, dance, music and digital culture. The volume also makes available an interview with Guattari which clearly restates the 'aesthetic paradigm' that organizes both his and Deleuze's work.

*A Shock to Thought* will be of interest to all those in philosophy, cultural studies and aesthetics.

**Brian Massumi** is in the Department of Communication at the Université de Montréal. He is the translator of Deleuze and Guattari's *A Thousand Plateaus* and the author of *The User's Guide to Capitalism and Schizophrenia: Deviations from Deleuze and Guattari* and *Parables for the Virtual: Movement, Affect, Sensation.*

# A SHOCK TO THOUGHT

Expression after Deleuze and Guattari

*Edited by Brian Massumi*

London and New York

First published 2002
by Routledge
11 New Fetter Lane, London EC4P 4EE

Simultaneously published in the USA and Canada
by Routledge
29 West 35th Street, New York, NY 10001

Reprinted 2003

*Routledge is an imprint of the Taylor & Francis Group*

Typeset in Bembo by Taylor & Francis Books Ltd
Printed and bound in Great Britain by
Biddles Ltd, Guildford and King's Lynn

*British Library Cataloguing in Publication Data*
A catalogue record for this book is available from the British Library

*Library of Congress Cataloging in Publication Data*
A shock to thought: expression after Deleuze and Guattari /
[edited by] Brian Massumi.
p.cm.
Includes bibliographical references.
1. Literature–Aesthetics. 2. Aesthetics. 3. Deleuze, Gilles–Criticism and
interpretation. 4. Guattari, Félix–Criticism and interpretation. I. Massumi, Brian.
PN45 .S416 2002
801′93–dc21                                          2001058882

ISBN 0–415–23803–X
ISBN 0–415–23804–8

# CONTENTS

# CONTENTS

# CONTENTS

\*ANTONIN ARTAUD, CITED IN CATHERINE DALE

# ILLUSTRATIONS

# CONTRIBUTORS

**Paul Bains** is the translator of *Power and Invention* by Isabelle Stengers (1997) and of Félix Guattari's *Chaosmosis: An Ethico-Aesthetic Paradigm* (with Julian Pefanis) (1995). His recently completed doctorate from Murdoch University, Australia was on *The Primacy of Relations*. He continues to research the topic of minds and their brains with the invaluable guidance of the Center for Neurobiological Investigations, Ministry of Health and Welfare, Argentine Republic.

**Alan Bourassa** is an assistant English professor at St. Thomas University in Fredericton, New Brunswick. He is currently working on a book entitled *Writing the Non-Human: Faulkner, Wharton and the Anglo-American Novel.*

**Catherine Dale** is a doctoral student in the English Department at the University of Melbourne.

**Aden Evens** is a postdoctoral fellow at the Pembroke Center at Brown University. His book-in-progress reflects his interests in philosophy, cultural theory, music, mathematics, and the sciences. Like many interdisciplinary scholars, he moves around a lot, but his family and piano are in Boston.

**Gary Genosko** is Canada Research Chair in Sociology at Lakehead University in Thunder Bay, Ontario. He is the author of *Félix Guattari: An Aberrant Introduction* (forthcoming), and the editor of *The Guattari Reader* (1996) and *Deleuze and Guattari: Critical Assessments* (Routledge, 2001).

**José Gil** is professor of philosophy at the University of Lisbon and at the Collège International de Philosophie in Paris. He is the author of *Metamorphoses of the Body* (1998) and *Fernando Pessoa ou la métaphysique des sensations* (1988).

**Mani Haghighi** lives in Tehran and Toronto. He is the Persian translator of Michel Foucault's *Ceci n'est pas une pipe*, and has edited an anthology of postmodern texts, *The Aporia of Signs* (1995).

**Michael Hardt** is associate professor of literature at Duke University. He is the author of *Gilles Deleuze: An Apprenticeship in Philosophy* (1993) and co-author with Antonio Negri of *Labor of Dionysus* (1994) and *Empire* (2000).

**Thomas Lamarre** is associate professor of East Asian Studies at McGill University. He is the author of *Uncovering Heian Japan: An Archaeology of Sensation and Inscription* (2001) and *Shadows on the Screen: Tanizaki Junichirô on Cinema and Oriental Aesthetics* (forthcoming). He is currently co-editing a volume on 'The Impacts of Modernities' for *Traces: A Multilingual Series of Cultural Theory*.

**Bracha Lichtenberg Ettinger** is an internationally renowned artist, feminist theorist, and psychoanalyst. She is Professor of Psychoanalysis and Aesthetics at Leeds University. Her recent solo exhibitions include The Drawing Center (New York), Museum of Modern Art (Oxford), The Israel Museum (Jerusalem) and the Palais des Beaux Arts (Brussels). She is the author of *Regard et Espace-de-bord matrixiels* (La Letter Volée), forthcoming from the University of Minnesota Press under the title *Matrixial Gaze and Borderspace*.

**Brian Massumi** teaches in the communication department of the Université de Montréal. He is the author of *Parables for the Virtual: Movement, Affect, Sensation* (2002), *A User's Guide to Capitalism and Schizophrenia: Deviations from Deleuze and Guattari* (1992), and (with Kenneth Dean) *First and Last Emperors: The Absolute State and the Body of the Despot* (1993).

**Melissa McMahon** is completing a Ph.D. on Deleuze and Kant in the Department of Philosophy at the University of Sydney. She is translator of numerous published articles in the area of modern French philosophy and film theory, and most recently translated and introduced an article by Antona Soulez on Wittgenstein for a special issue of *Hypatia* on contemporary French women philosophers.

**Andrew Murphie** is a Senior Lecturer in Media and Communications at the University of New South Wales, Sydney. He has published on a range of issues: performance and the visual arts, popular music, contemporary cultural theory, virtual media and digital aesthetics. He is currently writing a book in the area of culture and technology with John Potts and is working on two other books on machines, ethics and aesthetics. He has in the past worked as a marketing manager and production manager for arts companies, and as a freelance theatre director.

**Steven Shaviro** teaches in the Cinema Studies Program at the University of Washington. He is the author of *Passion and Excess* (1990), *The Cinematic Body* (1993) and *Doom Patrols* (1997).

**Stephen Zagala** (né O'Connell) is currently pursuing a Ph.D. in the Centre for Cross-Cultural Research at the Australian National University. His thesis is concerned with the cultivation of dynamic visual forms in the Melanesian archipelago of Vanuatu. He continues to travel with Deleuze, but prefers to keep him concealed under a newly acquired pith helmet.

# INTRODUCTION

## Like a thought

*Brian Massumi*

because they've said too much to be born
and said too much in being born
not to be reborn
and take a body

(Artaud, 1999: 88)

### The world does not exist outside of its expressions[1]

A clearer statement of the importance of the concept of expression for the philosophy of Deleuze and Deleuze–Guattari would be hard to find. Their entire ontology, this formula proclaims, revolves around it. A less fashionable concept, for late twentieth-century European thought, would also be hard to find. For many years, across many schools, 'expression' has been anathema. The underlying assumption has been that any expressionism is an uncritical subjectivism. Expression conjures up the image of a self-governing, reflective individual whose inner life can be conveyed at will to a public composed of similarly sovereign individuals – rational atoms of human experience in voluntary congregation, usefully sharing thoughts and experiences. In a word: 'communication'. Communicational models of expression share many assumptions. These include the interiority of individual life, its rationality, an effective separation into private and public spheres, the voluntary nature of the collective bonds regulating that separation, the possibility of transparent transmission between privacies or between the private and the public, and the notion that what is transmitted is fundamentally information. All of these assumptions have been severely tested by structuralist, poststructuralist, post-modern, and postpostmodern thought. Communication has long since fallen on hard times and with it, expression.

Communication, Deleuze and Guattari agree, is a questionable concept. Yet they hold to expression. *'What takes the place of communication is a kind of expressionism.'*[2]

## Neither common form nor correspondence

So closely bound have the concepts of expression and communication become that Deleuze and Guattari's insistence on discarding one while retaining the other might well seem quixotic. There are certainly consequences to going that route, and Deleuze and Guattari are not shy about them. A willingness is required to forego certain bedrock notions, with potentially unsettling repercussions even for anti-communicationalists.

'One can never', Deleuze and Guattari begin, 'assign the form of expression the function of simply representing, describing, or averring a corresponding content: there is neither correspondence nor conformity' (1987: 86). So far so good. This is a restatement of the well-known critique of the referential function of language that is presupposed by the communicational model, and the renunciation of which unites its foes. Deleuze and Guattari join the critics, then step away. They go on to say that 'it would be an error to believe that content determines expression by causal action, even if expression is accorded the power not only to "reflect" content but to act upon it in an active way' (1987, 89).

The assertion that expression is actively formative of its content, or its 'objects', is a constructivist strategy underpinning most contemporary anti-communicational semiotics. It performs a causal twist enabling semiotically savvy ideology critique. 'Discourse', by this account, constructs the subject by constructing the objects in polarity with which the subject forms. The subject's expression is still causally linked to its content, but the nature of the link has changed. What traditionally appeared as a one-way determination of expression by a mirroring of or a moulding by its content (the correspondence or conformity of 'representing, describing, or averring') reappears as a formative polarity (a subject–object dialectic). It is less that the subject willfully speaks its contents than that it is spoken, unwitting, by its discursively orchestrated object-relations. If the spoken subject expresses anything, it is – indirectly – its own circuitous determination: the anything-but-transparent dialectic of its orchestrated formation. The ultimate content of all expression is this occulted determinative power incumbent in discourse – which the critic has the counter-power, if not political duty, to uncover.

When Deleuze and Guattari call into question this dialectical solution, they are abandoning ideology critique along with its communicational nemesis. Why throw out baby-ideology with the dirty communicative bathwater? If you choose to abstain from both communication and ideology, what's left? Not 'postmodernism'.[3] From a Deleuze–Guattarian perspective these three approaches, for all their differences, have too much in common philosophically. What they share is an attachment to a concept of determination predicated, in one way or another, despite any protestations to the contrary, on conformity and correspondence.

Traditionally, for communicational purposes, expression is anchored to a 'content'. The content is viewed as having an objective existence prior and exterior to the form of its expression. The assumed solidity of the content transfers, across the mirror-like correspondence or moulded conformity, into a trustworthiness of the subjective expression. Moulded, mirroring, expression faithfully conveys content: re-presents it at a subjective distance. This enables communication, understood as a faithful exchange of contents transmitted at a convenient distance from their objective emplacement. In this model, content is the beginning and end of communicative expression: at once its external cause and its guarantee of validity. This causal guarantee is crucial, because the subjective distancing upon which communication is predicated enables deception no less than exchange. If there were no common form or correspondence, who could say? And what? Anyone, anything – out of control. The 'postmodern' is an image of communication out of control. Seeming to have lost its mooring in objective conformity or correspondence, it appears uncaused, unmotivated, in endless, unguaranteed 'slippage'.

One of the reasons Deleuze and Guattari find the basic communicational model questionable is that it assumes a world of already-defined things for the mirroring. Expression's potential is straight-jacketed by this pre-definition. In *Logic of Sense* (1990a), Deleuze confronts the 'propositional' view of language underpinning this model, arguing that it allows three fundamental operations, none of which are up to the measure of expression's potential: a three-sleeved straight-jacket. The first cuff, 'designation', concerns the faithfulness of the expression to the *particular* state of things with which it is in conformity or to which it corresponds: its objectivity. 'Manifestation' is the subjective correlate of designation. It pertains to the *personal* desires and beliefs owned up to by the designating 'I'. 'Signification' is founded on the capacity of designation to apply beyond particulars to kinds, in other words to *general* ideas and their implications: 'it is a question of the relation of the word to universal or general concepts, and of syntactic connections to the implications of the concept'.[4] If designation concerns the true and the false, signification concerns the *conditions* of truth and falsehood: 'the aggregate of conditions under which the proposition' would be 'true'. 'The condition of truth', it must be noted, 'is not opposed to the false, but to the absurd' (Deleuze, 1990: 14–15).

The wilful absurdism of postmodernisms of the Baudrillardian kind took off from signification. The 'simulation' they celebrated is an unmooring of the conditions of truth from the true and the false: from designation. Unhinged from designation, lacking a referent, the productive operation of the conditions of truth becomes indistinguishable from a proliferating absurdity: an absurdity by 'unmotivated' excess of signification. These particular counterconditions of absurdity, however, were staged by postmodernists insufficiently unbuttoned from the true – and arguably nostalgic for it – as a parody or ironic subversion of the truth rather than something other than it, to which it is 'opposed'. Both parody and irony covertly conserve the true. They need the idea of a conformity or correspondence between expression and content as a

foil. Ultimately, the postmodern absurdity is to retain the true *in order*, repeatedly, to lampoon it by bracketing its objective anchoring. Why not just be
done with it?[5] From a Deleuzian perspective, parody and irony protest too
much. The way in which they performatively foreground the signifying virtu-
osity of the speaking or writing subject seem distinctly to manifest a personal
desire for a certain kind (a cynical kind) of masterful presence. The 'nostalgia'
their postmodern practitioners have sometimes been accused of may have
betokened, even more than a residual attachment to the truth, an investment
in manifestation: a nostalgia for the master-subject whose 'death' postmodernism manifestly announced.[6] The same might be said of a precursor of this
form of postmodernism, surrealism. More sober postmodernisms were to find
somewhere seriously absurd to take the unanchoring of the true: into the
sublime.[7]

The ideological approach is in many ways closer to Deleuze and Guattari's
approach than either the communicational or postmodern, in spite of their
frequent criticisms of it. It has major advantages over them. For one thing, it
links the workings of language to a problematic of power, insisting on the
intrinsic connection between language and extra-linguistic forces. It also
breaks the symmetry between expression and things 'as they are' already.
Models of mirroring or moulding – in a word, representational models – see
the basic task of expression as faithfully reflecting a state of things. They focus
on the 'as is', as it is taken up by language. Ideology critique focuses on the
'what might be'. Its preoccupation is change. To open the way for change, it
must break the symmetry between the saying and the said. It does this by
transforming the content-expression correspondence into an asymmetry, as
subject–object polarity. The question is displaced onto what governs their
dialectic: how the two come together, or what mediates their interaction.
Mediation steals centre stage from conformity and correspondence.

The problem for Deleuze and Guattari is that conformity and correspondence sneak back in through the back door. The subject formed through the
dialectic does not simply mirror its objects. It embodies the system of mediation. It is a physical instantiation of that system. That is the ideological
proposition: that a subject is made to be in conformity with the system that
produced it, such that the subject reproduces the system. What reproduces the
system is not what the subject says *per se*. The direct content of its expressions
do not faithfully reflect the system, since the relation of the system to its own
expressed content has been 'mystified' by mediation. The fundamental mystification consists in making the subject's adhesion to the system appear as a
choice. Mystified, the subject must be trained to truly express the system it has
unwittingly been reproducing. This is the role of critique.

The subject does not express the system. It *is* an expression of the system.
The system expresses itself in its subjects' every 'chosen' deed and mystified
word – in its very form of life (its habitus, as Pierre Bourdieu (2000: 256–85)
would say). Where, in the conformity and correspondence between the life-

form of the subject and the system of power that produced it, has the potential for change gone? Conscious critique seems an unloaded weapon in the face of the relentless acting out of powers of conformity on the preconscious level of habitus. The only conscious force strong enough to counter those powers is self-interest: a subject must come to an unmystified consciousness of its own interests as occupying the position it does. But doesn't that lock the subject all the more firmly into position? And aren't decisions truly motivated by self-interest a matter of choice? Doesn't making a true choice depend on seeing through mystification to an analysis of the real state of affairs (designation), then faithfully conveying the general applicability of the ideological propositions arrived at (signification) to others of your class, as one sovereign individual in voluntary congregation, usefully sharing thoughts and experiences (manifestation)? Aren't we back at the same old communicational model? Designation, manifestation, signification resurgent. Perhaps insurgent. But is this change enough?

The move to save change by breaking the symmetries at the basis of the propositional view of language has back-fired. They return, in conformity and correspondence, as if in confirmation of the doctrine that production is always actually, systematically, reproduction. If production is reproduction, then life is trapped in a vicious circle: that of the systemic repetition of its own formation (wholesale or in self-interested part). Still the initial emphasis has shifted from form, as mirrored or moulded, to form*ation* And it has done so in a framework that broadens the vistas of expression. It is no longer a question of language narrowly defined. It is also a question of extra-linguistic forces operating through language, as well as unspoken systems of signs (what the configuration of objects in the social field, and their patterns of accessibility, indirectly 'tells' the subject-in-the-making of its assigned position). As we will see in the course of this introduction, Deleuze and Guattari agree that the subject is in a sense spoken by extra-linguistic forces of expression, and that this impersonal speaking is not a matter of choice. But they do not see anything 'hidden' to uncover, nor are they willing to reduce the expressing individual to an instantiation of a system. From their perspective, the force of expression and the linguistically formed exercises of power it often fuels are painfully evident. The force of expression, however, strikes the body first, directly and unmediatedly. It passes transformatively through the flesh before being instantiated in subject-positions subsumed by a system of power. Its immediate effect is a differing. It must be made a reproduction. The body, fresh in the throes of expression, incarnates not an already-formed system but a modification – a change. Expression is an event. The ideological question of how to think open a space for change in a grid-locked positional system is turned on its head. The task for a theory of expression is how to account for stability of form, given event. The key is to remember that 'emergence, mutation, change affect composing forces, not composed forms' (Deleuze, 1988: 87).

## A net on potential

Form*ation* cannot be accounted for if a common form is assumed, whether between content and expression or subject and system. If the world exhibits conformities or correspondences they are, precisely, *produced*. To make them the principle of production is to confuse the composing with the composed, the process with the product. Deleuze and Guattari call this 'tracing' (*décalque*) (1987: 12–15). A tracing approach overlays the product onto the process, on the assumption that they must be structurally homologous. The assumption is that you can conceptually superimpose them to bring out a common logical outline. When this procedure is followed, product and process appear as versions of each other: copies. Production coincides with reproduction. Any potential the process may have had of leading to a significantly different product is lost in the overlay of what already is.

Deleuze and Guattari take a simple step that carries them a long way from this procedure: they say that there is more than one form. The cornerstone of their theories of expression, in their solo as well as collaborative writings, is the principle that contents and expressions do not share a form. They each have their own form (or forms). Loosely basing themselves on the work of the linguist Louis Hjelmslev, they contend that there are any number of forms of content and forms of expression, each with their own substance or specific materiality. The tricky part is that there is no form of forms to bridge the gap. Deleuze and Guattari do not make this move in order to ascend to some meta-level. Between a form of content and a form of expression there is only the process of *their passing into each other*: in other words, an immanence. In the gap between content and expression is the immanence of their mutual 'deterritorialization'. This blurring of the boundaries is *in addition to* their formal distinction.

In dialogue with Michel Foucault, they use the example of the prison (1987: 66–7). The prison itself is the form of content. Of course a prison building is not a prison without prisoners. The prisoners' bodies are the substance of content for the prison as form of content. Of course not only prisoners' bodies enter a prison, guards and visitors do also. A body in a prison is not a prisoner unless it has been condemned for a crime. The judge's pronouncement of guilt contributes a substance to the form of content. A verbal expression has, in effect, passed into content. The pronouncement of guilt is a performative use of language, defined as an utterance which transforms the attributes and physical conditions of a body or state of things simply by being said. The performative is a direct avenue for the passage of expression into content. Deleuze and Guattari argue that every use of language carries a certain performative force, if only because it presupposes a conventional context of intelligibilty, and that conventional girding brings pressure to bear toward a certain manner of response. Every utterance is an 'order-word' in the sense that it moulds, subtly or directly, the potential actions of its addressees. This 'moulding' by language is very different from the mirror-like moulding of the communicational model. There is no resemblance between a pronouncement of guilt and an emprisonment. The performative relation of the expression to its content is not representational. The performative is a speech *act* which modifies the target body's own potential for action: it is an action on an action. As in the ideological model, the content is actively modified by expression. It is also not without return channels for affecting expression. However, whatever back-action there may be does not set in motion a dialectic. The reciprocal actions of content and expression have to pass a gap of non-resemblance which breaks not only the symmetry between content and expression assumed by the communicational model, but also the polarity on which ideological models' dialectical method is based. What happens in the break is the crux of the matter for Deleuze and Guattari.

The pronouncement of guilt is not the form of expression for the prison regime, but a linguistic contributor to its content. What then is the form of expression? What it is decidedly not, according to Foucault, is the meaning of the word 'prison'. Construing it that way limits expression once again to the conceptual or semantic level of designation, manifestation and signification, entirely missing the 'action on action', the direct, mutual involvement of language and extra-linguistic forces. In Foucault's analysis in *Discipline and Punish* (1977), as read by Deleuze and Guattari, the form of expression for which the prison is the form of content is 'delinquency'. The actions in the social field leading to the emergence of the modern prison system were most effectively expressed in a varied and widespread discourse on delinquency, not through philosophical or semantic reflections on the meaning of 'prison'. There was no essential connection between delinquency as form of expression and the prison as form of content. There is no logical or teleological reason why that particular articulation had to be. Its power was the cumulative result of a thousand tiny performative struggles peppered throughout the social field. The connection was *made*, and it was made collectively, under the control of no individual subject.

As aggregate formations, expression-content articulations have a tendency to drift over time. 'Delinquency' would subsequently migrate, extending to a new form of content: the school. The school-form owed not a little to the strategies of containment implemented in the prison. Content and expression were re-articulating themselves, toward a new aggregate result. How it would all re-crystallize into a functioning system of power was at no point a foregone conclusion. Which content elements would make the migration? How would they re-couple with what expressive elements? What new expressions might pass over into content? Which might cease to? What elements from forms of expression other than delinquency and forms of content other than the prison would make contributions to the mix? Another thousand tiny struggles. For a re-articulation of this kind to eventuate, for anything new to arise in the social field, established forms of content and expression must give of themselves. They shed functions, like so many seeds in search of new soil, or like branches for the grafting. It is of their cobbled-together nature to do so: to disseminate. And it is the inconstant nature of their sheddings to mutate as they disseminate. This mutational dissemination of transplantable functions is an instance of what Deleuze and Guattari call a 'deterritorialization'.

The point for Deleuze and Guattari is that in the drift of power formations 'there exist *intermediate states* between content and expression, expression and content ... through which a stratified system passes' (1987: 44). The system of established articulations passes into a mutational gap-state, filled with shed functions fallen free from their former implantations.[8] A deterritorialized function is no longer a function in the normal sense. What can you do with something that hasn't yet decided if it is to fall back in on the side of content or expression? What aim or object can it have as yet? What meaning? Nothing determinate. The articulatory sheddings are functions without the determinate functioning they will come to have: in a state of potential. Deleuze and Guattari call articulatory functions in an in-between state of mutational potential 'particles' of expression or 'asignifying signs'. If there is no individual subject capable of governing their drift, then what determines where they fall and what they grow into? What determines how they recombine and settle into an actual functioning as part of a new articulation or 'regime of signs'? Deleuze and Guattari call the orchestrator of expression the 'abstract machine'.

The 'machine' is abstract because the asignifying signs with which it concerns itself lack determinate form or actual content definition. Though abstract, they are not unreal. They are in transport. They constitute the dynamic 'matter' of expression. When they settle into rearticulation, they become 'substances': formed, functional elements of either content (a prisoner, for example) or expression (a phoneme perhaps). Deleuze and Guattari's matter of expression correlates with Hjelmslev's 'purport' (for which the French translation is *matière*). Purport, Hjelmselv writes, 'has no possible existence except through being substance for one form or another' (1969: 52)[9] It has no existence − only dynamic potential. It *comes into* existence through its capture by a content-expression articulation, as in a 'net'. Hjelmslev emphasizes the 'arbitrary' nature of this process. What is 'arbitrary' about it is the oddness of a quarry whose species does not preexist its capture, a prey whose determinate existence results from the casting of the hunter's net. Deleuze and Guattari do not favour the term arbitrary. It has too wan a logical ring for such an ontologically fraught struggle. From a Deleuze–Guattarian perspective, it would be better to say that the actual content of expression − what effectively comes to be signified, manifested, designated; its 'object' − *emerges* from expressive potential through a process of the capture of that potential, and that this emergence into being-determinate necessarily crosses a zone of systemic indeterminacy by virtue of which the whole affair is tinged with a passing element of chance. To the logical ring of the arbitrary, Deleuze and Guattari respond with a contingent tinge to the emergent.

## The primacy of expression

'There is a primacy of the collective assemblage of enunciation over language and words' (Deleuze and Guattari, 1987: 90). The 'collective assemblage of enunciation' is the prong of the abstract machine that settles asignifying signs back into a functional form of expression (the 'machinic assemblage of bodies' is the prong that does the same for content). It is not only the emphasis on the collective nature of the process that is worth remarking. More radically, Deleuze and Guattari are suggesting that there is an impersonal expressive agency that is not only not restricted to language, but whose process takes precedence over its operations. Expression is not in a language-using mind, or in a speaking subject *vis à vis* its objects. Nor is it rooted in an individual body. It is not even in a particular institution, because it is precisely the institutional system that is in flux. Expression is abroad in the world – where the potential is for what may become. It is non-local, scattered across a myriad struggles over what manner of life-defining nets will capture and contain that potential in reproducible articulations, or actual functions. Determinate minds, subjects, bodies, objects, and institutions are the result. The subject, its embodiment, the meanings and objects it might own, the institutions that come to govern them, these are all conduits through which a movement of expression streams. Expression adopts them for its temporary forms and substances, towards its own furtherance, in ongoing self-redefintion. 'The expressive is primary in relation to the possessive' (1987: 316).

It was a moral precept of a certain era that one must 'own' one's enunciative position. An imperative was issued to speak responsibly from personal experience. But if expression is abroad in the world, it is not fundamentally ownable. It may well be morally domesticatable under certain conditions – many a moralizing capture through the ages attests to this – but only secondarily. 'The "first" language, or rather the first determination of language, is "*indirect discourse*" – expression that finally cannot be attributed to a particular speaker. "Language is not content to go from a first party to a second party, from one who has seen to one who has not, but necessarily goes from a second party to a third party, neither of whom has seen"' (1987: 76–7). Expression is always on the move, always engrossed in its own course, over-spilling individual experience, nomadically evading responsibility. It is self-transporting, serially *across* experiences. 'There is a self-movement of expressive qualities' that momentarily crystallizes into actual objects and associated subject positions: 'expressive qualities are auto-objective' (1987: 317). Expression is captured in passing by its auto-objectifications, but only ever provisionally. In C.S. Peirces's terms, it operates in the element of

'thirdness': already included in every passage from one to another is a potential relay to a third. Even as expression settles into a particular articulation, it is
already extending what Deleuze and Guattari call 'probe-heads' to a next, as-
yet unknown destination: already shedding of itself, in the interests of its
moving on.[10] Expression's self-movement is a continual stretch. Expression is
tensile.

> 'To express is not to depend upon; there is an autonomy of expression'.
>
> (1987: 317)

What expression is most emphatically not dependent upon in the first
instance is any purportedly generally applicable moral rule assigning responsibility for it or toward it. There is indeed an ethics of expression, which
Deleuze and Guattari acknowledge and accept as a central problem. They
insist on the term 'ethics', as opposed to morality, because the problem in
their eyes is not in any primary fashion that of personal responsibility. It is a
basically pragmatic question of how one *performatively* contributes to the
stretch of expression in the world – or conversely prolongs its capture. This is
fundamentally a *creative* problem. Where expression stretches, potential determinately emerges into something new. Expression's tensing is by nature
creative. Its passing brings into definite being. It is *ontogenetic*. To tend the
stretch of expression, to foster and inflect it rather than trying to own it, is to
enter the stream, contributing to its probings: this is co-creative, an aesthetic
endeavour. It is also an ethical endeavour, since it is to ally oneself with
change: for an ethics of emergence. The English translators of Guattari's last
work were right to subtitle its project an 'ethico-aesthetic paradigm'.[11]

## Stretch to intensity

Pragmatically, an ethics of expression involves producing 'atypical expressions'.

> The atypical expression constitutes a cutting edge of deterritorializa-
> tion of language, it plays the role of *tensor*; in other words, it causes
> language to tend toward the limit of its elements, forms, or notions,
> toward a near side or beyond of language. The tensor effects a kind of
> transitivization of the phrase, causing the last term to react upon the
> preceding term, back through the entire chain. It assures an intensive
> and chromatic treatment of language.
>
> (Deleuze and Guattari, 1987: 99)

'Agrammaticality' brings out the tensile dimension of language by stretching
its elements beyond the limit of their known forms and conventional functions. The atypical expression pulls language into a direct contact with its own
futurity. It forcibly twists it into glints of forms, hints of contents, as-yet func-

tionless functions which, however 'unmotivated' or 'arbitrary', *could be*. Because they just were, after a fashion (germinally). The atypical expression puts the screws on the system of language in a way that forces its actual operation to overlap with its zone of potential. The same experimental torture also brings out the transitive element of thirdness, in a recursive mode, by 'causing the last term to react upon the preceding term, back through the entire chain'. The combined result is a *recursive futurity*. Language folds back on its own unfolding. Wrapped up in itself, language falls into a state of utter tension: intensity. Language has been made to coincide, 'on the near side or beyond' of its conventional usage, with its own *intensity*.

A recursive futurity is one of the ways Deleuze and Guattari talk about the *virtual*. It is a crucial element of their theory of expression that ethico-aesthetic practices of expression can directly access virtual forces. These are the forces of ontogenesis responsible for the stream of novation, caught at the moment of their just emerging: expression's momentum.[12] Certain practices of expression are capable of actualizing the momentum of emergence *as such*, uncaptured. This is expression in its free state, under formation, tortured but unbound (tortured and for that very reason unbound). The hitch is that to catch expression in the forming requires allying with forces of systematic *de*formation. It takes stretching and twisting: pain. The agrammatical experiment is a cry of expression.

Bearing in mind the performative dimension of expression, the 'atypical expression' could as well be a gesture, operating on systematizations of non-verbal expression. More challengingly, it could address the hinge between non-verbal and verbal expression, experimenting with the limits not only of a certain form of expression, but with the very nature of the content-expression articulation itself: how bodies and words couple and struggle; whether or in what circumstances they might pass into each other, as in expression's performative passing into content; how their mutual immanence must be *lived*, experienced most directly and intensely. If the agrammatical verbal expression is an ontogenetic cry, then the gestural atypical expression is its accompanying dance. So deforming can this 'tarantella' be that its asignifying violence can wrack the body and risk the life lending themselves to the process: a danger named Artaud. 'He danced his did'.[13]

## The autonomy of expression

It was said earlier that the 'abstract machine' was the 'expressive agency'. This is misleading. Putting it in those terms risks 'hypostasizing' the *process* that is expression: treating it as a substantive. To do so is to commit the 'tracing' error of placing the process of emergence on a level with its substantial products.

There is no entity to expression. There is no super-subject behind its movement. Its emerging into words and things is always an *event* before it is a designation, manifestation, or signification propositionally and provisionally attached to a subject. There is no 'form of forms' underneath or beyond, however such a thing might be conceived (whether as an ideological system, transcendental ego, or collective unconscious). While there is no form of forms, there *is* the event of events: a coming to pass through comings to be; the world as becoming. Hypostasizing process into a super-subject is the error of idealism (the 'ideo–' is in 'ideology' for a reason). Deleuze and Guattari's expressionism is in no way an idealism. It is an ontogenetic process philosophy: a philosophy of the event concerned directly with becoming.

Still, the 'production of subjectivity' is a central preoccupation of Guattari's work in particular, and within his corpus most particularly of *Chaosmosis* (1995). By 'production of subjectivity' Guattari does not only mean the actual subjects that emerge in the ontogenetic net articulating content and expression, determining their potential. He also means that the movement of expression is itself subjective, in the sense that it is self-moving and has determinate effects. It is an agency, only without an agent: a subjectless subjectivity.[14] The 'production of subjectivity' is also the self-production of expression's momentum.

There is nothing mystical in this notion. It is entirely natural (or: it is as natural as it is cultural). Nietzsche used the example of lightning to make the same point about the error of hypostasis, associating it as do Deleuze and Guattari with the propositional logic that necessarily attributes expression to a subject:

> It is ... only owing to the seduction of language (and of the fundamental errors of reason that are petrified in it) which conceives and misconceives all effects as conditioned by something that causes effects, by a 'subject' ... the popular mind separates lightning from its flash and takes the latter for an *action*, for the operation of a subject called lightning ... as if there were a neutral substratum behind [it] ... But there is no such substratum; there is no 'being' behind doing, effecting, becoming ... the deed is everything.
>
> (Nietzsche, 1967: 45)

The event is everything. There is no subject before or behind it whose deed it would be. It is an autonomous doing. Before the flash there is only potential, in a continuum of intensity: a *field* of charged particles. The triggering of the charge is a movement immanent to the field of potential, by which it plays out the consequences of its own intensity. The movement involves the field in its entirety. It is non-local, belonging directly to the dynamic relation *between* a myriad of charged particles. The flash of lightning expresses this non-local relation. Expression is always fundamentally of a *relation*, not a subject. In the expression, process and product are one. But this is a different process–product unity than the tracing kind. It is the unmediated unity of a processual immanence, involving neither external resemblance nor structural homology.[15] The lightning strike doesn't resemble, represent, or reproduce the charged field. It doesn't conform or correspond to it. It culminates it, in a playing out or performing of its intensity. Only with the culmination will the field have effectively been what it was: the conditions for lightning. The field of potential will have been determined. The deed is definitive. There is no going back on a strike of lightning. The doing of the did says it all. It is its everything.

And more. On top of everything, the flash can *also* be captured. All is not yet done and culminated if, for example, the movement is caught by a human eye. Having passed into that perception, the flash is a product separate from its process. It has passed from an autonomous expression into the content of a body and a life. Its now perceptual intensity (immanent to the neuronal field of potential of the brain) may seed, for example, a myth.[16] The event of the flash may be prolonged, becoming a content for a mythic form of expression. Zeus, for example, emerges to take the credit. A creator now owns the deed. A subject has been added to the expression, a doer to the deed. The energies creative of the flash have extended into myth creation: from physical ontogenesis to mythopoiesis. Once the heroic subject has emerged to claim his object, a 'tracing' relation may be established between the two substantives. Zeus is 'like' the lighting. He is as decisive and unforgiving as his thunderbolt. They share properties. They conform and they correspond. Properties: the flash has gone from the expressive to the possessive. The products of the creative process now seem to contain its intensity in their mutual reflection. They jointly own it, as if they contained the principle of their reciprocal formation in their own likeness. This is the derivative level of symmetrical process–product unity associated with the propositional model. When subject-Zeus next throws his object-thunderbolt, he expresses something other than that deed: he expresses his anger. The flash is now a proposition: a manifestation of his mood. The resemblance to lightning has passed from whole to part, from the god to his emotion. Expression is now more narcissistic than ontogenetic: all it can do is spin off further resemblances (in accordance with a rhetorical structure, in this case through a synecdoche).

All that expression is not, it has become. Creative to the last: so generously creative is expression that it agrees to its own conversion. It allows its process to be prolonged into a qualitatively different mode of operation. It flows into rhetorical captivity, possession by a form of content and a form of expression in narcissistic reflection. There is little use in critiquing this 'annulment' of expression in a perceptual separation of its product from its process.[17] In one way or another, expression always self-converts upon reaching perception. This is its way, and it is the way of perception: both are predicated on the independence of the product from the autonomy of the process. What expression loses in ontogenetic vivacity, it gains in longevity. The flash doesn't disappear into the black of night. It continues. Its pick-up by a different process is the price of its continuing. Its culmination, the effect of its playing out (in this case a strikingly optical effect), feeds forward into another productive process for which it provides a content. In this example, the process that picked up the flash and converted it from an autonomous form of expression into a form of content is creative in its own way: of myth. The capture of the content in 'narcissistic' rhetorical structure culminates the mythopoeic process. This second culmination, in the anti-flash of manifested resemblance, is also in fact productive, in a weak (homologous) way. It produces rhetorical figures. These readily form relays among themselves which settle into conventional circuits of association (structural propositions) constituting a self-reproducing system (for example, an oral or literary tradition). The violence of the flash has been domesticated to serve the functioning of a system operating according to its own rules of formation, at a certain level of reality. Lightning's capture has contributed to the addition of an organizational level to the world. The intitial ontogenesis, its continuation in mythopoiesis, and its second coming to an end in rhetorical poiesis are interlocking 'strata' of expression. Expression's impulse travels through the chain, creatively changing forms along the way, passing between content and expression as it crosses the gaps between the strata.

Deleuze and Guattari's ethics favours *affirming* expression, across all its meanderings, up to and including its annulment. Ethics is not about applying a critical judgement to expression's product. It is about evaluating where its processual self-conversions lead. The basic question is: does process continue across its capture? Is the crossing of the gaps, the transformative feed-forward between strata, drift enough to keep it creative? Or has it really reached the end of the stream? Has it entered an oxbow of stagnant resemblances where it can do no more than eddy in its own likeness, producing self-reflective homologies? Has its ontogenesis ceased to be a *heterogenesis* to become, systematically, a reproduction? Does the success of the system's self-reproduction create such a logjam that it backs up the flow of expression, spreading stagnation along its entire course, preventing still-striking autonomies of expression from making perceptual waves?

The next question is: can the logjam break? How can the stratified system be deterritorialized – made to pass into an 'intermediate state' between its established contents and their ordered expressions so that it crosses back over into a zone of systemic indeterminacy, re-tingeing with chance? How can expression rejoin a continuum of potential? How can its self-conversion to reproduction be reconverted to emergence? Can it reintensify? This is the entirely *pragmatic* question of how to perform an atypical expression capable of diverting the process into rebecoming. Emitting what experimental 'particles' of expression will recharge the creative field? Can the ontogenetic force be regained, out the far end of the strata, in flashes of language and gesture?[18]

## Sense and singularity

What Deleuze called the propositional model of language was characterized earlier as a three-sleeved straight-jacket on expression's movement: designation, manifestation, and signification; the particular, the personal, and the general. What every propositional system puts the squeeze on is the *singular*.

An approximation of the concept of the singular can be arrived at simply by considering a state of things not as a member of a class, or a particular instance of an existing type but (as was just done in the preceding example) as an occurrence.[19] An occurrence always presents chance-inflected variations, 'accidents' not exhibited by other occurrences with which a propositional system might be tempted to group it according to its order of resemblances. Confronted with these ungroupable aspects, the system can only apprehend them negatively, as anomalies. As anomalies, they can be systematically brushed aside as insignificant. The atypicalities slip out of signification's sleeves.

This asignified fall-out, however, is precisely what made the occurrence what it was: an event. Not just an event: *this* event. *This* event is its own every-thing, its own happening, a singularity. The singular is not reducible to a particular thing or state of things belonging, according to a logic of resem-blance, to a general type. It is not defined by what it shares with others of a kind. It is a self-defining field. It belongs only to its own field conditions of anomaly.

The singular is exactly as it happens. Other events may follow. Its happening may prove to have been the first in a series of occurrences carrying what may well be considered, under systematic comparison, the 'same' acci-dents. These cease retrospectively to be anomalies, becoming identifiable traits. On the basis of the shared properties lately assigned to them, the series of occurrences can now be grouped together as belonging to a type: a new type (a new form of content for the propositional system's forms of expression). The event has passed from the status of a singularity to that of a particular instance of a general type: a member of a collection. Propositional systems are type-casting collector mechanisms.

Paradoxically, this means that with the singular appears the potential of a collection to come. Another way of putting it would be to say that the singular includes a *prospective* generality. Something that has an eventful prospective on generality – but on which generality has as yet no compre-hending perspective – is 'exemplary'. Earlier, the atypical expression was characterized as a 'recursive futurity'. It was recursive in that its coming to pass enveloped a series of prior events, in an intense revisiting of the move-ment leading to its own emergence, from a last to a next-to-last, back up the chain of expression. Now it can be seen that the atypical expression is doubly intense. It also prospectively envelops a series.[20]

Deleuze and Guattari use the exemplary nature of singular expression to argue that even the most ostensibly personal expression may be directly polit-ical, in that it envelops a potential collective. For example, the subject of literary expression, to the extent that it is effectively creative, is not the indi-vidual author but a 'people to come' (1987: 345).[21] The atypical expression emits the potential for an unlimited series of further (collective) expressions by individuals who will retrospectively be assigned by a propositional system of capture to membership in a group (psychosocial type, class, ethnicity, nation). An order of allowable designations, manifestations, and significations will settle around their type-casting. A complementary order of conventional performative expressions will help manage this new form of content. The force of collective, expressive emergence will be streamed into stratified functions of power. Unless: the collectivity in the making resists pick-up by an established stratum, insisting on defining its own traits, in a self-capture of its own anomaly. In this case, they will retain a shade of the unclassifiable and a margin of unpredictability in the eyes (or net) of existing systems of reference, no matter how hard those systems try fully to contain them. The collection will appear as what it is, a multiplicity in flux, an expressive 'movement' or 'orientation' still under formation (especially if the collective learns to creatively shed its traits as confidently as it cultivates them).

In Guattari's terminology, the atypical expression is a 'nucleus of expression' that may evade capture long enough to continue its autonomous formation as a 'node' of self-creative or 'autopoietic' subjectification.[22] It is because the subject of a singular expression continues under formation, still yet-to-come, that its autopoiesis must be considered a 'subjectless' subjectivity. Shy of its definitive capture at the reproductive end of its stream, it is a process without a fully determinate agent or product (an open-ended subjectification).[23]

That the singular event belongs only to its own conditions of anomaly means that it is prior to and independent of the conditions of truth or falsehood that will be assigned to its unfolding once its collective has come (to an end). Deleuze links the concept of the people to come, the collective of expression still in throes of continuing formation, to the creative 'powers of the false'. Given the distinction he often makes between the generative nature of force on the one hand and power as containment on the other, and his statement cited above about the opposite of the truth, it might actually be better to call it a productive 'force of absurdity'. [24]

The singular's conditions of anomaly are counter-conditions of absurdity, but in an entirely different way than the postmodern. They are absurd not because they produce an *excess of* signification, but because what they produce is, as potential, *in excess* of it.[25] As it happens, the exemplary expression signifies nothing. Which is not to say it expresses nothing. It expresses, in and as its own event, even before any eventual capture or continuation, the field conditions that gave rise to it and the collective potential its occurrence envelops. This doubly intense 'absurdity' of ontogenetic conditioning and unrealized potential, wrapped anomalously in *this* event, is what, on broadest general level of his theories of expression, Deleuze calls *sense* (Hjelmslev's 'purport' as the net is just being cast but before it has closed definitively on its prey). Deleuze's logic of seriality and potential is what allows him to make sense of asignifying expression. In turn, it is the idea of asignifying expression that allows him to argue that speech and gesture can be literally (or is it literarily?) creative: ontogenetic; adding to reality.

It is important not to think of the creativity of expression as if it brought something into being from nothing. There is no *tabula rasa* of expression. It always takes place in a cluttered world. Its field of emergence is strewn with the after-effects of events past, already-formed subjects and objects and the two-pronged systems of capture (of content and expression, bodies and words) regulating their interaction: nets aplenty. In order to potentialize a new type, the atypical expression must evade these already established articulations. It must extract itself from captures ready and waiting, falling for an instant through the propositional mesh. 'Extracted from the proposition, sense is independent of it, since it suspends the proposition's affirmation and negation' (Deleuze, 1990: 32). It has entered the gap, the deterritorialized in-between of strata: the absurdity of the excluded middle. We may add propositional logics obeying the law of the excluded middle to the list of things expression is not fundamentally (but often and inevitably becomes): information, communication, ideology, rhetoric, postmodern slippage.

The evasive in-betweenness of expression's emerging into and continuing through a cluttered world is why it is never 'autonomous' in the sense of being a separate entity. Only a *process* is autonomous. A process is by nature relational, from its first strike to its recharging for more. The only autonomy is of unfolding relation. A corollary to this principle is: only an autonomy can be captured.

## Like a thought

The continuing of expression across experiences means that it is too big to fit the contours of an individual human body. Its moving-through envelops the sky-like immensity of its field conditions of emergence, and the numberless collectivity of a people to come. But in order to move through, it must move in. If expression's charge of potential were not incarnated in an individual body capable of renewing it, it would cease to be expressed. It would dissipate, unperceived, like the lightning flash you just missed seeing. Expression's culmination effects consent to perceptual pick-up by the human body. Not only, of course: non-human expression, including captures effected by other organisms, and even non-organic formations, are a recurring concern of Deleuze and Guattari.[26] There are any number of non-human strata in the world, with their own 'perceptual' mechanisms: means for picking up a charge of potential aflow in the world and capturing it in a stratum-forming self-production or reproduction. Many of these non-human formations are in fact integrated in the human body. A ray of light passing into the human eye strikes on the level of physics. Its impulse passes through many an interlocking level, from the physical to the chemical to the biological. On each level, it produces a dedicated effect that is captured as a content, and around which certain functions alimenting the self-regulating system will come to revolve. The cascading generation of alimentary effect and functional capture continues across the gaps between bodily strata. When it reaches the brain, the whole series repotentializes. Brain functioning serves as a hinge between the internal stratifications contained by the skin and the wider systems of capture into which the human organism as a whole is in turn integrated.

Deleuze, following Leibniz, considers every step along the chain a 'perception'. Before the perception reaches the 'molar' level where it can be experienced as a memory, thought, or sensation consciously belonging to the life of the organism as a whole, it has already been these partially and nonconsciously. It has been a crowd of stratum-specific 'molecular' or 'micro' perceptions. Each stratum has its own rules of content formation to feed its level-specific functioning, as well as unique forms of expression to transmit the generative impulse to other levels. Each stratum has its own self-generating mode of activity and effectivity: each is a mini-subjectivity. Or to use the term Guattari designed to foreground the autonomously relational nature of the interlocking strata, each is a 'part-subject'. The micro-perceptions occupying the rungs of this step-ladder of self-generation are and remain non-conscious. Their content is stratum-specific, and cannot be passed on as such. Only an aggregate effect of their busy populating of the body is transmitted. This cumulative crowd-effect is vague, but upon impact on each level it catalyzes a self-organizing of that stratum.[27] Effective but lacking content, the 'transmission' is not a communication. It is a 'transduction': a self-propagating movement seeding serial self-organizations, each differing in nature from the last but connected by a shared generative impulse.[28]

Expression's moving-through is non-consciously inflected in the body by a cascade of repeated determinations, no sooner followed by passings into the gaps of systemic indeterminacy between its strata. The body's layered processing injects as much chance inflection as it does serial definition, branding the cumulative effect of any entering impulse with a productive margin of unpredictabilty. The brain thrives on it. Creative uncertainty, according to Deleuze and Guattari, is in fact the brain's chief product. It is a specialized organ for producing functionless functions alimenting expressive experimentation. The brain, claimed Henri Bergson, is *the* organ of intensity, enveloping self-magnifying potential in its convoluted folds. Its operation, Deleuze and Guattari suggest, is 'a bit like tuning a television screen whose intensities bring out that which escapes the power of objective definition' (Deleuze and Guattari, 1994: 209). The brain itself is a subjectless subjectivity – all the better to relay with other autonomies of expression (in relation to which the human organism itself will be in operational continuity as a part-subject). 'From the cosmological to the microscopic, but also from the microscopic to the macroscopic' (Deleuze, 1993: 87). That was the story of the lightning, from the sky, in the eye, through myth to literary tradition: in a nature–culture continuum (the field of emergence that is the world).[29]

If expression were not incarnated in the human body in a way that doesn't just passively receive but actively repotentializes its moving-through, it would come to a stand-still on the retina. The human problem is that the charge of potential its perceptual apparatuses take in, to say nothing of the cerebral intensity they add, is too big to be contained in the body. Expression's passing through the body envelops, prospectively and retrospectively, levels cosmological and macroscopic. If the expressive momentum hits the body with its full ontogenetic force, it produces a compression shock. To convey the expressive potential 'faithfully' (with sufficient, creative absurdity) the body must transmit the reality of the shock. It's a torture, a multi-level, interlocking, self-magnifying torture.[30] The body is wracked. A tarantella of atypical expression pours forth, deforming. Its outpouring relays the torture to the conventional forms of content and expression with which or to which the body is expected to speak and gesture. The body has become an expressive event: a voluble singularity.

The calming alternative is to brush off the impulse as a mere anomaly. It all depends on which nervous system is hit: whether it can live with expressive turbulence, or has learned to divert it into placid ox-bows of complacency. Habit is the body's defence against shocks of expression. It 'recognizes' every arriving perception it can as being 'like' an impulse the body has already integrated as a functional life content. It contains potential with resemblance. Any number of singular bodily events will automatically be grouped together, soliciting the same type of response. The resemblance is in this redundancy of response: it is in on the level of the event's effect. In other words, it is a produced resemblance – of the body's elicited actions to each other – rather than a formal likeness between the 'stimulus' and the response.[31] The sameness of the response depends precisely on disregarding the singular contours of the arriving impulse: dismissing its potentially torturous anomalies as functionally insignificant.

Deleuze writes that a body does not choose to think, and that the supreme operation of thought does not consist in making a choice. A body is 'forced to think' by its implication in a self-propagating, serially self-organizing generative movement (Deleuze, 1994: 138–40). Thought strikes like lightning, with sheering ontogenetic force. It is *felt*. The highest operation of thought is not to choose, but to harbour and convey that felt force, repotentialized. The thinking is not contained in the designations, manifestations, and significations of language, as owned by a subject. These are only partial expressions of it: pale reflections of its flash. The thinking is all along the line. It *is* the process: its own event. To think along the line, conveying and magnifying its creative momentum, does not involve a mastery of it. To the contrary, it involves submitting to it, consenting to participate in it, letting its self-propagating movement pass through, transducing it. The tarantella of thought is a mimickry of that *event*, not a mirroring or moulding of expression to content. There is nothing, actually, in thought as such with which to conform or correspond. It only has force to *de*form to. Thinking is of potential. The wrackings of the thinking body mimic the excess of potential it hosts. The mimickry is not of any form, but of the process of formation itself, its actual products aside. It is a performance of the ontogenetic force of the process as such. That forced movement overspills the particular body. It overspills its generality as well, its assigned class or type – the 'subject-position' from which it conventionally speaks and acts – continuing uncertainly, violently across anything we might habitually construe as personal experience, evading definitive capture in already established forms of content and expression. The body's mimickry of the event makes it a lived 'analogy' of it, not in the sense that it in any way resembles it, but in the sense that it really (not truly) repeats its operations (of transformation). To live 'like' a thought: in *operative* identity with emergent expression. Thought does not reflect the real. It *is* real. It has a reality on a par with the world's becoming.[32]

## A genesis of the definite

Artaud was right: expression 'says too much to be born, and says too much in being born'. Its expressive momentum carries a charge of potential too great to be absorbed in any particular thing or event: too much to be born(e). It is for this very reason that it has to take body: so as to continue, generating a more to reality to absorb the excess. What absorbs the excess of potential are the determinate functionings of the host body. These actualize the potential in determinate forms of content and expression. That actual definition says too much in being born: it annuls the potential, bringing a current of expression to the end of the stream. So the movement must rebegin. Its determinate products must pass again into an intermediate state where they are repotentialized. Expression regains momentum, cascading through the body's many levels, like a contagion. If the result is an exemplary expression convoking of a collectivity, the contagion will spread. Expression will take another body. Across an indefinite series of such incarnations, it will not only have taken bodies, it will have taken on a life of its own. What each host body receives in return for its service to expression is a quantum of that vivacity: a quantum of potential to feed into its own growth and functioning. What expression spreads when it says too much are forces of existence. It disseminates life. It comes to be determined, and exceeds its determinations to become.

The theory of expression, according to Deleuze and Guattari, is not concerned with the communication of information but with the genesis of the definite (Deleuze, 1990b: 135). It should be sufficiently clear by now that the emphasis is on the genesis: its continuing across defining events. Determination is a necessary concept for the theory of expression: its problem is how determinate beings, or being-determinate, serially emerges. What makes it a theory of change was announced at the beginning: the insistence that what emerges does not conform or correspond to anything outside it, nor to its own conditions of emergence. A determination of being is not a tracing. Determination is a differing. Emergence is always of the different: every genesis a heterogenesis. A thing's form does not reflect its formation. It inflects it.

Conditions of emergence are an existential opening for determinations to come. This means that their mode of reality follows a different logic from that of the constituted beings to which it gives rise, with their reproductions and closed operational loops. If Deleuze and Guattari's theories of expression are an ontology, it is of a very special kind: what Deleuze calls a 'superior' or 'transcendental empiricism'.[33] A transcendental empiricism takes it to heart that formation and form, the emerging and the emerged, pertain to different modes of reality, even if they both belong to the same reality (there being only one world).[34] It is an 'empiricism' in that it is experimental and pragmatic. It is an expanded empiricism, in fact, in that it accepts the reality of the potential from which determinate being arises. Potential, it says, is no mere 'possibility'. Traditionally in philosophy, it is said that there is no difference between a determinate being and its possibility, other than existence. In other words, if you bracket the thing's being its idea remains the same. Its ceasing-to-be subtracts nothing from its concept. There is no real difference. Between potential and being determinate, on the other hand, there is all the difference in the world: coming to be. Ultimately, what is bracketted by possibility is becoming. The actual existence of the thing is irrelevant because whether it happens to exist or not there is still a correspondence between the content of the idea that may be had of it, and the form it would have were it to be. Possibility is the tracing power of thought to mirror things formally while bracketing their reality. Deleuze and Guattari do not wish to bracket reality in thought. They want to open bodies to the reality *of* thought. This requires operating in the element of potential.

The empiricism of their theories of expression is 'transcendental' by virtue of the transitivity and excess that come with potential. Potential carries too high a charge of reality not to be reborn and take another body: not to go beyond any determinate incarnation of it. The conditioning of emergence that is potential, is a 'lived transcendental'. Its always going beyond is not into a separate reality any more than it is a lack of reality. It is an always-more *in* this reality. Its going-beyond is a moving-in: a movement of immanence. This immanence of the transcendental, this always more to lived reality, may be summed up as: the inclusion of conditions for new emergence in the world that determinately emerges, and reciprocally the inclusion of the determinately emerged in the field conditions for new emergence. Potential rolls in to roll on, in an experiential openness of clutter and invention.

That openness, once again, is an autonomy of relation. The idea suggested earlier that the event of the singular is 'accidental' needs to be reappraised in light of this. What makes a singularity unique – fully and only its own event – is an accident only from the perspective of the already-operating type-casting collector mechanisms to which it gives pause. What is accidental is *their* momentary failure to recognize. The accident is their negative observation that the event does not immediately provide more grist for their alimentary operations: more substance for their established forms of content. From the point of view of emergence, on the other hand, the 'accidents' are a necessity. They are precisely what make the event an expression of potential. They are its openness to being otherwise; to becoming. 'Relation is not an accident *vis-à-vis* a substance, it is a structuring, energetic, and constitutive condition that extends into the existence of constituted beings' (Simondon, 1995: 81). Determinate being is an extended expression of its constitutive conditions. A transcendental empiricism recognizes 'accidents' of birth as an extending, expressive necessity. It is every being's exemplary fate to be born a singularity, for more to come.

## Please continue

The essays presented in this book deal with a wide range of subject matter. They are not organized around a common theme. What brings them together is a willingness to process the shock of Deleuze and Guattari's transcendental empiricism. Most of the essays include relatively little direct commentary upon Deleuze and Guattari's work. They are extensions of it, more than reflections on it. In this, they are faithful: in their refusal to take Deleuze and Guattari's thought as a model to conform or correspond to. Although it is not always reflected in their current affiliations, a large majority of the authors in this volume have worked from a base in Canada or Australia. The reception of Deleuze and Guattari's work occurred in those countries under local conditions lending themselves (perhaps more easily than was elsewhere the case) to the perception that its refusal to communicate, judge correctness, and moralize was not an abdication but an ethics and that the ethics was also and immediately an aesthetics. That this volume should reflect this particular geographical clustering is, of course, no accident. I have had the benefit of living and working under both sets of local conditions – a 'fate' for which I am more than editorially grateful.

The preceding introductory essay does not presume to explain or represent the essays in the volume. Its relation to them is purposely tangential. The introduction follows its own itinerary, taking a pass at many of the preoccupations that the reader will encounter again in the essays, approached in them from different and original angles. It is hoped that the (undoubtedly idiosyncratic) linking of the concepts in the introduction will not constrain the reading of the essays, but instead will suggest to readers the potential for making their own 'tranversal' links between them: creative relays across the diversity of the essays' subject matter and the originality of their approaches.

The point was not to pre-form, but to invite more of the different, along 'analogous' lines. Please continue.

## Acknowledgements

This book first took shape as a special issue of the *Canadian Review of Comparative Literature* (volume 24, no. 3, September 1997). I would like to thank the editors and administrators of that journal for their invitation to guest edit and their expert follow-through. I owe a particular debt of gratitude to Shane Wilcox, whose industry, expertise, and attention to detail as my research assistant benefited the project incalculably. The work of editing the journal issue and refashioning it as a book was carried out under grants from the Australian Research Council and the Social Sciences and Humanities Research Council of Canada. My research activities in Australia were hosted by the English Department of the University of Queensland and the Humanities Research Centre of the Australian National University. Andrew Murphie kindly contributed the idea for the book title. Finally, I would like to thank my editor at Routledge, Tony Bruce, and his assistants Zoe Drayson and Muna Khogali, for gently ushering the book into existence.

## Notes

1 Deleuze (1993:132).
2 Deleuze (1995: 147). For Deleuze and Guattari's dismissal of communicational and informational models, see Deleuze and Guattari (1987: 75–85).
3 See for example, Guattari (1996: 109–13).
4 Deleuze, (1990: 14). In the English translation, *désignation* is rendered as 'denotation'.
5 For a nostalgia-less, Deleuze–Guattari inflected appropriation of the notion of 'simulation' for inter-cultural politics, see **Mani Haghighi** in this volume.
6 'Irony … determines … the whole of the possible as a supreme originary individuality … [it] acts as the instance which assures the coextensive of being and the individual within the world of representation … [rendering] possible the ascent of the individual', (Deleuze, 1990a: 138).
7 The current of postmodernism following from Baudrillard was perhaps given its most surrealist-absurd formulation in the work of Arthur and Marilouise Kroker. Seriously absurd currents pivot on the later work of François Lyotard on Kant. The sublime is absurd by Kantian definition. As a 'concept without an intuition' to ground it, it carries an empty excess of signification (like Lévi-Strauss's mana, the sublime object of anthropology). For an alternative to the postmodern sublime centring instead on the analytic of the beautiful, see **Melissa McMahon, Steven Shaviro**, and **Stephen Zagala** in this volume.
8 For a sustained discussion of how content and expression can be made to pass into intermediate states that fuse them into mutational 'matters of expression' see Deleuze and Guattari (1986: 3–8).
9 Cited in Genosko (2001: 916).
10 On 'probe-heads' or 'cutting edges of deterritorialization', see Deleuze and Guattari (1987: 189–91).
11 Guattari (1995). On the shift in Guattari's thinking to an aesthetic paradigm, see Félix Guattari in this volume. **Stephen Zagala** also develops an ethico-aesthetics

in his contribution. **Thomas Lamarre** analyses the streaming of the world as expression, through bodily fostering sensation, into the brush-stroke of the Japanese calligrapher.

12 There is a tension in Deleuze and Guattari's work over the relation between potential and virtuality. They are often treated synonymously, especially in passages where the influence of Gilbert Simondon's energeticism is evident. Elsewhere, where the influence of Bergson's concept of 'pure memory' is predominant, the virtual is treated as non-dynamic or anenergetic (a 'sterile' double of the actual in the vocabulary of *Logic of Sense*). These tensions are not necessarily contradictions. The non-dynamic treatment of the virtual imposes itself where it is a question of the differential mode of reality of the virtual in itself. Potential comes in where it is a question of the differentiating passage of the virtual into actuality (emergence). It may be productive to think of potential as the transition state between the virtual and the actual, logically distinct from both. For more on these issues see Brian Massumi (2002). **Andrew Murphie**, in this volume, offers a detailed analysis of the relation between the virtual and expression.

13 This is Deleuze and Guattari's example of an atypical expression, drawn from e.e. cummings (Deleuze and Guattari, 1987: 99). On the tarantella as a zone of dynamic indistinction effecting a becoming between established forms–contents, see Deleuze and Guattari (1987: 305). On the 'schizophrenic' ability of words and things or bodies to cross over into each other, see Deleuze's analyses of Lewis Carroll and Louis Wolfson in 1990a: 82–93. See also the appendix to *Logic of Sense* on 'Klossowski or Bodies-Languages' (1990a: 280–300). In *Francis Bacon. Loqique de la sensation* (1981), Deleuze's analyses the deformational force of expression. On the cry of expression, see the discussion of Bacon's scream portraits in the same volume, as well as Deleuze and Guattari, *Kafka* (1986: 6) and *Logic of Sense* (1990a: 89–90) (the schizophrenic 'howl'). On Artaud and the 'cruelty' of expression, see **Catherine Dale** in this volume.

14 On cognition, the brain, and subjectless subjectivity (a concept drawn from the work of Raymond Ruyer), see **Paul Bains** in this volume.

15 On the 'primary process' as involving a certain product–process unity, see Deleuze and Guattari, (1983: 7).

16 On perception, the brain, and the subject, see Deleuze and Guattari, (1994: 208–12) where the brain is described as a 'form in itself' or immanent 'self-surveying' (autonomous) field of relation productive of events – flashes of thought. The immediate reference in this passage is again to the work of Raymond Ruyer and subjectless subjectivity.

17 On the perceptual 'signal' as a 'flash' simultaneously culminating in the expression of difference and marking its cancellation in determinate being, see Deleuze, (1994: 222–3, 228).

18 Rather than doing away with the notion of critique, Deleuze himself prefers to renew it and use it. He goes back to its Kantian sense of 'the determination of the genetic elements that condition … production'. Deleuze turns Kant's meaning against him by construing the conditions in question as those productive of 'real' rather than 'possible' experience. See Daniel Smith's translator's introduction to Deleuze (1997: xxiv). The reconversion of a stratified system of expression into a 'pre-individual' field of emergence is an instance of what Deleuze calls 'counter-actualization' (1990a: 150).

19 This is using 'singularity' in a sense closer to Deleuze and Guattari's usage in their later works (see Guattari, 1995: 7) than to the 'singular points' of *Logic of Sense* or *Difference and Repetition* (these latter pertain less to dynamic potential on the edge of emergence, than to the differential nature of the virtual as such). For a treat-

ment of the concept of singularity closer to the way it is used in *Logic of Sense* and *Difference and Repetition*, see **Alan Bourassa** in this volume.

20  Deleuze develops the serial logic of expression at length throughout *Logic of Sense*.

21  Also on the subject of expression as a 'missing people' to be invented, see Deleuze, (1997: 4). What is being termed the 'exemplary' here also figures in the work of Deleuze and Guattari in the guise of the 'anomalous individual' serving as a pivot for a collective becoming. See Deleuze and Guattari, 1987: 243–8 and Deleuze and Parnet 1987: 42.

22  On autopoietic expression, approached from a Guattari-inflected Lacanian perspective, see **Bracha Lichtenberg Ettinger** in this volume.

23  'Nucleus of expression', 'node of subjectification', and 'autopoiesis' feature in the vocabulary of Guattari's *Chaosmosis*. In his earlier vocabulary, the captured collective of expression is a 'subjugated group' and the continuing collective expression is a 'group-subject'.

24  On the powers of the false, see Deleuze, 1989: 147–55 and 1997: 104–5. Actually, the ambiguity of calling them 'powers' of the false does not occur in French. In French there are two terms for power. *Puissance* connotes potential, a 'power to'. *Pouvoir* connotes 'power over'. The 'powers of the false' are *les puissances du faux*.

25  Deleuze's *Logic of Sense* approaches 'sense' through paradox (rather than parody or irony). See in particular 1990a: 74–81.

26  See in particular 'The Geology of Morals' (Deleuze and Guattari, 1987: 39–74). On the human/non-human and expression, see **Gary Genosko** and **Alan Bourassa** in this volume.

27  On micro-perception and the distinctiveness of its 'confused' expressive impact, see **Aden Evens** and **Andrew Murphie** in this volume.

28  The term 'transduction' is borrowed by Deleuze and Guattari from Gilbert Simondon. They use it for the mode of operation of becoming. Deleuze and Guattari's concept of deterritorialization is also in dialogue with Simondon's concept of 'dephasing'. An ontogenetic field, he argues, is dephased in the sense that it envelops the potential for what will in actuality separate out as separate temporal phases as well as distinct organizational strata. A transductive process crosses intervals of dephasing where it is repotentialized for a next emergence. See Simondon 1995: 30–2.

29  In order to sustain a nature–culture continuum it seems necessary to posit 'feed-back' mechanisms whereby the formed products specific to a stratum cascade back down the chain, retransforming into 'functionless functions' contributing to conditioning the field of emergence for each stratum. In the absence of this recursive causality, the system of interlocking organizational levels risks becoming a hierarchical 'chain of being' with human reason once again at the pinnacle. On this idea of a 'feed-back of higher forms', see Massumi, (2002), introduction and chapters 1, 6, and 8.

30  **Michael Hardt**, in this volume, writes of the 'exposure' of the flesh to the violence of expressive incarnation.

31  On habit, see Deleuze, 1994: 70–9. Deleuze's treatment of habit rightly emphasizes that it is not just a passive response to a stimulus, but is inventive in its own containing way: the resemblances are *produced* (by the repetition of the response, as spontaneously preserved by a self-organizing memory of the flesh). Unlike the ideological notion of habitus, Deleuze's account of habit emphasizes that it belongs as much to the organic stratum, to the productive, physiological capacities of the flesh, as to cultural systems of reproduction.

32  On the analogic reality of thought, see Simondon, 1995: 263–8 and Deleuze, 1981. On mimicking the event, see Deleuze, 1990a: 150–1 and 178–9 (on the 'actor-dancer'). In this volume, **José Gil** analyses Merce Cunningham's dance practice as

a 'mimesis' enjoining forces of deformation in order to compose, in the artistic event, a virtual body-double.

33 Deleuze, 1994: 143–8. 'The aim [of a transcendental empiricism] is not to rediscover the eternal or the universal, but to find the conditions under which something new is produced (*creativeness*)', Deleuze in Deleuze and Claire Parnet (1987: preface to the English edition, vii).

34 The 'univocity' of being, in all its multiplicity (the 'One-All'-ness of the world), is a major concern for Deleuze throughout his writing life. It is a particular concern of *Expressionism in Philosophy* (1990b), *Logic of Sense* (1990a), and *Difference and Repetition* (1994): 'arrive at the magic formula we seek – PLURALISM = MONISM' (Deleuze and Guattari, 1987: 20).

# References

Artaud, Antonin (1999) 'Dix ans que le langage est parti', in Stephen Barber, *The Screaming Body*, New York: Creation Books.

Bourdieu, Pierre (2000) *Esquisse d'une théorie de la pratique*, Paris: Seuil, 256–85.

Deleuze, Gilles (1981) *Francis Bacon. Logique de la sensation*, Paris: Ed. de la Différence.

—— (1988) *Foucault*, trans. Seán Hand, Minneapolis: University of Minnesota Press.

—— (1989) *Cinema 2: The Time-Image*, trans. Hugh Tomlinson and Barbara Habberjam, Minneapolis: University of Minnesota Press

—— (1990a) *The Logic of Sense*, trans. Mark Lester with Charles Stivale, ed. Constantin V. Boundas, New York: Columbia Unversity Press.

—— (1990b) *Expressionism in Philosophy: Spinoza*, trans. Martin Joughin, New York: Zone Books.

—— (1993) *The Fold: Leibniz and the Baroque*, trans. Tom Conley, Minneapolis: University of Minnesota Press.

—— (1994) *Difference and Repetition*, trans. Paul Patton, New York: Columbia University Press.

—— (1995) *Negotiations*, trans. Martin Joughin, New York: Columbia University Press.

—— (1997) *Essays Critical and Clinical*, trans. Daniel Smith, Minneapolis: University of Minnesota Press.

Deleuze, G. and Guattari, F. (1983) *Anti-Oedipus*, trans. Robert Hurley, Mark Seem, and Helen R. Lane, Minneapolis: University of Minnesota Press.

—— (1986) *Kafka: Toward a Minor Literature*, trans. Dana Polan, Minneapolis: University of Minnesota Press.

—— (1987) *A Thousand Plateaus*, trans. Brian Massumi, Minneapolis: University of Minnesota Press.

—— (1994) *What is Philosophy?*, trans. Graham Burchell and Hugh Tomlinson, London: Verso.

Deleuze, G. and Parnet, Claire (1987) *Dialogues*, trans. Hugh Tomlinson and Barbara Habberjam, New York: Columbia University Press.

Foucault, Michel (1977) *Discipline and Punish*, New York: Pantheon.

Genosko, Gary (2001) 'Guattari's Schizoanalytic Semiotics: Mixing Hjelmslev and Peirce', in *Deleuze and Guattari: Critical Assessments of Leading Philosophers*, vol. 3, ed. Genosko, London/New York: Routledge, 2001: 916.

Guattari, Félix (1995) *Chaosmosis: An Ethico-Aesthetic Paradigm*, trans. Paul Bains and Julian Pefanis, Sydney/Indianapolis: Power Publications/University of Indiana Press.

—— (1996) 'The Postmodern Impasse', *The Guattari Reader*, ed. Gary Genosko, London: Blackwell.

Hjelmslev, Louis (1969) *Prolegomena to a Theory of Language*, trans. Francis J. Whitfield, Madison: University of Wisconsin Press.

Massumi, Brian (2002) *Parables for the Virtual: Movement, Affect, Sensation*, Durham: Duke University Press.

Nietzsche, Friedrich (1967) *On the Genealogy of Morals*, trans. Walter Kaufmann and R.J. Hollingdale, New York: Vintage.

Simondon, Gilbert (1995) *L'individu et sa genèse physico-biologique*, Grenoble: Millon, 2nd edn.

# Part 1

# THAT THINKING FEELING

*… everything which introduces doubt
about the position of mental images
and their relationship to one another …*

# 1

# BEAUTY

## Machinic repetition in the age of art[1]

### *Melissa McMahon*

The rising ground is no longer below, it acquires autonomous existence; the form reflected in this ground is no longer form, but an abstract line acting directly upon the soul. When the ground rises to the surface, the human face decomposes in this mirror in which both determinations and indetermination combine in a single determination which 'makes' the difference.

(Deleuze, 1994: 28)

## Prologue

I wait for the 'best' moment. Yes, I say to myself, there will come a moment when I will be able to gather my forces, have a vision of the Whole, and from this place and this time will emerge The Act. Every day I wait. I try to egg it on with cigarettes and coffee, or by not smoking and not drinking coffee. I'm waiting for my freedom, waiting for all the conditions to come together that will make possible what I want to do. Time passes. A lot of time passes. I'm waiting for it to stop, for it to gather itself into an image, of myself, of my life, of the world. I'm waiting for the movement to stop and reflect itself back to itself – reflection is the condition of action, isn't it? But it turns its face away, dissolves into a hundred tiny details on a cruelly indifferent time-line, dissolves me into a hundred tiny details, pure moving mass. It is true that in trying all of these different postures, I might just crack the code, it might all 'come together'. But it is undeniable that this moment will not have been one of discovery but of invention.

## Introduction

If Kant had had any sense of marketing, he might have called his *Critique of Judgement*: 'The Work of Art in the Age of Mechanical Reproduction'. This book and Benjamin's canonical essay of that name share a specifically modern problem that does not seem to go away: faced with a seemingly boundless homogeneity, how do you *make a difference*? The recent comeback of Kant's

3

sublime would be in part because it seems to capture, redeem, and even glamorize this pathos of individual impotence in the face of a gormless modernity. Beauty, smaller in scale and of course happier in affect, does not seem to sit so well with either a modernity that is nothing if not 'big', or the seriousness that seems called for in response.

Both the *Critique of Judgement* and Benjamin's essay deal with the tensions between a dominant mechanical paradigm and an organic model of cohesion. But while Benjamin finds no viable reconciliation between a fragmented modernity (carried by mechanization), and a lost pre-modern idyll of holistic coherence (home of the traditional work of art), Kant creates a third term between the organic and the mechanical which is precisely the aesthetic.

Or indeed the 'machinic'. Kant's beauty is too easily reduced to a languid reflection on natural forms. It seems that Benjamin has this in mind when he uses as a model of pre-modern aesthetic contemplation a 'man, who, one summer afternoon, abandons himself to following with his gaze the profile of the mountainous horizon or the line of a branch which casts its shadow upon him' (Benjamin, 1970: 224–5). But what is 'form'? and by what power does it distinguish itself, demand and grip attention? To say: 'because it is beautiful' just begs the question. Kant's beauty is much better 'dramatized' by Deleuze's 'spiritual automaton', whose encounter with a chance singularity suspends the world and sets off a chain reaction in which a new power of thought is engendered. The problem of modernity itself is dramatized through these competing figures of the 'individual' and what it means for them to think.

What the modern (non-) artwork seems most to lack, in Benjamin's eyes, is the ability to provide an *image*. The artwork as 'image' is not about it being imitative or 'realist', but about the role of the aesthetic as a synthesizer of values, relations and forces. To provide an image is to provide a point of reflection, identification and orientation for the subject in relation to its community and to the world. It gives *form* to these latter, and is inseparable from their backdrop.

In this model is a portrait of what it means to think; an 'image of thought'. The term Benjamin uses for 'contemplation' in the original French publication is *receuillement*: 'gathering together'. The subject has the distance and the freedom to appraise the whole and assign the parts, including itself, to their proper place. The 'here and now' of the aesthetic experience is not just an isolated moment but the repository of a history and a culture. It is an 'organic' logic, to borrow Kant's term, where the particular is embraced by the principle of the whole that precedes it (Kant, 1987: 253 [§77]).

By contrast, the mechanism displays an impeccable, but 'dumb' rationality, insensitive and unresponsive to its context, unreflective of itself or anything around it, proceeding indefinitely by identical fragments, too small and too large to be synthesized into a meaningful whole. It's subjective correlate, for Benjamin, is the stupefied spectator or 'mass', caught up in the movement for better or worse, but unable to assign a place of arrest, a beginning or end, from which it could orient and reflect itself.

The traditional notion of 'alienation' is precisely this absence of an ability to grasp the whole, but perhaps more profoundly, the alienating character of the mechanism is its inability to give back an image, to serve as a reflective mirror. Unlike other 'others', the mechanism is not just *not* me, but profoundly and essentially *indifferent* to me (no chance for a dialectic of recognition). Worse, this indifference overrides any sense of distance: I distinguish myself from the mechanism; 'it', however, does not return the favour. It is a portrait of cruelty, as Deleuze describes it: 'There is cruelty, even monstrosity, on both sides of this struggle against an elusive adversary, in which the distinguished opposes something which cannot distinguish itself from it but continues to espouse that which divorces it' (Deleuze, 1994: 28). Even in Nature the subject can 'find' itself, under the auspices of a englobing notion such as God.[2] The face of the mechanism, however, turns away, dissolves the human in its unreflective opacity. For Kant, for example, mechanism in nature is an obstacle to the difference human freedom could make not because it *excludes its possibility* (reducing all to determinism), but worse, because it *ignores its existence* (Kant, 1987: 14–15 [Introduction]).

And yet in this formula, where the human face is dissolved in a depthless indetermination, how can we not see, aside from the figure of a homogenizing mechanization, the typical traits of the modern artist and artwork which finds in the blind and inhuman – pure chance, drugs, madness, the machine itself – the conditions of a higher individuality? Benjamin is not ignorant of these forms, but because he makes economic and technological changes (the rise of Capital) the agent of modernity, he is incapable of seeing these as posing a properly *artistic* problem, except that of its own death or compromise.

The emergence of the modern 'individual' is contemporaneous with the emergence of mechanistic paradigms: nowhere is this more apparent than in modernist art. It is an error to understand the notion of the individual by placing it alongside existing values, whether these be of the 'community' in a traditional sense, or the capitalistic-mechanistic ones of modernity, in such a way that the individual embodies the *negation* of these latter: the 'avant-garde' formula of transgression and transcendence. We have learnt well that to negate something (history, society, modernity itself) is just another way of affirming it, a childish 'denial'. It is no doubt in this way that many representatives of the avant-garde themselves conceive individuality. The question remains as to whether it is in this relation that the problem of individuality is really posed: is anything really constituted or created through saying, or even *being*, a yes or no? *What difference does it make?*

Kant's beauty is nothing if not a discourse on individuality: an imperative that resonates from a contingent singularity (by contrast, the sublime still operates with a – doomed – imperative to reproduce the Whole). The condition for this experience is neither the backdrop of existing cultural values nor their negation, but precisely a kind of indifference: 'disinterestedness'. This famous notion of Kant's is poorly understood as a disaffected or casual attitude: the 'spectator' removed from the action. The 'interest' that is lacking in the aesthetic experience is an investment in the object from a moral, utilitarian or theoretical perspective: *what* the object is, or what it is *good* for (Kant, 1987: 44–53 [§1–5]). And *who* has such concerns if not a spectator, or perhaps the careful customer? Such attitudes give a 'perspective' on the object, a correct distance. They precisely enable us to *recognize* the object, situate it in a world and ourselves in relation to it. Such interests precede the object and attenuate its contingency by integrating it into a pre-existing material or cultural whole.

In this sense, Kant's notion of 'disinterest' marks not a distance but its loss, an encounter which precisely strips the subject of its habits of thought. In fact it is no longer clear that in the absence of such interests the 'what' that is operative in the aesthetic experience is an 'object' at all: it is more a 'sign', a trigger. The attribute of beauty attaches not to the object but to the 'event' of the beautiful (Kant, 1987: 30 [Introduction]).

We can see already how this aesthetic contracts the twin destiny of the modern work of art. On the one hand, its entry into the machinery of capital and commercialization, negligent of tradition and original or destined context, losing its status as object to become commodity and abstract (market) 'value'. On the other hand, the imperative to disorientation and novelty in art (novelty being another value that is shared by both commerce and creativity) and the decline of object-based and representative art forms. It is as if Kant's aesthetic was itself a sign, enveloping two tendencies: 'one by which, as sign, it expresses a productive dissymmetry, the other by which it tends to annul it' (Deleuze, 1994: 20).

The complicity of a mechanistic paradigm and the concept of creation is expressed well by Deleuze in his *Cinema* books, and in a way that aligns itself with the dynamic of Kant's beauty (Deleuze, 1986: 3–8). Deleuze, following Bergson, traces the genesis of modernity to the *analysis* of movement into equidistant points. This flattening of movement means that a moving body can be intercepted at 'any-moment-whatever' in order to yield information, as opposed to the ancient *synthesis* of movement into *privileged* moments (Origin, Telos, Apex, etc.).

As a form of representation or reproduction of movement, the 'modern' model holds little interest: it reduces movements to homogeneous and immobile points. And yet this indifference is the basis for the creation of an interesting body at any-moment-whatever. It is for this reason that Deleuze sees in this model a 'total conversion of thought'. Thought would no longer rely on a pre-existing determined order which it would stand back and 'reflect', but remains indeterminate until an encounter at a contingent moment (an 'interception') obliges it to *make* a difference.

In effect, Kant replaces Benjamin's loaded term of the 'here and now' with the 'any-moment-whatever' as emblem of artistic individuality and image of thought. For Benjamin, the 'here and now' which constitutes the 'aura' of the work of art is the summit of a culture, 'eternal and immobile', ineffable and untranslatable. It is a dead end, impotent to reproduce itself without rerouting through its conditions of possibility. The removal of the beautiful, in Kant's aesthetic, from any given cultural or scientific context, by virtue of its lack of a determinate concept and hence an interest, seems also to isolate and immobilize the aesthetic in an affective ineffability. But on the contrary, it is this quality that produces the dynamism of the beautiful, and its capacity to provoke *thought*.

The beautiful obliges us to think (its singularity poses a *problem*), without there being any concept for thought to settle on. The thought of the beautiful is identical with the series of incomplete determinations it gives rise to, in which it creates and indefinitely recreates itself; it is identical to the repetition of its singularity in an open-ended movement. In his anthropological writings, Kant analyses the affects of pleasure and displeasure entirely in terms of stimuli that may or may not lead to a change of state. This is the formal 'play' of Kant's aesthetic, which is not a static formalism devoid of 'content', but the fusion of content with a process. The event of the beautiful marks a beginning rather than an end-point, without the pretension of being an Origin, as it happens just any time. The principle of the 'any-moment-whatever' enfolds both an indifference and an obligation to differentiate, an impersonality and total individuality.

In this way, the problem of artistic individuality escapes on the one hand the heroism and pathos of the avant-garde subject which affirms itself against an image of the whole, and on the other the autism that results from confining individuality to a purely affective and ineffable moment. Both notions in the end make of the individual the great 'spectator', the visionary for whom action naturally follows or else is not the point. Benjamin himself presents action and thought as dependent upon having access to 'the big picture', and the 'small picture' that is subjective self-reflection: the image being what mediates between the two. Against the 'big picture', Kant's beautiful presents the individual as necessarily working from a fragment, a 'cut', not exactly removed from the whole, but from which the whole is itself removed. Against the 'small picture', the beautiful does not stop but starts with this moment. While it refers to no external goal or concept, neither is it an 'end in itself'. It is a vector, a 'clue', inseparable from the action it unleashes; a 'problem' which lances an imperative to change. Modern individuality constructs itself *au courant* ('on the run') in a heightened sensibility to the actual that is inseparable from a movement of actualization.

## Conclusion

It is not simply that Benjamin poses the problem of modernity in a way that prejudices the possibility of a 'solution'. It is more that he does not pose it as a 'problem' at all, but as a 'theorem': modernity (as also the pre-modern) is summed up as a given state of affairs, as *how things are*, and it remains for us to draw out the endless consequences. If modernity is 'how things are', then there can ultimately be no modernity, no novelty, in thinking or art, except as a simply empirical/historical qualification, simply contemporary with and reflective of changes that happen elsewhere. This is the fate of an image of thought and of art based on contemplation.

But by what strange power is it that Capital and the machine, any of these 'things' or 'states of affairs' (History, Society, my parents, etc.), effect change, in a way that is denied to thought, art, the individual? The indifference of 'what is' is conceived along the lines of an objective necessity, an inevitability, a power of determination, in relation to which we are forced into a reactive position. What is properly 'human' or 'personal' can only be reactive then: what interprets, synthesizes, affirms or negates what 'is'.

In Kant's beauty this indifference is harnessed as a subjective principle, an *in*determination 'actualized' at a contingent point of encounter which creates a problem. Beyond what follows the lines of this event, which extend indefinitely, what 'is' is of no interest. Of course, it still exists. Creation does not happen in a vacuum, it is simply the perspective in which the determining power of what 'exists' is suspended, in order to plug into forces and arrangements of things more interesting than that of 'existence'. This refusal to take 'what is' as given in advance, and as the 'ground' for thought, action, and art is the *critical* imperative that unites Kant and Deleuze as philosophers of modernity.

## Notes

1 This article, in slightly different form, originally appeared in *Globe E-Journal of Australian Visual Arts* 3 (<http://www.monash.edu.au/visarts/globe/ghome.html>) and is reproduced with the kind permission of Robert Shubert, the general editor, and Stephen Zagala, the editor of that particular issue dedicated to the theme of beauty. I would like to give special thanks to Stephen for his personal support and help in writing this article.
2 See Deleuze and Guattari's face-landscape formula (1987: 167–94).

## References

Benjamin, Walter (1970) 'The Work of Art in the Age of Mechanical Reproduction', in *Illuminations*, trans. H. Zohn, London: Fontana.
Deleuze, Gilles (1986) *Cinema 1: The Movement-Image*, trans. Hugh Tomlinson and Barbara Habberjam, Minneapolis: University of Minnesota Press.
—— (1994) *Difference and Repetition*, trans. P. Patton, New York: Columbia University Press.
Deleuze, Gilles and Guattari, Félix (1987) *A Thousand Plateaus: Capitalism and Schizophrenia*, trans. B. Massumi, Minneapolis: University of Minnesota Press.
Kant, Immanuel (1974) *Anthropology from a Pragmatic Point of View*, trans. M. J. Gregor, The Hague: Martinus Nijhoff.
—— (1987) *Critique of Judgement*, trans. W.S. Pluhar, Indianapolis/Cambridge: Hackett.

# 2

# BEAUTY LIES IN THE EYE

*Steven Shaviro*

1   It has become quite fashionable to talk about the Sublime, as it is presented in Kant's *Critique of Judgement*, in relation to postmodernism. But it is rare to find anyone who similarly considers Kant's presentation of the Beautiful.

2   The Sublime seems more appropriate to contemporary taste because it is an aesthetic of immensity, excess, and disproportion. Whereas the Beautiful is one of harmony and proportion. It is as if Beauty were somehow old-fashioned, whereas the Sublime is considered more radical.

3   Among recent theorists, Jean-François Lyotard is the one who has talked most interestingly about the Sublime. In his account, the Sublime is what invokes the unpresentable, what keeps open that which would otherwise be foreclosed by information technologies and by commodification. The postmodern sublime, he writes, 'would be that which in the modern invokes the unpresentable in presentation itself, that which refuses the consolation of correct forms, refuses the consensus of taste permitting a common experience of nostalgia for the impossible, and inquires into new presentations – not to take pleasure in them, but to better produce the feeling that there is something unpresentable'.

4   The Sublime in Kant is a double movement: a rupture followed by a higher recuperation. Postmodernists want to affirm the first moment, but defer or avoid the second. The breakdown of the imagination in the sublime can be compared to Bataille's notion of expenditure without return. It is an opening. But the appearance of Reason is a restoration of order and of closure.

5   But is it really possible to separate out the parts of the Kantian movement like this? Neil Hertz suggests that even the first moment of the sublime, the imagination's distress, seems 'slightly factitious, staged precisely in order to require the somewhat melodramatic arrival of Ethics'. Hertz has an important point here, though it is unfortunate that he chooses to denigrate melodrama.

6   Lyotard, unlike many recent commentators, respects both moments in the unfolding of the sublime. But such a reading has its own problems. Lyotard valorizes the Sublime only at the price of entirely devalorizing the aesthetic and the Beautiful. According to Lyotard, 'Kant writes that the sublime is a *Geistesgefühl*, a sentiment of the mind, whereas the beautiful is the sentiment that proceeds from a "fit" between nature and mind ... This marriage or, at least, this betrothal proper to the beautiful is broken by the sublime ... the sublime is none other than the sacrificial announcement of the ethical in the aesthetic field. Sacrificial in that it requires that imaginative nature ... must be sacrificed in the interests of practical reason ... This heralds the end of an aesthetics, that of the beautiful, in the name of the final destination of the mind, which is freedom'.

7   Beauty seems to offer none of these sublime possibilities of rupture and openness, however dubious they may be. Beauty is too ordered and harmonious for that. Nonetheless the topic of beauty continues to come up, both in everyday discourse (when we find some work of art – though probably not nature – beautiful) and in the overt strategy of many postmodern works.

8   Consider, for instance, Prince's underappreciated 1986 film, *Under the Cherry Moon*. This film is beautiful, and not sublime. It is set in a fantasy version of the French Riviera: a place where rose petals flutter through the air, and where men and women alike wear the most elegant costumes. This is a high-society world, and it is lily-white. The 'butterscotch' Prince and his 'chocolate' sidekick Jerome Benton are almost the only people of colour around. As if to underscore this, the film is shot in sumptuous black and white. The screen is suffused with light, which vanquishes all shadows. Sometimes this light is dazzling, at other times muted and low-key. But even the night is luminous. Everything is posed for maximum visibility. Everything glows, from the white bedding and white dresses that the women favour, to the black sheen of Prince's conked, pomaded hair.

9   Throughout the film, Prince cultivates the art of being on display. He fashions himself into an exotic Other. His body, clothed in glamour, is the focus of all glances. We see him in bed, in the bathtub, at the piano, on the dance floor, and driving a car. Everywhere he manifests the same delicious languor. He moves with a slow, stylized grace. It's as if he were waiting to be ravished. He disdains work, he tells us, and lives only for 'fun'. The camera moves caressingly up the length of his body. It dwells longingly on the ample folds of his ass. His feet are sheathed in high-heeled shoes. His pants are flared at the legs, but nicely tight around the buttocks. His jackets and shirts feature rows of big buttons, and leave his chest or midriff bare. A single lock of hair curls daintily over his forehead. Sometimes his eyes are hidden behind sunglasses. Other times, he bats his eyes coyly, or opens them wide in mock horror.

10   *Under the Cherry Moon* is also noteworthy for its exceedingly postmodern strategy of pastiche. It evokes in turn various past eras: the 1920s, the 1930s, the 1940s. But we are not sure if these decades are being alluded to as they were in life, or just as they were in film. This sort of evocation is quite different from modernist nostalgia. For, far from being about somehow lacking those pasts, Prince's pastiche of styles is about having access to them to an excess, and even to the point of boredom. This is why Prince feels so free to mix and match past styles almost at random, without any coherent principle or criterion to guide him. The sublime grows out of an anxiety about representation and its inadequacies; but in this beautifully simulacral film, representation just is not an issue at all.

11   *Under the Cherry Moon* is beautiful (and not sublime) even in its confrontation with death. Toward the end of the film, Prince is killed by a single bullet. He drops to the ground ever so gracefully. You'd think he had merely fallen into an affected swoon. His limbs are carefully arrayed upon the ground. His lover cradles his head in her arms. He mutters a few last words; then his head daintily droops. In this film, death is not a limit-experience, much less a contact with the beyond. It is rather just another moment of immanence. Death is just another pose in the film's recycling of a previous *fin de siècle*'s aestheticizing, posturing, and posing. (Indeed, the film critic J. Hoberman rightly saw Prince in this film as a *poète maudit* in the tradition of Baudelaire and Lautréamont).

12   Seen in this light, Beauty is quite strange. It is a matter of great difficulty and great fragility. And yet its very difficulty is insubstantial. There is no more egregious and sterile waste of time than that spent by the dandy in front of the mirror, or parading his beauty for others to view. Yet in the perspective of beauty, even this waste of time doesn't matter. Warhol: 'If people want to spend their whole lives creaming and tweezing and brushing and tilting and gluing, that's okay too, because it gives them something to do'.

13   The flat immanence of beauty contrasts sharply with the residues of transcendence (even if only a negative transcendence) that continue to haunt the Sublime.

14   This strangeness, wastefulness, and sterility has something to do with the disinterest that for Kant is crucial in any judgement of beauty.

15   Melissa McMahon writes thus of Kantian disinterest: 'the "interest" that is lacking in the aesthetic experience is an investment in the object from a moral, utilitarian, or theoretical perspective … Kant's notion of disinterest marks not a distance [such as that of the aura in Benjamin] but its loss, an encounter which precisely strips the subject of its habits of thought. In fact it

11

is no longer clear that in the absence of such interests the "what" that is operative in the aesthetic experience is an "object" at all; it is more a "sign", a trigger. The attribute of beauty attaches not to the object but to the "event" of the beautiful'.

16    The flatness and immanence of beauty is a different sort of stripping away than the one that occurs in the sublime. Beauty cannot be identified with the aura that Benjamin posited in older, pre-industrial art. (Which is how Lyotard sees it when he praises the sublime for marking an end to any aesthetics of the beautiful.) Beauty rather implies, quite strongly, the loss of the aura. But this loss is not the modernist and Benjaminian one of shock or trauma. It is more like a blasé shrug of the shoulders, or like Andy Warhol's bland and oft-repeated judgement: 'it's great'.

17    By virtue of this indifference, the beautiful is more resistant than is the sublime to being appropriated by the discourses or forces of morality. Beauty, Kant says, is as free from any notion of goodness or perfection as it is from any notion of utility. A sensitivity toward the beautiful may, he suggests, indicate a disposition toward the good. But that is as far as Kant is willing to go. The aesthetic taste itself may not be subordinated to any pre-existing criterion of morality.

18    Melissa McMahon sees Kant's aesthetics of the beautiful as 'replac[ing] Benjamin's loaded term of the "here and now" with the "any–moment–whatever" as emblem of artistic individuality and image of thought'. This 'here-and-now' is quite close to Lyotard's reading of the sublime as an event (Heideggerian *Ereignis*), a kind of open question: 'is it happening?' The contrary notion of the 'any-moment-whatever', is taken by McMahon from Deleuze's *Cinema* volumes. It is related less to Heidegger and to Benjamin than to Giorgio Agamben's sense of 'whatever being' in *The Coming Community*. (Benjamin and Heidegger are indeed Agamben's greatest influences, but his peculiar inflection of them moves in a very different, more Kantian direction).

19    As a state of detachment from utilitarian and especially from moral concerns, Kant's disinterest is a kind of impassivity or indifference, something that is at once otherworldly (since it is detached, other-than-concerned-with-the-here-and-now, in terms of affect) and yet still very much of this world (since it is rooted in the immediacy of an event, and denies any *telos* or transcendence).

20    Beauty, therefore, is everything and nothing at once. Like the disaster invoked by Maurice Blanchot, it 'ruins everything while leaving everything in place'. In Kant's own terms, the beautiful involves an antinomy. On one hand, the judgement of beauty is entirely singular. There is no concept to determine

it. On the other hand, we see such a judgement as universal, and we demand assent from others regarding it.

21   The first half of the antinomy works like this. An aesthetic judgement must be made without a concept to determine it. This means that it is entirely singular. No rule can be applied to it or generalized from it. The singular object of aesthetic judgement cannot even be called a particular, because that would imply some sort of relation to more general instances.

22   The beautiful is composed of examples that nevertheless cannot be reduced to rules. Instances of the beautiful are examples in themselves, but not examples of anything. They are copies for which there is no original, or secondaries for which there is no primary. You can point to them as examples; but you cannot point to that of which they are examples. Each is a singularity: an instance that can be emulated, but not imitated.

23   Kant also expresses this paradox as follows. The Beautiful leads to aesthetic Ideas, intuitions for which there are no adequate concepts. Whereas the Sublime leads to rational Ideas, concepts for which there are no adequate intuitions.

24   Kant's idea of the singular aesthetic Idea, as an intuition for which there can be no concept, is quite close to the notion of singularity in Deleuze. Something absolutely singular breaks away from the hierarchical conceptual relations of genus to species, or of general to particular.

25   What is a singularity in Deleuze? A point in the graph of a function for which there is no slope or derivative; a point of phase transition in matter like the boiling and freezing points of water; a bifurcation point in chaos theory; a mutation in biology, understanding that, as Richard Dawkins says, the effect of a gene can be understood only differentially, in relation to all other alleles at the same location in the genome.

26   Or take the example of gender. Male and female are conceptual categories; neither could be called a singularity. They are particulars in relation to the 'bi-univocal' generality above them. And they are generic terms which regulate the particulars or individuals beneath them. Both sides of this hierarchy are expressed in the Law (as Lacan might say) of gender: that every human being must have a gender, must be one or the other.

27   The two genders are privileged points, conceptual hinges around which everything else is organized. They are foci of stabilization. For that very reason, they are not what Deleuze in *Logic of Sense* calls remarkable points, points of transformation and of singularity. The singularity in Deleuze is not a specially privileged 'here and now'. For singularity can precisely arise

at 'any-moment-whatever'. Any moment, unpredictably, can turn out to be a remarkable point where concepts break down, where the intuition exceeds the concept, where the distributive characterization operated by a bi-univocal arrangement like male/female (the concept of gender) stops working. The machinery gets jammed, and something else passes through. There is a scattering of singularities, an interpenetration between genders, their aconceptual transformations into one another.

28   The other side of Kant's antinomy is that the aesthetic judgement claims universal validity. But universality is not the same thing as generality. There is no mediation, no measured ascent from the immediate to some higher or broader point. The aesthetic judgement remains singular and subjective, Kant says; it refers only to this one singular point, even as it demands the assent of others. 'Nothing is postulated in a judgement of taste except a universal voice about a liking unmediated by concepts'. This voice requires assent from everyone, but it cannot postulate such assent as actually existing. We cannot prove that the other must agree with us, since there is no concept to argue from. We are impelled to posit universal agreement, but we cannot actually enforce any such agreement.

29   As McMahon puts it, 'the beautiful obliges us to think (its singularity poses a problem), without there being any concept for thought to settle on'.

30   Thomas Wall suggests, in an unpublished essay, that the claim to universality in a judgement of beauty is, actually, an active demand. I actively impinge upon the Other. I insist that she share my judgement that something is beautiful. The aesthetic judgement is not my spontaneous thought, so much as it is something that forces me to think. And even more, it forces me to demand the Other to participate together with me.

31   Why this turn to the Other? It is a question of communication. In the absence of any concept it is as impossible to communicate an aesthetic pleasure to myself as it is for me to communicate it to someone else. In an aesthetic judgement, I only demand of others what I first demand of myself. In the aesthetic experience, I am being obliged to conceptualize and communicate, while the very means to do so are withheld from me.

32   Kant's very demand for the universal communicability of aesthetic judgement thus presupposes its own conceptual impossibility. The actual pleasure or sensation of beauty cannot be communicated. It is precisely the singularity left over when all concepts are removed.

33   This argument has much in common with the question of private language in Wittgenstein. In *Philosophical Investigations*, he writes, speaking of

the inner sensation of a toothache, or of the colour red: 'It is not a something, but not a nothing either! The conclusion was only that a nothing would serve just as well as a something about which nothing could be said'.

34   For Kant, too, the singularity is not a something, but not a nothing either. Communication can neither grasp it nor exclude it. It is an excess in relation to what language can express. So it is impossible to talk about it directly. But it is equally impossible not to endeavour to refer to it. What IS communicable and communicated in the aesthetic judgement must be 'the subjective conditions for the possibility of cognition as such'.

35   How, then, can I make the demand for agreement in matters of taste? How can I posit aesthetic universality? Kant says that the universality of a subjective aesthetic judgement must reside in whatever of it is universally communicable. The trouble is that communication almost necessarily involves cognition, but the aesthetic judgement is non-cognitive. What is communicated in an aesthetic judgement, therefore, is not the singular experience of beauty itself, but merely the harmonious free accord of the powers of the mind that is the condition of possibility for there to be such a thing as a disinterested and singular judgement of beauty. Beauty is always singular, and what is communicated of this singular beauty is the presupposition that alone makes it possible: the presupposition of a *sensus communis*.

36   Lyotard links Kant's insistence on communicability – his positing a *sensus communis* – with Adorno's insistence that 'no work of art should be described or explained through the categories of communication'. What such (seemingly opposed) formulations have in common, Lyotard says, is that they alike reject the universality of the concept, and of conceptual communication, such as one finds in Hegel and Habermas. According to Lyotard, Kant and Adorno share 'a thinking about art which is not a thinking of non-communication but of non-conceptual communication'.

37   The universal communication of a free harmony of the faculties thus paradoxically implies a pre-existing separation. Indeed, what is communicated publicly is the formal condition of possibility for there to be such a thing as a private aesthetic pleasure at all. But only that private pleasure, incommunicable in itself, is the actual precondition that can impel me to endeavour to communicate in the first place, or to posit possible comprehensibility for my communication.

38   This paradox is similar to the one that animates the writings of Pierre Klossowski. He draws a distinction between the unique sign – the height or depth of affect, which is entirely singular and incommunicable – and the meaning that is communicated through the exchangable signs of language.

The latter presupposes the former, but also marks the former's otherness to, and exclusion from, any possible discourse.

39   This Klossowskian exclusion is the flip side of the Levinasian obligation, the demand upon the Other, that Wall sees in the paradox of the aesthetic judgement. Both of these dimensions imply the need for a radical separation.

40   How can Kant's antinomy be used to help define a postmodern or Deleuzian notion of Beauty? I can only sketch out some of the places in which we might begin to look for such a notion.

41   In *The Fold*, Deleuze sees modern and contemporary art as a sort of neo-Baroque, akin to the Baroque of Leibniz's time. With the difference, of course, that modernist music rejects the pre-established harmony of Baroque music, and instead affirms a primordial dissonance.

42   But there is another way that Deleuze conceives dissonance, this time in association with Kant. In *Kant's Critical Philosophy*, he remarks that 'the faculties confront one another, each stretched to its own limit, and find their accord in a fundamental discord: a discordant accord is the great discovery of the *Critique of Judgement*, the final Kantian reversal … A new music as discord, and as a discordant accord, the source of time'.

43   According to Deleuze, the whole problematic of Western philosophy changes with Kant. In his theory of the beautiful, Kant gives a new status to the notion of harmony. Harmony is no longer pre-established, as it was in all thinkers from Plato to Leibniz. Kant does not see harmony as given or intrinsic. Instead, he claims to trace its actual genesis. Harmony is now seen as a product of the free accord of the faculties (rather than as the source of their accord). This reversal is the great accomplishment of the critical programme.

44   Deleuze further recounts how the post-Kantians reproached Kant, but only for betraying his own critical programme. They 'demanded a principle which was not merely conditioning in relation to objects but was also truly genetic and productive … They also condemned the survival, in Kant, of miraculous harmonies between terms that remain external to one another'.

45   In Deleuze's account of the history of philosophy, it is left to Nietzsche to fulfil the demands of the post-Kantians, and to carry out the critical project in its full radicality. This is the repeated theme of *Nietzsche and Philosophy*. Nietzsche stands to Kant, in this early book, much as, later in *The Fold*, Whitehead stands to Leibniz, or Boulez to Bach.

46   According to Deleuze, Nietzsche performs 'a radical transformation of Kantianism, a re-invention of the critique which Kant betrayed at the same time as he conceived it, a resumption of the critical project on a new basis and with new concepts'. And again: 'Finally, Nietzsche's relation to Kant is like Marx's to Hegel: Nietzsche stands critique on its feet, just as Marx does with the dialectic'.

47   The interrogation of limits in Kant is rewritten in Nietzsche as affirmation, instead of as self-reflection. As Deleuze says: 'A thought that would go to the limit of what life can do, a thought that would lead life to the limit of what it can do? A thought that would *affirm* life instead of a knowledge that is opposed to life ... Thinking would then mean *discovering, inventing, new possibilities of life*'.

48   The will-to-power is, according to Deleuze, the differential and genealogical element behind manifestation. As such, it is Nietzsche's rewriting of Kant's transcendental syntheses in the First Critique.

49   Similarly, the Eternal Return is read by Deleuze as a principle of selection and singularization. A such, it is Nietzsche's rewriting of the categorical imperative in the Second Critique. It is a new conception of universality. We must will, not the event's generalizability as a law of reason, but its singular return, that is to say its literal infinite repetition.

50   Though Deleuze does not do this explicitly, we could similarly extend Nietzsche's rewriting of Kant to the Third Critique. The *sensus communis* would be seen as the cultivation and sharing of the highest possible degree of singularity, rather than as something generalizable into a 'community'. Aesthetic Ideas are what Deleuze elsewhere calls Powers of the False. They are modes of the virtual, as projected by the imagination. As Brian Massumi puts it: 'Imagination is the mode of thought most precisely suited to the vagueness of the virtual'.

51   Postmodern art might then bear the same relation to the severe, dissonant 'neo-Baroque' late-modernism favoured by Deleuze, as the 'romanticism' of Kant (revised and extended by the post-Kantians, and especially by Nietzsche) bears to the Baroque of Leibniz. In *The Fold* and other late works, Deleuze expresses his fondness for such artists as Samuel Beckett, Carl André, and Pierre Boulez. A postmodern sensibility might prefer to dwell on such figures as Kathy Acker, Cindy Sherman, and Sonic Youth. Their postmodern works would give singularity a new status, one that transforms, or goes 'beyond', modernist dissonance.

52   Postmodern beauty would be the event in which the free play of the faculties turns inside out to affirm singularity and multiplicity. The faculties are not harmonized, but each is pushed to its limits. In the beautiful this interrogation of the limit, turned into an affirmation, takes place entirely immanently, without the negativity and the hints of transcendence that are still present even in Lyotard's postmodern sublime. Beauty will be singular and immanent, or not at all.

53   All this points to an aestheticism somewhat similar to that of the late Barthes and the late Foucault. Such aestheticism is often criticized as being apolitical. But it stands as a reproach to the endeavours of William Bennett and others on the Right to reduce culture and beauty to matters of virtue and morality.

54   'Beauty Lies in the Eye' is a song from Sonic Youth's 1987 album *Sister*. The sound is dissonant and thickly layered. There is no melody to speak of. The tempo is moderately slow. Steve Shelley's drums keep up a steady beat. Thurston Moore's and Lee Ranaldo's guitars twang in unison. The guitars have been treated to produce a muddy, reverberating sound. They drone through a series of unresolved minor chords. Everything seems fuzzy, slightly out of focus.

55   This music doesn't go anywhere. It doesn't build to a climax. It ends as uncertainly as it began. It just drifts, for two minutes and fifteen seconds. Yet it is not laid back. It is too nervous and edgy. It exudes an air of restlessness, with a hint of violence. Something could explode at any moment. Something has just happened, or is about to happen. The music is heavy with premonitions. Overtones ring out. The drums speed up to double time. A single note insistently repeats. An extra guitar line snakes through the wall of sound. These variations unfold at the very edge of hearing. They appear briefly. Then they fade back into the mix. They seem to portend a greater change in the offing. But the future they look forward to does not arrive. The song remains distant and impassive. It inhabits an empty time, a time that never passes. This music lies suspended between memory and anticipation.

56   The video for 'Beauty Lies in the Eye' confounds things even further. It is a dazzling blur of strobe effects, overlaid images, and vivid colours. Dropped frames make for ripples of jerky motion. The camera tilts to extreme angles. It zooms in on the smallest details. Thurston Moore's fingers pick out chords on the guitar. Kim Gordon's lips caress the microphone. Waves churn in the ocean. Two, three, or more images appear at once on the screen. They pass through each other, like ghosts. They bleed into each other, leaving tracks of light in their wakes. They melt into smears of highly saturated colour. Everything wavers and flows. Everything dissolves into a synesthetic haze.

57   Kim Gordon's voice alone emerges intact. Her words come through clearly, with an almost palpable presence. She speaks the lyrics, more than she sings them. She recites them slowly, nearly without expression. Her intonation is flat and matter-of-fact. The blankness of her voice seems at odds with what she is saying. For the lyrics themselves are laden with emotion. They are all about loss, regret, and yearning. Kim is taken by surprise. An old, forgotten love comes back to haunt her. 'Something in the air there ... brings you back to me. It's been so long'. The past returns, unbidden and unwanted. 'It's coming coming down over me'. It sweeps through her, in an overwhelming rush. It seizes her, beyond all hope of forgetting. She is troubled by feelings long dead and gone. She is seduced by a lover who is no longer there. She searches out the eyes of someone who cannot return her gaze.

58   That is why Kim Gordon's voice is blank. The passion is real enough. But she cannot claim it as her own. This love does not unfold in the time and space of the present. It happens in an empty time, a time that is not now. It takes place in a space removed, a space that is not here. It draws Kim outside of herself. It lures her into its own alien depths. She cannot contain the 'explosions in [her] eye'. She cannot possess the vision that drives her mad. She can neither recover the past, nor free herself from its spell. The memories that haunt her belong to somebody else. 'Beauty lies in the eyes of another's dreams. Beauty lies lost in another's dream'.

59   No song has the power to recover such a dream. No song can compensate for loss. No song can bridge the gap between one person and another. 'Beauty Lies in the Eye' does not even try. Its words, like its sounds, are forever incomplete. Beauty is not a recompense for anything that has been lost. Beauty is rather the pang of loss itself, its truest expression. It cannot be shared, and it cannot be preserved. It vanishes in the very act by which I apprehend it. I can only cry out, a witness to its passing. At the end of the song, there's a subtle shift in tone. Kim Gordon's voice is no longer entirely blank. It becomes imploring, almost wistful. She calls to someone who is not there and who will never answer: 'Hey baby ... Hey sweetheart ... Hey fox come here ... Hey beautiful ... Come here, sugar'.

61   Any theory of beauty is always inadequate to its examples.

62   I would like to thank Thomas Wall, Stephen Zagala, Melissa McMahon, and William Flesch. This essay could not have been written without them.

# 3

# AESTHETICS

## A place I've never seen[1]

### Stephen Zagala

> The work of art, for those who use it, is an activity of un-framing, of rupturing sense, of baroque proliferation or extreme impoverishment which leads to a recreation and a reinvention of the subject itself.
>
> (Guattari 1995: 131)

> The white walls of the gallery become the page that must be read with both hands, if not the whole body's caress.
>
> (Jones 1993)

## Deleuze and Guattari's ethico-aesthetic paradigm

In his final work, *Chaosmosis:An Ethico-Aesthetic Paradigm* (1995), Félix Guattari suggests that aesthetics might occupy a privileged position for a radical ethics in our *fin de millénaire*. In principle, aesthetics has no more transformative power than philosophical thought, scientific knowledge or political action, but for Guattari it highlights a creative process necessary for ethical activity in all of these fields. It highlights an ethic of experimentation that can free us from the 'fogs and miasmas' which obscure the creative possibilities of the future. Art, as such, does not have a monopoly on creativity. Guattari is not referring to institutionalized art but to an 'artistry' or 'power of emergence' which traverses all domains (Guattari, 1995: 102). In short, his ethic is the creative production of the *new*. Consequently, his writing moves quite freely between poetry, psychotherapy, economics and ecology, fashioning new modes of practice and different ways of thinking.

This transversal conception of aesthetics is particularly obvious in Guattari's collaborations with Deleuze, where the movement of animals is discussed alongside the rhythms of writers and musicians, or where the behavioural patterns of sub-atomic particles have no more or less significance than a film plot. In their separate vocations, as psychiatrist and teacher, similar assemblages of creativity emerge. At La Borde, the psychiatric clinic which Guattari helped to establish in 1953 and where he worked until his death in 1992, functional roles were created throughout the day's activities, rather than

20

determined in the context of the analyst's couch: 'The kitchen then becomes a little opera scene: in it people talk, dance and play with all kinds of instruments, with water and fire, dough and dustbins, relations of prestige and submission' (1995: 69). The seminar conducted by Deleuze at Vincennes in the early 1970s was equally informal and experimental. With frequent questions and interruptions, discussions 'would range from Spinoza to modern music, from Chinese metallurgy to bird-song, from linguistics to gang warfare … The rhizome would grow' (Deleuze and Parnet, 1987: xii).[2] Artistry, in this general sense, is concerned with creating new modes of existence.

Like many French philosophers, Guattari and Deleuze have also written specifically about fine art. Guattari has published articles and reviews on single artists and on the state of cinema, literature and the plastic arts. Deleuze has written major studies on the painting of Francis Bacon, the art and architecture of the Baroque, the history of cinema, and the literature of Marcel Proust, Leopold von Sacher-Masoch and Lewis Carroll. Deleuze and Guattari's small collaborative study on Franz Kafka specifically addresses issues of interpretation and expression in literature, and their larger collaborations include lengthy discussions of art and artists of all types. There is also a tendency, moreover, to make passing reference to an extensive range of painters, musicians, architects and film-makers as they weave their creative rhizomes. Yet despite these transversal assemblages, which might seem to diminish the fine arts within a broader project, Deleuze and Guattari do not simply let the concept of 'art' dissolve into an undifferentiated amalgam with other practices. In *What Is Philosophy?* they demonstrate that art, philosophy and science have different objectives and different limits which makes them irreducible to each other. While philosophy is concerned with the form of concepts, and science with the function of knowledge, art is concerned with the force of sensation (Deleuze and Guattari, 1994: 216). Which is to say, *thought* is not co-extensive with *knowledge*: philosophy thinks with concepts, science thinks with functions, and art *thinks* with sensations. These different planes of practice interfere with each other, producing frames and interfaces which connect them. For example, philosophers create concepts of sensation, just as artists create pure sensations of concepts (as in the work of certain abstract painters like Mondrian and Malevich). But art does not *need* concepts in order to think. In other words, an artist can take a concept from philosophy, but only on the condition that it is recreated as a sensation. Painters think in terms of colours and lines, musicians think in terms of sounds and rhythms, sculptors think in terms of volumes and textures. When an art object uses a concept of philosophy or a function of science to prop itself up, it unnecessarily subordinates itself to another plane of activity. The artist's essential task is to create blocks of sensation, and 'the only law of creation is that the compound must stand up on its own' (Deleuze and Guattari, 1994: 164).

The emphasis that Deleuze and Guattari place on the autonomy of art often sounds quite conservative to those of us who associate this with the aesthetic idealism of late modernism, but at the genesis of modern aesthetics, the theory of art's autonomy has a more complicated dynamic. When eighteenth-century German philosophers such as Alexander Gottlieb Baumgarten, Friedrich Schiller and Immanuel Kant began using the term 'aesthetic' to designate a specifically artistic quality, they were moving away from the tendency in enlightenment thought to rationalize all of nature.[3] Questions of aesthetics are separated from questions of epistemology (or aesthetics is given its *own* truth as in Baumgarten) so that the specificity of the beautiful in nature and art can be recognized. In other words, these philosophers were thinking of how art could stand up by itself. The philosophical consideration of art's autonomy at this point in history brings with it a number of basic changes in the understanding of high culture, which heralds a truly modern conception of art.[4] In pre-modern societies the arts belong to *tradition*, that is to say, they are fixed memories of exemplary deeds and accomplishments. With the development of modern societies the arts are divorced from a direct embeddedment in definite social functions and contextualized as valuable cultural commodities worthy of accumulation in themselves. Moreover, *novelty* becomes a constitutive requirement for cultural production. In other words, a demand for originality in modern art replaces the respect for origins in pre-modern art. But the aspect which is particularly relevant to an understanding of Deleuze and Guattari's ethico-aesthetics is the modern value of *autonomy*.

It is simplistic to reduce the notion of artistic autonomy to later modernist theories of *ars gratia artis* or self-referential formalism. The autonomy of aesthetic pleasure, which lies at the heart of the modernist crisis in culture, does not necessarily deny sociological or psychological factors, but it recognizes that the aesthetic is not just a derivative of such extraneous functions. This is helpful in appreciating Deleuze and Guattari's frequent attention to modernists such as Paul Klee, Jackson Pollock, Claude Debussy and Samuel Beckett, who create abstract languages that have a certain autonomy from representational systems of reference. In these artists Deleuze and Guattari observe an engagement with the 'new' as something which is essentially disruptive, rather than a desire for transcendence and aesthetic idealism.[5] Furthermore, the disruption that they pose for Deleuze and Guattari is not explained in terms of a logical critique or subversion of tradition. Deleuze and Guattari clearly have no interest in participating in, or even reacting against, the avant-garde notion of dialectical Hegelian 'progress' which is frequently used to contextualize the project of modernist abstraction. For Deleuze and Guattari the 'new' is not simply the negation of something already known, but an encounter with something unthought. In order to understand how Deleuze and Guattari use this modernist notion of aesthetic abstraction, to treat art as both autonomous from other modes of thought and yet linked to a general power of emergence in all fields, I want first to briefly consider how Deleuze's theory of art might be related to Kant's *Critique of Judgement*.

As Hugh Tomlinson and Barbara Habberjam write in their translators' introduction to Deleuze's 1963 study on Kant, 'It is difficult to think of two philosophers more apparently opposite than old Immanuel Kant, "the great Chinaman of Königsberg", and Gilles Deleuze, the Parisian artist of nomadic intensities' (Deleuze, 1984: xv). Reflecting on the book ten years after its publication, Deleuze explains that it was a 'book on an enemy', but Deleuze does not react or rebel against his enemy. He learns to love him even if it requires 'all sorts of shifting, slippage, dislocations, and hidden emissions' (Deleuze, 1995: 6). In this sense, Deleuze is quite a traditional philosopher because he sees rich possibilities for opening up the past and finding loose threads in the fabric of philosophers who have been hemmed in by history.[6] This critical approach is not a deconstruction of Kant as much as a willingness to encounter Kant and connect with him in a joyful or productive way. It amounts to a Nietzschean ethic of affirmation. The slave fears the past and asserts himself by reacting against it, treating it as a master discourse that must be negated. 'This inversion of the value-positing eye', Nietzsche explains, 'is of the essence of *ressentiment*: in order to exist, the slave morality always first needs a hostile external world' (Nietzsche, 1967: 39). Deleuze, on the contrary, subscribes to Nietzsche's master morality: 'he can endure no other enemy than one in whom there is nothing to despise and very much to honor!' (Nietzsche, 1967: 39). Deleuze's survey of Kant's three *Critiques* provides a clear explanation of the essential themes, a sensitivity to the problems which are being pursued, and an ability to extend Kant's concepts in a creative way.[7] But we can draw out the aesthetic component in Kant's work more specifically by way of an observation that Deleuze makes in *The Logic of Sense*:

> Aesthetics suffers from a wrenching duality. On the one hand, it designates the theory of sensibility as the form of possible experience; on the other hand, it designates the theory of art as the reflection of real experience.
>
> (1990: 260)[8]

Kant's theory of experience defines the term 'aesthetic' in two distinct ways. In 'The Transcendental Aesthetic' of the *Critique of Pure Reason*, 'aesthetics' refers to a science of sensibility or sense perception. In this context Kant deals with the possibility of experiencing sensible objects, and more specifically with how these are given to the subject in the *a priori* forms of spatial extension and temporal duration. The human capacity for sensation is defined as purely receptive or passive, and all experience can be anticipated as conforming to their *a priori* conditions of possibility.

In the *Critique of Judgement*, on the other hand, 'aesthetics' refers to the faculty of judgement whose domain is feelings of pleasure and displeasure, not as conditions of possible experience but in order to respond to the variations of *real* experience that cannot be anticipated by conditions of possibility. This latter type of experience is discussed in relation to the appreciation of art, or more generally, to judgements of beauty and the sublime in both art and nature. Kant describes such aesthetic experiences as 'disinterested' because there is no theoretical or practical interest in the object.

Deleuze argues that these two aspects of the aesthetic need to be reunited in some way, so that a science of the sensible can account for the conditions of real experience. It is the *real* that must be accounted for by metaphysics. This involves reconfiguring Kant's philosophical project so that the transcendental conditions become immanent to the real. They cannot be understood as if from outside, as Kant attempted to do, nor are they directly accessible to experience or reducible to it. Deleuze argues that transcendental conditions must be experienced in the real events that they give rise to, though these conditions never actually appear in their totality, precisely because they have no actual totality. In this scheme of things, the higher form of aesthetic experience is continually diagrammed by the repetition of encounters with the real. Art works themselves become explorations of this transcendental realm of sensibility. In his early work Deleuze refers to this orientation in his philosophy as a 'transcendental empiricism', and although Guattari uses different terminology, it is also this experimental dynamic that is outlined in his ethico-aesthetic paradigm.

Deleuze summarizes his aesthetic project with the following imperative: 'The conditions of experience in general must become conditions of real experience; in this case the work of art would really appear as experimentation' (1990: 260). If we are only concerned with the conditions of possible experience, all experiences are predictable to some extent because they are always in the *a priori* coordinates of space and time. If, on the other hand, we refuse to consider conditions as determining what is possible, then the real becomes an arena for experimentation. This experimental dynamic is glimpsed, if not fully developed, in Kant's attempt to describe how aesthetic judgements are not regulated by one faculty or another but are brought into play by a free and unregulated operation of the faculties.

It is this possibility of a disjunctive use of the faculties that Deleuze extends, so that the critical project of metaphysics becomes a process of negotiation and invention rather than one of common principles. In the first two *Critiques* the relationship between the different faculties is determined by one of those faculties: understanding legislates in the theoretical interests of knowledge (*Critique of Pure Reason*), and reason legislates in the practical interests of desire (*Critique of Practical Reason*). In the *Critique of Judgement*, however, there is a free and indeterminate accord of the faculties. In its presentations of feelings of pleasure and displeasure, aesthetic judgement only expresses a relationship between the faculties, it refers only to itself. It is at this point that Kant's metaphysical system begins to resemble the Deleuzean schema of ideas or concepts being developed from within a distribution of singularities.

Kant argues that the only pure judgements of taste are those which formally exhibit what he calls 'free beauty' (Kant, 1987: 76). His examples of free beauty include sea shells, flowers, linear ornament *à la grecque*, crystals and bird song. These instances are 'free' because their form of beauty is independent of any interest we might have in them, and independent of any definite concept which might determine what the thing ought to be. Having disallowed its sources of subjective and objective determination, Kant argues that the judgement of beauty finds its coherence in the play of 'shape', 'composition' or 'design' (1987: 71–2).

Melissa McMahon has given an analysis of Kant's account of the beautiful which brings it close to a Deleuzo–Guattarian conception of the aesthetic, and which I would like to draw on here. As McMahon argues, the 'play' of the faculties in relation to the formal qualities of the aesthetic presentation open them both out as a 'process' or 'tendency', independent of its product or producer, subject or object (McMahon, 1995: 5).[9] It is here, in Kant's attempt to elaborate a tendency or process in artistic form, that he prefigures the dynamic of aesthetic experimentation which Deleuze and Guattari delineate as an assemblage of percepts and affects. In order to demonstrate the significance of this dynamic in Kant's modern aesthetic, we need to be clear about what he means by formal qualities. Kant does not consider the stiff regularity of geometric shapes, nor the functional symmetry of organic forms as constituting beautiful presentments (1987: 91–5). Kant suggests that such forms are ultimately boring. They suggest a determinate concept which regulates their composition, making them static or else uniform in their movement. In the case of a square, a circle or a cube, for example, a mathematical measurement defines its coherence. With an organic form, which is to say any part that is organized within a whole, the thing is accompanied by an idea of its functional purpose which allows us to cognize all the parts in their systematic combination. To consider form rather as a dynamic play, with no conceptual resolution, would be to understand it as a perpetual self-preserving instability. In this sense, Kant's 'beautiful form' approximates a Deleuzean notion of difference because it is endowed with an *internal* difference; difference which differentiates itself and affirms its difference without negation. Drawing out this point of convergence with Deleuze and Guattari's philosophy, McMahon explains that there is 'a paradox in the presentation of the beautiful, as the absence of a determinate concept entails both its singularity and its repeatability' (McMahon, 1995: 5). The beautiful's singularity means that it has an internal coherence which cannot be assessed in terms of a transcendent concept. We cannot, for instance, isolate something in the art work as inessential or superfluous by applying external criteria. The beautiful, as Deleuze says of the cinema, 'is always as perfect as it can be' (Deleuze, 1986: x).[10] But the absence of a determinate concept also gives rise to an infinite succession of incomplete determinations. We do not know what an art work can do in advance because, unlike an organic thing, the beautiful brings into play all manner of things, contracting them in its own way.

This repeatable singularity of the art work brings us back to the conception of aesthetics developed in Deleuze and Guattari's paradoxical treatment of art and artistry. The singularity of art means that it stands up on its own and does not need to be propped up by science or philosophy, but it also opens it up to endless connections with other practices, including philosophy and science. The political import of these principles is pointed to quite clearly when Deleuze elaborates them in his 1962 study, *Nietzsche and Philosophy*. Deleuze explains that Nietzsche's 'tragic conception of art' rests on two notions: first, an art work raises a world of artifice or objecthood, that is to say, it is a superficial body without a higher essence; and second, art excites an affectivity, or what Nietzsche calls a 'will to power', which maximizes the desire to overcome the organism and unfold subjectivity in material expression (Deleuze, 1983: 102–103). Or to put this another way, art has the power to recreate both the objective world and subjectivity in an ongoing dynamic of experimentation.

Throughout Deleuze and Guattari's writing on fine art, 'artistry' is not circumscribed by the artist's studio or the museum. Deleuze and Guattari seek out and develop an aestheticism in all spheres of life. But with a certain amount of clarity, art itself discloses the procedures that will allow new subjectivities and 'existential Territories' to be created in the coming millennium (Guattari, 1995: 98–118). In the section that follows, I explore the transformative political power of art's autonomy, as it is elaborated in Deleuze and Guattari's conceptual assemblage of percepts and affects, by considering an installation project by the Australian artist and gay activist Mathew Jones. In other words, my research on Jones is introduced as an evaluator of Deleuze and Guattari's artistic vitalism, prolonging their theory of aesthetics in order to spread out a conceptual plane for art-writing.

## The beautiful body of activist art

Mathew Jones has a reputation for withdrawing. In the face of activists who call for an audible gay voice he celebrates the elusive silences of homosexuality. At public lectures he retreats from the opportunity to speak, sending someone else to read his paper. And in artist's statements he often distances himself from the work, as if to avoid the role of authorial interpreter. Jones's critics have construed this 'pulling out' as an act of arrogance or cool indifference (e.g. Phillips, 1992; Baranowska, 1992), but it is much more complicated and perilous than that. Rather than establishing a safe distance, the withdrawal creates a turbulence in its wake. Twists and folds of matter are drawn out along the movement of bodies and this instability complicates any clear division between subject and object, speaker and audience, artist and art work, or active and passive roles. As Jones explains, 'pulling out before cumming is not as safe as it looks' (Jones, 1992). Jones's peculiar form of activism is generated around installation practices which evoke movements and sensual dynamics. By withdrawing from the scene, he leaves behind an art work that has a life of its own. It does not simply illustrate a pre-existing idea or intention, and it is not a static object designed for our passive contemplation. The art work stands up on its own and assembles itself in relation to the encounters that the installation-event precipitates. It is a body of sensation.

In a range of projects Jones has worked with different types of gay bodies: the ACT UP activist, the AIDS 'victim', the dual-income-no-kids consumer. And in various ways he introduces the sensual dynamism of his style to these different corporealities. The project that I want to concentrate on in this study is an installation called *A Place I've Never Seen*, which revolves around the 'erotic' body of gay pornography. To date, *A Place I've Never Seen* has been reworked and installed on five occasions, in three different countries.[11] A number of elements have changed in these successive displays, including the materials, the scale, and the composition itself, but the basis of each installation is a large braille text running around the wall of a gallery space, which describes a photograph of gay anal sex. Although this work is primarily about the 'erotic' body of pornography, Jones traces the genealogy of *A Place I've Never Seen* back to 1990,[12] when he participated in an AIDS education survey. This survey and the subsequent education campaign posed the problems that were eventually addressed in 1992 by Jones's first braille installation, *To Be Illiterate Is to be Blind*.[13]

Unlike *A Place I've Never Seen*, which is accompanied by a reproduction of the braille alphabet, the only introduction Jones offers for *To Be Illiterate Is to Be Blind* is an artist's statement discussing the relationship between two posters: an AIDS Council of New South Wales (ACON) safe-sex poster and a USSR literacy poster. Both posters carry a very similar picture of a blindfolded man walking off a cliff. Jones became aware of this image when ACON used it in 1990 with the caption, 'Pulling out before cumming is not as safe as it looks'. This was part of an education campaign which responded to a study 'examining the thought processes that enable gay men to decide to have unsafe sex in a given sexual encounter' (Gold, 1991: 3). The aim of this particular poster was to counter what was found to be a widely held misconception among gay men that withdrawal ensured safe sex. At a later date Jones discovered that the image used on ACON's poster was originally designed in the early 1920s by A. Radakov, and circulated in the context of revolutionary Russia with the slogan, 'To be illiterate is to be blind: on all sides lurk failure and unhappiness'. Jones's approach to the two posters is characterized by uncertainty. What does a blindfolded man walking off a cliff have to do with anal intercourse? Why did ACON appropriate an image from a USSR literacy poster? And why does being blindfolded make you illiterate? Or more generally, a problem which runs through a number of Jones's projects: what does representation have to do with desire? For Jones

*Figure 3.1* Mathew Jones, *A Place I've Never Seen* (detail), Braille alphabet printed on tissue

Source: Mathew Jones (1993) *A Place I've Never Seen*

it is exactly this uncertainty – the indeterminacy of his desire's relationship with representation – that is being denied by these propaganda posters. ACON's intention is to create boundaries which educate and organize gay desire. Both posters call for scopic certitude concerning the limits of safety; to feel your way is to fail. Rather than anxiously acting against the uncertainty of the body, Jones reclaims tactility as a process to live by. He says, 'put me on the other side of safe, dancing the chocolate cha-cha in the places that don't get a look-in' (Jones, 1992).

The installation which responds to the artist's statement consists of a strip of nodules and coloured dots that run around one corner of the room at eye level. This band of blotches is the complication of two discourses, one visual and the other tactile. The swarm of yellow-orange and purple-grey dots corresponds with the types of visual charts used to test for colour blindness.

And the raised nodules are the embossed language of braille, communicating the ironic message to those who read through touch that, 'to be illiterate is to be blind – like love'. The multitude of coloured dots confuses the systematic pattern of the braille, concealing the tactile message from those who privilege sight. And the optical text only conveys the redundancy of vision anyway, because the purple-grey dots don't make up a hidden message as they would in regular colour blindness charts. The eyes fail gallery-goers who keep their hands in their pockets: stop it or you'll go blind! Appearing like a rash on the gallery wall, this is a text of corporeal indeterminacy. Meaning has to be constructed at close range, where borders and limits are always being undone by bodies that do not know where they stand or how they should feel.

In retrospect, *To Be Illiterate Is to Be Blind* can be seen as a rehearsal for *A Place I've Never Seen*. Extending the formal composition of the first braille installation, *A Place I've Never Seen* explores the indeterminate relationship of desire and representation by introducing tactile movement to gay pornography. The main formal modification in *A Place I've Never Seen* is to discard colour and use black–white tonal variation to complicate the message of the braille text. Appearing like the cross-section of a molecular substratum, the twelve-centimetre-high strip opens up a chaotic multiplicity along the gallery's imaginary horizon line. In fact it is a horizon line that no longer delimits distance or perspective, ground or background. It constitutes what Deleuze and Guattari, after Aloïs Riegl, call haptic-vision: 'it does not establish an opposition between two sense organs but rather invites the assumption that the eye itself may fulfill this nonoptical function' (Deleuze and Guattari, 1987: 492). Or to put this another way, the space opened by the image is 'fascinating', in the sense that Blanchot writes about a depthless depth which we experience with a certain proximity but no measurable distance: 'But what happens when what you see, although at a distance, seems to touch you with a gripping contact [*par un contact saississant*], when the manner of seeing is a king of touch, when seeing is a *contact* at a distance?' (Blanchot, 1982: 32). Some of the swarming spheres are raised nodules protruding into the space of the gallery, but they jostle with photographic and computer-generated orbs which seem to reveal an illusionistic space beyond the room's existential coordinates.[14] A booklet, posing as the exhibition catalogue, gives us a way into this fascinating band of activity by reproducing a copy of the braille alphabet and introducing the raised nodules as the embossed language of the blind.[15] So with the directions in one hand and groping the wall with the other, 'viewers' are encouraged to actively insert themselves in the installation. But the decoded text complicates our sense of depth further, with irregular pronouns and a description which has no apparent beginning and end as it circles the circumference of the room. In a roundabout fashion, it evokes a sensation that is unphotographable, unrepresentable: passive anal sex.[16]

[T]his photograph you can't see his cock rammed huge hard lost in a place I've never seen, distended, wet with cum, the kid's thick white cream spewing hot and just their churning nuts bouncing that dude all the way to the root shooting[17]

Jones maintains that this work is pornographic because it is designed to be sexually stimulating, but it deserves to be portrayed differently given that it avoids the simplicity of most pornography. Following Gilles Deleuze we could call it 'pornology' because instead of ordering and describing sexual activity, it explores how desire and representation work. It is still 'porn' in that it still excites the body, but in such a way that interacting with the image itself becomes stimulating. We need to be clear with our definitions here because pornography is defined very differently by liberals, the moral right, and amongst feminisms. Deleuze's understanding of pornography is associated with the feminist observation that certain forms of representation violently simplify the world and encourage the viewer to act in accordance. As Deleuze explains, pornography exists to be grasped readily; everything is 'reduced to a few imperatives (do this, do that) followed by obscene descriptions' (Deleuze, 1989b: 17). Deleuze puts forward the idea of a pornology in order to recuperate the images of sex and violence that are found in the writings of Leopold von Sacher-Masoch and the Marquis de Sade. He argues that pornology produces an internal splitting of language such that it no longer functions to relate the reader to the world in a rudimentary way. It is 'aimed above all at confronting language with its own limits, with what is in a sense a "non-language" (violence that does not speak, eroticism that remains unspoken)' (Deleuze, 1989b: 22).

Critics of visual pornography who take their lead from Laura Mulvey's analysis of visual pleasure rely on the model of a scopophilic male-voyeur in command of the woman-objects being represented. The voyeur is said to internalize or conform to this abstract structure and then project it onto women in other contexts: pornography is theory, rape is practice. Mulvey explains that this voyeuristic relationship is constructed by disavowing both 'the material existence of the recording process [and] the critical reading of the spectator … in order to create a convincing world in which the spectator's surrogate can perform with verisimilitude' (Mulvey, 1975: 18). Jones's installation challenges these pornographic conventions because it refers to its material construction and the movement of readers who cross its surface. The unsafe sex scene found in the text communicates Jones's desires, but it cannot be taken as a personal imperative by the reader because its complexity returns the audience to the act of decoding the braille rather than the act of conforming to its description. In other words, the material recording process complicates a voyeuristic relationship with gay sex. The first generation of gay activists could embrace homosexual porn as an act of rebellion. As Ethan Morden explains, 'in the first days of Stonewall porn promised to be the most

*Figure 3.2* Mathew Jones, *A Place I've Never Seen* (installation view)
Source: Museu de Arte Moderna do São Paulo, 1994

immediate source of gay independence, symbolically the unique defiance' (Morden, 1986: 78). Jones, however, belongs to a generation that is more cautious of how gay culture is simplified and objectified by AIDS-related imagery, the clichés of the entertainment industry, and the postmodern taste for freak show perversity. Jones expresses gay desire as something that needs to make its presence felt without offering itself up as a spectacle.

The instrumental form of the catalogue, and the systematic pattern of the braille, suggest the need to interpret and analyse the installation. Jones notes how people move back and forth searching for the dirty bits, as if trying to dissect the bodies in the photograph (personal correspondence, 13 May, 1993). In the end though, the work moves beyond this function and becomes sensuous in itself. Rather than impersonally objectifying something else, the text frustrates the pornographic desire for simple relationships with the world. The irregular use of possessive pronouns confuses subject positions, and the text begins and ends at the same place in the installation, leaving us to continually search for linguistic clarity. The audience is forced to stumble over their reading process. Orientations are confused so that looking, touching, and reading correspond with a disjunctive body, trying to construct itself around the paradoxes of gay erotics.

As Nietzsche argues, art excites activity and 'arouses the will'. It therefore needs to be defined in terms of artists and creators rather than recipients

,967: 103–6). Perception is not passive recording, but enhance-
consecration. Traditional visual analyses negate the movement
,1 an interaction with porn, so that the meaning of the image can be
,rom a pre-constituted subject structure. Jones withdraws from the
,1emanded by this type of pornography. His withdrawal does not enact
,m shot' as a climactic moment when everything is visible; the moment
w1ı, / the spectacle of ejaculation measures out one body as active and the
other as passive. Jones's withdrawal produces an image which is more like a
sticky splotch that lubricates, but is also inseparable from the fluctuating
contours of interacting bodies. The 'sticky splotch' of *A Place I've Never Seen*,
alongside the previous discussion of Kant's beautiful form, allows us to draw
out the political dynamism of Deleuze and Guattari's assemblage of percepts
and affects.

## Percepts and affects

In *What Is Philosophy?* Deleuze and Guattari argue that the sole definition of
art is composition. And like Kant, citing bird song and the eccentric forms of
'nature' as examples of beautiful form, Deleuze and Guattari suggest that
perhaps the essence of art is given to us in the habitats carved out by animals.

> Every morning the *Scenopoetes dentirostris* [or brown stagemaker], a
> bird of the Australian rain forest, cuts leaves, makes them fall to the
> ground, and turns them over so that the paler, internal side contrasts
> with the earth. In this way it constructs a stage for itself like a ready-
> made; and directly above, on a creeper or a branch, while fluffing out
> the feathers beneath its beak to reveal their yellow roots, it sings a
> complex song made up from its own notes and, at intervals, those of
> other birds that it imitates: it is a complete artist.
>
> (Deleuze and Guattari, 1987: 184)

The animal that constructs a house, or composes a territory, allows a pure
body of sensation to emerge. This body of sensation is *pure* because it does not
refer to the perception of an object, nor to the affections of a subject. The
percept has been wrested from perception and the affect has been wrested
from affection, so that the art work is an autonomous composition of sensation. Art defined in this way, as a block of affects and percepts, has the power
to create new functional assemblages that are not predicated on a concept of
identity. The *Scenopoetes dentirostris*'s performance-installation does not constitute a perception of the rainforest, but the forest has entered into a
relationship with the bird, such that the bird has passed into the forest itself.
Nor does the *Scenopoetes dentirostris* express its affection for the other birds or
plants in the rainforest. Instead, it creates an indiscernibility between species
that allows them all to pass into an enterprise of co-creation. The territory of

the *Scenopoetes dentirostris* expresses the singularity of percepts which contract the landscape to produce an internal coherence, while also forming a repetition of affects that open onto the forest and even the cosmos in multiple ways.

When Jones wraps a ribbon of swarming spheres around the wall of a gallery he also carves out a territory. *A Place I've Never Seen* is a block of affects and percepts that allows gay sex to take on a life of its own within the installation. The braille text ironically refers to a photograph, but Jones actually gives us a percept of flesh, not a perception. He clinches the forces of anal eroticism in the autonomous framework of the habitat. Rather than giving us a window through which to perceive a body, Jones gives us a series of planes or sections which provides flesh with a framework. The body becomes part of the wall, defined by the dovetailing of different orientations: the hands, the eyes, the imagination. This scene of gay sex finds its support in the finite junction of the territory in which we participate. Accompanying this contraction of flesh in the installation's architecture, is a dissipation of the habitat. The stark white expanse of the wall highlights the sovereignty of the molecular

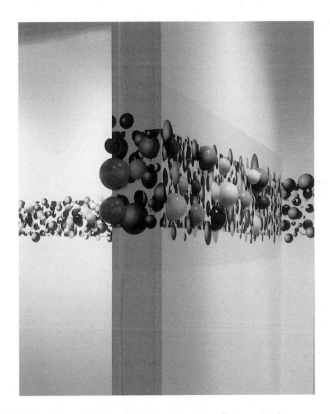

*Figure 3.3* Mathew Jones, *A Place I've Never Seen* (installation view)
Source: Toronto Photographer's Workshop, 1995

horizon, but it simultaneously infuses it with an inner light which beckons the braille to scatter itself across the dimensionless background. The forces that have been clenched by the intense band of movement threaten to spread like a rash across the walls, and the spheres bulge into the gallery, opening up the installation to envelop the outside in its compound. The audience becomes part of the work, and this expansion of the territory makes a whole range of unpredictable connections possible.

We can plot the rhythm of the habitat through a number of Jones's earlier projects to show how affects and percepts can be composed around a range of political problems. *Over My Dead Body* is the first of Jones's solo shows to explicitly deal with a political issue, but we can already see the dynamic of the territory operating in the pre-activist period of *Tableau Historique: Interior/Design*.[18] In this early body of work, the rhythmic contraction and expansion of the habitat pivots on the motif of the fold, particularly as it appears in Rococo architecture and design. *Tableau Historique* includes two painted chairs, a painted door, and several large drawings. The two 1950s style chairs, with chrome armature and vinyl panels, have been inset with lunettes of Rococo paintings by François Boucher and Jean-Paul Fragonard. The carved panel includes a Boucheresque inset within a sinuous gilded cartouche. And the drawings subtly link the scrolling lines of Rococo architecture, decoration, and landscape across a juxtaposition of vertical panels and stage screens. The pictorial space of Rococo art knots together natural form, architectural volume, and shallow design space to draw everything into a cosmos that endlessly folds one territory into another. In his early affection for the Rococo, we can see Jones's sense of form being related not to an essence or idea, but to a function of folding habitats. *Tableau Historique* animates the world with peristaltic turns and hysterical twists. The chaos contracts and expands through decorative furnishings and rhythmic territories that open back onto the surging surfaces of the cosmos.

*Tableau Historique* is primarily concerned with the fold which goes to infinity, but in subsequent work Jones attempts to localize the fold, or just give us a segment of its surface tension, in order to delineate specific territories for gay subjectivity. The projects that follow strategically generate new habitats for existence within the context of contemporary gay politics. *Tableau Historique* critiques the idea of measuring things out in relation to an ideal, while the work that follows explicitly focuses on the singularities involved in encountering the real and the habitats that cohere around them. As I have argued above, *A Place I've Never Seen* withdraws from a pornographic ideal and invents an experimental eroticism that functions as a perpetually mobile habitat. In the white canvases done between 1989 and 1991,[19] Jones withdraws from the reductive discourse of gay identity, especially as it is expressed in ACT UP slogans such as 'Silence = Death', and creates a space where silence is pregnant with new possibilities for subjectivity. The most developed installation from this period of work, *Silence = Death*, juxtaposes simplistic activist slogans with freshly primed canvases that have been stretched and stuffed to create enigmatic objects: a painting that looks like a piece of furniture, a body bag whose proportions would suit the death of art, a stretcher bed that would be impossible to lie on. The need for political action in the face of the AIDS pandemic is expressed in these limp sculptural bodies. The objects grip the forces of the disease, gathering percepts of the situation: the loss, the silence of mourning, the need to do *something* even though all action seems dubious. The surfaces of tucked and folded canvas contract the chaos in a chilling way,[20] but they also open up a space for habitation and experimentation. As Jones explains, this interval or gap of silence is 'like a place for me and other gay men – to fill up, to write in, or to keep empty' (Jones, 1991: 1).

Jones's more recent projects tend toward a colourful and camp style rather than the cool minimalist aesthetic of the work done between 1989 and 1991. *Poof!*, for example, fashions a comical response to the American trend in contemporary gay culture to identify as 'Queer'.[21] Under the logo of a cartoonesque 'Poof' explosion, Jones installs a large cloud of dacron and paints the walls of the gallery bright pink. The involuted contour of the explosion is a simple affect; a zone of indetermination, a becoming imperceptible. The sickly pink interior is a simple percept; an intense vision of gay kitsch and its forces of clichéd identification. Resounding between the percept and the affect is the rhythm of a new body. It is a body of sensation which calls into question any easy definition of gay identity and opens up a space for experimental individuations. To take another recent example, *I Feel Like Chicken Tonight*[22] withdraws from the ideal of a socially integrated homosexuality by carving out a territory for desires which remain unspeakable in queer politics. In this installation, Jones fills the gallery with flags and placards that might be used to display allegiances or incite a crowd, but who would wave these banners brandishing nothing but abstract patterns? He provides clues: 'Chicken' is gay slang for adolescent boy; the designs are taken from the school ties used to string the pennants together; and the exhibit includes newspaper articles on pederasty illustrated with retouched photographs of ACT UP demonstrators bearing Jones's schoolboy emblems. For Jones, paedophilia gestures toward an ethic that is essentially incomplete, a politic without people speaking on behalf of others. Shortly before *I Feel Like Chicken Tonight* opened, the International Lesbian and Gay Association lost consultancy status with the United Nations because of their affiliation with groups that advocate paedophilia. As Félix Guattari remarked in the mid-1970s, paedophilia constitutes a sort of 'jewishness' [*juiverie*] which provokes racist reaction, even within the gay community (Guattari, 1975: 14–15). In lieu of subjectivities that might activate them, the objects in his installation take on a life of their own. Eluding the world of guilt and justice, Jones turns its symbols into abstract a-signifying fluxes. He creates a body of sensation that unspeakable passions can occupy in flight.

## The community of sensual bodies

Deleuze and Guattari's aesthetics cannot be reduced to a theory of the art object *per se*. They understand aesthetics to be concerned with the dynamic of sensible assemblages. As I have argued above, this approach has its genealogy in a traditional definition of the discipline as a 'science of sensibility'. And because of this, aesthetics is a recurring theme in Deleuze and Guattari's work which not only pertains to art objects, but also introduces transversal linkages with ethics, ontology, epistemology, and historiography. They are 'aesthetical' philosophers, primarily concerned with creative encounters that are not preceded by a concept of identity. As Guattari explains, 'aesthetics isn't something that gives you recipes to make a work of art', it is a 'speculative cartography' which constructs coordinates of existence at the same time as those coordinates are lived (Guattari, 1993: 240–1). When Deleuze and Guattari write specifically about art objects, their aim is to diagram the speculative cartographies laid out by artists and open these territories up onto other practices in the arts, sciences, and philosophy. Deleuze's two books on cinema, for instance, release those temporal structures 'that the cinematographic image has been able to grasp and reveal' (Deleuze, 1989a: xii). This is not simply a history of cinema, but rather a taxonomy of cinematic habitats which resonate with concepts of being and functions of vision. To take another example, Guattari's article 'Cracks in the Street' examines the territories of subjectivity expressed in three paintings by Balthus, and shows how these echo certain formations of subjectivity in music, fractal geometry, and linguistics (Guattari, 1987: 82–5). In my discussion of *A Place I've Never Seen* I have attempted to map the operation of a territory, show how this opens onto new possibilities for political practice, and allow this aesthetic to resonate with the transformative power of sensual habitats developed in Deleuze and Guattari's work.

The concept of art itself remains quite nominal in this approach to art writing. The difference between art and non-art is unclear, which is to say, art does not have a determinate concept. But whenever an assemblage of affects and percepts appears, we have evidence of art differentiating itself as it develops an internal coherence of sensation. It is organized from within and, as I have demonstrated in relation to the autonomy of the beautiful in Kant, this also implies that art can link up to all manner of things. Deleuze and Guattari's preference for animal examples in their discussion of aesthetics points to the problem of defining or classifying art. 'We can not decide whether animals have painting', they confess in *A Thousand Plateaus*, because 'there is little foundation for a clear-cut distinction between animals and human beings' (Deleuze and Guattari, 1987: 301). And in *What Is Philosophy?* they tentatively suggest that 'perhaps art begins with the animal' (Deleuze and Guattari, 1994: 183). The hesitation that Deleuze and Guattari express in these instances is an indication that it is a false problem to try to define art in advance. Instead, they proceed by mapping the expanding territories of art wherever they might be encountered.

In no way do we believe in a fine-arts system; we believe in very diverse problems whose solutions are found in heterogeneous arts. To us, Art is a false concept, a solely nominal concept; this does not, however, preclude the possibility of a simultaneous usage of the various arts within a determinable multiplicity.

(Deleuze and Guattari, 1987: 300–301)

Using the work of Mathew Jones, I have shown how a single art work can function as a determinable multiplicity. The dynamic territories that we find in his work draw together the pre-individual singularities of percepts and affects such that new subjectivities and existential territories might individuate themselves. The singularities provide an intensive consistency of differences in which new formations crystallize. We could say that the singularities precede a concept of activist art and a concept of gay politics, coming together in a spatio-temporal dynamic that allows these practices to be individuated in 'new' or aberrant ways. This same principle of individuation can be related to the 'simultaneous usage of various arts' in Deleuze and Guattari's work. Singularities are extracted from painting, music, architecture, cinema, and bird song as a 'diverse problem' plots these singular points together in a 'determinable multiplicity'. In the process of writing about territories Deleuze and Guattari actually create their own habitats. The very nature of their collaboration also elaborates this process. It is difficult, if not impossible, to isolate the individual voices in Deleuze and Guattari's collaborations. They cease being 'authors', or subjects of enunciation, in order to function as 'temporary, transitory and evanescent points of subjectification'. The points of subjectification are not even what matters. What is important is the multiplicity which passes 'between the points, carrying them along without ever going from one to the other' (Deleuze and Parnet, 1987: ix).

'As soon as there is this type of multiplicity', Deleuze insists, 'there is politics, micro-politics. As Félix says: before Being there is politics' (Deleuze and Parnet, 1987: 17). Guattari has elaborated the political power of these fluxes that precede Being quite extensively in his commentaries on social institutions and revolutionary movements. In his 1985 collaboration with Toni Negri, Guattari explains that these habitats of singularities provide us with the basis for a truly liberationary communism. This habitat-communism has nothing to do with the collective barbarism of communist states, rather, it 'consists in creating the conditions of emergence of a permanent renewing of human activity and social production through the deployment of processes of singularization, auto-organization, auto-valorization' (Guattari and Negri, 1985: 11). It is no longer a matter of the universality of man, or the sharing of wealth, but 'rather of manifesting the singular as multiplicity, mobility, spatio-temporal variability and creativity' (26). The politics of multiplicities does not function prescriptively nor representationally. The task is not to legislate rules for 'correct' behaviour, nor to identify with someone and speak on their

*Figure 3.4* Mathew Jones, *A Place I've Never Seen* (installation view)
Source: The Clock Tower Studio, PSI, New York, 1996

behalf (even if you call that person 'I'). The micro-politics of the habitat works through the experimental formation of communities which can stand up by themselves without a transcendent ideal or determinate concept. The installational multiplicities of Mathew Jones are directed toward the production of these communities of singularities. They liberate desires which have not been reduced to social castes, sexual rituals or political practices. Desire consists of the singularities which overflow us and constitute us outside of ourselves, unlike sexuality, which is already specified. As Guattari argues, 'desire is everything that exists *before* the opposition between subject and object, *before* representation and production' (Guattari, 1979: 57).[23] The liberation of desire, rather than the liberation of sexuality, produces transversal connections that recreate existence as the singularities of real encounters are actually lived.

Art itself highlights this ethic of experimental politics. Jones's installation practice provides us with an example of art works which realize this in relation to issues that are obviously political, but the ethico-aesthetic paradigm also reverberates beyond preconceived notions of 'art' and 'politics'. Given that the coordinates of this paradigm are plotted at the same time as they are lived, it is not enough for art writers to simply be the representatives of a politic that they find elsewhere, in art works or in political science. It is necessary for art writers to create their own aesthetic multiplicities and their own micro-politics. A micro-politics of art scholarship would involve constructing writer-subjects and art-objects in the process of plotting the sensual habitats that distribute images and concepts, exhibitions and history, performance and ideas. To write 'about' art would be actually to pass into an aesthetic territory such that subject and object positions do not precede the habitat, but are extracted from it. In fact, it is no longer a matter of writing *about* art, but of writing *with* art, constructing concepts and identities through an aesthetical empiricism. Deleuze and Guattari do not simply use art works to illustrate the dynamic of artistry, they actually create themselves as aesthetic multiplicities. They distribute themselves in a community of sensual bodies. Guattari claims that 'the infinite body of man moving through all the incredible mutations of any one life time', is 'the true art work' (Guattari, 1984: 237). The subject becomes an artistic territory that is immanent to other artistic territories. Unlike theories of aestheticism that glorify the human subject, this is a pre-humanist aestheticism. It is an aestheticism which precedes Being and makes it possible.

Kant's attempt to theorize the autonomy of aesthetics at the dawn of modernity helps clarify the rigour with which Deleuze and Guattari approach the power of sensuous forms, but the sentiment of their aestheticism owes a great deal to Nietzsche, the artist-philosopher *par excellence*. Deleuze cites Nietzsche as the philosopher who gave him a taste for speaking through 'affects, intensities, experiences, experiments' (Deleuze, 1995: 6). And in his early study on Nietzsche, Deleuze positions him as the philosopher who completed the project which 'Kant betrayed at the same time as he conceived it' (Deleuze, 1983: 52). Kant introduced the problem of how to critique faculties from the inside, where aesthetics would have a certain autonomy from enlightenment thought, but in *Nietzsche and Philosophy* Deleuze argues that it was Nietzsche who realized this project (Deleuze, 1983: 91–4). Nietzsche is gripped by the need for a tragic submission to the forces of encounters, a need to become *immanent* and invent new possibilities for existence from within life itself. Nietzsche is a thought-artist, thinking through what Deleuze calls a 'method of *dramatisation*'. It is in this vein that Nietzsche applauds art for its ability to magnify falsehood, to raise a world of pure appearance and open-ended truth. It is art 'in which precisely the *lie* is sanctified and the *will to deception* has a good conscience' (78). And it is this pre-human aestheticism which Jones's activism tenders so well; the body as an artistic territory, truth as a continually reconstituted fiction. The formation of a body, whether human, animal or artistic, is a mysterious synthesis in a world where anything can happen and already is. The sensuous body of percepts and affects displaces all fixed notions of identity to make room for a rich community of creative intensities.

> One should have more respect for the bashfulness with which nature has hidden behind riddles and iridescent uncertainties … What is required … is to stop courageously at the surface, the fold, the skin,

to adore appearance, to believe in forms, tones, words … to be superficial – out of profundity.

(Nietzsche 1974: 38)

## Notes

1  I would like to thank Melissa McMahon for her thoughtful comments and
suggestions on this essay and her assistance with French translations.
2  Deleuze reflects on the Vincennes classroom in similar terms (1995: 139). Deleuze
also provides an explanation of his philosophy of teaching in *Vincennes ou le désir
d'apprendre* (1979: 120–1).
3  Baumgarten initiated the use of the term 'aesthetics' in this way. He goes beyond
the previous use of the term 'aesthetics' to designate the realm of sense perception
towards its use in relation to artistic considerations by designating as 'aesthetic
truths' the non-conceptual appreciation we have of individuals, as opposed to
'logical truths' which understand objects conceptually, but only at the expense of
their individuality. The feeling of beauty is the paradigmatic form of 'aesthetic'
truth; see his *Aesthetica*. Also see Kant's footnote to Baumgarten in *Critique of Pure
Reason* (Kant, 1933: 66–7).
4  In this sense Kant is extending the modern conception of philosophy inaugurated
by Descartes into the consideration of art. With modern or so-called Christian
Philosophy 'there is no longer even a need for a transcendent centre of power'
(Deleuze and Guattari, 1987: 129–130).
5  Deleuze's interpretation of artistic abstraction as a-signifying rather than transcendent is brought out quite clearly in his discussion of Christian art in *Logique de la
sensation*: by depicting God in Christ, painters gave form a certain autonomy from an
Ideal order, planting the seeds of modern abstraction, 'the germ of a tranquil atheism'
(Deleuze, 1981: 80). On this point also see Deleuze and Guattari (1987: 178–9).
6  Deleuze cites Hegel, a thinker who relentlessly hems in history, as the one
philosopher too detestable for this treatment (Deleuze, 1995: 6). For a discussion
of Deleuze's ethic of affirmation and its implicit critique of Hegel see Michael
Hardt: 'we can see why Deleuze might choose not to address Hegel's
master–slave dialectic directly, because the entire discussion is directed toward self-
consciousness, toward interiority, a condition antithetical to joy and affirmation'
(1993: 42).
7  In *Nietzsche and Philosophy*, published the year before *The Critical Philosophy of
Kant*, Deleuze assumes a more critical tone in relation to Kant. Given the subsequent importance of Kant to Deleuze's elaboration of a transcendental
empiricism, I take his reproach of Kantianism in this earlier context to be an
expression of Deleuze's desire to affirm and even identify with Nietzsche's voice
in the process of writing a book on Nietzsche.
8  Deleuze writes about this same dualism in *Difference and Repetition* (1994: 56–7, 68).
9  Also see McMahon in this volume.
10  It should be noted that Kant defines the term 'perfection' in a different way from
Deleuze, using it to describe the geometric or organic unity which prevents the
emergence of 'beautiful form'.
11  Jones, *A Place I've Never Seen*: Australian Centre for Photography, Sydney, February
1993; Museu de Arte Moderna de São Paulo, São Paulo, October–December
1994; Ace Art, Winnipeg, January–February 1995; Toronto Photographer's Workshop, Toronto, September–October 1995; The Clocktower, Studio 11, New York,
December–April 1995 (under the title 'Pornograph').

12 Jones traces this genealogy in his artist's statement for the exhibition of *A Place I've Never Seen* in Toronto.

13 Jones, *To Be Illiterate Is to Be Blind*, Room 4, Linden Gallery, Melbourne, April–May 1992.

14 In the first version, at the Australian Centre for Photography, the two dimensional dots are photogrammed hemispheres and the raised dots are plaster domes stuck to the surface of the photographic paper. Jones then digitalizes a cropped panoramic photograph of the first installation, and builds up the congestion of spheres with a computer graphics program to create a fifteen-foot refrain that can be plan-printed to the necessary length as the background for subsequent shows. In these later shows the plaster dots are replaced by polystyrene spheres of various dimensions.

15 The braille alphabet catalogue accompanied the first installation of the work in Sydney and the Toronto exhibition. In the New York installation the braille alphabet was stamped onto tissues that were strewn around the room. In other manifestations of this work no decoding key was offered to people who do not read braille.

16 It is unrepresentable in the sense that it does not conform to a concept that creates a distinction between subject, image and object – a concept of representation.

17 The description itself varies, partly to suit the length of the installation and the local language. Sydney: 'this photograph of my lover's cock lost in a place I've never seen this photo of this arse of mine distended by cock wet with cum you can't see'. São Paulo: 'perdido nesta fotografia você não pode ver o pau dele perdido em um lugar que nunca vi distendido pelo pau úmido de porra este meu cú você não pode ver esta fotografia'. Winnipeg: 'lost in this photograph you cant see his cock lost in a place Ive never seen distended by cock wet with cum this arse of mine you cant see this photograph' (no punctuation). New York: 'a photograph, up real close, or some guy's ass with some other cock up it, distended, wet with cum, unspeakable and lost to the logic of vision, half a hand cropped by a column of text, also meant to excite the body, drags across the skin raising pimply lumps'. Toronto: quoted in the body of my text.

18 George Paton Gallery, Melbourne, May–June 1988. Work from this period was also exhibited in a group show which toured Australia in late 1987, *Mirabilis: Post-Appropriation* (Cameleon Gallery, Hobart; Museum of Contemporary Art, Brisbane; George Paton Gallery, Melbourne).

19 Early versions of the white canvases from this period appear in the following group shows: *Imaging AIDS*, Australian Centre for Contemporary Art, Melbourne, January–February 1989; *Moët Chandon Touring Exhibition*, national tour, 1990. A more substantial series of white canvases was developed for a touring solo exhibition *Silence = Death*: 200 Gertrude Street, Melbourne, May 1991; Institute of Modern Art, Brisbane, July 1991. A selection of the works in *Silence = Death* was exhibited under the title *Over My Dead Body* at Artspace, Sydney, March–April 1991. A scale model of the Gertrude Street installation was also displayed at Microscope, Melbourne, May 1991. And a final series of white canvases, titled *What Is This Place?*, were produced for the Australian Perspecta 1991, Art Gallery of New South Wales, Sydney, August–September 1991.

20 Jones compares the chilling silence of the white canvases with the ACT UP strategy of playing dead in public spaces: 'I've seen this bureaucrat after she's dealt, deftly, confidently with our spokesperson in front of the TV cameras, stopped in her tracks as she turned towards her office by a couple of people lying down. A miniature die-in. And I saw that hurt, that registered, just her having to step

around this dumb body, ... and that's what *you're* doing, when you're looking at these ... paintings' (Jones, 1991: 1).

21 Jones, *Poof!*: Australian Centre for Contemporary Art, Melbourne, May–June 1993; *Australian Perspecta 1995*, Art Gallery of New South Wales, Sydney, February-March 1995. In the Sydney version, sequin, glitter and the theatrical architecture of the gallery's vestibule were substituted for the glitzy pink walls of the Melbourne version.

22 Jones, *I Feel Like Chicken Tonight*: Tolarno Galleries, Melbourne, October–November 1994; Artspace, Sydney, January–March 1995; Canberra Contemporary Art Space, Canberra, May–June 1995.

23 Michael Ryan's translation of this text (*Communists Like Us: New Spaces of Liberty, New Lines of Alliance*[1990], New York: Semiotext[e]) unfortunately deletes and distorts important phrases from the original French edition. My citations are translated directly from the French.

# References

Baranowska, Carmela (1992) 'Mathew Jones', *Agenda: Contemporary Art Magazine* 25: 31.

Baumgarten, Alexander Gottlieb (1961) *Aesthetica*, Hildesheim: Georg Holms Verlags-buchhandlung.

Blanchot, Maurice (1982) *The Space of Literature*, trans. Ann Smock, Lincoln: University of Nebraska Press.

Deleuze, Gilles (1979) 'En quoi la philosophie peut servir à des mathématiciens, ou même à des musiciens – même et surtout quand elle ne parle pas de musique ou des mathématiques',in *Vincennes ou le désir d'apprendre*, Jean Brunet, B. Cassen, François Châtelet, P.Merlin and M. Reberioux (eds), Paris: Alain Moreau, 120–1.

—— (1981) *Francis Bacon. Logique de la sensation*, Paris: Editions de la Différence, vol. 1.

—— (1983) *Nietzsche and Philosophy*, trans. Hugh Tomlinson., New York: Columbia University Press.

—— (1984) *The Critical Philosophy of Kant*, trans. Hugh Tomlinson and Barbara Habberjam, Minneapolis: University of Minnesota Press.

—— (1986) *Cinema 1: The Movement-Image*, trans. Hugh Tomlinson and Barbara Habberjam, Minneapolis: University of Minnesota Press.

—— (1989a) *Cinema 2: The Time-Image*, trans. Hugh Tomlinson and Robert Galeta, Minneapolis: University of Minnesota Press.

—— (1989b) 'Coldness and Cruelty', in *Masochism. With Leopold von Sacher-Masoch's Venus in Furs, trans. Jean McNeil, New York: Zone.*

—— (1990) *The Logic of Sense*, trans. Mark Lester and Charles Stivale, ed. Constantin V. Boundas, New York: Columbia University Press.

—— (1994) *Difference and Repetition*, trans. Paul Patton. New York: Columbia University Press.

—— (1995) *Negotiations 1972–1990*, trans. Martin Joughin. New York: Columbia University Press.

Deleuze, Gilles, and Guattari, Félix (1987) *A Thousand Plateaus*, trans. Brian Massumi, Minneapolis: University of Minnesota Press.

—— (1994) *What is Philosophy?* trans. Hugh Tomlinson and Graham Burchell, London:Verso.

Deleuze, Gilles and Claire Parnet (1987) *Dialogues*, trans. Hugh Tomlinson and Barbara Habberjam, New York: Columbia University Press.

Gold, Ron (1991) 'Places, Times, Reasons Revisited: Report on the Sydney Study', *National AIDS Bulletin* 5 (9).

Guattari, Félix (1975) 'Une sexualisation en rupture', interview by Christian Descamps in *La Quinzaine Littéraire* 215: 14–15.

—— (1979) 'A Liberation of Desire', interview by George Stambolian, *Homosexualities of French Literature*, George Stambolian and Elaine Marks (eds), Ithaca: Cornell University Press, 56–69.

—— (1984) *Molecular Revolution: Psychiatry and Politics*, trans. Rosemary Sheed, New York: Penguin.

—— (1987) 'Cracks in the Street', trans. Anne Gibault and John Johnson, *Flash Art* 135: 82–5.

—— (1993) 'Pragmatic/Machinic: Discussion with Charles Stivale', *Pre/Text* 14 (3–4): 215–50.

—— (1995) *Chaosmosis: An Ethico-Aesthetic Paradigm*, trans. Paul Bains and Julian Pefanis, Indianopolis/Sydney: University of Indiana Press/Power Publications.

Guattari, Félix and Toni Negri (1985) *Nouveaux espaces de liberté*, Paris: Dominque Bedou.

Hardt, Michael (1993) *Gilles Deleuze: An Apprenticeship in Philosophy*, Minneapolis: University of Minnesota Press.

Jones, Mathew (1991) *Over My Dead Body* (catalogue) Sydney: Artspace.

—— (1992) *To Be Illiterate Is To Be Blind, or, Pulling Out Before Cumming is Not as Safe as it Looks, or, Getting Off at Redfern* (catalogue) Melbourne: Linden Gallery.

—— (1993) *Press Release: A Place I've Never Seen*, Sydney: Australian Centre for Photography.

Kant, Immanuel (1933) *Critique of Pure Reason*, trans. Norman Kemp Smith, London: Macmillan.

—— (1987) *Critique of Judgement*, trans. Werner S. Pluhar, Cambridge: Hacket.

McMahon, Melissa (1995) 'Kant's Critique of Judgement: The Question of the Mediating Role of Aesthetic Judgements', unpublished typescript, Department of General Philosophy, University of Sydney.

Morden, Ethan (1986) *Buddies*, New York: St Martins.

Mulvey, Laura (1975) 'Visual Pleasure and Narrative Cinema', *Screen* 16: 6–18.

Nietzsche, Friedrich (1967) *Genealogy of Morals*, trans. Walter Kaufmann and R.J. Hollingdale, New York: Vintage.

—— (1974) *The Gay Science*, trans. Walter Kaufmann, New York: Random.

Phillips, David (1992) 'Rhetorical Silence', *Eyeline* 18: 18–21.

# Part 2

# THE SUPERIOR
# EMPIRICISM OF
# THE HUMAN

*...everything which disrupts the relationship between things
and puts us in touch with certain more acute states of mind...*

# 4

# A BESTIARY OF TERRITORIALITY AND EXPRESSION

## Poster fish, bower birds, and spiny lobsters

### Gary Genosko

I first employed the concept of the bestiary in relation to classic psychoanalytic texts (Genosko, 1993). My goal was to reveal the 'moral' tales – the pillars and remarkable caninophilia of the Freudian bestiary – told by the reproduction of animals found therein, as well as in the professional and domestic lives of analysts such as Freud, Ernest Jones, and Marie Bonaparte (Genosko, 1994). I later suggested, somewhat schematically, that the psycho- and schizoanalytic bestiaries of Freud and Guattari overlap on the matter of how they do things with horses and porcupines (Genosko, 1996). From the very beginning, however, I was inspired by the extraordinarily insightful and provocative plateau 2 ('One or Several Wolves') of Deleuze and Guattari's *A Thousand Plateaus* (1987), on Freud's case of the Wolf-Man. It seemed to me that they showed for the first time how productive the close scrutiny of the animal life of a text could be. Subsequently, scenes of animal reproduction became for me a way of reading Deleuze and Guattari's own writings; a way, then, of tracking their arguments across the plateaux by means of signs left by the animals of their own theoretical bestiary.

While this sounds remarkably simple – as simple as following fresh tracks in the sand – it takes practice, as any bird or butterfly enthusiast will tell you, and a firm grasp of the identifying features of the species at issue. Even a textual bestiary makes demands on animal fanciers, especially since the species at issue in this paper are as diverse as poster fish, bower birds and spiny lobsters. Contextual or field conditions are not, of course, the issue, nor is it a question of mastering a scientific literature; rather, the bestiarist is called upon to track these creatures as they perform varied theoretical work for Deleuze and Guattari (1987), and to bring to bear a certain amount of background knowledge, in the manner of a naturalist, upon the discussion of the services performed by such creatures. An example is in order. It took me a long time to see what is now obvious – that the lobster of plateau 3 ('On the Geology of Morals') is a true lobster and not the spiny lobster that most readers of plateau 11 ('Of the Refrain') will remember from the fascinating footnote on the cosmic dimension of its migration.

The concept of the bestiary requires a certain amount of zoological knowledge, to be sure. Identification is not an easy matter, in the field, as in the text. After a confirmed sighting has been made, the issues to which the bestiarist must attend only increase, especially since my interest in this paper is to track the relationship between territoriality and expression through the uses (Deleuze and Guattari's eclectic borrowing from the ethograms of a variety of animals) made of the three species mentioned in my title, across plateau 11, while simultaneously attending to the critique of the presuppositions of the ethological understanding of territoriality. There are not only three species at issue here; animals tend to multiply and, before long, one finds onself in the company of monkeys, chaffinches, spiders, etc.

## How to build a territory

In general, one may say of any bestiary that it is a machine for theory-making. The study of territoriality has traditionally been the province of ethology and behavioural ecology, which explains, in technical terms, the presence of Deleuze and Guattari's animals. Deleuze and Guattari advance an argument against the Austrian ethologist Konrad Lorenz which I will examine through a consideration of three references. Lorenz thinks that aggression is the basis of territoriality; more precisely, as Deleuze and Guattari note: 'Lorenz has a constant tendency to present territoriality as an effect of intraspecific aggression' (1987: 548, n. 9). Keep in mind that it is standard in ethology to first think of the demonstration of territoriality through the overt aggression between animals, before considering the second manifestation of boundaries by means of various signals. Deleuze and Guattari specifically reject the 'dangerous political overtones' (i.e., the escalation of violence) of Lorenz's controversial thesis that the value of intraspecific aggression lies in population distribution and regulation, selection of the strongest and the best defence of the young. For Lorenz, aggression is an instinct whose function is to preserve the species. Deleuze and Guattari maintain that this thesis presupposes territory rather than explains it (1987: 316); indeed, in the ethological literature it is generally the case that aggressive behaviour presupposes that an animal is in its familiar territory. Recall the pain they took to show that 'territorialization is an act of rhythm that has become expressive, or of milieu components that have become qualitative' (315). Deleuze and Guattari's critique of Lorenz begins by loosening territoriality from aggression, and bringing the ethological presupposition of territory into the foreground in order to give it new connections.

First reference: Deleuze and Guattari turn to Lorenz's *On Aggression*, against which they argue, for an example of a matter of expression, 'a territorializing mark': that of poster-coloured coral fish (1987: 315, 547 n. 6). This example, in Lorenz's work (1966: 14–15), both presupposes territory (the colours that a territory has found an owner) and is explained by intraspecific sion. From this material Deleuze and Guattari extract their counter-reading that poster-colouring is not tied to a specific function (aggression) which they identify with transitoriness, but rather, with temporal constancy and spatial range: the day-time coloration of these fish (which changes during sleep) and the visibility of the colours at long distances.

Second reference: The becoming-expressive of a component such as coloration marks a territory. Deleuze and Guattari populate their bestiary with selective examples from the ethograms (the inventory of patterns of behaviour) of certain species of birds, rabbits, and monkeys, many of which are borrowed from Irenäus Eibl-Eibesfeldt's *Ethology* (Deleuze and Guattari, 1987: 315, 547 n. 7). In particular, they employ the example of genital displays by so-called 'guard' monkeys in which the penis becomes a 'rhythmic and expressive colour-carrier that marks the limits of the territory' (see Eibl-Eibesfeldt, 1970: 428). But like Lorenz, Eibl-Eibesfeldt treats territoriality (the ownership of a territory may be temporally defined and consist of marked and unmarked paths rather than rigid boundaries, as well as including neutral areas) under the heading of intraspecific aggression. While borrowing what they need to reconnect territoriality to rhythm and expressive marking, they let stand the standard ethological presupposition, present in Eibl-Eibesfeldt no less than in Lorenz. Deleuze and Guattari have, in a sense, already fried the bigger fish.

Third reference: Deleuze and Guattari remark 'how quick' the becoming-expressive-territory of a component may be with respect to the ornithological example of the Brown Stagemaker: 'The Brown Stagemaker … lays down landmarks each morning by dropping leaves it picks from its tree, and then turning them upside down so the paler underside stands out against the dirt: inversion produces a matter of expression' (1987: 315). They borrow this example from W. H. Thorpe's *Learning and Instinct in Animals* (1956). Ronald Bogue adds the following clarification: 'Each leaf is a milieu component that has been removed from its milieu and converted into a quality, and the Stagemaker's action comprises a rhythm that is no longer simply a function of a milieu, but one that has become expressive' (Bogue, 1991: 89). In other words, the bird cuts a leaf from its tree, and deposits it, pale-side up, on its display ground at the base of the tree. It would be premature to conclude that Deleuze and Guattari are only interested in the visual elements of the Stagemaker's behaviour. As we will see, they are also concerned with its sonorous dimension. Thorpe does not elaborate upon this example, but a photograph of the bird's display ground or stage appears in his discussion of play in birds (Thorpe, 1956: 323, fig. 2). This activity of the Brown Stagemaker is a display activity in the strict sense – a species-specific behaviour pattern used in communication between both groups and individuals (i.e., in courtship rituals) – which also has an element of freedom. For Thorpe this is the critical element in true play found in those behaviours loosened from the restrictions imposed by the necessity of attaining specific goals (1956, 85). Deleuze and Guattari are only exaggerating a little when they refer to this leaf-turning activity as '*art brut*' (Deleuze and Guattari, 1987: 316) and find themselves in the company of zoosemioticians who recognize that birds have an aesthetic 'sense', both visual and musical, which thus breaks the anthroposemiotic hold on art (Sebeok, 1979). Deleuze and Guattari write: 'Artists are Stagemakers, even when they tear up their own posters. Of course, from this standpoint art is not the privilege of human beings' (1987: 316). Artists and birds: the frontispiece of 'Of the Refrain' (1987: plateau 11) is, after all, Paul Klee's *Twittering Machine* (1922).

Thorpe borrowed the photograph of the Brown Stagemaker's stage from A. J. Marshall's book on *Bower-Birds* (1954), to which Deleuze and Guattari later refer (1987: 331 n. 34). The Brown Stagemaker is included among Bower-birds even though it is technically a Cat-bird. It lives in wild ginger-shrubs, among other trees, in the rainforest in Northeast Queensland, Australia, and is also known for the 'melodious noise' of its display call in which it mimicks the calls of neighbouring bird species. The visual and auditory displays run parallel with its sexual cycle. The key point for Deleuze and Guattari is that territory (possession) emerges with expression, a reading which Marshall confirms with an important proviso: 'Whilst it cannot be denied that the birds get aesthetic pleasure from their stage-decoration and from the song that they produce from above it, these activities, extraordinary as they are, form essentially a highly specialized mechanism that ensures the acquisition and establishment of territory, the attraction of a mate in dense rainforest, and the synchronization of the male and female reproductive processes before the female can be inseminated' (Marshall, 1954: 63). The matter of the temporal constancy of expression is related, then, to the parallel display and nesting seasons, after which time the display ground falls into disrepair. But Deleuze and Guattari take a further, more radical step in making territory the result of art. Simply, if territory is the result of the becoming-expressive of milieu components, which means that expressive qualities (produced or selected) can be called art, then territory is the result of art, which is far removed from basing it on aggressiveness. This is what Deleuze and Guattari affirm, unlike Marshall, who merely does not wish to deny it in the case of the Brown Stagemaker.

The three references are, then: poster fish, guard monkey penis, Stage-maker's stage. Territoriality is, over the course of Deleuze and Guattari's readings of these animal references, turned from a presupposition tied to aggression to a form of art tied to expression.

Deleuze and Guattari then drift slowly back to Lorenz, having established the terms of their relationship with his work. Matters of expression, they maintain, form shifting relations with one another, expressing a twofold relation of territory: to an interior milieu (impulses or drives) and to an exterior milieu (circumstances or environmental variables). The internal relations of matters of expression constitute territorial motifs which are not pulsed; that is, non-pulsed motifs are independent of what Lorenz calls the 'big four' drives (hunger, sexuality, flight, aggression) (Lorenz, 1966: 89). What Deleuze and Guattari call territorial motifs, Lorenz refers to as 'special drives', independent variables arising from conflicting drives, some of which, as Deleuze and Guattari note, arise in territorial counterpoint with circumstances of the external milieu (Deleuze and Guattari, 1987: 317). Both territorial motifs and counterpoints 'explore potentialities of the interior or exterior milieu' (318). Lorenz treats this phenomenon as ritualization, and it is a simulation, with modifications (exaggeration, repetition), of original non-ritual behaviours in conflict (Lorenz, 1966: 90). Deleuze and Guattari consider the concept of ritualization to be 'not necessarily appropriate' to the independence of the non-pulsed motifs and counterpoints which, rather, form rhythmic faces or characters and melodic landscapes, respectively (Deleuze and Guattari, 1987: 318), even though Lorenz admits that 'new drives' can 'shout down' opposing impulses. What is at issue here is whether or not Lorenz accounts for, and in Deleuze and Guattari's estimation he does not, the variability and fixity of non-pulsed motifs and counterpoints. The hypothesis of simulation does not interest them, because this hypothesis makes it impossible to loosen rhythmic faces from drives and melody from landscape; for Lorenz uses the concept of the copy to relate new drives to a pattern of movement arising from the conflict of several original drives. In other words, Deleuze and Guattari are not fooled by this ruse of backward connection. In Deleuze and Guattari's terms, melody constitutes its own sonorous landscape and rhythm its own character. What was the mark, the signature or poster, becomes style, as they put it, when motifs, having become autonomous from impulses, conjoin on their own plane, and enrich their internal relations; in addition, characters do not refer – they autodevelop (319).

Deleuze and Guattari are content to group together artists and birds because they take the same route to motifs and counterpoints: via the posting of placards and the maintenance of a critical distance which, between members of the same species in different territories, is rhythmical, and between members of different species in the same territory, melodic. There is an intimation of the cosmic function in what is described as the opening of a territory for a mate (1987: 320). Recall their initial description of the third aspect of the refrain in plateau 11: the circle opens a crack, but not at the place where chaos presses in most strongly, and one 'joins the world' by 'fan[ning] out to the sphere of the cosmos' (312). Reproduction opens doors. They borrow from Lorenz the idea that territorial borders oscillate according to the rhythm of intraspecies movement across the boundary of two adjacent territories (Lorenz, 1966: 29). Territorialization changes existing functions and provides for the emergence of professional or work-functions. The first effect of territorialization discussed here, that of professionalization (or specialization,

:ological niche), continues Deleuze and Guattari's efforts to chal-
's presupposition of territory while adhering to his presentation
including professionalization) and even citing as an example of
ation of functions, owing to their territorialization, Lorenz's
upation with the selective advantage or 'survival value' of intra-
--ggression (competition) over interspecies aggression (predator–prey)
(Deleuze and Guattari, 1987: 321; Lorenz, 1966: 17ff). A further effect of
territorialization relates to religion and the intensive grouping of the forces of
the earth locked in battle at a particular place, an intense centre. The development of marks to motifs and counterpoints, to the reorganization and
regrouping of functions, Deleuze and Guattari state, 'already unleashes something that will surpass it [territory]' (1987: 322). In order to further express
this idea of 'unleashing' they adopt the language of the assemblage: the movement from the infraassemblage (posters) to the intraassemblage (motifs and
counterpoints) puts one on 'the passage of the Refrain' [a sonorous assem-
blage] (323). The organization of the intraassembalge is 'rich and complex',
and includes the territorial assemblage and territorialized functions.

When a territorial function acquires sufficient independence to constitute
a new, more or less deterritorialized assemblage –'more or less' in the sense
that it is not yet a question of leaving the territory – there is a passage from
the intra- to the inter-assemblage by means of a particular component.
Incidentally, this passage from intra- to inter- reverses Lorenz's inter- to intra-
paradigm. Deleuze and Guattari cite both colour and 'grass stem behaviour' of
Australian grass finches as deterritorialized components of passage from territorial to courtship assemblages (1987: 324); in the latter case, the grass stem
held by the male during the initial phases of courtship is no longer tied to
nest building (males no longer make nests), but rather enables nesting to
become an element of another assemblage, courtship. The 'grass stem' is an
'assemblage converter' (325). In the first instance and as a consequence of
their ethological examples, Deleuze and Guattari describe the territory of one
sex opening onto another; in the example cited above (in addition to an
earlier use of a species of wren in which the male built the nest before the
arrival of the female; 323) and the subsequent discussion, the territory of the
male opens onto the female (324–5); this is also the case in the example of the
Brown Stagemaker. If passages between assemblages take place on a 'case-by-
case basis' (325), we expect that the same holds true on a 'species-by-species
basis' with regard to who builds the nest, incubates the eggs, cares for the
young, etc. Deleuze and Guattari's claims cannot be generalized across bird
species, in other words.

In their characterization of territorial functions which suddenly acquire
autonomy and enter into new assemblages in a variety of ways, Deleuze and
Guattari constitute a rich vocabulary of 'opening': 'swinging'; 'draw a line of
deterritorialization'; 'take wing'; 'take off'; 'budding' (1987: 326). Deleuze and
Guattari revisit here the question of the intense centre of a territory as the

ambiguity of the Natal which is exterior to the territory, but the focal point of many different territories (325–6), and they cite several examples of 'prodigious takeoffs from the territory, displaying a vast movement of deterritorialization directly plugged into the territories and permeating them through and through', among which is the 'march of lobsters' (326). This march leaves the question of passage between assemblages behind: 'there is something of the Cosmos in these more ample movements' (326). 'Unleashings' become 'unclaspings' as deterritorialization dramatically affects 'bundles' of territorialized components.

## In search of the cosmic lobster

What is this cosmic lobster? The photograph of the underside of a lobster, bearing the subtitle 'double articulation' appears at the outset of plateau 3, '10,000 BC: The Geology of Morals' (Deleuze and Guattari, 1987: 39). The authors turn a classic linguistic concept from Louis Hjelmslev's glossematics to geological ends (linguistics and geology are, after all, concerned with stratification) through the mediation of a lobster. 'God is a lobster', they write, 'or a double pincer, a double bind' (40). It has two prominent claws, each with pincers. Just like two strata, each with its own layers, not to mention the expression and content planes described by Hjelmslev: within each plane there is both form and substance. This is commonly called a double dichotomy. God may be a lobster because all strata are his/her/its judgements, but is this the cosmic lobster? The question of the cosmic lobster is tied less to divine stratification, coding and territorialization than to destratification, decoding and deterritorialization, without forgetting the reterritorializations relative to them. This can't be it, as I indicated in my introductory remarks about distinguishing between different sorts of lobsters.

In an important footnote, Deleuze and Guattari refer to the speculations of marine biologist, scientific adventurer, and inventor of the aqualung, Jacques Cousteau, in his film on the march of lobsters (1987: 549 n. 26). A spotty description of spiny lobster mass migration follows. This is it: the cosmic lobster lacks prominent pincers. The mass migration of spiny lobsters off the coasts of the Yucatan, the Bahamas, and Florida, among other places, takes place in the autumn. The nocturnal 'queuing' (in single-files) begins before the autumn storms and may take several weeks to complete. These queues have many lengths (as little as two lobsters) and their formation each autumn is a seasonal refrain. The march of the queuers is connected with cosmic forces, with tellurian pulses. Migration over long distances takes place after periods of stormy weather. What attracts Deleuze and Guattari to this example is that it is not tied to a reproductive function (pre- or post-reproductive) and remains somewhat of a mystery, although there is no shortage of suggestions about its adaptive significance in the literature on animal migration (see Herrnkind, 1969; and for a summary of the literature, Rebach and Dunham,

1983: 234–5). Perhaps, Deleuze and Guattari note, following the American lobster expert William Herrnkind, whose writings on spiny lobster populations near the Bahamas are extensive, it is a ' "vestige" from the last ice age'; the phrase used by Rebach and Dunham is 'remnant from glacial times.' This idea is suggested by Herrnkind and Kanciruk who state: 'The hypothesis most clearly fitting present data is that the mass migration is a concentrated seasonal movement adapted to moving the population from the shallow banks, subject to severe cooling, to the oceanic fringe where conditions are suitable to over-wintering. Clearly, shallow waters over much of the range of the species cooled to temperatures of 10°C or less for long periods during glacial winters' (1978: 435). Below 12–15°C, the spiny lobster can neither feed nor complete moulting.

Perhaps, following Cousteau, 'it is a premonition of a new ice age' (Deleuze and Guattari, 1987: 549 n.22). Deleuze and Guattari prefer a forward-looking rather than a backward-looking interpretation. Whatever the case may be – it is understood that the earth is between ice ages – this phenomenon reveals the passage from a territorial assemblage to a social assemblage connected with cosmic forces ('pulsations of the earth', to use Cousteau's suggestive language, but which Herrnkind believes may be wave surges along the ocean floor, coupled with a decrease in temperature, and a lower light level all through October during the night queuing period and later in the month, during the mass migration itself; for the biologist, tellurian pulses are 'stimuli' to be tested). This constitutes the fourth kind of refrain of departures from a territory 'that sometimes bring on the movement of absolute deterritorialization' (Deleuze and Guattari, 1987: 327). Such absolute deterritorializations are dangerous. In the case of the cosmic lobster, a mass slaughter by fishermen ensues, a seasonal depopulation for the sake of their tails.

What is the relation between the cosmic lobster and the rock and roll saviour identifed by Cavale in Sam Shepard's *Cowboy Mouth*? The Lobster Man moults to a rock song played by Cavale and her putative saviour, Slim, whom he replaces. The Lobster Man is the rock and roll saviour. Earlier, Slim, sensing the power of the Lobster Man, threatened to kill him, acknowledging the 'ancient sea-green strength' of lobsters (Shepard, 1976: 212). The Lobster Man is the cosmic artisan capable of harnessing prehistoric forces, in Slim's estimation, and in Cavale's, he is the one who can capture, that is, 'reach out and grab all the little broken, busted-up pieces of people's frustration' (214). The Lobster Man doesn't found, he doesn't create; instead, he captures and assembles frustrations. He is a rocking lobster who makes consistent molecularized frustrations. He makes sonorous the non-sonorous, and proceeds by subtraction, simplification, by moulting. This is no rock and roll hootchy-koo. It's a rock lobster!

Cavale the schizo, the criminal, the dreamer with a '45 at her side only acknowledges her name with the emergence of the Lobster Man. *Etre en cavale*: to be on the lam. She found her name, she explains:

Nerval. He had visions. He cried like a coyote. He carried a crow. He walked through the Boulevard Noir inhuman like a triangle. He had a pet lobster on a pink ribbon. He told it his dreams, his visions, all the great secrets to the end of the world. And he hung himself on my birthday. Screaming like a coyote. The moon was cold and full and his visions and the crow and the lobster went on *cavale*. That's where I found my name. Cavale. On my birthday. It means escape.

(Shepard, 1976: 216)

Nerval and Dali may have walked their lobsters, but this lobster runs with the mass migration toward the reefs adjacent to the gulf stream. The cosmic lobster doesn't wear a leash and, instead of being on the lam, is open to the cosmos.

## From syntheses to synthesizers

Before picking up once more the theme of the deterritorializing Cosmos, consider the return of the Brown Stagemaker in Deleuze and Guattari's discussion of the holding together of heterogeneous components in a territorial assemblage as a kind of consolidation: a creative, machinic synthesis of heterogeneities (1987: 330). The Stagemaker is the bird, as they say, of the machinic opera. It lacks brilliant coloration, with the exception of the yellowish throat feathers it reveals while singing. Perched on its 'singing stick' above its display ground, the bird weaves into its loud vocalization pattern the sounds of other species (other birds, frogs and cicadas; see Marshall, 1954: 159). For Deleuze and Guattari the consolidation ' "consists" in species-specific sounds, sounds of other species, leaf hue, throat colour: the Stagemaker's machinic statement or assemblage of enunciation' (1987: 331). There is a kind of opening at work: the territorial assemblage is opened (deterritorialized by the insertion of a machine) to interspecific assemblages through mimickry (although Deleuze and Guattari consider imitation to be a matter of occupying a frequency in order to either advantageously restrict or open the assemblage). They also note the adaptive value of mixed calls in those species which otherwise have no other (visual) way to distinguish themselves and communicate with one another in the dense rainforest environment, which is precisely Marshall's point (1954: 163).

A further example of consolidation is adapted from Thorpe's study of chaffinch songs. For Deleuze and Guattari, there is consolidation in the passage from sub-song to full song, that is, from marks and placards to style and motif (1987: 330). But a brief look at Thorpe reveals that this gradual passage consists largely in the dropping out of what is not a necessary part of the extreme frequencies characterizing sub-song (373–4). When Deleuze and Guattari return to the question of bird song a page later in a discussion of imitation, they pick up Thorpe's idea of the occupation of a specific frequency in full songs by means of the selective process of leaving out imitative sounds available in the sub-song (331). Consolidation, in the case of chaffinches, is a matter of restriction, and in the Brown Stagemaker, a matter of expansion. And there are advantages to both. The concept of consolidation is employed by Deleuze and Guattari to suggest a solution to the problem of consistency. The issue here is which model best explains 'what holds things together?' Arborescent or rhizomatic? Deleuze and Guattari distinguish between the arborescent ethological model, a hierarchical and centralized model constructed of binary mechanisms such as inhibitors–innate releasing mechanisms, and the rhizomatic model, which postulates coordination between functional centres rather than causation from higher to lower centres. The rhizomatic model does not replace the ethological model, but criticizes it on the basis of its mistaken reliance on the 'oversimplified binarities' of a tree model. As I have shown, their argument with and against Lorenz involved three selected references to the ethograms of poster fish, guard monkeys, and Brown Stagemakers, as they slowly loosened territoriality from aggression, shifting it to expression through select ethological examples. Deleuze and Guattari do not work a logic of replacement: this for that; neither do they merely invert terms (minor for molar, root-stem for tree). While ethologists 'risk reintroducing souls and centres at each locus and stage of linkage' (1987: 328), for their part Deleuze and Guattari posit *transversals* whose function is to hold together components, thereby risking the creation of special components of linkage with a special property (a 'vector of deterritorialization'). Even in their reading of the hierarchized, linear causality of the molar ethological model, Deleuze and Guattari present a component which may be, they admit, 'highly determined', like the leaf-turning activity of the Brown Stagemaker in relation to its toothed beak (336).

Deleuze and Guattari's opening to the deterritorializing Cosmos is not a radically indeterminate openness. The opening to the Cosmos is not an oceanic feeling, just as the queuing of lobsters is in no way indeterminate. Recall Freud's reflection in *Civilisation and Its Discontents* on the prototypical new age narcissism of the ego-feeling of oneness with the world. Freud denied that this feeling was the origin of religious belief, and instead, traced it back to an earlier phase before the ego's boundaries were built up during maturation. He did not deny that it might co-exist with the bounded adult ego since such feelings may co-exist alongside stricter delimitations. Freud's scepticism serves me well. The cosmic 'breakaway' of Deleuze and Guattari is a matter of precision and localization, of 'queuing.' They move from the cosmic lobster to Paul Klee, for whom the forces of the Cosmos are harnessed in a work (1987: 337). Deleuze and Guattari work, then, in the inter-discipline between the study of the behaviour of the higher *Crustacea* and painting; there is no discipline *per se* in this space, but it is not without its rigors; nor is it a question of the analysis settling in one or the other area of study.

The issue is sobriety. Deleuze and Guattari urge sobriety because they want to avoid new age narcissism and noodling in the proliferation of lines, as well as cultish devotion to machines (my Ferrari, your Bang & Olufsen, etc.). On the matter of the synthesizer, and in particular Edgar Varèse's use of it, Deleuze and Guattari write:

> We thus leave behind the assemblages to enter the age of the Machine, the immense mechanosphere, the plane of cosmicization of forces to be harnessed. Varèse's procedure, at the dawn of this age, is exemplary: a musical machine of consistency, a *sound machine* (not a machine for reproducing sounds), which molecularizes and atomizes, ionizes sound matter, and harnesses a cosmic energy. If this machine must have an assemblage, it is the synthesizer.
>
> (Deleuze and Guattari, 1987: 343)

Noodling means reproducing sounds (strings, percussion, etc.) and combining them in a fuzzy way. The agglomeration of reproduced, synthesized sounds is a 'scrambling', a progressive rock jam: brain salad surgery. The least interesting thing about a Moog is that it can reproduce sounds. The formation of a rhythmic substance from the sonorities of thirty-seven percussion instruments, as Varèse demonstrated in his composition *Ionisation* of 1931, constitutes a sober synthesis of disparate elements.

## Concluding remarks

The issue of sobriety is closely related to that of subtraction. In the passage from sub-song to full song, as I noted in my discussion of Deleuze and Guattari's use of chaffinch songs, certain imitative sounds disappear. The plane of consistency is defined in terms of subtraction, simplicity, and sobriety in the making consistent of the multiple (molecularized and ionized sound matter, for example). Subtract against every inclination to add. Moult, like a lobster. Recall what Marshall McLuhan had to say about Klee's *Twittering Machine*: 'Preview of the TV aerial, electric configuration patterned to pick up nonvisual energy' (McLuhan and Parker, 1968: 189). These birds on the wire render non-visible energy visible; just as the synthesizer makes the sound process audible (Deleuze and Guattari, 1987: 343). McLuhan got it partially right: it is a question of energy, of forces, of picking them up: harnessing. Don't reterritorialize deterritorialization, Deleuze and Guattari advise, on madmen and children: 'your synthesis of disparate elements will be all the *stronger* if you proceed with a sober gesture, an act of consistency, capture, or extraction that works in a material that is not meager but prodigiously simplified, creatively limited, selected' (344–5).

For Deleuze and Guattari, the 'deformations' of the great cosmic deterritorialized refrain that flies from the earth and remains unsystematized are contained in assembled refrains like the rondo. The cosmic is contained in the territorial, and the latter is opened to the former. Deleuze and Guattari admit their tendency to privilege the sonorous over the visual. The latter 'clings' to territoriality, and tends to dissolve when it is deterritorialized (1987: 347). In *What Is Philosophy?* they provide numerous examples from painting and literature to show that they are not elevating music above all the other arts. Examples abound of the deterritorialization of the house: Matisse's windows opening 'onto an area of plain, uniform black' (Deleuze and Guattari, 1994: 180); the head of Kafka's ' "Shamefaced Lady" ... goes right through the ceiling' (184). The Brown Stagemaker returns here as a 'complete artist' of the house-territory. The emphasis on sound rather than colour in the discussion of certain birds, especially the Brown Stagemaker, is determined by the features of the birds themselves rather than by Deleuze and Guattari's preferences; poster fish, of course, are dealt with in terms of their visual qualities.

Deleuze and Guattari present, in plateau 11 (1987), a detailed argument for a territoriality made by expressive qualities, selected or produced, on the basis of a critique of the ethological theory that territoriality is an effect of aggression. The expressive qualities with which I have dealt have been colour and sound, although expression is not limited to these; the introduction of other species of animals (or, just as well, further research into the ethograms of the existing species under discussion) would undoubtedly expand the range of qualities into the chemical-olfactory realm. Since selected or produced qualities constitute a territory, this makes artists, Deleuze and Guattari add, of certain species, especially birds. It may be surprising for some readers of Deleuze and Guattari that I have reversed the relationship between music and animals that one commonly finds in discussions such as those of Bogue, on the musical interests of Olivier Messiaen, particularly his orthino–musico–graphical incorportions. This is an effect of my concept of the bestiary, wherein animal sounds are not incorporated into compositions according to a logic of reproduction, but music emerges from the consideration of birdsong, and the like, with a concomitant interest in visual elements as equal matters of expression.

## References

Bogue, Ronald (1991) 'Rhizomusicosmology', *Substance* 66 20 (3): 85–101.

Deleuze, Gilles and Guattari, Félix (1987) *A Thousand Plateaus*, trans. Brian Massumi, Minneapolis: University of Minnesota Press.

—— (1994) *What Is Philosophy?* trans. Hugh Tomlinson and Graham Burchell, London: Verso.

Eibl-Eibesfeldt, Irenäus (1970) *Ethology*, trans. E. Klinghammer, New York: Holt.

Freud, Sigmund (1930) *Civilisation and Its Discontents*, trans. Joan Riviere, *Standard Edition of the Works of Sigmund Freud*, vol. 21, London: Hogarth. 57–145.

Genosko, Gary (1993) 'Freud's Bestiary: How Does Psychoanalysis Treat Animals?' *Psychoanalytic Review* 80 (4): 603–32.

—— (1994) 'Introduction', *Topsy: The Story of a Golden-Haired Chow*, Mary Bonaparte, New Brunswick, NJ: Transaction.

—— (1996) 'Introduction', *The Guattari Reader*, Gary Genosko (ed.), Oxford: Blackwell.

Herrnkind, William (1969) 'Queuing Behaviour of Spiny Lobsters', *Science* 164.3886 (20 June): 1425–27.

Herrnkind, William, and Paul Kanciruk (1978) 'Mass Migration of Spiny Lobster, Panulirus argus (Crustacea: Palinuridae): Synopsis and Orientation', *Animal Migration, Navigation, and Homing*, K. Schmidt-Koenig and W. T. Keeton (eds), Berlin: Springer, 430–9.

Lorenz, Konrad (1966) *On Aggression*, trans. Marjorie Latzke, London: Methuen.

Marshall, A.J. (1954) *Bower-Birds: Their Displays and Breeding*, Oxford: Clarendon.

McLuhan, Marshall and Harley Parker (1968) *Through the Vanishing Point: Space in Poetry and Painting*, New York: Harper.

Rebach, S., and Dunham, D. (eds) (1983) *Studies in Adaptation: The Behaviour of Higher Crustacea*, New York: Wiley.

Sebeok, Thomas A (1979) *The Sign and Its Masters*, Austin: University of Texas Press.

Shepard, Sam (1976) *Angel City and Other Plays*, New York: Urizen.

Thorpe, W. H. (1956) *Learning and Instinct in Animals*, London: Methuen.

# 5

# LITERATURE, LANGUAGE, AND THE NON-HUMAN

*Alan Bourassa*

'In literature the human reveals itself through language.'

'Or rather, in literature, language creates the human.'

'Literature is the intersection of language and the human.'

'The human, which has its possibility in language, extracts from the possibilities of language to create literature.'

'Literature extracts the human from language to give the human its own voice.'

'The subtraction of literature from language, leaves us with all that is non-human.'

'Language, literature and the human fight pitched battles of mutual capture, shifting alliances and attrition, punctuated by periods of peace or uneasy truce.'

Nowhere does the human seem more the cornerstone of literature than in the novel. If the novel is an escape, it is an escape *into*: meaning, sense, the human. Madame Bovary. Isabel Archer. Gatsby. Ahab. Hester Prynne. It is the great *characters* of the novel that we remember, and the emotions that spring from the human encounter with all that is outside of it. Greed, obsession, sin, regret and pride assign a value to the humanity of fictional characters. Their triumphs are the human triumphs of understanding, reconciliation, creation; their defeats are equally human: despair, loneliness, loss.

In these terms the relationship between the human and literature is almost one of identity. The literary is that which shows forth the humanness of the human; it is the human activity *par excellence*. And the human is but the creation of a system of meanings and values that must in large part be called literary. The human takes shape among an endless proliferation of stories, characters, mythologies. There is no story without the human, no human without stories: one reality with two modalities.

But how much more complicated the picture becomes when the human/literary becomes the triad of language/literature/human.

Language shatters the easy equivalence of literary and human by opening up a dimension of the non-literary in literature (that is, everything that lies outside the scope of the literary but on which the literary depends) and of the non-human in the human (that is, all that lies outside the scope of the human, but nonetheless makes it up).

The question of the non-human is central here. It is a question posed by language itself, and one that can be phrased in terms of language. What is the non-human, and why must it be invoked by the question of language?

If we insist on phrasing the question of the non-human in affirmative terms (that is, if we insist on seeing in the 'non' of 'non-human' negativity rather than difference) we will find ourselves back at the three great figures of the non-human: the animal, the machine and the divinity. These three figures are not, of course, *essentially* non-human. They are not, in other words, defined by their deviation from the human. They are, at best *accidentally* non-human. The non-human, as something that can be spoken of, that can act and appear, is caught within the disjunction of the three, the empty space created and enclosed (but not occupied) by their imperfect overlap.

And these three figures of the non-human are paralleled by three kinds of language, three powers that can be assigned to language and between which our own thinking about language negotiates its uneasy path: semiotics, information and revelation.

The animal: pure semiotics. Language as a system of recognizable signs. As Agamben tells us, 'Animals do not enter language. They are already inside of it' (1993: 52). Semiotics is grounded in recognition rather than understanding. The animal recognizes a certain sign – the beaver's tail-slap on the water, the honeybee's signal indicating the presence of pollen – because the sign is repeated, either genetically in the animal's innate responses or experientially in its ability to learn. Our own response to language, our ability to make sense of it, depends upon our semantic skills, the ability to figure meanings in sentences we have never encountered. You can understand the sentence 'My daughter repaired the refrigerator although she was sick with the palsy' even though it is unlikely that you have encountered this sentence in the past. But this semantic competence rests on a certain level of semiotic efficiency, recognizing certain letters as signifiers for certain sounds and recognizing words as distinct signs. This is the first language we encounter.

The machine is language as information. Information differs from simple signification in that it relies upon a kind of coding that can intensify the signifying function of language. Félix Guattari uses the example of the bank card: 'The asignifying semiotic figures don't simply secrete significations. They give out stop and start orders, but above all activate the "bringing into being" of ontological Universes' (1995: 49). There is something immediately physical about this kind of coding; the most privileged example of it is the DNA double helix, information as chemical bonds. There is also something brutal about this kind of language, its atheistic immediacy, its relentless attachment to the actual. Information is a step up from the pure sign, calling on higher levels of organization and memory, but neither form of language can justify a claim to truth. Semiotics deals only with recognition and misrecognition, information only with correctness.

It is only a divine language (whether that divinity is God, the Idea, or transcendence itself) that can begin to make a claim to truth. This is our third language, the language of revelation. In his essay 'On Language as Such and the Language of Man', Walter Benjamin traces a line that runs through knowledge, language and divinity: 'God rested when he had left his creative power to itself in man. This creativity, relieved of its divine actuality, became knowledge. Man is the knower in the same language in which God is creator' (Benjamin: 1986, 323). This language, in its myriad forms, is the language of creativity and truth. It snatches the human up from above. It grounds the human in that which infinitely surpasses it: '*language as such* is the mental being of man; and only for this reason is the mental being of man, alone among all mental entities, communicable without residue' (1986: 318).

We open our mouths to speak and what issues forth? Signs? Information? Names that are grounded in our privilege as humans, our hegemony over a nature that communicates itself to us in order to be named? When we write, where do we locate ourselves? In the position of masters who control a circus of unruly signs, or as bodies through which something is written or writes itself?

This is the paradox of language. It is what we control – and there is no doubt that skill does tame the flux of language, makes it into an instrument – but it is the very same language that can suddenly show itself to us as a relentless revelation, a lighting that withdraws from understanding as it founds the very possibility of understanding.

Human or non-human? Our own creation or a gift that obsesses us? We might think of language as we would think of an apparition out of the darkness of an empty road. Is it a fellow wanderer? Does it share my nature and is it haunted by the silence and mystery of the darkness? Does it fear and ward off the imminent reality of the outside? Is it powerless to fight the spirit that possesses it? And can I speak to it? Gain comfort in a shared humanness? Or is this figure itself a secretion of the darkness? A ghost sent to haunt and possess me? Even if it shows compassion for my plight, will its infinite power over me always make it a stranger?

The question in short, is this: is language itself a force or is it taken up by forces? It is well to remember that Derrida's 'force is the other of language' comes in an essay entitled 'Force and Signification' (Derrida, 1978). When language signifies, that is, when it assumes its role as producer of signs and information, it will be open to questions of the other, it will be material haunted by the mystery of its own life, its own animation. But if language is itself a force, if it is language that opens a space of being, or language in which all of nature rests, then it is far more than instrument, but carries with it, in mediating immediately the communication of mental being, what Benjamin boldly has called its magic.

Although the hard and fast distinction between these three types of language breaks down almost as quickly as it is proposed, it still leaves us with a new perspective on literature. Information carries semiotics along with it, depends upon it, and, by the same token, the language of revelation takes up signification. No discourse, no matter how factual, how technical or how prosaic can escape being taken up by the revelatory power of language. And it is this taking up of everyday language that *is* the language of revelation. Benjamin speaks of mental being communicated *in* and not *through* language. Language as such, the language of revelation, is language *in which* mental being is communicated, but which is not separate from that which fills it up. Language, as Benjamin reminds us, communicates itself. Our third kind of language, then, is a kind of operation upon the first two, a modification of them, an intensive occupation. In a sense this was Benjamin's great project. In his attempt to imbue historical materialism with the power of messianic cessation of happening, he was forced away from speaking in conventionally religious terms, even though in the 'Language' essay he gives religion pride of place in the communication of the highest mental being. His attempt in 'On the Mimetic Faculty' to trace a line from occult practices to language through mimesis, suggests that Benjamin was searching for ways to speak of the revelatory and creative power of language without having to resort always to the language of theology (Benjamin, 1985). It is this ambivalence that gives so much uneasy energy to Benjamin's thinking, and gives so much compressed power to his political and aesthetic writing.

Intensive language, language possessed by a power from which it cannot divide itself, gives us, finally, a way to talk about literature. Literature is nothing but this intensity. It is never to be found without it. And more important than establishing the difference between literature and other uses of language is the naming of the intensities that are put into play in literature. And if literature is about the human, if it is always speaking in the voice of the personal, the subjective, the psychological, the moral – all the crowning achievements of the human – then the movement whereby language is taken up by what is other is paralleled by a movement in which the human is taken up by all that is non-human. And just as the language of revelation is a kind of possession of utilitarian language, a possession that is more a mutual capture than a domination, so the non-human is a possessing of the human by something that nonetheless retains the deepest intimacy with it. It is in this sense that we can say the human is created and sustained by the non-human, and that literature is maintained by a language that overflows and escapes it.

This possession of language by its other takes on many forms. We can speak of it in terms that may seem to belong more to physics or in terms that evoke a transcendence far beyond the traditional western conception of Being.

## Affect

For Deleuze, what possesses language is sensation and affect, which cannot be far from what Derrida means when he says that *force* is the other of language.

> The writer uses words, but by creating a syntax that makes them pass into sensation that makes the standard language stammer, tremble, cry, or even sing: this is the style, the 'tone', the language of sensation.
> … The writer twists language, makes it vibrate, seizes hold of it, and rends it in order to wrest the percepts from perceptions, the affect from affections, the sensation from opinion.
>
> (Deleuze and Guattari, 1994: 176)

'Sensations, percepts, and affects', Deleuze is careful to explain, 'are *beings* whose validity lies in themselves … They could be said to exist in the absence of man, as he is caught in stone, on the canvas, or by words, is himself a compound of percepts and affects' (Deleuze and Guattari, 1994: 164). In other words, in order to form language, the human must already be constituted by affects and percepts. And although the language of revelation (which we have said is language caught up by what is in excess of it) can be argued to be coterminous with affect (the language in which Agamben's animals are caught up is certainly nothing but relations of affecting and being affected) it is equally true that language as information and language as sign *becomes* more than itself when we consider it from the point of view of the force that takes it up. It is only because signification is exceeded by affect that we can make the same words the basis for different speech acts. 'I shall return' might be a promise, a threat or a citation, but it is only in abstracting it from a context – that is, a set of affects – that we can consider it 'purely' as signification.

Derrida, in his critique of Austin in 'Signature, Event, Context', correctly notes that Austin has managed to overlook the iteration of the signifier, a repetition upon which the speech act is based (Derrida, 1988). What is most interesting about this critique is that, in taking Austin to task for attempting to bypass the problem of signification, Derrida is forced to hand signification over to a power that exceeds it far more than any idea of speech act ever could, the power of repetition. For there to be signification, there must be an affect – repetition – that already holds sway over the signifier, indeed, that defines the signifier as signifier. There is no signifier that is spoken only once. To signify is, in a sense, to repeat, to be caught up in cycles of repetition whose power extends beyond signification.

Repetition, sensation, action can all be the basis of affect, and affect, as Deleuze has described it, is whatever comes into being when something is affected or affects something else. More than that, it is the determination (which must always be actual) that founds all potentiality. Language is filled with affects, and indeed, would have no existence without them. But this also means that language is not a homogeneous and empty space in which various affects can be displayed like paintings on a wall. Language-as-affect (which we will see later is the same thing as language-taken-up-by-affect) is so various that it begins to seem more and more misguided to see language as a genus (or a system, a *langue*) into which individual events (or speech acts, or *parole*) are gathered. A love sonnet, a battle cry, a judgement from the bench, a mass, do not seem to be convincingly related by tarring them with a brush called 'language'.

However, if affect is an affecting or a being-affected, then all that makes language possible, all those forces that link up with it, become part of it. Emotion, sensation, possibility, material, force, all have their place in language. And though we may argue along with Benjamin that it is only in the human that the most perfect language takes place, we must also argue (and not against Benjamin) that human language has nothing to communicate of the non-human world without that non-human world communicating itself to him. What, for example, is less human that light? Less removed from the fleshy weight of the body, the torpidity of muscle? And yet what is more the basis of human knowledge and understanding, Heidegger's *Dasein* standing in the lighted clearing of Being? How much is clarity, uncovering, dispelling of darkness the proudest achievement of the human mind? This is what I mean when I say that affect is non-human, yet, far from being hostile to the human, gives it the gift of possibility.

With 'affect' we have the first of what I will call the six modalities of the non-human. 'Affect' allows us to think of the human in terms of what surpasses it, undermines it, fragments it, but also in terms of what simultaneously supports its, energizes it and holds it together.

Each of the modalities of the non-human cover the entire field of the human/non-human relation. In other words, each modality can work independently of the others and can lay claim to giving a perspective on the human that needs no supplementation. But at the same time each modality allows for others. It is, for example, not a contradiction to say that the human exists and is constituted within a plane of affect and to say that the human is constituted by the events that make it up. Event and affect are two modalities of the non-human, but taken together they do not give us a more 'complete' view of the human or non-human. The modalities of the non-human do not 'add up', one might say. They are not meant to be a cumulative taxonomy of the non-human, but rather exist in relations of resonance with each other, of differential repetition, of imperfect overlap, of mutual intensification, and, at times, of mutual capture.

## The event

Events, much like affects, are difficult to define according to the traditional formula of 'it is an A, which has the differentiating attributes of X, Y, Z'; but the event, as it has been described by Deleuze in *Logic of Sense* does have an intimate relationship with language, even though it is difficult to speak of it in terms of being, in terms of any actually existing state of affairs. Defining the event, Deleuze tells us, is much like hunting Lewis Carrol's Snark. Events are both real and non-existent, both realizable and unfulfilled in their realization.

It is important not to confuse the event with a state of things, with bodies and materials that come together to produce results. Rather than being a set of bodies and things, rather than being the mingling and colliding of these bodies, the event is the *effect* of their mingling and colliding. Events are what Deleuze, after the Stoics, calls 'incorporeal entities', which are 'not physical qualities and properties, but rather logical or dialectical attributes' (Deleuze, 1990: 4–5). Existing and not existing; non-corporeal, yet the effect of bodies; neither active nor passive, yet the result of action and passion, the event is always paradoxical. And its greatest paradox is its relation to language. Deleuze takes us through a description of the event that makes of the event a kind of complex: event-sense. Sense is what is expressed in a proposition. So we are faced with a kind of becoming of the event. We have the event, which is sense, which is the expressed (or expressible) of a proposition. If we ask what independence the event then has from the proposition that expresses it, we will be on the right track and will be prepared for Deleuze's paradoxical response.

> What is expressed does not exist outside its expression. This is why we cannot say that sense exists, but rather that it inheres or subsists. On the other hand, it does not merge at all with the proposition, for it has an objective (*objectité*) which is quite distinct. What is expressed has no resemblance whatever to the expression.
>
> (Deleuze, 1990: 21)

To call the event ideal is not at all to call it unreal. It may not exist, it may not act or suffer action, it may not even be found to exist outside of a proposition. But if the event teaches us anything, it is that existence itself is a narrow slice of the real. The event does not exist, it does not act, but it does 'make possible', it does have force. In fact, for Deleuze, it is the sense-event that makes language itself possible. How, Deleuze asks, does sound, which issues from bodies, become separated enough from those bodies to be organized into propositions and expressions? How, in other words, do the body's sounds cross the threshold from grunts of pleasure or pain, from the tearing and chewing of food, to the relative autonomy required for language? Something must separate the proposition-sound of language from the corporeal-sound of the body. Something must separate the proposition from the state of affairs. And this something must turn one face toward language and one toward states of things. It must use this double aspect to organize the relationship between language and the state of affairs, but be neither one nor the other (for if it were one or the other it could not separate and organize the two series language and states of affairs; it would merely homogenize them so that we would be left with the need to say that all states of affairs are language, or that language is simply another state of affairs, both of which beliefs have been followed fruitlessly for decades). 'It operates', Deleuze tells us, 'on both sides by means of one and the same incorporeal power' (Deleuze, 1990: 183).

From Blanchot to Deleuze to Foucault, the perfect model of the Event has always been death.

> Death has an extreme and definite relation to me and my body and is grounded in me, but it also has no relation to me at all – it is incorporeal and infinitive, impersonal, grounded only in itself. On one side, there is a part of the event which is realized and accomplished; on the other there is that 'part of the event that cannot realize its accomplishment'.
>
> (Deleuze, 1990: 151–2)

It is no wonder that the event is so often spoken of in terms of its imminent terror. It is ghostly, crossing the threshold from the non-existent to the existing world, making possible and exerting force while powerless to act. Finding its way into the world through the walls and traps of existence. It is the ideal model of the relationship of human and non-human. The objection that the non-human does not exist must be met head on with a claim that renders the objection irrelevant. The non-human does not exist, does not act, but, like the sense-event, *makes possible* the human. It has force that is not of existence, and it holds together the human and the non-human in two resonating series that make the human possible. And if the human (in its guise as the psychological, the personal, the ego) finds this relationship disconcerting, it is the understandable fear that comes from the encounter with the overwhelming force of the real that exceeds existence.

## Force

Force is our third of the six modalities of the non-human. I have chosen the term 'modality' because, as shall become apparent, the six modalities are different perspectives, or perhaps different realizations of one diagram, one event. Already we can begin to ask questions about the relation between affects and events, and now between affect–event–force.

We can begin with a kind of approximate commonsensical description of force, if only to bring to the surface some of the prejudices of the everyday understanding. We tend to see force as the most actual of things, the most unproblematically real. We speak of the transfer of force in physics as something that happens at the level of actual bodies; the gathering of forces in a political or military sense, which again has to do with actual bodies in the world; or the force of compulsion taking place on existing bodies and psyches.

However, force, much like the event, is more of a real non-existence at the heart of power and of formations of power. In *Foucault*, Deleuze says again and again that force comes from the outside (1988a: 101). This is not simply to say that the force of one entity may impinge on the force of another entity exterior to it, but rather that force lies outside of (and not merely exterior to) that in which it inheres.

> The power to be affected is like a *matter* of force, and the power to affect is like a *function* of force. But it is a pure function, that is to say a non-formalized function, independent of the concrete forms it assumes, the aims it serves and the means it employs ... And it is also a pure unformed matter independent of the formed substances, qualified objects or beings which it enters: it is a physics of primary or bare matter.
>
> (Deleuze, 1988a: 71–2)

If there are echoes of Aristotle's Prime Matter here it should not be surprising. Like prime matter, force is a reality whose freedom from form puts it below the threshold of existence, but which nonetheless cannot be simply called nothing, or unreal. Structures, institutions, stratified relations do indeed capture and shape forces (and indeed could not exist without force), and forces can only ever be seen within stratified formations, but, as with the event and the state of affairs, force subsists and insists. Language, literature, and the human are clearly such stratified formations. And just as '[w]e can already foresee that the forces within man do not necessarily contribute to the composition of a Man-form, but may be otherwise invested in another concept of form' (Deleuze, 1988a: 124), so we may say that literature and language are also possessed of these forces that may enter into relations with other forces of the outside. Literature and language envelop unformed matters and non-formalized functions.

As a means of naming these unformed forces Deleuze gives us the concept of the diagram. And as his example of a functioning diagram, Deleuze gives us Foucault's Panopticon, a 'pure function' of imposing behaviours or taste upon an enclosed and limited group. It matters little how and when this diagram is realized (like the event and force it is never exhausted by particular actualizations), in a prison, in school, in advertising, or in an office. The diagram, then, can be defined in several ways.

[I]t is the presentation of the relations between forces unique to a particular formation; it is the distribution of the power to be affected; it is the mixture of non-formalized pure functions and unformed pure matter.

(Deleuze, 1988a: 72–3)

Of course the question for the human becomes, into what diagram does it enter, what non-localized, infinitive relation of forces does it depend upon? And for literature the question is, what diagrams are enclosed by and enclose the text? And can the text itself be a diagram, a distribution of powers to be affected, of singularities, of unformed matters? Apart from the ideological presumptions that literary theory often loves to tease out of texts, apart from the reflected images of the human, apart from the recognizable complexes of the unconscious, what else subsists in and with the text, the story, the poem, and the novel? The concept of the diagram makes one suspect that there is much that has been overlooked.

## Singularity

The novel encloses singularities, singular points. This seems a truism if, by 'singularity', we understand 'individual' defined psychologically. The individual never accounts for all the singularities she encloses. Much that goes to make up the human is lost in the human's account of itself. It is for this reason that singularity is defined as 'pre-individual, non-personal, a-conceptual' (Deleuze, 1990: 52): 'one must remember that the psychological and moral characters are also made of pre-personal singularities, and that their feelings or pathos are constituted in the vicinity of these singularities' (55).

As with our other modalities of the non-human, the singularity is caught up in paradox. On the side of the individual we must say that it is not that particular quality that makes something belong to a class (we might ask what, in other words, makes any particular human belong to 'humanity'). But neither is it simply an entity that is absolutely unique, so unique that it does not belong to any class. What would this even mean? To the extent that we consider a thing as actually existing we cannot help at the very least categorizing it as a 'thing'. So the singularity does not belong to the individual in which it is held any more than the event belongs to the proposition that expresses it.

On the other hand, the singular is not the universal, even though the singular does have a kind of generality about it, the same generality of the event: 'Singularities are the true transcendental events' (Deleuze, 1990: 103). Pre-personal, and pre-individual, the singularity can burst from the individual that contains it; singularities, or singular points, make up individuals, but they also communicate, at another level, with other singularities outside of the individual:

> singularities-events correspond to heterogeneous series which are organized into a system which is neither stable nor unstable, but 'metastable', endowed with a potential energy wherein the differences between series are distributed. (Potential energy is the energy of the pure event, whereas forms of actualization correspond to the realization of the event.)
>
> (Deleuze, 1990: 103)

If we wish to describe the singularity in terms of existence we might say, with Deleuze, that they are '[t]urning points and points of inflection; bottlenecks, knots, foyers, and centres; points of fusion, condensation and boiling; points of tears and joy, sickness and health, hope and anxiety, "sensitive" points' (1990: 52). There is a near infinity of ways in which these modes of singularity can be translated into the language of the personal – 'I have my limits', 'this is a sensitive area for me', 'I just can't get past this', 'I'm reaching my breaking point'. But there is also a near infinity of ways that the language of the personal fails to give a name to the singularities it encloses. When there are unrecognized or barely recognized perceptions, when there is language that only gestures to something that it cannot name, when there are effects that seem unrelated to any discernible causes – there the force of the singularity is at work.

The problem of the singularity is to give it a name. The human, language, and literature all enclose singularities, all are partial realizations of singularity-events. But it is not as identity that the human breaks open to let loose its singularities; it is not as ideological manipulation that the novel resonates with singularity-events. And it is not as a mechanism of subjectification that language reveals the pre-individual and apersonal forces that give it life. It is for these reasons that we must avoid reading novels in terms of identity, ideology or subjectivity. The novel does not represent the human, it does not trace itself back to an ideology that places the human at the centre of society and the universe, but it is clearly concerned with the human. But this is because both the human and the novel are constituted in the vicinity of the same sets or series of singularities. Needless to say, in crossing over from the human to the literary to the outside of both, these singularities reveal themselves as non-personal, non-subjective, and non-human.

## The outside

Just as the event is not to be confused with a state of affairs, or a singularity with an individual, so the outside must be distinguished from a simple exteriority. A body can be said to have an inside and an outside which meet at the surface of the skin. In a field of interacting bodies, then, each body will encounter others that are outside of it, exterior to it. This is not, however, the exteriority, or the outside to which I am referring. The sense in which one body is outside another, or one is outside of an institution, or the unconscious contents are outside of consciousness, are what we might call relative exteriority. But there is another outside, another exteriority that is at once further away and more intimately close. Deleuze does not often speak of it in his work, though so many of his concepts – the virtual, singularity, the event – rely on it, and in some books (*Difference and Repetition*, *Foucault*) he has acknowledged the importance of Blanchot for a thinking of the outside.

Not surprisingly, it is impossible to say what exteriority *is*. Nor is it surprising that Deleuze, Blanchot and Lévinas make different uses of the concept, uses that overlap but are far from identical. When Deleuze says that 'it is always from the outside that a force confers on others or receives from others the variable position to be found only at a particular distance or in a particular relation' (Deleuze, 1988a: 86) we see an exteriority which is, more than anything else, the outside particular determinations. There are, as we have seen, formed matters and formalized functions that make up not only particular institutions, but even what is recognizable to us as actuality. We do not *see* unformed matters, or forces directly. They are outside not only of institutions and formations, but outside actuality as well. It is, however, an outside that forms the interiority of thought:

> If thought comes from the outside and remains attached to the outside, how come the outside does not flood into the inside, as the element that thought does not and cannot think of? The unthought is therefore not external to thought, but lies at its very heart, as that impossibility of thinking which doubles or hollows out the outside.
>
> (Deleuze, 1988a: 97)

For Blanchot, this outside takes on a more haunting aspect, which is that of death. Death haunts Blanchot's work, not as the final possibility toward which we move, not as an imminent necessity to which we must surrender, but as the ultimate *impossibility*, indeed as the very model of impossibility. Death is both the most certain and uncertain of all things. It is true that it will come, but doubtful that I will be there to greet it, to grasp it and make it my own death. Since dying is the very non-being of the 'I' that it takes away, it is not the 'I' that dies. There is not a trace of action in dying. It is pure passion, pure passivity, and hence, radically separated from any subjectivity. And this relationship (or non-relationship) to death is paralleled in the subject's relation to language. As Foucault tells us in 'Maurice Blanchot: The Thought from the Outside', 'The being of language only appears for itself with the disappearance of the subject' (Foucault, 1987: 15). The writer is caught up by language. Her writing is in no way an act of mastery or control, but rather a kind of deathlike passivity, a contention with impossibility. This is why Blanchot can draw his rather disturbing comparison between the artist and the suicide.

Both the artist and the suicide plan something that eludes all plans and if they do have a path, they have no goal; they do not know what they are doing. Both exert a resolute will, but both are linked to what they want to achieve by a demand that knows nothing of their will.

(Blanchot, 1982: 106)

Clearly, the writer's great disturbance is not the facing down of the dreaded dragon called death. Death is not to be feared as the relentless enemy; rather, it refuses to engage in battle. It slips away, but in slipping away draws one after it. It is the impossibility, yet the reality, of that which lies beyond the actual. And we have seen, in so many modalities of the non-human (the event, singularity, force) the same kind of disjunction between the actual and a non-existence that is nonetheless real. The writer's relation with force, the singularity-event, takes on the same impossibility as his relationship with death. It is for this reason that death, the event, exteriority, force, are modalities or aspects of the non-human: 'In the work man speaks, but the work gives voice in man to what does not speak: to the unnamable, the inhuman, to what is devoid of truth, bereft of justice, without rights' (Blanchot, 1982: 232).

Lévinas expresses, in a more 'properly' philosophical discourse, the same concern with what lies on the outside of the actual. But the 'beyond' of which he speaks is the beyond of Being itself, if Being is totality:

The visage of being that shows itself in war is fixed in the concept of totality, which dominates western philosophy. Individuals are reduced to being bearers of forces that command them unbeknown to themselves. The meaning of individuals (invisible outside this totality) is derived from the totality.

(Lévinas, 1969: 21–2)

There are, of course, many totalities that dominate western thought. Almost every system tries to impose coordinates that totalize the field of existence: the unconscious, history, even capital have taken on the role of totalizing forces that cover the entire field of nature/culture. But, for Lévinas, Being is the grandfather of them all. But there is a beyond of this totalized and total-izing Being,

a surplus always exterior to the totality, as though the objective totality did not fit out the true measure of being, as though another concept, the concept of infinity, were needed to express the transcendence with regard to totality, non-encompassable within a totality and as primordial as totality ... It is reflected within the totality and history, within experience.

(Lévinas, 1969: 22–3)

This 'beyond', this 'otherwise than being', takes on the form not of Blanchot's Outside, but of alterity, the otherness of ethical face-to-face encounter. The issue of language, then, becomes largely the issue of speech and communication. All language is taken up by the ethical relationship with the Other: 'Language is not enacted within a consciousness; it comes to me from the Other and reverberates in consciousness by putting it in question. This event is irreducible to consciousness' (1969: 204). In *Otherwise than Being*, Lévinas introduces the distinction between the Said and the Saying, and explains that, while the Said can always be assimilated to being, can always be taken up in a theme, the saying escapes the said at every point. 'Saying signifies otherwise than as an apparitor presenting essence and entities' (Lévinas, 1981: 46).

Of course we already understand the infinite modalities of the said. They are called themes, subjects, contents. But we have little sense of the modalities of saying.

Lévinas leaves us with several problems, some concerning literature, others concerning the human: to what extent does literature embody the face-to-face of the ethical relationship, to what extent is it an address to the transcendence of the other, and to what extent can literary criticism see literature as a saying rather than a said? And if it can address itself to the saying of literature, what tools does it have at its disposal? And does it need to create new tools that will at least take some trace of the saying of literature? And if literature is indeed, as I have said, about the human, how does Lévinas's human intersect with the novel? For although Lévinas is by no means an anti-humanist – and in fact he might be said to be the twentieth-century philosopher most firmly committed to humanism – his human is certainly not a human-*being*. The human face encountered in the face-to-face of the ethical relationship is taken up by the transcendence of the otherwise-than-being. If we are to define the human as the personal, the psychological, the social, then this transcendent human that overlaps it can only appear in the world as the non-human, that which is not personal, not psychological, not a subject in society, but rather a kind of virtual human that can only actualize itself in the human-being by differing from itself.

## The virtual

Our sixth, and last, modality of the non-human is the virtual. As we have seen most of the modalities of the non-human are related to approximate everyday definitions from which they must be distinguished: affect is not emotion; an event is not a state of things; force is not physical; the singular is not the individual; and exteriority is not merely the space outside a delimited body. In the same way, we must understand the difference between the virtual and the term with which it is too easily confused, the possible. The virtual in many ways has a wider scope than the possible because it can cross the space of difference. Perhaps the best elaboration of the limitation of the possible is Aristotle's in *Metaphysics*. His two great examples of the limitations of the possible are the transformation of wine into vinegar and of the human seed into a human being. Aristotle tells us, first of all, that wine is not potentially vinegar. Wine as a substance, as a *this*, does not *become* vinegar. Wine may become many things – hot, cold, sour, agitated, mobile – and all the while remain wine. So this is the first condition of possibility: a thing may manifest as many possibilities as it will, so long as it remains itself. Consequently, wine does not have the potentiality to cross the threshold that makes wine wine. But we know that wine does in fact turn into vinegar, it does in fact cross the threshold, but only by differing from itself. So we might say as a first rule that the limits of substance are the limits of possibility, whereas the virtual proceeds by differentiation. Aristotle also tells us that the seed is not potentially a human until it has been fertilized, indeed it is not potentially human until it has started irrevocably (except by external accident) on the process of becoming human. It is almost as if Aristotle is saying that the seed is not potentially human until it is actually human. This is overstating the case, but it does point to our second rule, which is that potentiality becomes real by a process of resemblance. The actuality is essentially the same as its possibility. My actual ability to speak French is almost identical to my potentiality to speak French. This resemblance is the source of Bergson's critique of possibility as merely a retroactive projection of the present moment into the past. Only when I can actually speak French, in short, do I project backward into the past and say 'there must have been a potentiality to speak French present all along!'

The virtual contrasts with the possible on these two main points – sameness/difference and resemblance/disjunction. The virtual is not, like the possible, contrasted with the real, but with the actual (Lévy, 1998: 23–7). The virtual is perfectly real *qua* virtual, but as it begins to actualize it differs from itself. The actualization of the virtual does not resemble the virtuality from which it springs because, in actualizing, it crosses the threshold within which it is identical to itself. It therefore becomes *problematic* to understand the relation of the actual to its particular virtuality, and indeed, the *problematic* is the form of the virtual.

> Unlike the possible, which is static and already constituted, the virtual is a kind of problematic complex, the knot of tendencies or forces that accompanies a situation, event, object, or entity, and invokes a process of resolution: actualization.
>
> (Lévy, 1998: 24)

The real, Lévy tells us, *resembles* the possible, but the actual *responds to* the virtual (25). Certainly, the process of actualization of the virtual is far more unpredictable than the movement from possible to real. One name for this unpredictability is *creation*: 'The virtual … does not have to be realized, but rather actualized; and the rules of actualization are not those of resemblance and limitation, but those of difference and divergence and of creation (Deleuze, 1988b: 97). Creative, mobile and non-actual, the virtual presents a new set of problems for the human, language and literature, or rather it turns these three into problems rather than simply facts. If the human is an actuality springing from virtuality, if, as Deleuze says 'an organism is nothing if not the solution to a problem' (Deleuze, 1994: 211), then we must trace back the human to the non-human forces that have followed a ramifying line of differ-entiation to cross, perhaps only for a moment, the threshold of humanity (on their way who knows where). If language is caught up by virtuality it may be that we must also follow the line of actualization back across the threshold of language, to the non-linguistic or pre-linguistic forces that are contained in it. And perhaps most importantly, virtuality brings the truism of the novel – that it must begin with and elaborate a problem – to a new level. If the novel is a problem then just as 'the virtual possesses the reality of a task to be performed or a problem to be solved' (Deleuze, 1994: 212), so the novel becomes a great virtuality and criticism becomes the problem of differentiating the virtualities contained in the novel, of bringing the novel beyond its own thresholds, of making the novel into the most perfect diagram of the forces and events that intersect with it. No longer caught in a linear relation that forces us to ask fruitless questions of order (which came first, which is the cause of the other), the human, language, and literature are all taken up into that timeless time, that abstract yet real time between a past that has just disappeared and a future that will just begin. All three are caught up at once in the modalities of the non-human, and to properly understand any of them, and especially their relationship, we must be prepared to let them unfold, unmake themselves as they will.

## Literature/language/human

I have said that the language of revelation is the taking up of semiotics and signification by a force that is outside it. When it is caught up by a modality of the non-human, a force, and event, language is not other than that force, that event. It maintains no autonomy. And indeed, if we ask whether there is a 'pure' language, a language free of the intensive possession by the non-human, we must answer that such a language could neither refer, express, or in fact even appear. Although, as we have seen, the modalities of the non-human possess a paradoxical reality that is not of existence, the existence of language would vanish into nothingness if it were cut off from what lies beyond it.

There is no reason the triumvirate of literature, language and the human need be the only constellation with which we are concerned. Certainly language and the human have their roles in many formations – plastic arts, war, nature. But surely literature most directly takes language as both its medium and its matrix. And it can be argued that it is in the novel that language and the human form their strongest alliance (since poetry so often concerns itself with the other-than-human, and film has made its mark by raising physical objects to a new level of expressiveness).

The question that remains for us is not whether or not the modalities of the non-human have something to contribute to criticism but what new affects can we find mapped out in our most familiar masterpieces, what new forces will we finally see shooting across the whiteness of the page, what great and singular events will be hovering in the infinitive spaces of the most classic stories, what free-floating crystals of exteriority shall we find in the characters whose worlds seem so closed, what virtualities await us, unactualized and, even so, haunting the familiar forest paths, the elegant parlours, the dark mansions that we dream of together?

# References

Agamben, Giorgio (1993) *Infancy and History*, trans. L. Heron, New York: Verso.

Benjamin, Walter (1985) 'On the Mimetic Faculty', *One Way Street and Other Writings*, trans. Edmund Jephcott and Kingsley Shorter, London: Verso. 160–3.

—— (1986) 'On Language as Such and the Language of Man', *Reflections*, P. Demetz (ed.), New York: Schocken. 314–32.

Blanchot, Maurice (1982) *The Space of Literature*, trans. A. Smock, Lincoln: University of Nebraska Press.

Deleuze, Gilles (1988a) *Foucault*, trans. S. Hand, Minneapolis: University of Minnesota Press.

—— (1988b) *Bergsonism*, trans. Hugh Tomlinson and Barbara Habberjam, New York: Zone.

—— (1990) *The Logic of Sense*, trans. M. Lester, New York: Columbia University Press.

—— (1994) *Difference and Repetition*, trans. Paul Patton, New York: Columbia University Press.

Deleuze, Gilles, and Guattari, Félix (1994) *What is Philosophy?* trans. Hugh Tomlinson and Graham Burchell, New York: Columbia University Press.

Derrida, Jacques (1978) 'Force and Signification', *Difference and Writing*, trans. Alan Bass, Chicago: University of Chicago Press.

—— (1988) *Limited Inc.*, 'Signature, Event, Context', Evanston, IL: Northwestern University Press, 1–25.

Foucault, Michel (1987) 'Maurice Blanchot: The Thought from Outside', trans. Jeffrey Mehlman, *Foucault/Blanchot*, New York: Zone Books. 9–58.

Guattari, Félix (1995) *Chaosmosis: An Ethico-Aesthetic Paradigm*, trans. Paul Bains and Julian Pefanis, Sydney/Indianapolis: Power Publications/Indiana University Press.

Levinas, Emmanuel (1969) *Totality and Infinity*, trans. Alphonso Lingis, Pittsburgh: University of Duquesne Press.

—— (1981) *Otherwise than Being or Beyond Essence*, trans. Alphonso Lingis, Boston: Martinus Nijhoff.

Lévy, Pierre (1998) *Becoming Virtual: Reality in the Digital Age*, trans. Robert Bononno, London: Plenum.

# 6

# EXPOSURE

## Pasolini in the flesh

*Michael Hardt*

*for Giorgio Agamben*[1]

| | |
|---|---|
| *La crocifissione* | *Crucifixion* |
| Ma noi predichiamo Cristo crocifisso: scandalo pe' Giudei, stoltezza pe' Gentili. | But we preach Christ crucified: scandal for the Jews, folly for the Gentiles. |
| Paolo, *Lettera ai Corinti* | Paul, *Letter to the Corinthians* |

Tutte le piaghe sono al sole
ed Egli muore sotto gli occhi
di tutti: perfino la madre
sotto il petto, il ventre, i ginocchi,
guarda il Suo corpo patire.
L'alba e il vespro Gli fanno luce
sulle braccia aperte e l'Aprile
intenerisce il Suo esibire
la morte a sguardi che Lo bruciano.

All His wounds are open to the sun
and He dies under the eyes
of everyone: even His mother
under His breast, belly, and knees,
watches His body suffer.
Dawn and dusk cast light
on His open arms and April
softens His exhibition of death
to gazes that burn Him.

Perché Cristo fu ESPOSTO in Croce?
Oh scossa del cuore al nudo
corpo del giovinetto ... atroce
offesa al suo pudore crudo ...
Il sole e gli sguardi! La voce
estrema chiese a Dio perdono
con un singhiozzo di vergogna
rossa nel cielo senza suono,
tra pupille fresche e annoiate
di Lui: morte, sesso e gogna.

Why was Christ EXPOSED on the Cross?
Oh, the heart shudders at the naked
body of the youth ... atrocious
offense to its raw modesty ...
The sun and the gazes! The ultimate
voice asked God forgiveness
with a sob of red shame
in a sky without sound,
between His fresh and weary
pupils: death, sex, and pillory.

Bisogna esporsi (questo insegna il povero
Cristo inchiodato?),
la chiarezza del cuore è degna
di ogni scherno, di ogni peccato
di ogni più nuda passione ...
(questo vuol dire il Crocifisso?

You must expose yourself (is this what the
poor nailed-up Christ teaches?),
the clarity of the heart is worthy
of every sneer, every sin,
every more naked passion ...
(is this what the Crucifix means?

77

| | |
|---|---|
| sacrificare ogni giorno il dono | sacrifice every day the gift |
| rinunciare ogni giorno al perdono | renounce every day forgiveness |
| sporgersi ingenui sull'abisso). | cast yourself ingenuous over the abyss). |
| | |
| Noi staremo offerti sulla croce, | We will be offered on the cross, |
| alla gogna, tra le pupille | on the pillory, between the pupils |
| limpide di gioia feroce, | limpid with ferocious joy, |
| scoprendo all'ironia le stille | leaving open to irony the drops |
| del sangue dal petto ai ginocchi, | of blood from the breast to the knees, |
| miti, ridicoli, tremando | gentle and ridiculous, trembling |
| d'intelletto e passione nel gioco | with intellect and passion in the play |
| del cuore arso dal suo fuoco, | of the heart burning from its fire, |
| per testimoniare lo scandolo. | testifying to the scandal. |

(Pier Paolo Pasolini, 1993: 376–7)

## Incarnation

Paul wrote from his prison cell to the Philippians:

> Adopt towards one another, in your mutual relations, the same attitude that was found in Christ. Although he was in the form of God, he did not regard this divine equality as a precious thing to be exploited. Instead, he *emptied himself* by taking the form of a slave and being born like other human beings. And being in human form, he humbled himself and became obedient to the point of death, even death on the cross.

Abandon me! Incarnation is all about abandonment – abandonment to the flesh. Paul writes that in becoming flesh Christ abandoned the form of God; he emptied himself by taking on a limited materiality. This self-emptying is the exposure of the flesh. It is a kind of slavery that appeared to Paul in prison as liberation. What exactly did Christ abandon when he emptied himself? Certainly he did not abandon divinity as such; rather, he emptied the transcendental *form* and carried divinity into the material. From one perspective this abandoned being might seem precarious, foundationless, cast over the abyss, but really this abandonment testifies instead to the fullness of the surfaces of being. The self-emptying or *kenosis* of Christ, the evacuation of the transcendental, is the affirmation of the plenitude of the material, the fullness of the flesh.

Incarnation is first of all a metaphysical thesis that the essence and existence of being are one and the same. There is no ontological essence that resides beyond the world. None of being or God or nature remains outside existence, but rather all is fully realized, fully expressed, without remainder, in the flesh. Incarnation means that the absolute oneness of all being, infinite and eternal, coincides completely with the constant becoming-different of the modalities of existence. The figure of Christ has often been understood as a point of mediation of the external relationship between divine essence and worldly existence. But the incarnation, the self-emptying of Christ, denies any possible exteriority and hence any need for mediation. Any imagined transcendent substance, separated from the world, is merely a hollow husk, a form emptied of all being. Or better, the transcendent is more properly understood as residing within the material, immanent, as its in-dwelling potentiality.[2] Transcendence, the condition of possibility of being, should not be imagined as above or below the material – it dwells, rather, precisely at its very surface. Incarnation is the claim that there is no opposition and no mediation necessary between the transcendent and the immanent, but an intimate complementarity. This immanent transcendence is the innermost exteriority of being, the potentiality of the flesh.

Incarnation is also a theological proposition: The plenitude of materiality, the fullness of existence is divine. But why should we even speak about divinity here, when the form of God has been completely emptied out, abandoned? Because divinity marks the essential vitality of existence. The surfaces of the world are charged with a powerful intensity. Divinity resides precisely in the boundaries or thresholds of things, at their limits, passionate and exposed, as if surrounding them with a halo. Incarnation abandons any notion of a hidden God, any transcendental notion of a divinity that remains 'pure' outside the exposure of materiality. This is the good news whispered to us by the 'impure angel' that Pasolini loves. In the incarnation the divine becomes flesh with an electric vitality; and in turn our innocent limbs become divine, 'con le carni brucianti / di splendidi sorrisi' [with the burning flesh of splendid smiles] ('Carne e cielo' in Pasolini, 1993: 341).

Finally, incarnation is an ethical injunction: empty yourself, become flesh! This is the lesson the poor nailed-up Christ teaches us. (How little we have realized our flesh! We don't even know what flesh can do!) Incarnation is an option of joy and love. And the ultimate form of love is precisely the belief in *this* world, as it is.[3] So be it. (What else could Spinoza have meant by the love of God?) Our belief can finally have no object other than the flesh. Becoming flesh will be our joy.

Christ's life in the flesh plays out this drama. The metaphysical emptying-out which takes place in the incarnation at the beginning of Christ's life is perfectly balanced by the recognition at the end of his life of abandonment on the cross. Or rather, the birth of Christ is merely a formal incarnation, a nominal abandonment to this world. The real incarnation takes place on Calvary. Only hanging on the cross does Christ realize the flesh. When the naked body exposed on the cross cries with its ultimate voice, 'Why have you forsaken me?', the question can only be rhetorical. The abandonment took place long before; the incarnation at birth was symbol of the emptying out of any possible addressee. What happens on the cross is that Christ fully fulfills that abandonment in the flesh. Christ was abandoned to the divinity of the flesh, in love and joy.

## Exposure

Take me now! Pasolini is fascinated with the immodest offering of Christ's body on the cross. His wounds are open. His entire body – breast, belly, sex, and knees – is burning under the gazes of the crowd and the elements. At the point of death, Christ is all body, an open piece of flesh, abandoned, exposed. This is when Christ's emptied divinity, its radiant surfaces shine forth most brightly.

The exposure of flesh is erotic. The divine charge that courses through the surfaces of being creates this intensity, this excitement. Eroticism, as Georges Bataille tells us, is assenting to life up to the point of death (1986). Christ's incarnation is this pure affirmation of life, even to the point of death on the cross. Death functions here, however, not as the point of fascination nor as an instinct or drive of life, but merely as a negative limit that highlights in contrast life's affirmation. The erotic points us toward the vital continuity extending across the surfaces of being. It breaks down or dissolves the separateness, the self-possession, the discontinuity that exists among individual entities and things. It strips them naked, empties them, and puts them in common. Eroticism is thus a state of communication that testifies to our striving toward a possible continuity of being, beyond the prison of the self.[4] The limits or boundaries of individual entities become open thresholds that feel the pleasures – the rise and the recess – of flows and intensities.

Erotic exposure, paradoxically, does not really involve seeing and being seen. In fact, exposure subverts a certain regime of vision. The exposed flesh does not reveal a secret self that had been hidden, but rather dissolves any self that could be apprehended. We not only have nothing left to hide, we no longer present any separate thing for the eyes to grasp. We become imperceptible. In the erotic we lose ourselves, or rather we abandon our discontinuity in a naked and divine communion.

Christ's crucified body is exemplary of this eroticism. For Pasolini, however, in contrast to Bataille, the erotic is not predicated on any kind of transgression. Transgression always functions in relation to (or in complicity with) a norm or taboo, negating the dictates of the norm and yet paradoxically re-enforcing the norm's effects. The transgressive act does not simply refuse the norm, but rather negates it, transcends it, and completes it. It exceeds a limit, but in its excess verifies the limit itself. Transgression always operates through a dialectic of negations. If the norm were destroyed, the transgression itself would lose all value. Pasolini's erotics depend not on transgression but exposure. No norm or taboo forms a negative foundation and no synthesis transcends the opposition. Exposure operates rather on a purely positive logic of emanation. It involves casting off, or really, emptying out all that is external to its material existence and then intensifying that materiality. What is exposed is naked flesh, absolute immanence, a pure affirmation.

Exposed flesh is not transgression but scandal. In other words, exposure does indeed oppose and negate the norms of propriety, but its effect does not depend on that opposition as a support. Violation of the norm is not primary to exposure; the negation is secondary, an afterthought, an accident. It turns its back on the norm – that is its great offence. Exposure operates in ignorance of the norm, and thus conducts, in the only way possible, its real destruction. Christ's body testifies to the scandal, the scandal of the cross.

## Crucifixion

In the act of incarnation Christ takes the form of a slave and renounces any divine separation not as a demonstration of ascetic denial but rather in search for the continuity of life and community. This being in common is an escape from prison. Sacrificing the gift is an option of joy. The exposure in the form of a slave that we all share, however, carries with it always and necessarily the potential of the most horrible torments, to the point of torture on the cross.

The effect of torture is always separation and discontinuity even in situations of extreme proximity and intimacy. Often we cannot even recognize our torturers as human; they are irremediably other to us. (We tend to think of them as dogs or beasts, when really those animals never separate themselves in such a way.) And at the same time the torture makes it impossible to recognize the continuity of our own lives. It's not me he's fucking, it isn't me they're burning with that iron prod – they can only touch my body. Torture forces us out of the flesh, it forces us to separate from our bodies, to make ourselves other. The experience of torture is a form of exile, at the most intimate levels of being – an exile from living. Torture makes impossible the exposure of the flesh, even when paradoxically our torturers try to strip us naked.

The miracle of Christ is to take the flesh back from the soldiers of empire who nailed him to the cross. Even in his torment Christ lived the flesh in all its intensity. The critique of torture does not require that we should live in such a way as to avoid all violence and all pain – that would be a life without intensity, always already separated from the violence of experience. Rather, we should refuse the separation from the flesh that torture entails: live the violence of experience in the flesh, make our pain a mode of intensity and joy. This is the miracle that Pasolini sees in the crucifixion. The pain of the crucifixion does not fall back into a private language of isolated individuality, but rather opens up to a common language. Precisely to the extent that they create such a common language and a shared experience of the flesh, pain and violence can be erotic, because the erotic is nothing other than that shared intensity of our experience, that common electric charge coursing through our flesh.

Consider, for example, how authors such as the Marquis de Sade and Leopold von Sacher-Masoch construct a kind of ritual violence through various institutions and contracts in an effort to invent common languages of the flesh. Their ritual and imaginary dramas of victimizer and victim seek to overcome or vanquish the separation that characterizes our daily torture. This violence thus points toward an erotic continuity, an affirmation of life. Pasolini's notion of exposure shares this project to discover an antidote to torture and separation, but it does not create an imaginary plane or a theatre of representation. Representation still implies too much separation. Exposure, then, does not recreate the scene of torture but rather seeks to dissolve its boundaries and its effects of discontinuity. The violence of the exposed flesh does not separate into passive and active roles, but moves united in an erotic affirmation. Through exposure violence becomes again our own as a common language, a vital power of creation, a life force.

## Flesh

Abandonment to the flesh is a form of freedom. Exposed, the passions of the flesh are released from any normative structures or organic functions. This is Pasolini's continual call to the utopia of youth: 'Allora la carne era senza freni' [Back then flesh had no brakes] ('La religione del mio tempo' in Pasolini, 1993: 492). Becoming-flesh is a form of forgetting – a forgetting of self, propriety, discontinuity. Impure carnality, or rather the divine exposure of the flesh enacts its own logic of passions. This abandonment is the joy that Pasolini sees in Christ's example.

In un debole lezzo di macello
vedo l'immagine del mio corpo:
seminudo, ignorato, quasi morto.
E' così che mi volevo crocifisso,
con una vampa di tenero orrore,
da bambino, già automa del mio amore.

In the faint stench of a slaughterhouse.
I see the image of my body:
half-naked, forgotten, almost dead.
This is how I wanted to be crucified,
with a flash of tender horror,
since childhood, already an automaton of my love.

('L'ex vita' in Pasolini, 1993: 400)

The abandoned body is set free – released from the prisons of separation, immersed in the impurity of this world, or rather in the maniacal love of this world, in the form of a slave, a love automaton.

Even the term 'body' often seems insufficient for Pasolini. It is too caught up in the discontinuous and hierarchical functionings of various organs, too detached from other bodies and things, too implicated in that dialectical coupling with consciousness. Any residues of mind/body dualisms are completely out of place here. Even referring to ourselves as embodied seems too tied to those paradigms, as if we could imagine some spirit or mind potentially separate from corporeality so that we now had to insist on its unity with matter.

Pasolini prefers to think of 'members' and 'limbs' [membra] or simply 'flesh' [carne]. Flesh is the vital materiality of existence. Flesh certainly refers to matter, a passionately charged, intense matter, but it is always equally intellectual. It is not opposed to or excluded from thought or consciousness. Rather, the paths of thought and existence are all traced on the flesh.[5] Flesh subtends existence; it is its very potentiality.

Flesh is the condition of possibility of the qualities of the world, but it is never contained within or defined by those qualities. In this sense it is both a superficial foundation and an immanent transcendence – alien to any dialectic of reality and appearance, or depth and surface. It confounds all of these anti-nomies. Flesh is the superficial depth, the real appearance of existence. That the world is, how the world is, precisely such as it is, is exposed perfectly and irremediably in the flesh. (Is this what Spinoza meant when he said that reality and perfection are the same thing?) The exposure of the flesh is indeed the mystery of life, or rather the miracle of the world.

How do we love in the flesh? What is the flesh's desire? In erotic exposure the boundaries or discontinuities between self and other are broken down and dissolved to open a kind of communication or communion. This love cannot really be conceived as an encounter with the other because the self has already been completely emptied out, abandoned. Similarly, the desire cannot really be conceived as a becoming-other of the self because that too depends on fundamentally stable discontinuities, and implies in the end a return to self. We are only able to love in abandoning ourselves to the flesh.[6] In the flesh I lose track of which is your arm and my arm, your leg and mine, a tangle of limbs and members. Take me! Exposure is anonymous. It brings both an intensification of experience and an undifferentiation of matter. It sets in motion a wild proliferation of erotic zones and modes of intensity across the surfaces of the flesh (the warmth of your lips, the subtle vibration of my tongue), and at the same time brings about a tendential unification or communion. Hence the ecstasy of exposure.

## Notes

1  I would like to thank Gail Hamner, Frank Lentricchia, Michael Moon, Karen Ocaña, Karen Pinkus, and Steve Shaviro for their comments on earlier drafts of this essay. All translations of Pasolini's texts are my own.

2  'The transcendent is not a supreme entity above all things; rather, the pure transcendent is the taking-place of every thing' (Agamben, 1993: 14–15).

3  'Only belief in the world can reconnect man to what he sees and hears. The cinema must film, not the world, but belief in this world, our only link ... Whether we are Christians or atheists, in our universal schizophrenia, *we need reasons to believe in this world*' (Deleuze, 1989: 172).

4  'The transition from the normal state to that of erotic desire presupposes a partial dissolution of the person as he exists in the realm of discontinuity ... It is a state of communication revealing a quest for a possible continuance of being beyond the confines of the self' (Bataille, 1986: 17).

5  'There are intellectual cries, cries born of the *subtlety* of the marrow. That is what I mean by Flesh. I do not separate my thought from my life. With each vibration of my tongue I retrace all the pathways of my thought in my flesh' ('Situation of the Flesh,' Artaud, 1988: 110).

6  'I have become capable of loving ... by abandoning love and self' (Deleuze and Guattari, 1987: 199).

# References

Agamben, Giorgio (1993) *The Coming Community*, trans. Michael Hardt, Minneapolis: University of Minnesota Press.

Artaud, Antonin (1988) *Selected Writings*, trans. Helen Weaver, Berkeley: University of California Press.

Bataille, Georges (1986) *Erotism*, trans. Mary Dalwood, San Francisco: City Lights.

Deleuze, Gilles (1989) *Cinema 2: The Time-Image*, trans. Hugh Tomlinson and Robert Galeta, Minneapolis: University of Minnesota Press.

Deleuze, Gilles, and Guattari, Félix (1987) *A Thousand Plateaus*, trans. Brian Massumi, Minneapolis: University of Minnesota Press.

Pasolini, Pier Paolo (1993) *Bestemmia: Tutte le poesie*, vol. 1, Graziella Chiarcossi and Walter Siti (eds), Milan: Garzanti.

# 7

# CRUEL

## Antonin Artaud and Gilles Deleuze

*Catherine Dale*

Everything in the order of the written word which abandons the field of clear, orderly perception, everything which aims at reversing appearances and introduces doubt about the position of mental images and their relationship to one another, everything which provokes confusion without destroying the strength of an emergent thought, everything which disrupts the relationship between things by giving this agitated thought an even greater aspect of truth and violence – all these offer death a loophole and put us in touch with certain more acute states of mind in the throes of which death expresses itself.

(Artaud, 1970–4, vol. 1: 92)

The question of what Antonin Artaud means by positing a compatibility between goodness and cruelty is taken up at the end of his infamous last public reading, 'The Story Lived by Artaud Mômo' where he said, 'I put myself in your place, and I see very well that what I am saying isn't interesting at all, it's still theatre. What can I do to be truly sincere?'[1] After an hour of inundating his audience with poems, travel experiences, and stories of black magic, Artaud spoke for another two hours of his psychiatric incarcerations, his vehement refutations of death, and generally flailed about making wild gestures, cries and screams.[2] Having posed his curious question of sincerity, Artaud, who had dropped all his papers, read his final poem, 'Artaud the Mômo', glaring at the audience as he uttered the words, 'the filthy meat', and abruptly left the stage (Artaud, 1995: 117). Disabused of its saccharine associa- tions, Artaud's sincerity is an 'affective' theatrical plea that could just as well be a specious glance toward authenticity. What would be the difference? In a letter to André Breton, Artaud writes, 'I left because I realized that the only / language I could use on an audience was to / take bombs out of my pockets and throw them / in their faces in a gesture of unmistakable / aggression' (Artaud, 1989: 183). And yet there is this refrain, this bow, this histrionic collapse in front of nine hundred people. Artaud's plaintive interrogation of the constitution of truthfulness is a burden to the audience and to himself, (a rhetorical question, or more precisely, part of Artaud's interrogative practice of disciplined cruelty) and more importantly a repetition, a repetition of the creation of the ideal kernel of pure thought itself.

Artaud's concern with sincerity poses a difficult problem. Is 'truly sincere' simply a rhetorical device or is it literal? While he endeavours to explain the relationship between thought and violence, the way thought impinges itself on the mind (a thinking thing) and erupts in the mind to split open thought itself, Artaud also attempts miserably or successfully (the answer will not concern us) to demonstrate truth. There are two ways to approach this problem. We can view Artaud's 'truly sincere' as a tautology. Here 'truly' is the prefix of a gracious and passional generosity while 'sincere' is a demand and challenge to the audience (language) to uphold such an impossible truth. Tautologically, of course, this equation will work equally well in reverse. 'True' is generally presented in opposition to 'false' but if we oppose it to 'sincere' it becomes interrogative of sincerity itself. Sincerity, on the other hand, is most often protected by the idea of personal sanctuary, and is therefore difficult to question. Tautology ignores the existence of a first principle of truth and sincerity; truth arrives without reason but very soon becomes reasonable. What is most scandalous about Artaud's 'truly sincere' however is not that Artaud synthesizes the good and the bad on this single and desperate night – as if this were – anomalous to the rest of his work, work which incessantly calls into question notions such as true and sincere – but that this determination of the true could well *be* his work (the true is all there is is true).

In *The Logic of Sense* (1990) and *Difference and Repetition* (1994), Deleuze follows Artaud's pursuit of 'the terrible revelation of a thought without image, and the conquest of a new principle which does not allow itself to be represented' (Deleuze, 1994: 147). In addition, Deleuze and Félix Guattari employ Artaud as a model for their conception of an alternative mode of thought which they call schizoanalytic. This mode of thought promotes the freedom of desire as a productive force traversing the segmented lines of habitual thought as so many intensities. Thus 'truly sincere' appears as a dialectical 'attitude' which would be incongruous with the kind of schizophrenic thought Deleuze and Guattari put forward in *Anti-Oedipus* (1983). Schizoanalysis repudiates the notion of self-identification of a self which is gained through the working of social structures, the family in particular. It is possible to view Artaud as injecting the audience not with the personal, but with the impotence of the personal in proposing the existence of the sincerity of truth itself. At first glance 'truly sincere' demonstrates the perilous probity of the integrity of a madman, poet, and actor: a little sincerity is dangerous, warns Oscar Wilde, but a lot is fatal. By 'pulverizing' the fatal oneness of a true sincerity, Artaud creates a little sincerity overdoing (overcoming) the qualifications of both true and sincere.

Artaud is ever vigilant against the 'image' of thought, accusing it of fixing itself to habit 'so that thought is not in immediate and uninterrupted communication with things – this fixation and this immobilization, this tendency of the soul to construct monuments occurring, as it were, BEFORE THOUGHT. Evidently this is the right condition for creativity' (Artaud, 1976: 79). What Artaud does, as exemplified in his famous poem, 'To Have Done with the Judgment of God', is to overcome the distinction between true (correct) and false (wrong) thought. Artaud throws both mind and body into consternation accusing man of thinking along the organized lines of the organism, that is, of thinking in the same way as he is constructed and vice versa. 'Man is sick because he is badly constructed'(Artaud, 1982: 79).[3] In opposition to thought's presupposition of good and evil Artaud writes, 'in a manifested world, metaphysically speaking, evil is the permanent law, and what is good is an effort and already one more cruelty added to the other' (Artaud, 1958: 103). Artaud's will to 'goodness' becomes a fundamental problem in relation to a 'true sincerity' seen as a naive idea. But Artaud's goodness is the desire of a will to cruelty, a disruption of continuous evil. Artaud-the-philosopher approaches thought acting as one who does not know what to think, as one who is ignorant of thought's presuppositions, of thought's knowledge of the true and the good. This is why he is pleased when he finds that he has missed out on the subjective or private presuppositions which prohibit the game of philosophy (Deleuze, 1994: 130). It is the cruelty of calling thought into ques-tion, of attacking thought with problems, or what Deleuze calls 'fortunate difficulties' by which 'our efforts to overcome these obstacles allow us to maintain an ideal of the self as it exists in pure thought' (1994: 147). Morality separates truth and thought because it requires that each one judge the other by its own standard (identification). But thought and truth are inseparable, illegitimate children. It is evil, not to be confused with error or falsity, that maintains a sense of progression, a logical direction, while goodness, the vital force between bodies, moves along the edge of their depths, between form and ground, at the juncture where language and the body meet.

Artaud is an embarrassment to philosophy. He makes philosophy cringe when he flaunts his sincerity and truth. Even more persistently he is the philosopher who, through a restructuration of the actions and passions of the body, produces a discreditable practice of thought, and chastises both philos-ophy and its audience for their pre-philosophical presuppositions, their predictable emotions and physical reactions. Artaud's sincerity becomes a theatrical phylogeny, a set of vibrations designed to connect all the audiences that have ever lived. Infectious thought staves off the dictation of reason, just as disease repudiates the liberal parasite of medicine. 'I have not become a poet or an actor in order to write or recite poems, but to live them. I read a poem not to milk applause but to feel the bodies of men and women – and I mean their bodies – throb and quiver in harmony with mine' (Artaud, 1970–4, vol. 2: 191). This is the principle of Artaud's famous 'theatre of cruelty' which generates a dramaturgical force of life forced to think. Through his 'sincere' peroration Artaud flees a philosophical idealism where reactions dissolve into relative truths. But this is not because he proscribes truth; Artaud is confident that 'the public, which takes the false for the true, has the sense of the true and always responds to it when it is manifested' (Artaud, 1958: 76).[4] Artaud abolishes the kind of theatre which prepares itself for an audience that privileges the senses first. He replaces this 'ordinary psychological theatre' with 'the Theatre of Cruelty [that] proposes to resort to a mass spectacle; to seek in the agitation of tremendous masses, convulsed and hurled against each other, a little of that poetry of festivals and crowd when, all too rarely nowadays, the people pour out into the streets' (1958: 85). In this sense Artaud is the tormentor, tormented, and fool who thrives precisely because as ridiculous as he is on stage, he is dangerously sincere and so frightens, confuses and dismays his audience. Artaud wants to hold the body's attention, he wants to both affect and correct the anatomy (recall his famous body without organs).[5]

Like Deleuze, Artaud regards sense as that which separates the body from language, life from thought; sense is facilitated by affections at the level of the unexpected, of the new. And this passing on to the senses is a contagious, or a resonant, passing of the interminable new. Artaud's theatre is not designed to represent or reproduce (describe) man but to create a being which moves. The language of Artaud is a symbiosis of technologies – asignifying semiotics, affective gestures, violent sounds and painful noises – challenging the organization of the organism in its collectivity (audience, participant, body) and in its singularity (event), occurring at the chasm between language and the body. It is, after all, Artaud who presents Deleuze with a combination of literature, schizoanalysis and the anguished inability of thought to think. And it is also Artaud who gives us the clinical and the critical in a single unthinkable and unproductive body without organs, and who most contributes to our sense that madness, philosophy, and literature are not three ways toward the same thing. Although the Idea of the colossal unthought appears as an immense and unified hope of communication (three ways toward the same thing), Artaud shows us that the experimentation of thought and the new can only be entered by innumerably disparate and invented paths, can only be entered by the shock of the new.

Artaud is the claimant of his own creation.[6] His self-birth and his begetting of thought suggest that there is nothing intrinsic about thinking, about attaining and containing a thought. At the limit of thought, along its separated line, Artaud imagines an 'uncreated conception', where the limit of thought is its immanence. In a letter to Jacques Rivière Artaud writes,

> I am innately *genital*, and if we examine closely what that means, it means that I have never made the most of myself. There are some fools who think of themselves as beings, as innately beings. I am he, who in order to be, must whip his innateness. One must be a being innately, that is, always whipping this sort of non-existent kennel [*chenil*, also hole or hovel], O bitches of impossibility!
>
> (Artaud, 1970–4, vol. 1: 19)

Artaud rejects innateness as a natural and essential state, preferring to view the innate as the pure unthought within thought. This is because he disapproves of thinking of oneself as a being, as an innate being who is then able to represent/reproduce oneself. This type of innateness is synonymous with complacency, and habit, and must be whipped, stirred into being a being innately (the becoming of being innate). When Artaud places genitality beside innateness he is suggesting the birth of innateness which is the becoming innate of being born: there is nothing prior to innateness, and nothing after it in the form of the cultural. To whip the non-existent hole (the traditional image of thought) in order to be a being innately, means to force thought to its internal limit. Artaud struggles with the bitches of impossibility who suffocate the actualization (contemporaneity) of his potential for thought.

> I put myself into this state of impossible absurdity in order to try to generate thought in myself. There are a few of us in this era who have tried to get hold of things, to create within ourselves spaces for life, spaces which did not exist and which did not seem to belong in actual space.
>
> (Artaud, 1976: 79)

Having nothing to do with reproduction but everything to do with repetition (always whipping one's innateness), Artaud's innateness is 'genital' precisely because it is autonomous, just as Antonin Artaud is progenitor of himself.

On the subject of Artaud's 'innate genitality' Deleuze writes, 'to think is to create, there is no other creation — but to create is first of all to engender "thinking" in thought. For this reason Artaud opposes genitality to innateness in thought, but equally to reminiscence, and thereby proposes the principle of a transcendental empiricism' (Deleuze, 1994: 147). Why does Deleuze express Artaud's relation of genitality and innateness as an opposition? Transcendental empiricism is a crucial disjunctive synthesis which reduces the mode of the perceptual field which reasons from the empirical to the transcendental. Transcendental empiricism is the extreme point or limit of the sensible. What is sensed is the qualitative difference, rather than opposition, of genitality and innateness within creation. Artaud's transcendental empiricism calls into question the opposition between the 'natural' and the 'cultural' because the body becomes both. The body becomes indispensable and impulsive, distinct and assembled, inherent and assertive; it becomes self-culturing, it engenders its own innateness. Artaud embraces this engendering of self-birth in place of the oppositions of nature and culture which usually organize the body. If, therefore, Artaud really is opposing genitality and innateness perhaps it is because he is highlighting genitality and having it match innateness qualitatively and stylistically. In *A Thousand Plateaus*, Deleuze and Guattari write,

> It is true that Artaud still presents the identity of the One and the Multiple as a dialectical unity, one that reduces the multiple by

89

gathering it into the One ... But that is a manner of speaking, for from the beginning multiplicity surpasses all opposition and does away with dialectical movement.

(1987: 532 n. 16)

Could this 'manner of speaking' then be a 'speaking for' Artaud who clearly does not intend to put genitality and innateness into a dialectical relation? Artaud establishes an unusually direct alliance between the innate and the genital which circumvents the intercession of culture as it is understood as outside of the body. Artaud's theatre for example, 'takes gestures and develops them as far as they will go: like the plague it reforges the chain between what is and what is not, between the virtuality of the possible and what already exists in materialized nature' (Artaud, 1958: 27). This is Artaud's attempt to refigure the linkings, the autonomous pause, between life and death, language and the body, thought and its expression.

Because he disregards any notion of a psychological model of perception, sensation, thought, and understanding, Artaud's problem does not concern the orientation, expression, and method of his thought so much as the problem of being able to think at all. According to Deleuze, Artaud 'pursues in all this, the terrible revelation of a thought without image, and the conquest of a new principle which does not allow itself to be represented' (1994: 147). Artaud's impossible image of thought then is split in two, thought which struggles to exist and thought which is presupposed to exist, which for him is only vile and reasonable government. There is then only one thought, the multiple anarchic force of thought always at its limit, about to happen and having happened, an ungraspable image of thought. And it is precisely through Artaud's self-birth, his innate genitality, that he is able to take on the terror of thought without an image because in becoming violently new at every turn of his mind he never allows his new self to become incorporated.

I shall not command my desires and my inclinations, but neither do I want them to direct me, I want *to be* those desires and those inclinations, and this of course is difficult in a world which has never ceased to be under the command of the mind, and this to the imperilment of the soul and the loss of every body.

(Artaud, 1976: 446–7)

Artaud collapses the distinction between himself and his thought, annihilating the possibility of the domination of either. Artaud's sense of cruelty is a confrontation with the force of thought which in another sense confronts the mind (here mind is another word for the thought which presupposes good and evil) with the soul (another word for thought without an image).

Artaud is pleased to be wrong and stupid, he is pleased not to think if it means the pitiful huffing and puffing of language's straightforward denotations and expressions.[7] 'I suffer because the Mind is not life and life is not the Mind; I suffer from the Mind as organ, the Mind as interpreter, the Mind as intimidator of things, to force them to enter the Mind' (Artaud, 1976: 56). Artaud frees (liberates) thought by limiting the domination of its proper or prephilosophical image. Artaud does not reject the mind, he denounces it as an organ of the organized body and as an interpreter of meaning. What Artaud suffers to force into the mind is the mind's organizational presuppositions, which is to say that he suffers to force the mind's difference from itself to enter the mind.

When Artaud declares, 'I would rather work than feel myself alive' (1965: 222), this is hardly surprising for a man who says he can feel his thoughts stirring within him (can feel his mind move). But what does it mean to feel oneself alive? To feel 'oneself' is absurd but to feel oneself alive is truly abominable. 'The real pain', announces Artaud, 'is to feel one's thought shift within oneself. But thought as a fixed point', he adds, 'is certainly not painful' (1976: 84). It is this dimensionless point of thought that Artaud tracks, in the sense that he pursues the chance to show that it is there. Artaud follows the movement of change, the transformation or becoming of thought, as it eschews the distinguishable present along its mode of existence. Deleuze refers to this paradox, where that which happens differs from the materiality attributable to it, as an event or effect without a cause. An event is always destroyed when understanding or perception divide it into consecutive states that hide the inseparability of its continuous transformation of reality. Artaud dislikes the weakness of thought which cannot think without the interim necessary to distinguish objects from their repeated state of conversion. He is burdened by the inarticulation of the point of change. In *Theatre and its Double* he writes, 'from the aspect of our own existence, the most current philosophical determinism is an image of cruelty' (1958: 79). Artaud spies difference in itself as the act of cruelty in thought, and cruelty as the primary object of change. Recalling Artaud's idea that 'cruelty is nothing but determination as such', Deleuze writes, 'we should not be surprised that difference should appear accursed, that it should be error, sin, or the figure of evil for which there must be expiation. There is no sin other than raising the ground and dissolving the form' (Deleuze, 1994: 29). A point of change is the sudden shock when thought realizes itself in the body. As an autonomous affect this point is separate from the actions and the passions of the body. An affect is not nothing, it still produces signs. The affect is the implied relation between intensities of pure difference as it is experienced by the senses. These intensities become forces within a formless ground: in the vertiginous depths of the body desire materializes in Artaud's theatre 'on a level that is not yet human' (Artaud, 1976: 307).

Artaud's peculiar conception of cruelty devotes itself to a pitiless persistence toward the production of thought. Rather than relate simply to the production of pain and suffering where cruelty is regarded as cause, that is, as producing effective torment, Artaud's cruelty is a form of severity in thought, diligent and strict. 'Cruelty signifies rigor, implacable intention and decison, irreversible and absolute determination' (1958: 101). According to Artaud, we are in a degenerative state and so 'it is through the skin that metaphysics must be made to re-enter our minds' (1958: 99). Metaphysics enters the body as cruelty. Cruelty is a practice designed to force the mind to be affected, it is the production of a desire to become self-affected and active.[8] Artaud's cruelty has nothing to do with blood and war, it is 'the far more terrible, essential cruelty objects can practice on us' (1958: 79), because for Artaud, 'everything that acts is cruelty' (1958: 85). It is the movement (direction) of objects which determines our relationship to the world and to each other. Artaud's famous cane is an example of how objects move between us as so many trajectories deciding our lives. In 1934 Artaud read about the Jesus-stick of Saint Patrick. On his release from a drug detox centre in 1937 he was given a cane. Artaud claimed that this cane, due to its thirteen knots, was none other than the Jesus-stick, the staff of Saint Patrick. Artaud made extravagant, imposing and pretentious tours around Paris with his cane and it ruined his chance to marry, so scandalous was its appearance to his fiancée's family. He had the cane steel-tipped and also dipped in holy water and then he took it to Ireland. The cane allowed Artaud to replace Christ. Artaud said later that in Dublin it had been at the centre of street riots. The riots were 'in fact' imaginary and the cane was lost either in a Cathedral or a police station just before Artaud's deportation from Ireland in a straight-jacket.[9] The story of the cane invokes Artaud's 'theatre of cruelty' which reduces the role of understanding, shrinking the size of logic's importance and highlighting words as objects of cruelty and direction. 'Words will be construed in an incantational, truly magical sense – for their shape and their sensual emanations, not only for their meaning' (1958: 125). Cruelty makes us move, it wakes up the heart and nerves and tests our vitality in order to confront us with our potential, in order to force us into combat with our chaos. Deleuze follows Artaud's schizophrenic thought as it plunges into universal depths where the word loses its meaning but not its affect.

The unlanguage of howls and syncopated rhythms requires utter diligence and determination. Contrary to popular belief there is nothing sloppy about the workings of the depths. Artaud is not interested in a theatre of chance and improvisation, nor in the 'caprice of the wild and thoughtless inspiration of the actor, especially the actor who, once cut off from the text, plunges in without any idea of what he is doing' (1958: 109–10). In presenting the paradox of language and things, Artaud thwarts the collapse of the mind, but his intensity threatens to collapse even itself, and yet death can never die, and so Artaud's language of crazed cruelty is always accompanied by mercilessly direct and commanding writing.

Artaud intends to create signs rather than meaning. In the language of absolute depths these signs, the cruelty of objects, are 'false', which, it must be remembered, is not the same as evil. Artaud, like Nietzsche, sees evil as the opposite of good. Evil belongs to the man whose value system judges life from a moral origin of truth (Nietzsche, 1990: *passim*). Good, on the other hand, is not opposed to bad or false. The False is an eternal truth because 'it is the power of the false which supersedes the form of the true, because it poses the simultaneity of incompossible presents, or the coexistence of not-necessarily true pasts' (Deleuze, 1989: 131).

The good that Artaud distinguishes from continuous evil is the good which 'knows how to transform itself, to metamorphose itself according to its encounters … Of course there is no more truth in one life than in the other; there is only becoming, and becoming is the power of the false of life, is the will to power' (Deleuze, 1989: 141). According to Deleuze, 'Artaud is alone in having been an absolute depth in literature, and in having discovered a vital body and the prodigious language of this body. As he says, he discovered them through suffering' (Deleuze, 1990: 93). Artaud's language is intended to incite the body into action, to contaminate it like a disease through indigestible sounds and syncopated rhythms. Invented language, says Artaud, must issue from torment, words (Artaud's 'howl-words', which act at the level of pure phonetics and his unwritable 'breath-words') must have value in themselves, which in effect means that at some level they must be meaningless (Deleuze, 1990: 88). This 'value in itself' is the transcendent principle of the physicality of the word. The language of the depths of the body is before and after the judgment of man (it is not really God that Artaud rejects, but the judgment of god as instructed/constructed by man).

> What remains? There remain bodies, which are forces, nothing but forces. But force no longer refers to a centre, anymore than it confronts a set of obstacles. It only confronts other forces, it refers to other forces that it affects or that affect it.
>
> (Deleuze, 1989: 139)

Artaud's body, having lost its centre, its unvarying organization, becomes, like Deleuze's comment on Orson Welles's Don Quixote, 'the "goodness" of life in itself, a strange goodness which carries the living being to creation' (Deleuze, 1989: 142). In the depths of Artaud's language words become senseless and swamped by the harsh sounds and materiality of the body as so many phonetic elements which wound the body with unwieldy consonants and a plethora of bellows, yells and moans, and exhaust the body with breath-words and asphyxiation (Deleuze, 1990: 88–9).

The problem Artaud faces is that he cannot distinguish between an incorporeal event and the body's actions and passions. But truth, says Deleuze, is an undecidable alternative, it is not to be produced or achieved but to be created. 'There is no other truth than the creation of the New' (Deleuze, 1989: 146–7). Beneath the surface of language, between the actions and passions of the body, lies thought which can only be sensed, but which cannot be understood. Artaud writes, 'Above all else there is the wholeness of the nerves. A wholeness that includes all of consciousness, and the secret pathways of the mind in the flesh' (Artaud, 1976: 259). Artaud's pain, his inner feeling, no longer corresponds to images of sensation but only to sense. 'And it looks so good, I can see it / And it smells so good, I can smell it / And it sounds so good, I can hear it / And it feels so good, I can feel it / so why iye, iye, iye iyee / can't I touch it?'[10] Deleuze reiterates this when he writes, 'the eternal truth of the event is grasped only if the event is also inscribed in the flesh' (Deleuze, 1990: 161). Again we turn to Artaud's 'Theater and the Plague', where he writes, 'theater takes gestures and develops them as far as they will go: like the plague it reforges the chain between what is and what is not, between the virtuality of the possible and what already exists in materialized nature' (Artaud, 1958: 27). This is the flesh, the depth of bodies certainly, but at the synapses of the nerves which act as virtual intensities in continuous agitation (Artaud, 1976: 82).

Artaud's language of depth is related to Deleuze's commentary on the crack as the suddenness of the event within the flesh. In *Logic of Sense* (1990) Deleuze discusses the crack (named after F. Scott Fitzgerald's 'The Crack Up') which persists at the frontier of the depths and the surface. In the twenty-second series of *The Logic of Sense* Deleuze returns repeatedly to the problem of depth and surface, of Artaud's madness and senselessness and Carroll's humour and nonsense, of how to stay at the surface of the crack, at the incorporeal event without actualizing oneself in the quicksand and clamour of its body (1990: 154–61). Is Deleuze striving for a kind of balance between the two poles of surface and depth? He wills the crack and its perils and yet he warns us to stay at its edges like the paradox of the intrepid tourist.

All these questions point out the ridiculousness of the thinker: yes, they are always two aspects, and the two processes differ in nature. But when Bousquet speaks of the wound's eternal truth, it is in the name of a personal and abominable wound which he bears within his body. When Fitzgerald or Lowry speak of this incorporeal metaphysical crack and find in it the locus as well as the obstacle of their thought, its source as well as its drying up, sense and nonsense, they speak with all the gallons of alcohol they have drunk which have actualized the crack in the body. When Artaud speaks of the erosion of thought as something both essential and accidental, a radical impotence and nevertheless a great power, it is already from the bottom of schizophrenia. Each one risked something and went as far as possible in taking this risk; each one drew from it an irrepressible right. What is left for the abstract speaker once she has given advice of wisdom and distinction? Well then, are we to speak always about Bousquet's wound, about Fitzgerald's and Lowry's alcoholism, Nietzsche and Artaud's madness, while remaining on the shore? Are we to become the professionals who give talks on these topics? Are we to wish only that those who have been struck down do not abuse themselves too much? Are we to take up collections and create special journal issues? Or should we go a short way further to see for ourselves, be a little of an alcoholic, a little crazy, a little of a guerrilla enough to extend the crack, but not enough to deepen it irremedially? Wherever we turn everything seems dismal. Indeed, how are we to stay on the surface without staying on the shore? How do we save ourselves by saving the surface and every surface organization, including language and life? How is this politics, this full guerrilla warfare to be attained?

(Deleuze, 1990: 157–8)

The humour of this conundrum encapsulates a certain ironic burden toward change, toward the perception of knowledge and the knowledge of change (and a call to loosen up if not fall apart, to live a little if not on the edge, to want a little pain, if not to die from it). Deleuze and Guattari say that because of the infinite speeds of chaos and because of its shocks, we are always losing our ideas. We need a 'little order' in ideas, in things, in states of affairs, a little empirical imaging, a little sensation, as protection against plunging into black holes. In *What Is Philosophy?* (1994) it is the philosopher, the artist and the scientist who attempt to hold back opinion on the one hand, and chaos on the other. It is a precious juggling act. The fisherman who casts his net over concepts but risks being swept away is Deleuze's reiteration of concern at the loss of the shore. 'It is as if one were casting a net, but the fisherman always risks beign swept away and finding himself in the open sea when he thought he had reached port' (Deleuze and Guattari, 1994: 203). A little bit crazy, just enough to create. The question is, what does Deleuze see in Artaud's energy – life – chaos that he so admires? The second question follows, does he limit these 'Artaudian values', by means of his caution? But this is to position Deleuze on a rigid line of pedantic philosophy, and Artaud on some kind of fluid line of dissolution, when the two are really not all that opposed. Perhaps Deleuze's caution is a way of assembling life so that it can support the most extreme intensities, so that it can risk anything at all? Deleuze's desire for Artaud's craziness is still dangerous, in staying so stratified he risks repeating the banality of the destruction of a transvaluation of both their forces of life. Similarly, Artaud, even with his own position in the literary canon, can still be said to have written himself into dissolution.

In *their* quest for being a little crazy and a little alcoholic, Deleuze and Guattari favour Henry Miller who suggests getting soused on water, and William Burroughs, who tries thinking the possibility that things usually attained by chemical means are also 'accessible by other paths' (Deleuze, 1990: 161). Deleuze and Guattari, like the masochist, the schizo and the drug addict are hankering for a taste, for the effects of a practice. This is not to suggest that

Deleuze and Guattari ought instead to differentiate altered states by their causes (as if one could), but it is to point out that to get drunk on water is still to solicit (an) intoxication. In talking about a pure experience without drugs Deleuze and Guattari are the ultimate clichéd junkies 'just' hankering for an effect, an effect without a cause where intoxication has little, if nothing at all to do with supposed causal substances (except to suggest itself – junk, sex, alcohol) and more, or everything, to do with the active affections of the flesh of an inhuman body. Along a crack between the flesh and its sense (at its 'cutting edge'), Deleuze and Guattari

> cannot give up the hope that the effects of drugs and alcohol (their 'revelations') will be able to be relived and recovered for their own sake at the surface of the world, independently of the use of those substances, provided that the techniques of social alienation which determine this use are reversed into revolutionary means of exploration.
>
> (Deleuze, 1990: 161)

However, Deleuze and Guattari find the masochist and the drug addict hapless and empty because their 'sub-cultural' identities are ever reliant on the state. These failed bodies are said to produce the structured rigidities which a full body must eliminate.

What is problematic about this differentiation of the full and the empty (and should at all costs not be ignored) is that Deleuze and Guattari are proposing a dubious solution to the problem of the social order, an order where these empty bodies are also examples of socially stigmatized forms of subjectivity. It can be argued that the economies of drugs, pain and madness do not operate entirely as the effect of the substances or movements they take on any more than thought and writing do, but Deleuze and Guattari leave little room for anything other than the operation of the effect. Alternative operations by these empty bodies are regarded simply as processes of restrictive identification. And yet when Deleuze questions the paradoxical nature of the experimental, he cites its becoming within the aesthetic categories of madness (Artaud and Nietzsche), masochism or suicide (Bousquet) and drugs (Lowry and Fitzgerald). If this is a method of achieving a new intellectual record, what kind of record is it? The body without organs is described as 'the simple Thing, the Entity, the full Body, the stationary Voyage, Anorexia, cutaneous Vision, Yoga, Krishna, Love, Experimentation' (Deleuze and Guattari, 1987: 151). Because the masochist, the addict and the madman (as empty bodies without organs) are said to be degenerative and empty, they are only valuable because of the effects and ideas they engender in other visions and experimentations and not as experiments in themselves. Curiously, Deleuze and Guattari are all too happy to overlook the aesthetic practices of masochism, madness and alcoholism.[11] Concentrating on the adjectival force of 'a little', when executing a little cruelty, a little craziness and a little alcoholism, might enable the effect or the event of risk to be separated from its myriad nominal expressions, thereby acknowledging its applicability to any number of bodies.

The alcoholic's maxim is 'One thought is too many and a thousand is never enough'. Thought moves in both directions at once, like Deleuze's Alice who is becoming both larger than she was and smaller than she is becoming (Deleuze, 1990: 1).

> For the Large and the Small are not naturally said of the One, but first and foremost of difference. The question arises, therefore, how far the difference can and must extend – how large? how small? – in order to remain within the limits of the concept, neither becoming lost within, nor escaping beyond it.
>
> (Deleuze, 1994: 29)

'A little' is the seed of creation occurring on both sides of an opposition of too much and too little movement and rest, life and death. It is an implied limit, and difference, which is infinitely small and infinitely large is only ever implied. 'A little' is the presence of the actor in the event. In terms of a becoming crazy or alcoholic one is not a little crazy, one becomes a little crazy, which, like Alice, means that one can be a little crazy and a little stratified or cautious at the same time. 'A little' is neither particularly spatial nor temporal, it is not of the relations of subjects and objects, it is an affect and its sign.

What Deleuze regards as an *actual* or real problem is the imperial exigency of thought; it is a piece of chaotic reality that plagues our calculations and anticipations, and their habits. But what does this 'little piece of chaotic reality', this absolute and unthinkable chaos make us think? And what is its relation to the 'little order' so necessary for thought to become actual at all? Artaud parallels Deleuze's move toward a transcendental empiricism where order and chaos co-produce each other in an uncaused or self-propelling process. The 'little bit of chaotic reality' which forces us to think can only be sensed, it cannot be recognized. Deleuze's commentary on the image of thought and of thought without an image, tells us that if 'an encounter' with thought is invested in an object then it becomes recognized or recalled and is no longer an encounter, for it no longer forces us to think – it has become a product of common sense produced by a combination of the faculties (by their oppositions, their analogies, and their judgements) (Deleuze, 1994: 139). Artaud did not recognize his sacred cane, to others it was an old cane, but Artaud sensed, felt, intuited that it was more than (other than) a cane, it was magic. So what of the 'little bit of order' that stops us from thought rather than encourages it? Is it recognition itself and is it different from the bit of order? A 'little bit of order' prevents the loss of ideas, it is less order than before and also more order than 'a little chaos'.

If we construe order itself as a Kantian faculty then Deleuze's transcendental empiricism would take 'a little' of it, not as the overwhelming of another faculty as in the sublime, nor as a turning toward the other faculties (connection), but as the movement which extricates a single faculty out from all the others, 'in the presence of that which is its own' (Deleuze, 1994: 141). What concerns order essentially is creation. What is ordered in order is creation, the coming of the new, which in itself is forever coming, and has never been ordered. Similarly, what is not chaotic in chaos is a moment of creation, the chance swerve of an atom, the swing in a change of direction which necessitates that what is, is already no longer chaotic. The faculty of order then in confronting its own limit communicates to a little piece of chaotic reality, a little craziness and to a little alcoholism (and vice versa) only 'a violence which brings it face to face with its own element, as though with its disappearance or its perfection' (Deleuze, 1994: 141). This is the original necessity of violence inflicted in thought. The coexistence of the contraries of order and chaos or of crazy and secure are non-relational mad-becomings of philosophy. Following Deleuze we ask, what is it that can only be ordered, yet is chaotic at the same time. What is it that can only be drunken, yet is sober at the same time, and what is it that can only be crazy, yet is also sane or secure? (Deleuze, 1994: 143).

Artaud's well-documented mania parallels Deleuze's trancendental empiricism. Unable to think, Artaud strives to show that the unthought is there in thought. He tracks the unthought down, he raises thinking in thought to the level of the affect. This level of the affect corresponds with the 'just' of 'just a little order'. It is to 'just' that we must look in order to confirm, even in its imperceptibility, the event and its affect. Just crazy or just thinking implies an only just and a pure determined moment, an only crazy within the realm of a little crazy. It is Artaud's just madness, his very nearly more than mad and very nearly more than nonsensical that constitutes both his, as much as Deleuze's attachment to the shore. If a 'little' alcoholic is to be 'just' alcoholic then this is also to engender alcoholic or crazy, innately. 'Just' forces thought to its limit by creating 'just' such a limit within the unthought. Just is inconsiderable, small, it is also perfect and exact, choiceless and necessary, and it is not extreme. It is not extreme when it is revalued in relation to an 'extremity' specific to Artaud's project, which seeks to approach an immanent limit rather than to exceed its boundaries. 'Just' evokes a transcendental empiricism, it is the necessary determination of the imperceptibility of 'a little anything' because it bypasses the possibility of measuring the quantity and the quality of a sense of the affect. Artaud bypasses the crazy loop of death because he declares that his thoughts, although he can feel them stirring within him, are unthinkable.[12] He asks Rivière whether it is better to write something (the rejected poems that he sends him) than nothing at all.

> It is you who will give the answer by accepting or rejecting this little attempt. You will judge it, of course, from the point of view of the absolute. But I shall tell you that it would be a very great consolation

for me to think that even though I am not *all* of myself, not as tall, not as dense, not as wide as myself, I can still be something.

(Artaud, 1976: 36)

And he asks Rivière to judge it then, by being 'truly absolute'.

## Notes

1 Extracts from the various reports on Artaud's reading at the Vieux-Colombier 13 January 1947, at 9 pm are included in *Artaud on Theatre* (1989: 180–2).

2 This is quoted from a detailed description of Artaud's performance in Barber (1993: 136–9). Barber's text alludes to a number of commentators on the 13 January evening but credits no one in particular with having heard and relayed these words by Artaud.

3 Artaud chastised the surrealists for wanting a psychic revolution, when to alter the body was for Artaud to alter the world.

4 Lotringer (1996) comments on Artaud's bad acting style, he was the butt of theatrical jokes but his awkward gestures and his over-earnest attempts to portray a character were entertainingly far superior. Artaud's atrocious acting also refers to the diabolical performances of his own work, described by Madame Denise Colomb as being acted 'to the point of indecency' (Artaud, 1989: x).

5 See 'To Have Done with the Judgment of God'. The famous extract from the conclusion reads, 'Man is sick because he is badly constructed / We must decide to strip him in order to scratch out this / animacule which makes him itch to death, / god, / and with god, / his organs. / For tie me down if you want to, / but there is nothing more useless than an organ.// When you have given him a body without organs, / then you will have delivered him from all his automatisms and / restored him to his true liberty' (1982: 61–79).

6 The notion of self-creation may sound suspiciously like the classical notion of the creative genius, the autonomous artist fashioning his very own liberationist self, but this assumption misses the real aspect of Artaud's autogenesis. For example, when in his 'In Memoriam' Saillet discusses Artaud's observation of himself, the way Artaud addresses himself, Antonin Artaud by Antonin Artaud, he writes, 'His work is an inventory of himself' (quoted in Hayman, 1977: 152) and, I would add, an *invention* of himself. Artaud's self-invention is certainly not the self-production of the aspiring individualist. The individualist creates himself out of already self-proliferating and already public fragments. There is nothing new except, perhaps, Artaud's combinations of himself.

7 Artaud's approach to ignorance is perhaps evocative of Spinoza's. Both view ignorance or inadequate ideas as catalysts for creating active affections out of what Spinoza called joyful passions. Where Artaud cruelly confronts common forces of bodies, Spinoza who is also harsh, encourages everyone to work toward joyful relations between bodies, what he calls 'common notions'. Both are thinking of the energy of the forces of bodies.

8 'By affect I understand affections of the Body by which the Body's power of acting is increased or diminished, aided or restrained, and at the same time, the ideas of these affections. Therefore, if we can be the adequate cause of any of these affections, I understand by the Affect an action; otherwise, a passion'. Spinoza, *Ethics*, III D3 (Spinoza, 1985: 493).

9 A whole chapter devoted to Artaud's cane is in Rattray, 1992: 143–170.

10 Lyrics of 'Why Can't I Touch It?' The Buzzcocks. *Singles Going Steady* LP.

11 This is not always the case: in *Coldness and Cruelty* (1991) Deleuze studies the

aesthetics of masochism. On the discrepancy between the masochist in Deleuze's collaborations with Guattari, see Dale (1997). Of course, Deleuze and Guattari's caution can also be understood as a cruelty, something hard, a disciplinary masochism.

12 After writing my first draft on 'just', as a way of thinking about the affect, I found a similar use of the word in Deleuze's *Negotiations* in a discussion on the film-maker Godard. Deleuze talks about conforming and confirming ideas which he calls 'just' ideas, which he differentiates from a becoming-present, from a stammering of ideas which he calls 'just ideas', and which 'can only be expressed in the form of questions, that tend to confound any answers. Or you can present some simple thing that disrupts all the arguments' (Deleuze, 1995: 39).

# References

Artaud, Antonin (1958) *The Theatre and its Double*, trans. Clayton Eshleman, Los Angeles: Panjandrum.

—— (1965) *Artaud Anthology*, Jack Hirshman (ed.), San Francisco: City Lights.

—— (1970–4) *Antonin Artaud: Collected Works*, vols. 1–4, trans. Victor Corti, London: Caulder and Boyars.

—— (1976) *Antonin Artaud: Selected Writings*, Susan Sontag (ed.), trans. Helen Weaver, Los Angeles: UCLA Press.

—— (1982) *Antonin Artaud: Four Texts*, trans Clayton Eshleman and Norman Glass, Los Angeles: Panjandrum.

—— (1989) *Artaud on Theatre*, ed. and trans. Claude Shumacher, London: Methuen.

—— (1995) *Watch Fiends and Rack Screams*, ed. and trans. Clayton Eshleman with Bernard Bador, Boston: Exact Change.

Barber, Stephen (1993) *Antonin Artaud: Blows and Bombs*, London: Faber.

Deleuze, Gilles (1989) *Cinema 2: the Time-Image*, trans. Hugh Tomlinson and Robert Galeta, Minneapolis: University of Minnesota Press.

—— (1990) *The Logic of Sense*, trans. Mark Lester, ed. Constantin V. Boundas, New York: Columbia University Press.

—— (1991) *Coldness and Cruelty*, trans. Jean McNeil, New York: Zone Books.

—— (1994) *Difference and Repetition*, trans. Paul Patton, New York: Columbia University Press.

—— (1995) *Negotiations 1972–1990*, trans. Martin Joughin, New York: Columbia University Press.

Deleuze, Gilles, and Guattari, Félix (1983) *Anti-Oedipus*, trans. Robert Hurley, Mark Seem and Helen R. Lane, Minneapolis: University of Minnesota Press.

—— (1987) *A Thousand Plateaus*, trans. Brian Massumi, Minneapolis: University of Minnesota Press.

—— (1994) *What Is Philosophy?*, trans. Hugh Tomlinson and Graham Burchell, New York: Columbia University Press.

Hayman, Ronald (1977) *Artaud and After*, Oxford: Oxford University Press.

Lotringer, Sylvère (1996) 'One Hundred Years of Cruelty', conference paper Power House Museum, Sydney, Australia, 13–15 September 1996.

Nietzsche, Friedrich (1990) *Beyond Good and Evil*, trans. R.J. Hollingdale, London: Penguin.

Rattray, David (1992) *How I Became One of the Invisible*, New York: Semiotext(e).

Spinoza, Baruch (1985) *The Collected Works*, vol. 1, trans. Edwin Curley, Princeton: Princeton University Press.

# 8

# SUBJECTLESS SUBJECTIVITIES

*Paul Bains*

Self-present in the vertical dimension, overseeing themselves without taking any distance, these are neither objects that can explain perception, nor subjects capable of grasping a perceived object; rather, they are absolute interiorities that take hold of themselves and everything that fills them, in a process of 'self-enjoyment.'

(Deleuze, 1993: 102–3)

It appears to us that the only way of avoiding the absurdities of contemporary idealisms is by conferring a machinic status to subjectivity and accepting without reticence the existence of a proto-subjectivity, an economy of choice, a negentropic passion, at all levels of the cosmos – from the point zero of expansion of the universe to the blossoming of the most deterritorialized machinisms, such as those of poetry, music, and the sciences.

(Guattari, 1979: 165–6)

The recognition of a trans-spatial thematics indissolubly connected to spatio-temporal dimensions, does not mean accepting the old dualism of body and soul ... The organism is not a machine *plus* a soul. Organic existence only exists dynamically in an incessant flux that, to put it simply, renews all its molecules. It is constant activity, a permanence of dynamism, and not the permanence of a material reality, informed afterwards by an ideal form.

(Ruyer, 1956: 244)

Even the mind of God can only imagine
Those things that have become themselves

(D.H. Lawrence quoted in Ruyer, 1956: 263)

## Introduction

This essay intervenes in the growing field of Deleuze and Guattari studies and seeks to give expression to their ethico-aesthetic conception of subjectivity, its

101

political nature and distinction from classical, objectivist, scientific theories. What is disturbing about their endeavour is that it attempts to think that which cannot be thought and to write the unreadable. To think of a not-external outside and a not-internal inside: 'an outside more distant than any external world, because it is an inside deeper than any internal world: it is immanence' (Deleuze and Guattari, 1994: 59). A self-referential, autopoietic immanence that is not immanence *to* something (as to a purely ideal transcendent ego-onto-theological plane or Subject/Eye) but rather an autopoietic or self-producing/positing immanence *of* subjectivity. A plane of immanence or consistency 'which has no supplementary dimension to that which transpires upon it'. 'A what!?'

Such a project which poses 'absolute interiorities' and 'proto-subjectivities' sits uneasily within the contemporary humanities as over the last fifty years or so, with the notable exception of feminist theories that rethink subjectivity, a massive commitment has been made to deny, deconstruct or obliterate any concept of the 'subject' and 'interiority'. The traditional notion of the rational, conscious, Cartesian or phenomenological subject has been the intended target of poststructuralism and postmodernism in their differing guises and the current intellectual landscape seems to be imbued with the idea that any notion of subjectivity (which must surely be bringing a 'subject' or 'mind' in through the back door) is highly suspect and to be treated with derision or at the very least, suspicion. We are encouraged by some to believe that we inhabit a world of pure exteriority (whatever that is) and manipulable 'body parts' available for reconfiguration. (The fascination with cyborgs.) Or even a world where 'subjectivity' has been taken outside of the skin onto the internet (Stelarc) – on the apparent assumption that it had been originally like a gas 'inside' something called the 'body' which now becomes a purely material support. Dualism in and out through the bloody back door.

This prevailing suspicion of the concept of subjectivity remains operative despite the later works of Michel Foucault which develop the notion of 'the care of the self' (Foucault, 1986) and the whole corpus of Gilles Deleuze and Félix Guattari's work which has as its recurring theme *the autopoietic or self-referential production of subjectivity*. That is to say, the processes of the realization of autonomy understood as 'an event that is in-itself and for-itself, and not as from its aspect in the essence of another such occasion' (Whitehead, 1938: 89). Without being able to fully develop this concept right now, it should be immediately understood that such a definition of autonomy or autopoiesis distinguishes itself from any purely thermodynamic definition that is solely constituted by relational flows. An autopoietic event has an endo-consistency that is lacking in a vortex or dissipative structure defined only by its relational flows with the surrounding medium. A baby or a molecule or a paramecium is not in and of itself a whirlpool or vortex or a wave or a crystal although it involves dissipative structures and can display vortex-like 'behaviour'. It is a sovereign individual autonomy with an intrinsic existential reality or self-referential territory, *even though it has relations with other existential territories*. It is a value that is an end in itself – for its own sake. Very few philosophers or scientists (with the exception of Spinoza, Whitehead, Ruyer, Maturana and Deleuze and Guattari) have attempted to think the possibility of an existential integrity that is at the same time in relation with other self-referential territories or events. To think the possibility of creative affirmation and Joy in a world of suffering and resentment. It is easy to be against things but not so easy to be for something and know how to produce it.

There are significant differences between these three theorists (Deleuze/-Guattari and Foucault) but their fascination with the creative generation of subjectivity seems to have been ignored in over-emphasizing the deterministic construction of subjectivity and the subject by the symbolic order and power relations. In this respect it is striking that in his final work *Chaosmosis* (1995) (a meteoric text whose time has yet to come and which develops to an extreme degree material which is barely introduced here) Guattari gives an account of Daniel N. Stern's *The Interpersonal World of The Infant* (1985), which offers a brilliant portrayal of the non-conscious sense of self already available at birth. The fusional, transitivist 'emergent self' that ignores the oppositions self/other, subject/object.[1]

It is of course fair to say that a significant aim of Deleuze and Guattari's work (and Foucault's) has been to pulverize the traditional notion of the subject as the ultimate essence of individuation, pre-reflexively contemplating its own existence, and to develop a *schizoanalytic* subjectivity superposing multiple strata of subjectivation in a multicomponential cartography opposed to the Conscious/Unconscious dualism of the Freudian schema. This is not a denial of the process of individuation but the recognition that subjectivity deploys itself as much 'beyond' the 'individual' ('it is wrought by collective assemblages of enunciation') as 'before' it on the side of preverbal intensities. Pathic or prehensive events. This recognition of a multiplicity of subjective strata has often been interpreted as the primacy of something called *multiplicity* and the consequent denial of subjectivity or unicity, understood in a phenomenological or Cartesian sense, whereas the absolute *self-referentiality* of this ensemble of subjective strata and conditions is necessary for its emergence as an 'existential Territory, adjacent, or in a delimiting relation, to an alterity that is itself subjective' (Guattari, 1995: 9). The difficulty here is in recognizing that the multiplicity of heterogeneous components can emerge as a process of subjective self-reference through a kind of global transconsistency or existential grasping (Guattari, 1995: 113; Guattari, 1989: 82; following Whitehead's process of concrescence) whereby a fragmentary whole emerges, a *unitas multiplex*, a unity in multiplicity, an absolute survey that involves no supplementary dimension (Ruyer). A plane of consistency. Rational modes of discursive knowledge cannot adequately grasp this kind of metalogical approach which can only be fully appreciated through a non-discursive, affective pathic awareness. The *grasping* of real unity of feeling. You either get it or you don't. A particle of zen. A whole in all the parts. A holon. An endo-consistency in which the components are distinct but inseparable. A composite unity. A Whiteheadian event. A philosophy of organism. A body without organs.

I get the feeling that Deleuze's substantive, *multiplicity,* has been sometimes understood as a numeric multiplicity (the dialectical opposition of the one to the multiple) involving space and spatial divisibility, *partes extra partes,* as one of its conditions. But this is exactly what Deleuze (developing Bergson) and, as we shall see even more coherently, Raymond Ruyer (who posits a 'real extension' *partes in unitate*) seek to avoid, by positing a qualitative multiplicity involving duration as one of its conditions. A qualitative multiplicity is not an aggregate of parts with an apparent unity constituted by the relation of separate numerical or physical existents (the Galilean world of purely external relations) but an *event, an actual occasion of experience* (Whitehead, 1938). A processual pathic intensity. An eventity breaking down the ontological iron curtain between mind and matter. A desiring machine. A 'fusional' multiplicity. A zone of intensive continuity that is not spatially divisible. A quantal non-locality. A plateau. A real space.

> 'Rei's only reality is the realm of ongoing serial creation', Rez said. 'Entirely *process*; infinitely more than the combined sum of her various selves.'
>
> (Gibson, 1996: 202)[2]

What cannot be too strongly emphasized is that although for Deleuze and Guattari the individuated psyche is generated from a pre-individual autopoietic or self-referential node of events and intensive singularities, *these events are themselves subjectivities in absolute or non-dimensional self-survey.* The term 'absolute survey', which Deleuze and Guattari take from the French philosopher Raymond Ruyer, is introduced here as a kind of conceptual provocation. Its meaning and affect can only be apprehended through some engagement with Ruyer's 'biological philosophy' and its incorporation within the complex conceptual onto-ecology developed by Deleuze and Guattari, most notably in *The Fold: Leibniz and the Baroque* (1993) and *What Is Philosophy?* (1994).[3] There could be no subjectivity (a self-referential territory in-itself and for-itself) within a world composed of a numerical multiplicity of infinitely divisible physical existents related solely through cause and effect (the very notion of extension or substance evaporates with infinite divisibility – extension reduces to pure points, something that idealist philosophy was quick to notice in positing an a-spatial 'subject' or spirit to hold it all together). The early Greeks (not to mention non-Western thought) had no concept of a separate 'body' and 'soul'. Their cosmos was an 'animated' living whole without separation between 'matter' and 'mind.'[4] Pansychism. Brian Massumi claims that 'one of the things that distinguishes Deleuze's philosophy most sharply from that of his contemporaries is the notion that ideality is a dimension of matter (also understood as encompassing the human, the artificial, and the invented)' (Massumi, 1995: 97).

> Metaphysical, meta-semiotic, regardless of the name, I see no reason to refuse the existence of the equivalent of a subjectivity or proto-subjectivity, to material and living assemblages. This molecular economy cannot be assimilated to a micro-physics of passive elementary entities. Freud wasted his brilliant intuition concerning the existence of an unconscious subjectivity by trying to base it on thermodynamic analo-gies in a way that radically opposed a sphere of differentiated order to a sphere of undifferentiated primary energetic matter.
>
> (Guattari, 1979: 161)[5]

One of the challenges of this essay (which is only the introduction to a larger project) will be to articulate such a notion of subjectivity and its radical distinction from phenomenological accounts which distinguish an inert desubjectified 'in-itself' and a self-conscious 'for-itself' that creates the world by naming it (Heidegger). This phenomenological subjectivity is characterized by a particular (bizarre) understanding of visual perception and does not envisage the possibility of a subjectivity (Deleuze and Guattari emphasize the distinction between subjectivity and Cartesian consciousness – 'it's not enough to think in order to be'; 1989b: 23) that does not operate in the mode of phenomenology's understanding of visual perception but is rather a direct non-discursive auto-possession – a non-human for-itself (to be distinguished from an unconscious). A 'fourth person singular'. An in-itself that is for-itself. Auto-affection. A self-feeling unicity. A real space. Not a Cartesian or Bergsonian geometrical space.

For Deleuze and Guattari human subjectivity or interiority (before/beyond any internal Cartesian spectator/cinema complex or geometrical notions of spatiality) emerges as a self-referential existential Territory at the intersection of multiple components (material, semiotic, biological ... Casteñada's tonal-nagual: 'a fiber stretches from a human to an animal, from a human or an animal to molecules, from molecules to particles, and so on to the imperceptible – a universe of microperceptions'; Castañada, 1993: 249) which are themselves proto-subjectivies or intensive singularities. Singularities are pre-individual, non-personal, a-conceptual events or 'sensitive points'. The unity of mind and nature (Deleuze). The Body Without Organs/The Plane of Immanence. Absolute survey. Casteñada's sorceric account of perception and its Deleuzo–Guattarian appropriation, is, as will be become blindingly obvious, a practical philosophy that is profoundly Leibnizian–Spinozist. We are self-referential, autopoietic 'bubbles of perception' – whose 'assemblage point' can be radically shifted in order to free us from the fight or flight mentality (q.v. Car-los Casteñada). *This is in no way an idealistic subjectivism or solipsistic antirealism.*

In *The Three Ecologies*, Guattari emphasizes that such an approach is difficult to maintain in contexts where there is suspicion or even a rejection in principle of any specific reference to subjectivity (Guattari, 2000: 36–8). He argues (I am glossing on the French text) that even those who do deal with subjectivity take great care to never stray too far from pseudo-scientific paradigms, borrowed in preference from the hard sciences: thermodynamics, systems theory, linguistics, topology (Lacan), etc. As if a scientific super-ego required that psychical entities had to be reified and only understood in terms of extrinsic coordinates and physical forces. This is not to say that Deleuze and Guattari do not appropriate notions drawn from the so-called hard sciences but that this is done (as Guattari has emphasized, 1980) in terms of operational borrowings rather than in terms of a scientific super-ego.

Guattari further argues that in such conditions it is hardly surprising that the human and social sciences ignore the intrinsically creative and auto-positioning or autopoietic dimensions of processes of subjectivation (Guattari, 1989b: 25). He also suggests that the best cartographies of the psyche, or if one prefers, the best psychoanalyses, were written by Goethe, Proust, Joyce, Artaud, and Beckett, rather than by Freud, Jung and Lacan. And that in the work of the latter, it is the literary part of their work that remains the most valuable. For example, Sigmund Freud's *The Interpretation of Dreams* can be read as an extraordinary modern novel. By emphasing the creative possibilities inherent to subjectivity, Guattari is arguing that all those who intervene in subjective or psychical domains, whether individual or collective (in education, health, culture, sport, art, the media, the fashion industry, etc.) have an ethical responsibility which cannot be dissolved by a neutrality based on a claim to mastery of the unconscious or scientific knowledge. That is to say we have a politico-ethical responsibility for our creations or progeny whether virtual or actual.[6] For the way we invent/posit subjectivities and for our reappropriation of the means of production of subjectivity, which alone will enable us to deal with the eco-systemic crises already engulfing us and with those yet to emerge ('the chaosmic spasms looming on the horizon'; Guattari 1995: 135). Guattari distinguishes this aesthetic paradigm and ethico-political responsibility from classical scientific approaches which objectify or reify subjectivity in extrinsic coordinates and claim to act from a position of disinterestedness. An immanent proto-ethics that doesn't emanate from a transcendent plane. Freedom exists only within immanence (Spinoza). Guattari stresses that we should look to artistic and poetic practices for inspiration in the creative processes that are intrinsic to any reinvention of subjectivity or mentality. A reinvention that will involve the three ecologies of the environment, the socius and the psyche.

As Alain Badiou has argued, 'Deleuze is searching for a figure of interiority (or of the subject) that is *neither* reflection (or the cogito), *nor* the relation-to, the focus (or intentionality), *nor* the pure empty point (or eclipse). Neither Descartes, nor Husserl, nor Lacan' (Badiou 1994: 61). This essay will suggest/deduce that Raymond Ruyer's post-Leibnizian psycho-biology provides Deleuze and Guattari with their most compelling account of subjectivity (a spatio-temporal immanence of unity in multiplicity, or of interiority in exteriority) which achieves its expression in their final work *What Is Philosophy?* (particulary in the conclusion, 'From Chaos to the Brain', where the brain becomes subject in absolute-survey, an auto-possession or 'self-enjoyment', prior to the emergence of the phenomenal perceptual field – 'the brain is the *mind* itself'; 1994: 210–11). In *Difference and Repetition* (1994) and through his engagement with Bergsonian thought (things are luminous by themselves without anything illuminating them: all consciousness *is* something, not *of* something), Deleuze had sought to displace the notion of consciousness as illuminating objects or casting light on things (a theory of thought without image) and Ruyer provides the conceptual apparatus for this displacement as it is taken up in *What is Philosophy?*

*What is this brain becoming-mind/subject in absolute survey?* This absolute surface in self-possession? This immanent plane of consistency, or of Nature, that has no supplementary dimension to that which transpires 'upon' it ... this immanent survey of a field without any need of an ideal 'subject' giving it its unity.

## Memories of a plan(e) maker

It is a primary, 'true form' as Ruyer defined it: neither a Gestalt nor a perceived form, but a *form in itself* that does not refer to any exterior point of view, any more than the retina or striated area of the cortex refers to another retina or cortical area; it is an absolute consistent form that surveys *itself* independently of any supplementary dimension, which does not appeal therefore to any transcendence, which has only a single side whatever the number of its dimensions, which remains copresent to all its determinations without proximity or distance, traverses them at infinite speed, without limit-speed, and which makes of them so many *inseparable variations* on which it confers an equipotentiality without confusion.

(Deleuze and Guattari, 1994: 210)

This stunning expression will require unpacking! What are 'true forms' and how might they relate to 'equipotentiality'? In fact this essay may do no more nor less than attempt to explicate this Ruyerian concept of the mindbrain virtual–actual interface as appropriated by Deleuze and Guattari, and in so doing distinguish this approach to subjectivity from that of mechanistic, gestalt, Bergsonian[7] or phenomenological accounts. Deleuze and Guattari consider this to be Ruyer's singular achievement as manifested throughout his extensive oeuvre.[8] (What new ways of thinking and feeling can be experienced today?)

107

## Absolute survey and the myth of intentionality[9]

This is how the translators of *What Is Philosophy?* introduce the concept of 'survey':

> It is difficult to find a single English equivalent for the word *survol*. The word derives from *survoler*, 'to fly over' or 'to skim one's eyes rapidly over something'. However, the present use derives from the philosopher Raymond Ruyer. Ruyer uses the notion of an absolute or non-dimensional 'survol' to describe the relationship of the 'I-unity' to the subjective sensation of the visual field. This sensation, he says, tempts us to imagine the 'I' as a kind of invisible center outside, and situated in a supplementary dimension perpendicular to, the whole of the visual field that it surveys from a distance. However, this is an error. The immediate survey of the unity of the visual field made up of many different details takes place within the dimension of the visual sensation itself; it is a kind of 'self-enjoyment' that does not involve any supplementary dimension.
>
> (Deleuze and Guattari, 1994: ix–x)

Ruyer claims that although the concept of a Consciousness-entity has been universally rejected – and that this rejection is nothing new, finding its roots in Empiricism – it is often only rejected in words, being based on an illusion that has never been clearly eradicated (Ruyer, 1950: 52). We have the strong impression that our sensual/visual field is *in front* of us and that we *look at it* from a supplementary dimension. This is an error. Sensations are brain achievements and there is no brain behind the brain or eye behind the eye to look at its products. Vision or any other sensorial experience is existence rather than 'representation of'. There is no re-presentation of one world but only the multiple worlds our brains achieve. *This is not subjectivism – no philosophical or psychological subject is involved.* The brain or organism as an autopoietic, self-referential, primary true form, is naturally producing a virtual world (or actualizing a virtual world that is real but not actual; the indiscernible oscillation at infinite speed between the virtual/actual; chaosmosis). 'But really you do *not* see the eye. And nothing *in the visual field* allows you to infer that it is seen by an eye' (Wittgenstein, 1974: s. 5.633; Wittgenstein is very close to Ruyer in stressing that 'we' do not *observe* our consciousness; nor do we look out through our eyes! just in case we hadn't noticed).

Ruyer maintains that absolute overview or survey is the key, not only to the question of subjectivity and consciousness, but to the problem of life itself (Ruyer, 1952: 100). In order to clarify this concept and introduce his central thesis of *reversed epiphenomenalism* Ruyer, in a crucial chapter of *Néo-finalisme* – 'Surfaces Absolues et Domaines Absolus de Survol' (1952: chapter 9) – makes a distinction between the optical and the mental aspects of vision. Reversed epiphenomenalism claims that there would be no 'matter' or real extension if there were no autopoietic 'primary true forms' or subjectivities as indivisible unities (with an outside beyond any externality and an inside beyond any internal world). Pure Cartesian, geometrical extension has no real substance. (Deleuze follows Ruyer in arguing that the great dividing line is not between the organic/inorganic but between the individual or primary true form and the aggregate; 1993: chapter 8). The molar/molecular distinction. An elephant is molecular. Crowd phenomena are molar.

The illustration or beginner's guide to absolute domains of survey (which involves the example of visual perception, but only in order to go beyond it and demonstrate that there are absolute surfaces that do not involve vision or a contemplating subject or idealistic ego) unfolds something like this: If we are looking at a physical surface such as a checkered table-top – the checkers of which are all definable *partes extra partes* (i.e., exterior to each other, *they are all at different places on the surface*) – we must be positioned in space so that our retina is at some distance, and in a dimension perpendicular to the surface of the table. This is also the case for a camera. A living being, localized as a body, has to be in a second dimension to see or photograph a line and in a third dimension to see or photograph a surface. In brief, as Ruyer puts it, an observer must always be in $n+1$ dimension in order to be able to see, at once, all the constituant points of a being in n dimensions. However, Ruyer claims (and this is important so don't forget it) that *this geometrical law, which is valid for perception as a physico-physiological event, is not valid for visual sensation as a state of consciousness* (Ruyer, 1952: 96). However, if we shift our attention to our visual sensation *per se* then we don't have to be outside of our sensation, in a dimension perpendicular to it, in order to contemplate all the different details of which it is made up. We do not have to imagine a 'third eye' or super-retina in its turn perceiving our visual sensation. Thus the viewed-table as a visual sensation doesn't obey the laws of physical geometry. 'It is a surface seized in all its details, without a third dimension. It is an "absolute surface", that is not relative to any point of view exterior to itself, which knows itself without observing itself' (Ruyer, 1952: 98). Ruyer claims that visual sensation *has only one side*, somewhat like a mobius surface although the analogy should remain one. (Topological forms do not have an intensive, pathic, autopoietic dynamism. Neither will *purely algorithmic* infinitely unfolding fractals do the job – although self-referential fractal dimensions are pretty cool. Mandelbrot has argued that autopoietic molecular systems are not infinitely fractal. There is infinite fractality only in purely mathematical geometrical constructions.) This onesideness of visual sensation is due to the non-geometrical and non-dimensional character of survey. *If the sensible surface could be seen from both sides it would no longer be a sensation but an object.* The overviewing I/eye is metaphorical. Rather than being punctiform as suggested by the geometric optics of the sixteenth and seventeenth centuries, the 'I' (self-feeling multiplicity/unicity) is domainal and ubiquitous, copresent to sensation and having neither proximity nor distance from sensation. A decentred subjectivity with an always displaced periphery. The self awareness of our visual sensation is spatially and temporally ubiquitous. It is everywhere at once, being simultaneously in the multiple details of our field of vision. Whereas, in the physical surface the checkers are spatially separate and distinct, in the absolute surface there exists no such separateness: the various orders and relations of the checkers are immediately given in an absolute unity, without therefore being a fusion or confusion. For Ruyer, this means that one's sensation is a 'true form', and not a *pattern,* or a structure, or an aggregate of elements, or a Gestalt-form. What surprises Ruyer is that this revolutionary consequence of the negation of the subject for the nature of sensible extension was not recognized before. The possibility of an extensity that is in–itself and for–itself without being perceived by a spiritual subject.

In the *Logic of Sense,* Deleuze conceives of the brain in terms of the conversion of a cerebral surface into a metaphysical surface, 'the brain is not only a corporeal organ but also the inductor of another invisible, incorporeal, and metaphysical surface on which all events are inscribed and symbolized' (Deleuze 1990: 233). A topological surface. (Topological proximity is independent of distance or contiguity; Deleuze and Parnet, 1987: 104). In *Cinema 2,* Deleuze, drawing on the work of Gilbert Simondon, indicates that 'the cortex cannot be adequately represented in a Euclidean way' and that there is now the discovery/invention of a topological cerebral space which 'achieves the copresence of an inside deeper than any internal medium, and an outside more distant than any external medium' (see chapter 8, 'Cinema, Body and Brain, Thought'; Deleuze, 1989: 211). 'The image no longer has space and movement as its primary characteristics but topology and time'. (Topology is the study of those properties of geometric forms that remain invariant under certain transformations, such as bending, stretching, folding). 'To belong to interiority does not mean to "be inside", but to be on the "in-side" of the limit' (Simondon quoted in Deleuze, 1990: 104). The difficulty of finding non-dimensional or hyper-dimensional or transversal language. The problem with topology is that it remains a geometrical analysis of a non-geometrical non-dimension. The supreme act of philosophy is to think the unthinkable. As Spinoza did once and so, as it also seems, did Ruyer.

But I (as a non-punctiform, primary true form) digress. And isn't philosophy in a state of perpetual digression? (Deleuze and Guattari, 1994: 23) Let's return to the absolute surface and sort a few things out, like *infinite speed and equipotentiality.*

Because the 'I' or self-enjoyment of sensation (NB not the 'I' of commonsense or semiotic/psychoanalytic criticism) is in all 'places' at once, it is not constrained by the special theory of relativity which informs us that one cannot be in two places at once. There is no limit-speed for the domain of subjectivity. It doesn't respect Einstein's cosmological limit of the speed of light (quantum physics has now empirically verified non-local quantum entanglement that involves absolute simultaneity at a distance). Self-enjoyment is everywhere in the visual field. The checkered squares of the table-top vary in distance from each other but in visual sensation this isn't a real distance. Ruyer claims that the notion of absolute overview enables us to understand the difference between subjectivity (or primary 'subjectless' consciousness) and the secondary consciousness of a 'subject'.

Ruyer will accept the neurobiologist's account that our visual sensations (in fact all our sensations) are occurring in the brain as observed from outside. However, 'within' the brain there is no third eye that would scan the visual sensations as given in their immediacy. It surveys itself in absolute overview, without taking a dimension perpendicular to itself. It is not a Cartesian theatre. This suggests that at least a certain part of the organism is directly conscious of itself. Now if we take an organism without a nervous system such as the unicellular protozoa, can it 'see' itself directly, like our cortical tissue? The protozoan has no eyes or mirrors, but neither does our brain have eyes or mirrors to see what is presented to it. Ruyer infers that the protozoan has a 'self-enjoyment' or primary consciousness that doesn't perceive external forms but has an auto-subjectivity that constitutes its very being. The term 'self-enjoyment' is explicitly taken by Ruyer from the philosophy of Samuel Alexander and does not designate pleasure but rather an immediacy without objectification. This primary consciousness, manifesting itself as a unified dynamic form in micropsychic autopoiesis is coextensive with life, wherever formation and function are confounded. *The absolute surface (or volume) knows itself without observing itself.*

> There is no reason to deny to our non-cortical cells, even if they have no nervous system, a subjectivity, primary consciousness, self-survey, the *self-enjoyment* of their own form. 'I' don't participate in this *self-enjoyment* because 'I' am specialized in sensory consciousness.
>
> (Ruyer, 1952: 104)

Equipotentiality (a term coined by the neurophysiologist Karl Lashley in the 1920s and subsequently developed by his student Karl Pribram as the holographic theory of memory) means that in principle any part of the embryo can deputize for another and thus for the whole: a fact demonstrated by performing drastic surgery upon it. The embryonic surface does not respond like a surface with geometrical properties, *it is equipotential*. (This equipotentiality is the clue to absolute survey and non-locality.) This is also apparently the case for cerebral activity. Ruyer argues, with an abundance of material, that this equipotentiality is the actual manifestation of an absolute domain of survey, and that the embryo, from its start in space and time, must be in contact with a metabiological *trans-spatial* realm of mnemonic themes or morphic fields (the virtual or potential realm) that dominate the visible, structural transformations that later take place. An organic memory 'invents' the brain before making use of it. *The organism is a machine that has built itself.* Not a replica or copy of itself. It is a process of self-referential molecular production. A desiring machine. The 'product' is the process – is the product ... a tangled hierarchy like Escher's painting *Drawing Hands*, although dynamic and epigenetic. The hands can draw themselves differently as the process unfolds. (Distinguish autopoiesis from Derridian deconstruction. Derrida doesn't see that the self-referentiality of autopiesis also embodies the logic of the supplement, which is Derrida's main weapon *against* any claim to autonomous unity.)[10] Deleuze invokes Ruyer's work in *Difference and Repetition:*

> When a cellular migration takes place, as Raymond Ruyer shows, it is the requirements of a 'role' insofar as this follows from a structural 'theme' to be actualized which determines the situation and not the inverse. The world is an egg, but the egg is itself a theatre: a staged theatre in which the roles dominate the actors, the spaces dominate the roles and the Ideas dominate the spaces.
>
> (Deleuze, 1994: 216)

The actualization of the virtual. Deleuze further argues (in *Bergsonism*) that Ruyer is analogous to Bergson in appealing to an ' "inventive, mnemonic and trans-spatial potential", the refusal to interpret evolution in purely actual terms' (Deleuze, 1991: 132).

Rhenan Mysticism. Medieval Monopsychism. Carlitos Casteñada. Ruyer on microphysics and his consistency with current microphysics of the brain. Quantum brain dynamics!

> To continue Bergson's project today, means for example to constitute a metaphysical image of thought corresponding to the new lines, openings, traces, leaps, dynamisms, discovered by a molecular biology of the brain: new linkings and re-linkings of thought.
>
> (Deleuze, 1988: 117)

One place to look for this molecular biology of the brain is in the work of Stuart Hameroff and Roger Penrose. How to make yourself a microtubule. Biomolecular subjectivity at the quantum level. 'All becomings are already molecular'. Look out for Penrose's book *The Large, The Small, And The Human Mind* (1997). And Ilya Prigogine's *The End of Certainty* (1997). Prigogine proposes a unified formulation of quantum theory based on statistical mechanics in which the transition from potentiality to actuality is achieved by the irreversible 'holistic' *self-measuring* activity of complex dynamical systems. They measure themselves without distance from themselves. They are in absolute survey. A non-subjectivist, non-biocentric, interpretation of the so-called measurement problem that would have pleased Ruyer (who wrote about the measurement 'problem' and proposed a realist interpretation; Ruyer, 1970. Ruyer's son Bernard Ruyer has noted the connection between Raymond Ruyer and Roger Penrose's work). Primary true forms either require no collapse of the wave function (Prigogine, 1997) or they self-collapse it (Penrose, 1997). This requires a revolution in quantum theory that is occurring right now. 'We live in a privileged moment of the history of science' (Prigogine, 1997). A world reduced to neither deterministic laws nor pure chance. A world as rich in possibilities for creative development as for chaosmic implosion.

Ruyer argues that all the essential properties of the so-called 'psychological' or psychobiological domains, are already in the individualized spatio-temporal domains studied by microphysics: non-punctual localization or non-locality, and conjugated multiplicity of states, virtual presence of possible states (Ruyer, 1964: 75). According to microphysics the old opposition between matter and mind disappears.

> The fundamental paradox, which is the origin of all the others, is that a domain of primary consciousness is in 'absolute survey' – that is to say without any need of an external scanning – that it possesses a kind of *autovision without gaze*. This character has no analogy in classical physics, but it does in microphysics because the domains of consciousness come directly from microphysics, which are already in autosurvey.
>
> In order to 'speak' of primary consciousness, to evoke it, we are obliged to use expressions like a 'form perceiving itself', a 'form that sees itself without eyes'. First we transform the form into a 'visual image', primary consciousness into secondary consciousnes, then we emphasize that there is no secondary consciousness before primary conscious-ness...
>
> But it is very difficult, in spite of oneself, to not be led to think that a being that is conscious of its own form represents a more mysterious type of consciousness than a being that is conscious, through modulations of sensory information, of the form of exterior objects. It is very difficult to admit that a protoplasm, a molecular edifice, an embryo, an organic tissue or a cortex, are conscious of themselves (possess their own form) before becoming, by added modulation, conscious of the form of other beings, and without being obliged to pass by this detour.
>
> (Ruyer, 1966: 167)

Fade out.

Other than in the work of Eric Alliez there has been no discussion of Ruyer's important influence on Deleuze and Guattari. Only one other work in French engages with Ruyer's oeuvre (Chambon, 1974).

Are we ready for a non-reductionistic quantum molecular biology of the brain? Or can we be no more than apostles who draw nearer or distance themselves from the mystery of the cerebral folds. 'It is the brain that thinks and not man – the latter being only a cerebral crystallization' (Deleuze and Guattari, 1994: 210). The art of becoming like everybody else ... *becoming*

113

*everybody/everything*. An animal elegance that aesthetically combines the cosmos with its molecular components.

## Notes

1  Brian Massumi refers to Daniel Stern's work in his fine essay: 'One's sense of "aliveness" is a continuous non-conscious *self-perception (unconscious self-reflection)*. It is the perception of this self-perception, its naming and making conscious, that allows affect to be effectively analysed – as long as a vocabulary can be found for that which is imperceptible but whose escape from perception cannot but be perceived, as long as one is alive' (Massumi, 1995: 97). The opening onto the virtual.

2  In other places in *Idoru*, Gibson disconcertingly uses the term 'aggregates of subjective desire' to characterize his 'desiring machines'. A process is not an aggregate. It is an event or intensive multiplicity.

3  In fact references to Raymond Ruyer occur throughout Deleuze and Guattari's work (e.g. *Difference and Repetition, Anti-Oedipus, A Thousand Plateaus, Bergsonism*). In *Anti-Oedipus* the very distinction between micropsychic/molecular desiring machines (*where functioning and formation are still confounded* – which is the very nature of subjectivity for Ruyer; note this early version of *autopoiesis*) and the molar regimes, whether social, technical or organic, is explicitly drawn from Ruyer (Deleuze and Guattari, 1983: 283–7). Deleuze saw Ruyer as the latest of Leibniz's great disciples and felt that Ruyer's biological philosophy offered a profound analysis of the notions of the virtual and actualization. In *What Is Philosophy?* (1994) the very definition of a concept and cerebral activity are quite explicitly drawn from Ruyer's work and we are specifically referred by Deleuze and Guattari to chapters 7–11 of *Néo-finalisme* (1952) for an account of absolute overview and absolute surfaces or volumes as true beings. None of Ruyer's extensive oeuvre has been translated into English and all quotations have been translated by me.

4  Some theorists of contempory quantum brain dynamics have now accepted this 'fundamentality' (see Hameroff and Penrose, 1996). Aristotle appears to have invented the modern concept of 'matter' and the history of ideas has no single concept of matter. Paradoxically twentieth century microphysics has largely dissolved any relevance this term may have had. The elementary domains of microphysics are quantum monads. It is important to look at the neo-Platonism in Deleuze and Guattari, and its relation with Platonism. Especially the concept of 'immediate' or intuitive knowledge (cf. Alliez, 1996). Eric Alliez, a former student of Deleuze, has written the only study of Deleuze and Guattari that engages with the influence of Whitehead and Ruyer on their work (Alliez, 1993).

5  Here and elsewhere, the translation of the texts for which no published English translation exists is mine.

6  In *Chaosmosis* (1995) Guattari cites Hans Jonas on the ethical obligation we have with respect to our 'progeny'.

7  Ruyer distinguishes his theory of perception from that of Bergson. In fact he says Bergson 'is at the antipodes of the truth' (1988: n. 35). Ruyer insists that 'images' or sensations are 'in' our heads *not out there at the point* p *of emanation, even if we form a whole with the image à la Bergson*. Ruyer's approach has many similarities with contemporary developments in quantum brain dynamics. The world in its apparent 'out-thereness' is a brain achievement that involves no projection. Nor is it a re-presentation. 'Being in the World' is a brain achievement. Or perhaps the achievement of any autopoietic, self-forming, primary true form, with or without a nervous system (e.g. a subjectivity composed of quarks or galaxies).

8 Raymond Ruyer (1902–87) spent his whole teaching career at the University of Nancy. A conference was organized in his honour by the University of Nancy in 1993, the proceedings of which are available in print (Vax and Wunenberger, 1995). It contains an essay by Serge Valdinoci entitled 'Vers l'autre démarche. Ruyer, Merleau-Ponty, Deleuze.'

9 There are only two texts in English that deal with Raymond Ruyer's work (Wiklund, 1960; Tomlin, 1955). Only two short essays by Ruyer have been translated into English (Ruyer, 1980; Ruyer, 1988).

10 On the distinction between autopoiesis and deconstruction see Dupuy (1990).

# References

Alliez, Eric (1993) *La signature du monde; ou, Qu'est-ce que la philosophie de Deleuze et Guattari?* Paris: CERF.

—— (1996) *Capital Times: Tales from the Conquest of Time*, trans. Georges Van Den Abbele, foreword by Gilles Deleuze, Minneapolis: University of Minnesota Press.

Badiou, Alain (1994) 'Gilles Deleuze, *The Fold: Leibniz and the Baroque*', *Gilles Deleuze and the Theatre of Philosophy*, Constantine Boundas and Dorothy Olkowski (eds), London: Routledge, 51–69.

Casteñada, Carlos (1993) *The Art of Dreaming*, London: Aquarian.

Chambon, Roger (1974) *Le monde comme perception et réalité*, Paris: Vrin.

Deleuze, Gilles (1988) *Foucault*, trans. Sean Hand, Minneapolis: University of Minnesota Press.

—— (1989) *Cinema 2: The Time-Image*, trans. Hugh Tomlinson and Robert Galeta, Minneapolis: University of Minnesota Press.

—— (1990) *The Logic of Sense*, trans. Mark Lester with Charles Stivale, New York: Columbia University Press.

—— (1991) *Bergsonism,* trans. Hugh Tomlinson and Barbara Habberjam, New York: Zone.

—— (1993) *The Fold: Leibniz and the Baroque*, trans. Tom Conley, Minneapolis: University of Minnesota Press.

—— (1995) *Difference and Repetition*, trans. Paul Patton, New York: Columbia University Press.

Deleuze, Gilles, and Guattari, Félix (1983) *Anti-Oedipus*, trans. Robert Hurley, Mark Seem and Helen R. Lane, Minneapolis: University of Minnesota Press.

—— (1994) *What is Philosophy?* trans. Graham Burchell and Hugh Tomlinson, London: Verso.

Deleuze, Gilles, and Parnet, Claire (1987) *Dialogues*, trans. Hugh Tomlinson and Barbara Habberjam, New York: Columbia University Press.

Dupuy, Jean-Pierre (1990) 'Tangled Hierarchies: Self-reference in Philosophy, Anthropology, and Critical Theory', *Comparative Criticism* 12: 105–23.

Escher, M. C. (1988) *The World of M. C. Escher*, New York: Abradale Press, p. 175.

Foucault, Michel (1986) *The Care of the Self*, trans. Robert Hurley, New York: Pantheon.

Freud, Sigmund (1976) *The Interpretation of Dreams*, trans. and ed. J. Strachey, Harmondsworth: Penguin.

Gibson, William (1996) *Idoru*, New York: Viking.

Guattari, Félix (1979) *L'inconscient machinique. Essais de schizo-analyse*, Paris: Encres.

—— (1980) Untitled, *If You Love Me Don't Love Me: Constructions of Reality and Change in Family Therapy*, Mony Elkaim, New York: Basic, 181.

—— (1989) *Cartographies schizoanalytiques*, Paris: Galilée.

—— (1995) *Chaosmosis: An Ethico-Aesthetic Paradigm*, trans. Paul Bains and Julian Pefanis, Indianpolis/Sydney: University Indiana Press/Power Publications.

—— (2000) *The Three Ecologies*, trans. Ian Pindar and Paul Sutton, London/New Brunswick, N.J.: Athlone Press.

Hameroff, Stuart, and Penrose, Roger (1996) 'Orchestrated Reduction of Quantum Coherence in Brain Microtubules: A Model for Consciousness', *Toward a Science of Consciousness: The First Tucson Discussions and Debates*, S. Hameroff, A. Kaszniak, and A. Scott (eds), Cambridge, MA: MIT Press, 507–40.

Jonas, Hans (1994) *The Imperative of Responsibility: In Search of an Ethics for the Technological Age*, Chicago: University of Chicago Press.

Massumi, Brian (1995) 'The Autonomy of Affect', *Cultural Critique* 31: 83–109. Reprinted in *Deleuze: A Critical Reader*, Paul Patton (ed.), London: Blackwell, 1996, 317–39.

Penrose, Roger (1997) *The Large, The Small, And The Human Mind*, ed. Malcolm Longair, Cambridge/New York: Cambridge University Press.

Prigogine, Ilya (1997) *The End of Certainty: Time, Chaos and the New Laws of Nature*, New York: Freeman.

Ruyer, Raymond (1950) *La conscience et le corps*, Paris: PUF.

—— (1952) *Néo-finalisme*, Paris: PUF.

—— (1956) *La Genèse des Formes Vivantes*, Paris: Flammarion.

—— (1964) *L'animal. L'homme. La fonction symbolique*, Paris: Gallimard.

—— (1966) *Paradoxes de la conscience et limites de l'automatisme*, Paris: Albin Michel.

—— (1970) 'Le petit chat est-il mort?' *Revue Philosophique* 160: 9–33.

—— (1980) 'The Status of the Future And The Invisible World', trans. R. Scott Walker, *Diogenes* 109: 37–53.

—— (1988) 'There Is No Subconscious: Embryogenesis and Memory', trans. R. Scott Walker, *Diogenes* 142: 24–46.

Stern, Daniel (1985) *The Interpersonal World of the Infant*, New York: Basic.

Tomlin, W.F. (1955) *Living and Knowing*, London: Faber.

Valdinoci, Serge (1995) 'Vers l'autre démarche. Ruyer, Merleau-Ponty, Deleuze', in Vax and Wunenberger, *Raymond Ruyer. De la science à la théologie*, Paris: Kimé, 1995: 197–210.

Vax, Louis and Wunenberger, Jean-Jacques (eds) (1995) *Raymond Ruyer. De la science à la théologie*, Paris: Kimé.

Whitehead, A.N. (1938) *Science and The Modern World*, London: Penguin.

Wiklund, Rolf A. (1960) 'A Short Introduction to the Neo-Finalist Philosophy of Raymond Ruyer', *Philosophy and Phenomenological Research* 21: 187–98.

Wittgenstein, Ludwig (1974) *Tractatus Logico-Philosophicus*, trans. D.F. Pears and B.F. McGuinness, Atlantic Highlands, NJ: Humanities.

# 9

# THE DANCER'S BODY

*José Gil*

1 **Everyone is familiar with the general characteristics of Merce Cunningham's choreography**: its rejection of expressive conventions, the decentred stage space, the autonomy of the music and the movements, the incorporation of chance into choreographic method, etc. All of these characteristics submit to a coherent logic, which works on the principle that one can render movement in itself, without external references. The idea, for Cunningham, was to do away with mimesis in danced movements: the mimesis of 'figures', the mimesis of a stage space that reproduced outside space, and even a kind of mimesis of 'interiority', since the body was thought to be capable of translating the emotions of a subject or group.

These three aspects in turn conditioned others, such as the opening out of space. In Cunningham's words: 'The classical ballet, by maintaining the image of the Renaissance perspective in stage thought, kept a linear form of space. The modern American dance, stemming from German expressionism and the personal feelings of the various American pioneers, made space into a series of lumps, or often just static hills on the stage with actually no relation to the larger space of the stage area, but simply forms that by their connection in time made a shape. Some of the space-thought coming from German dance opened the space out, and left a momentary feeling of connection with it, but too often the space was not visible enough because the physical action was all of a lightness, like sky without earth, or heaven without hell' (Cunningham, 1992: 37).

The characteristics common to ballet and modern dance (that of Loïe Fuller, Isadora Duncan and Martha Graham) from which Cunningham is attempting to free himself, can be grouped according to three principles: a principle of expression, by which movement is supposed to express emotion; a principle of verticality, which although it may not always direct movement upward, denies the body's weight; and, a principle of organization, whereby the body of the dancer or group of dancers forms an organic whole whose movements converge towards a common goal.

These three principles are related. In *Embattled Garden*, choreographed in 1958, Martha Graham sought to have danced movements reproduce 'the interconnections of these emotions [sexuality, anguish, tension, intensity of

117

emotional experience] by delineating a relationship between the body's centre and its periphery, and between the pelvis and the rest of the torso' (Foster, 1986: 73). The organic body served to express feelings, whose quality and sublimity inflected the direction of gestures upwards, towards the pure sky. Moreover, the representation of the outer world was translated into situations and behaviours engaging bodies, often described by means of a narrative.

We know that Cunningham combats these three principles by employing two essential weapons: incorporating randomness into choreographic method, and decomposing 'organic' sequences of movement by multiplying traditional articulations.

The adoption of randomness as a choreographic method has wide-ranging effects: once it becomes open-ended, movement is no longer the product of a centralized will, that is, of a subject wishing to express personal feelings in a particular way. In fact, the very notion of a subject (or 'body-subject') tends to disappear.

The relation between music and choreography, two fields that have traditionally operated in unison, is also affected. Since chance is now what directs the changes in danced sequences, the connection to music no longer holds. No longer does music provide the 'signposts' by which dancers guide themselves through alterations in space, rhythm, or relations with the movements of other dancers. Cunningham has given chance such importance that dancers might not receive the musical score for a piece until the day of the première. The outcome is not hard to guess: music and dance become two divergent series that intersect only at certain 'structural points', and between which no relation is established. Cunningham comments that, 'It is essentially a *non-relationship*' (Cunningham, 1951a: 52). This Deleuzean term indicates to what extent Cunningham's choreography can be seen to resonate with a Deleuzean theory of series.

A third consequence of incorporating chance into dance is particularly interesting: the break it produces in the traditional frame (or code) governing corporeal possibilities, and how that opens the body out to other previously unexplored movements. This implies yet another break, this time with the traditional 'models' governing the co-ordination of movements. These models, used in ballet as well as in the school of Doris Humphrey, always presupposed an organic image of the body as a finished whole. 'That was surely one of the reasons I began to use random methods in choreography, to break the patterns of personal remembered physical co-ordinations', says Cunningham (1951a: 59).

The latter relates to another procedure Cunningham systematically employs to undo the organization of the body: by multiplying articulated movements, such that sequences are no longer co-ordinated organically, they gain a sort of autonomy stemming from the very autonomy of 'parts of the body'. It is the relation of whole-to-parts that is thereby dislocated.

Cunningham's technique gives as much freedom as possible to parts of the body, so that series of disconnected movements can take off and develop at the same time in the same body. Cunningham writes: 'This involves the problem of balance of the body, and the sustaining of one part against another part. If one uses the torso as the centre of balance and as the vertical axis at all times, then the question of balance is always related to that central part, the arms and legs balancing each another on either side and in various ways, and moving against each other. If one uses the torso as the moving force itself, allowing the spine to be the motivating force in a visual shift of balance, the problem is to sense how far the shift of balance can go in any direction, and in any time arrangement, and then move instantaneously towards any other direction and in any other time arrangements, without having to break the flow of movement by a catching of the weight, whether by an actual shift of weight, or a break in the time, or other means' (1951b: 253).

Once the centre of balance (torso or spine) has become an autonomous mobile force rather than a static vertical axis, it becomes possible to disarticulate movements from one another, since they no longer have to relate to a fixed body part, but can relate to one that is itself mobile. And since movement has been decomposed into multiplicities, a limb no longer has to align itself with only one body part and with that part in only one position to derive a sense of balance, when numerous parts are available. Any part of the body can now enter into composition with several mobile and plastic axes: movements of the arms and legs will anticipate future points of balance, while simultaneously balancing the body at 'this moment'. Call this a paradoxical or *metastable* sense of balance – as Deleuze would, after Simondon – presupposing tension and movement and especially a sort of decomposition of the whole body into its parts.

Once configurations of arms and legs on either side of the body dissolve, and movements of limbs disconnect, a mobile balance is achieved, inducing the simultaneous superposition of multiple positions in space. These movements achieve a maximum power of deformation and asymmetry through non-organic variation, as if many bodies were to coexist in a single body.

This increase in articulation allows divergent series of movement to arise at the same instant: a series of gestures disconnected from another series of gestures in the same body; the series wrought by any dancer's body in relation to another body; the music series and that of danced gestures, individually or in groups.

But, given that Cunningham has rejected all referents, meaning that he has rejected any motivation (be it emotional or representational) for movement other than movement itself, the question remains as to what triggers the series of gestures. How can movement, of itself, give rise to movement?

2 **Cunningham's greatest difficulty can be formulated as follows**: in performing a radical critique of traditional choreographic languages, and in rejecting any external referent other than movement itself, how was he able to transform what *remained* on the plane of movement after his critique, into the units of a new language?

In dance, the very notion of critique lends itself to debate. When everything takes place on the *practical* level of danced gesture, there can be no movements that signify negation (of other movements). There are no 'negative movements' – for all is affirmative and positive in the presence and fullness of danced movement. Then, what sense does it make to *refuse* or *deny* traditional choreographic languages? Even if one invents parodic or satiric movements (as is the case with many choreographers making fun of classical ballet), movement does not actively negate except when it becomes a sign, is doubled, and registers at the semiotic level. In itself, in its kinetic and muscular manifestation, movement is purely affirmative. A negative and negating movement would be one that is self-constraining.

Why would it be it necessary to negate traditional choreographic languages? Why not simply discard them? In fact, isn't this what Cunningham does?

The problem is this: if Cunningham invents a new language without referents, this can only be the outcome of the negation of referential languages, in other words of the negation of the referents of these languages. Such an operation, not restricted to the kinetic level, *would thus remain on the aesthetic plane*. While one can imagine pure movement without meaning (referent), as a kind of acrobatics or gymnastics (possessing meaning only as dictated by its aims), it is more difficult to conceive of pure movement that is also aesthetic, that is, movement unconditioned by any external elements, yet fulfilling a number of requirements – such as semantic saturation, infinitude or singularity – that make of it an object one could call 'aesthetic'.

The task, then, consisted in hooking the critique onto a sort of artistic metalanguage, to ensure the radical nature of the negation of all internal and external referents, in and by movement itself: a negation of movement by movement that would still preserve the formal aesthetic traits of negating movement.

Clearly, this 'artistic metalanguage' could be neither a true metalanguage, nor could it really be said to be artistic. Dance is not a language, first of all, the non-verbal nature of its movements rendering the idea of a *meta*-language inconceivable. Second, whatever the frame to which the movements were to remain attached while danced movements performed their necessary negations, its progressive dissolution had to achieve a sort of 'degree zero of art': the absolute prerequisite for the emergence of a virgin territory where a *new* language and a new aesthetic frame could come about. In other words, Cunningham's choreographic language springs at once from a critique of earlier languages and from virgin ground.

It is to this paradox that all of Cunningham's creative work has had to answer: how do you radically discard 'the old' without abandoning the aesthetic domain?

3 **One can also pose this question otherwise, by substituting 'linguistic unit' and 'metalinguistic unity' for 'language' and 'metalanguage'.** Though these expressions are as 'theoretical' as the ones they are replacing, they have the advantage of more adequately designating the reality:

the unit would simply be a minimum series of movements out of which the unity of a danced language would take shape.

The question then becomes: what metalinguistic unity does Cunningham create that is capable of transforming itself into (or acting as) the unit of a new language with no referent other than itself?

Remember that critical decomposition and construction are being undertaken in the name of a new unit(y) of movement which, in a sense, does not exist yet, for it is *also* the result of the destruction of the earlier languages.

Cunningham goes about it by making an empty space outside and inside.

Outside: He empties stage space (which is also the space of bodies, beyond the personal body that filled it in work such as Martha Graham's). This involves opening out the stage space so that all kinds of events can take place; 'A prevalent feeling among many painters that lets them make a space in which anything can happen is a feeling dancers can have too. Imitating the way nature makes a space, and puts lots of things in it, heavy and light, little and big, all unrelated, yet each affecting all the others', writes Cunningham (1992: 38).

Inside: He strips the dancer's experience of all representative and emotional elements that might drive movement (as in ballet or modern dance). He goes about this by forcing the dancer's attention to focus on pure movement, i.e. on 'the grammar'. *Awareness of the body* is focused on the energy, articulations, movements, and not at all on emotions or images constructing a narrative, in which case consciousness commands body awareness. Cunningham turns this around to make body awareness command consciousness.

In stripping away emotions and representations that might otherwise trigger movement, it is clear that Cunningham simultaneously empties the stage and the space of the body, which had always been an emotional space. In stripping away images and affect from corporeal experience and in emptying out space, grammar emerges, but what used to motivate or trigger movement has disappeared. For grammar to 'become meaning' as Cunningham loves to say ('the grammar is the meaning'), that is, for grammar to be able to become a constitutive element of movement, 'danced grammar' has to 'fill itself' with meaning; that is, this movement has to be *danced*, and has to invent its own logic, its own triggering elements, and its own orientation.

What then, one may ask, will replace the discarded elements? And, what will play the roles once assigned to the imagination, emotion and the space of the body? As discussed earlier, it appears that the roles will be taken up by the new unit (or unity) of movement itself, from which other new language combinations will emerge.

4 **What does it mean to 'empty out movement'?** The process entails creating vacuoles of time inside of movement, by means of techniques much like those used in yoga or Zen meditation. (The importance of both of these practices for Cunningham is well known.) This involves liberating the rhythms of thought from the movements of the body, especially from those of breathing.

Since thinking is no longer bound to the rhythms of the body, its base speed can slow down between one point and another, because space expands, whereas its surface speed may accelerate indefinitely. And since thinking is no longer swept along by breathing (since breathing is under control and independent of cardiac and other rhythms), it does not have to run, having nothing to follow but its own movements. Breathing, in turn, detached from thought, no longer speeds up with fear nor relaxes with feelings of serenity.

Isn't this what Cunningham does? He decomposes 'organic' gestures of the body through movement. He disconnects movements from one another, as if each movement belonged to a different body. Moreover, he assigns arbitrary periods of time to be 'filled up' with choreography. Finally, Cunningham makes thought espouse movement and movement only, and he does so in two ways: both in creating vacuoles of time between movements of the body, and in preparing for the construction of a plane of immanence where the actions of the body can no longer be distinguished from the movements of thought.

We can now understand what is involved in 'emptying out' or excluding emotions and images from the sphere of movements: by concentrating solely on movements, these two series can be freed from that of gestures. For their part, the void or vacuoles allow articulations to proliferate so that movements are no longer linked together on the surface, but are joined by means of a profound continuity. As has sometimes been said of Cunningham's style: his movements 'float'.

The question remains as to what makes these floating movements come together again on the surface to form danced sequences.

5  **Several pending problems have yet to be addressed:** (a) As we have seen, the emptying out and filling up of movements involved in the destruction and construction of a new language in turn imply the formation of a plane of immanence. For, in disconnecting movements from each other and in disconnecting these from thought, we are preparing a new osmosis whereby thought and the body become one, and whereby a new fluidity, a new kind of movement, may circulate on this plane of immanence that is dance.

This new osmosis comes about through *body consciousness*: having made itself a *body of thought*, consciousness orders and directs from within danced movement. What I mean is this: body consciousness implies a field of consciousness simultaneously constituted as a point of consciousness, which then becomes separate. The field of consciousness allows itself to be permeated by the body and thereby acquires two properties:

- it gains the plasticity, continuity, consistency, and pervasiveness of the self-awareness proper to the body;
- as it spreads throughout the body, it transforms into a map of the body; a whole cartography of the body and its movements is drawn.

The point-of-consciousness gains the power to influence the movements of the body by following this map.

(b) We seem to have located the unit of movement that maintains movement in the aesthetic sphere, even as it transforms and annuls itself in the process of negating earlier choreographic languages. It is a unity composed of *virtual movement*. It is an empty unit of (actual) movement.

The unity belongs to a virtual body whose composition takes place while the composing movements are themselves in decomposition. The multiplication of articulations and gestures (which will give birth to divergent series of movement) enable the construction of a body whose virtuality ensures the *profound continuity* of the movements that make up the dance.

Let us be more precise about the concept of a virtual body. As we have seen thus far, Cunningham decomposes gestures in the balancing act of the body-in-movement, so that the nexus of positions of bodily parts is no longer that of an organic body. One could even say that to each of the simultaneously held positions made up of heterogeneous gestures there corresponds a different body. (Organic, yes, but out of the multiplicity of organic virtual bodies that constitute one same body there emerges an impossible body, a sort of monstrous body: this is the virtual body.) This body prolongs gesture into virtuality, since what follows from gesture can no longer be perceived by and in an empirical, actual body.

It follows that there is no single body, like the 'proper body' of phenomenology, but rather multiple bodies. The body of the dancer, Cunningham's body, but in fact the body of all dancers, is composed of a multiplicity of virtual bodies.

The unit of virtual movement (or the virtual unity of movement) creates a space where 'everything fits', a space of coexistence and of consistency of heterogeneous series. It ensures several functions: as a non-actual movement stemming from the emptying out of movement, it guarantees that movement can 'reflect' back on itself, since every empirical movement is now doubled by a virtual entity to which it is linked. This means that there is a doubling of movement whereby it is now both virtual and actual; it can therefore 'double back on itself' from the virtual point of view. 'To double back on itself' can mean 'to negate itself' as well as 'to refer back to itself'. The virtual point of view becomes the source for a new type of actual movement and a new choreographic language.

The act of discarding certain classical movements can now be seen as equalling their negation, since the actual movements replacing the earlier ones have been achieved through the emptying out/exclusion of the earlier units, which is to say an emptying out/exclusion *for* the virtual-in-formation. The outcome is a unit(y) of virtual movement that makes the *transformation* (of the movements of classical languages) from actual to virtual take on a value of negation (the monstrous body as the negation of the organic body).

That is how the virtual unity of movement founds the complex 'metalinguistic' operations needed to posit a kind of non-verbal negation, and how it maintains movement, across its decomposition-negation, at the aesthetic level of dance.

6 **I would like to conclude by saying a few words about the plane of immanence of dance,** a notion I had surreptitiously introduced without justifying it. But first, I would like to summarize a few of our research results:

(a) The virtual ('meta-infralinguistic') unity of movement is what persists as 'pure movement' once one has discarded all of the emotional, representational and expressive motivations of the body;

(b) This enables the construction of a virtual plane of movement where all of the movements of bodies, objects, music, colour acquire a consistency, that is, a logic or a nexus;

(c) It also enables the re-organization of movements of the body without recourse to external elements, since the actual movements of the body of the dancer obtain their impetus from the virtual plane and from the tensions produced there.

The virtual plane of movement is the plane of immanence. Its tension or intensity $= 0$, but on it are engendered the strongest intensities. On it, thought and body dissolve into one another ('thought' and 'the body' as empirical facts); it is the plane of heterogenesis of danced movement. To paraphrase Deleuze, one could describe the characteristic immanence of this movement as follows: *what moves as a body returns as the movement of thought*. As Cunningham says: 'It is that blatant exhibition of this energy, i.e. of energy geared to an intensity high enough to melt steel in some dancers, that gives the great excitement. This isn't feeling about something, this is the whipping of the mind and body into an action that is so intense, that for the brief moment involved, the body and mind are one' (Cunningham, 1997: 98). In other words, intensities are circulating on the body-without-organs.

But, where is this plane of immanence located, and by what traits is it characterized? It is the virtual, invisible plane that founds the perception of a continuum of movements during a performance. In a fairly old text, Susanne Langer describes at length the perception of danced movement: 'The dance is an appearance, if you like, an apparition. It springs from what the dancers do, yet it is something else. In watching a dance, you do not see what is physically before you – people running around or twisting their bodies; what you see is a display of interacting forces, by which the dance seems to be lifted, driven, drawn, closed or attenuated, whether it be solo or choric, whirling like the end of a dervish dance, or slow, centred, and single in its motion. One human body may put the whole play of mysterious powers before you. But these powers, these forces that seem to operate in the dance, are not the physical forces of the dancer's muscles, which actually cause the movements taking place. The forces we seem to perceive most directly and convincingly are created for our perception: and they exist only for it. … Anything that exists only for perception, and plays no ordinary, passive part in nature as common objects do, is a virtual entity. It is not unreal; where it confronts you, you really perceive it, you don't dream or imagine that you do' (Langer, 1951: 341–42).

For Susanne Langer this plane of virtual forces is a 'dynamic image'. For us, it is clearly the plane of immanence.

Her very penetrating description shows to what extent dance is not, as per the old cliché, an art of the ephemeral. On the contrary, this virtual plane which we 'perceive' (with our eyes, but also with our whole bodies which tend to repeat the perceived movements) ensures the continuity of gestures and movements. Never has the spectator of a danced performance felt anxious about the disappearance of images in time. And it is not psychological memory which retains the passing moments, but rather the present gesture, which is incorporated into a more profound, virtual continuity.

It is the plane of immanence that lays out the profound continuity, as well as the consistency of all movements taking place in choreographic space. What we 'see' beyond and by virtue of the visible is not ephemeral as are the sequences of movements or the gesture-signs of the dancer. The plane of immanence is always there, and dance unfolds on its permanent surface, independently of its gestures and yet existing only by means of these gestures. The plane of immanence enables the coexistence of all of these movements though it never moves, and is also never still; empty, autonomous, enveloping signs and bodies, thought and movement, of dancers as well as of spectators, it is the ground zero of movement, never static, and consisting of a certain emptiness that constitutes its very texture.

To dance is to create immanence through movement: this is why there is no meaning outside of the plane nor outside of the actions of the dancer. Questions like, 'how do you achieve this kind of choreography?', 'how do you translate this kind of choreographic idea into danced movement?' or, 'how do you express that kind of feeling through movement?' deserve only one answer. As Cunningham would say: 'How do you do it? By doing it'. Because only danced gesture yields meaning: emotion is born of movement and not the reverse.

Cunningham wills immanence: for him, meaning does not transcend movement and life. The meaning of movement is the very movement of meaning. This is why, as he affirms, 'movement is, in itself, expressive'. Or, again: 'If the dancer … *dances*, everything is there. The meaning is there, if that's what you want. When I dance, it means: this is what I am doing' (Cunningham, 1997: 86).

7 **We now have a good idea why Cunningham, unlike Malevitch and Kandinsky,** never feels anxious about the absolute negation of danced movement (i.e. the 'death of dance'). There are two essential reasons for this: first, because there are no abstract movements and, second, because there is no

'degree zero of movement', *the annulment of actual movement coinciding with virtual movement*.

There are no abstract movements because the 'emptying out' of movements makes them most real and *concrete*, the most unburdened of possible emotional and imaginative charges. In their utmost concreteness, as they circulate on the plane of immanence, they carry in themselves all of the meaning, emotions, and images that movements, by virtue of their intensities, are capable of arousing: for it is precisely movements of meaning and emotion that pure movement deploys on the plane of immanence.

If there is no 'degree zero of movement', it is because the virtual unity of movement, as a residue of the operation of 'emptying out', coincides with a *remainder* which, in the danced movement of the production of signs, never fails to escape semiotization.

It helps to consider that, both in the case of representation and of danced signs, the body represents the world, and in so doing, represents itself. If it expresses emotions, it also expresses itself. The body plays the body, in playing the world. Because there is an imbrication or overlap between the played representation and the referent, dance always preserves a non-representational element that escapes the production of signs.

This *remainder* marks the inherence of gesture to its corporeal context: here, the sign and the sign's agent of contextualization are one (the body) or, rather, they are imbricated.

This explains why the emptying out of the body's gestures can never attain a 'degree zero of movement', or a 'degree zero of gestures'. If the body can negate the world and the representation of itself without self-destructing, it is because something of it escapes its self-representation. Something that resists, prior to representation. In taking a bow, a body is representing a body taking a bow, but the representing body never fully coincides with the represented body it is 'figuring'.

Something holds back, remaining outside the actualized image of the body: something that is not only of the order of actual movements, but also of the order of virtual movements; something that is neither represented nor representable, belonging to the blind zone of their imbrication.

What holds back is also what triggers the expressive or mimetic image. It is the body virtual.

The virtual unity draws upon this remainder of non-representable movement that is always there. It is what guarantees the 'reflection' of the body, or rather the 'meta-infralinguistic' operation of the body that preserves 'pure' movement while meaningful and expressive movements are being emptied.

This leads one to suppose that the imbrication of sign and context, body and consciousness, prepare the construction of a plane of immanence or consistency of movements. It is by virtue of the inherence of the agent of construction (movement) in the materiality of the plane (movement) that dance, more so than any other art, makes itself a plane of immanence directly, in the very act of dancing. To dance is to flow in immanence.

Translated by Karen Ocaña

## References

Cunningham, Merce (1951a) 'Choreography and the Dance', in Sorrell, *The Dance Has Many Faces*, New York: World Publishing.

—— (1951b) 'The Function of a Technique for Dance', in Sorrell, *The Dance Has Many Faces*, New York: World Publishing.

—— (1992) 'Space, Time and Dance', in Kostelanetz and Anderson, *Merce Cunningham: Dancing in Space and Time*, Pennington, NJ: A Capella Books.

—— (1997) 'The Impermanent Art', in Vaughn, *Merce Cunningham: Fifty Years*, New York: Aperture.

Foster, Susan (1986) *Bodies and Subjects in Contemporary American Dance*, Berkeley: University of California Press.

Kostelanetz, Richard and Anderson, Jack (eds) (1992) *Merce Cunningham: Dancing in Space and Time*, Pennington, NJ: A Capella Books.

Langer, Suzanne (1951) 'The Dynamic Image: Some Philosophical Reflections on Dance', in Sorrell *The Dance Has Many Faces*, New York: World Publishing.

Sorell, Walter (ed.). (1951) *The Dance Has Many Faces*, New York: World Publishing.

Vaughn, David (ed.) (1997) *Merce Cunningham: Fifty Years*, New York: Aperture.

# Part 3

# FORCES OF EXPRESSION

*... everything which provokes confusion*
*without destroying the strength of an emergent thought...*

# 10

# NEO-ARCHAISM

## Mani Haghighi

In September of 1998, a decade after the publication of Salman Rushdie's *Satanic Verses*, the Iranian President Mohammad Khatami announced that, as far as his government was concerned, the 'Rushdie Affair' was over. Even though the President did not have the power actually to revoke Ayatollah Khomeini's 1989 *fatwa* against Rushdie, he nevertheless declared that his government was no longer willing to support or promote the Ayatollah's edict. This development was of little practical consequence: so-called 'rogue Muslim elements', acting individually and in opposition to Khatami's government, still seemed determined to assassinate Rushdie and enjoyed the enthusiastic support of several senior members of the clergy in Iran. Furthermore, by the time Khatami made his announcement, the 'Rushdie Affair' had unwound itself to such a lugubrious torpor that it had virtually disappeared, without being actually resolved. As a result, commentators generally tended to forget that during the previous decade it had become increasingly senseless to demand a revocation of the *fatwa*. Every such demand, whether through an appeal to religious precedence or to international law, had proved futile in that time. Negotiations had been particularly difficult to sustain because the *fatwa* as well as the collective subject of its enunciation had proved to be operating within a self-contained and self-justifying discursive regime, one which tended to transform its postulates with a fluidity and a velocity that disoriented Rushdie's allies at every turn. The unlearned lesson of the Rushdie Affair, then, was that the formalization of a new strategy for undoing such a quandary must, above all, question the political assumptions that were at work in Rushdie's support and effectuate a radical break from the funereal humanism that animated those assumptions.

## The performative misrecognition

Khomeini's *fatwa* was by no means the originary moment of the Rushdie Affair. The *Satanic Verses*, which had been published in England in September 1988, had already been banned in India in October, burnt in Bolton in December, and again in Bradford in January. By the time Khomeini had decided to make his

contribution to the crisis on Valentine's Day 1989, at least six people had died
during riots against the book in Islamabad and Kashmir.

Khomeini's intervention redefined the protest against Rushdie by changing
its stakes: the task was no longer to ban the *Satanic Verses* in order to limit or
reverse the damage it had caused, but rather to obliterate its author in an effort
to fulfil a religious duty. The gesture displaced the performative function of
the protest away from the dialogical sphere of retribution and counter-attack
to the irreversible trajectory of sin. An essentially secular semiotic, governed by
the laws of exchange, was, in other words, suddenly deterritorialized by an
exorbitant line of divine annihilation: from the moment of its utterance, the
*fatwa* was treated as an irreversible and eternal judgement. This irreversibility
meant that no line of force issuing from outside the folds of the *fatwa* could
match its deadly force. Rushdie's death became a priceless commodity:
nothing in this world could match its worth. Thus, subverting the dialogical
structure of exchange, the *fatwa* became a gift of death, or a theft of life. The
notorious promises of a golden key to paradise, as well as the cash reward
which was subsequently offered to Rushdie's potential killer, were entirely
accidental and disposable attributes of this transcendental gift.

Sadly, all the reactions against the *fatwa* seemed to misrecognize this shift in
the performative dimension. An enormous transformation in a regime of
signification was reduced, in the liberal imagination, to an act of theological
machismo. This fatal oversight meant that the condemnations directed against
Khomeini's sentence were, in effect, orbiting an epistemological vacuum.
Rather than a new development, the *fatwa* was regarded by Rushdie and his
supporters as an intense and singular instance of all the violence and protests
that had preceded it.

It would be a further mistake to view this misrecognition as the symptom of
a particularly violent collision of two opposing and self-same cultural entities
named East and West, since the ethical commitments and rhetorical tactics
employed by Middle Eastern intellectuals in their denunciations of the *fatwa*
were consistently identical to those of their Western counterparts. The formula
they used is familiar by now: after an appeal to the universality of human rights
and an imperative to the freedom of speech, the *fatwa* was denounced as the
archaic pronouncement of a fossilized mind, and a demand for its immediate
revocation was coupled with an imaginary identification with Rushdie.
Rushdie's supporters, in other words, continued to address the *fatwa* as if it was
still operating within a sharply delimited and stratified field of expression: they
took the hostile otherness of 'fundamentalism' as a sign of its full determination.

## Spiral and speed

Prior to Khomeini's intervention, the protests against the *Satanic Verses* had
unfolded in a familiar field of signification. The organizers of the Bradford
bookburning, for example, had insisted that their protests were entirely legal

expressions of dissent, and had appealed to the British law against blasphemy, as outlined in the Public Order Act of 1986, to justify their efforts to ban the book (Bedford, 1993: 153). The fact that Christianity was the only religion protected by the Act had begun to shift the focus of the protests away from the question of blasphemy as such, and towards the question of the judicial prejudice against British Muslims.

Thus, in spite of appearances, the Bradford bookburnings can be regarded, in a specific sense, as attempts to invoke and reinterpret the notions of law and democracy. They were an attempt to ensure the right of expression of a *people*, that is, of a collective assemblage *as such*, rather than that of a person whose individual right of expression, under the liberal rubric, was to be safeguarded collectively. The concept of 'rights' as the supreme signifier of enlightenment was invoked not only by Rushdie's supporters, but also, in a new configuration, by those who were calling for the suppression of his book before the promulgation of the *fatwa*. While the former insisted on Rushdie's individual right to free speech, the latter were demanding that the explicitly legislated right to be protected from blasphemy be extended to Muslim citizens as a *people*. In spite of their obvious differences, what linked the strategies of these two groups was their willingness to inscribe their demands within the folds of a secular, and therefore historical and negotiable, code of law. Both groups, in other words, sought to infuse their demands with an authority whose source was external to the demands themselves.

Call this a spiralling semiotic regime.[1] The circulation of signs in this regime is dictated by two gravitational poles: the inner pole of the spiral is a relatively stable locus – usually empty – around which the drama of signification unspools. In a liberal democracy, this centre is actualized by the empty throne of power, occupied in brief intervals by the elected representative of the people. The other pole of the regime is defined by its outermost spiral, the most distant line beyond which the regime will mutate into something entirely different. Passing beyond this line amounts to a banishment or an exile – Deleuze and Guattari call it the 'scapegoat function' – and a massive legal bureaucracy monitors its proper functioning. But between these two poles, all manners of slippage and speeding is tolerated. Thus, bookburning as a rhetorical gesture aimed at revising the law is condemned but tolerated, while bombing bookstores results in immediate deportation; a group of demonstrators calling for Rushdie's death provoke moral outrage in the media, but actually going after him with a shotgun will land you in the goat's anus: 'Anything that exceeds the excess of the signifier or passes beneath it will be marked with a negative value. Your only choice will be between a goat's ass and the face of a god' (Deleuze and Guattari, 1987: 116).

The campaign to support Rushdie presupposed the spiralling semiotic all along and continued to function according to its rules, investing its signifiers with a negotiable meaning. Its principle themes had to do with apologies, amendments and retractions. For example, Rushdie, who had rejected the charge of apostasy by pointing out that he had never actually believed in the tenets of Islam, decided to 'embrace Islam' (Rushdie, 1991). But when the gesture proved futile in saving his life, he renounced the faith, causing the charge of apostasy to stick more firmly the second time. In similar fashion, he understandably interpreted and reinterpreted his novel in diametrically opposed ways, oscillating between reading it as a parody of the diasporic plight and an anti-clerical, political allegory. First, in a letter to Rajiv Ghandi, whose government had banned the *Satanic Verses*, he claimed that the book, as a fictional weave of schizophrenic fantasies and dreams, could not possibly have anything to do with Islam (Rushdie, 1988: A27). Six months later, once the *fatwa* had been issued and his apology rejected, he pleaded for the right to criticize Islam, arguing that the religion had been taken over by 'a powerful tribe of clerics' (Rushdie, 1989: 26).

These various prospective and retrospective movements, jumpings back and forth between several spirals of meaning, were coupled at every turn with a call for the retraction of the *fatwa*. A pure, authoritarian order-word, the *fatwa* seemed to hover about in the speeding semiotic, incapable of finding its rightful place of rest. An obscene phantom, a perfect example of an *objet petit a*, it refused to be framed and delineated in reference to other signs in the system: it announced a perfectly alien invasion, replacing the relatively foreign bookburners of Bradford who were being urged, ever so politely, by the British Home Office to calm down. The campaign to support Rushdie, therefore, amounted to a massive attempt to find a proper place for the *fatwa*, somewhere for it to be lodged and tamed, so that it could be discarded. But the *fatwa* presented itself as an impossibly elusive *neo-archaism*: an incomprehensible, ancient thing, fulfilling a shockingly novel function.

The pronouncement of the *fatwa* marked a shift of focus in the Rushdie Affair toward a speeding, linear semiotic. Here, '*a sign or a pocket of signs detaches from the irradiating circular network* and sets to work on its own account' (Deleuze and Guattari, 1987: 121). This gesture of detachment is already at work in the spiralling regime, but in a relatively compromised and delimited way. In Rushdie's case, for example, all the various riots, bookburnings and bombings are instances of such secession. But these are ultimately accorded a negative value under the spiralling semiotic, and their more violent perpetrators are marginalized and banished, sent down the line of flight as scapegoats. On the other hand, in the speeding semiotic, which emphasizes the more pronounced features of what Deleuze and Guattari have called the postsignifying regime, the situation is different: here the line of flight 'receives a positive sign, as though it were effectively occupied and followed by a people who find in it their reason for being or destiny' (1987: 121).

The difference in the value accorded to the line of flight is one of the important variables that distinguish the circular and dialogical character of the spiralling semiotic from the linear and irreversible arrangement of the speeding regime. While the former effectuates a ceaseless but more or less limited negotiation of signs in a bi-polar system between a centralized power and a banished scapegoat, the latter proscribes all such negotiation and redirects the movement of its signs toward a gravitational field outside the limits of the territory. In spite of its exorbitant nature, this line does seek its own regathering and reintegration into another spiral, with its own centre and its own bureaucracy – the positivity of the line's value depends on this desire for destination. But the delimitation desired by the line, the fulfilment of its desire for a territorialized circulation, is indefinitely postponed.

In this regime, what Kierkegaard has called the 'Apostle' replaces the central despotic bureaucracy: the codes of the spiralling regime – the constitution, for example, as well as various codes of judicial precedence – give way to a more mystical, and therefore a more explicitly authoritarian, vision. The apostle does not *interpret* God's message (the way a civil servant interprets the constitution, for example); instead, overwhelmed by the message, he merely *authorizes* it. He is not a hermeneutician, but a seer, smitten by a vision which 'no longer needs to be justified, for better or worse' (Deleuze, 1989: 20).[2]

For Kierkegaard, the authority of the apostle's statement resides in nothing other than the subject who utters the statement. The statement of the apostle, in other words, does not refer to an available system of verification beyond it in order to justify its content: the very fact that the statement has been uttered by the apostle is to be taken as the verification of its truth:

> It is not by evaluating the content of the doctrine aesthetically or intellectually that I should or could reach the result: *ergo*, the man who proclaimed the doctrine was called by a revelation; *ergo* he is an apostle. The very reverse is the case: the man who is called by a revelation and to whom a doctrine is entrusted, argues from the fact that it is revelation, from his authority.
>
> (Kierkegaard, 1962: 93)

The political consequences of Kierkegaard's argument are clear: He calls for an absolute and infallible faith in the imperatives of an authoritarian figure, and denies us every possible route for negotiating, let alone rejecting, these imperatives. Any attempt, on our part, to verify the truth or authority of these imperatives immediately betrays our aesthetic and intellectual predispositions and bars us from understanding the meaning of the imperative.

This formulation clarifies some of the peculiarities surrounding the Rushdie Affair. For one, it makes sense of the strange grammatical register of the *fatwa*, which presents itself not as a direct order, but as a transmission of information: 'I inform the proud Muslim people of the world that the author of the *Satanic Verses* which is against Islam, the prophet and the Koran, and all involved in its publication who were aware of its content, are sentenced to death' (Bedford, 1993: 130). Khomeini does not announce the *fatwa* in his capacity as a statesman; rather, he is a messenger or medium, an authority in matters divine, and nothing, according to Kierkegaard, can compromise this authority and this position.

The usual reductive interpretations of the *fatwa* ignore the manner in which it beckons one fuzzy set to transform another fuzzy set: 'the proud Muslim people of the world' are to kill 'all involved' in the publication of the book. The *fatwa*, literally *invents* these two sets: it extracts from the 'Muslim world' a 'proud' subset, and pits it against another set whose boundaries are just as vague. You are not a proud Muslim unless you set yourself against the Apostatic Rushdie Machine.[3] This, as will become clear, already precludes any straightforward interpretation of the *fatwa* in terms of a prefabricated topological category, such as a Nation, a Culture, or a Religion, since the delimitations of the topos in question are impossibly vague. The political character of the *fatwa* does not limit its productive operations to the stratified territory of the State, which is why governments are as helpless as individual subjects in pinpointing and undoing its fuzzy force.

The logic of the speeding semiotic aggravates this fuzziness: it makes the *fatwa*'s subject of enunciation (Khomeini) fade into the subject of its statement ('the proud Muslim people of the world') through a passional transubstantiation. In this regime, '*the subject of enunciation recoils into the subject of the statement, to the point that the subject of the statement resupplies subject of enunciation for another proceeding*' (Deleuze and Guattari, 1987: 129; emphasis in the original). The 'I' who issues the death sentence is already none other than the collective 'I' who is obliged to carry it out. The prophet or apostle who enunciates the sentence is a symptom of his people: his power to issue the sentence is guaranteed by their multiplicity. 'The subject of the statement has become the "respondent" or guarantor of the subject of enunciation, through a kind of reductive echolalia, in a biunivocal relation' (1987: 129).

Correspondingly, through his passional enfolding of an outside divinity, and by virtue of his people's performative affirmation of this link, the apostle marks the convergence of two different bodies. His earthly body, which perishes and passes away, is regarded as a vessel for actualizing a virtual and atemporal body: a divine or sublime body that, after the apostle's death, is to be reactualized by the body of his successor.[4]

The apostle's enunciations are therefore issued from a site woven out of a difference between two differences: the difference between his two bodies, and the difference between his double locutionary subjectivities. The Iranian revolutionaries' famous chant, 'You are my spirit Khomeini; you are the iconoclast, Khomeini', was the ideological proclamation of this double difference. It is no longer possible to distinguish the divine from the prophetic and the plebeian: 'there is no subject, only collective assemblages of enunciation' (Deleuze and Guattari, 1987: 130).

There is a significant contrast between the locus of locution in the speeding semiotic and the empty place from which democratic power issues its decrees. The place of power in the democratic order is always empty. Every quasi-occupant of this always-empty place is therefore a body in transit, a surrogate sovereign. The empty place is marked by pure negation, since the primary task of democracy is to prevent the absolute actualization of the sovereign. In the speeding semiotic, on the other hand, the negating emptiness of the demo-cratic structure is replaced with a differentiating void. Here, the passional God is an alien force that folds into the apostle's body, while the apostle's enuncia-tion recoils into the subjects of his statement. The apostle is regarded as the emissary of divine rays which give the people's line of flight its positive value. Unlike the despotic hermeneut, whose interpretations appeal to a transcen-dental system of verification, the imperatives of the passional seer are always the effects of a folding-in of the outside. The dogmatism of the apostle is indistinguishable from the force of his illuminations.

The vagueness of the void that transmits the apostle's expression is coupled with the suppleness of the line that weaves the divine ray into his body and folds him into the body of his people. This supple line incessantly forks out in two directions. On one side, it mutates into a rigid state-line, congeals the misty boundaries separating the apostle from his God and his people into a single authoritarian body-politic and reterritorializes the perpetual reprieve under which the people exist. On the other side, it follows its miraculous becomings further and takes new flights into the outside, *without a chance for retraction or return* (cf. Deleuze and Guattari, 1987: 203). This bifurcation explains why 'the people' constantly persist throughout 'the nation' as a vague subset, with individuals constantly shifting from one register to the other, incapable of coming to rest. This is not the case of a minoritarian or diasporic people resisting, or succumbing to, the authority of the Nation-State. Rather, it is a matter of the same body of people weaving a diasporic space *within* its own sedentary structure: a people permeating the body of an authoritarian Nation-State insisting on its incessant becoming-minor, speaking for itself out of its fuzzy site.

## The incorporeal transformation

The fuzziness of this void of illocution is what has lent the *fatwa* its strategic efficacy in the field of international politics. Issuing from a weave of differ-ences, the *fatwa* cannot be addressed in a zone of inter-subjective communication among individuated subjects or subject-nations. The source of its illocution is both *trans*-subjective and *sub*-subjective, and the effects, or the events, it produces are as vague and elusive as the place of its emission.

Khomeini's decree effectuated an extensive mobilization of bodies all around the world. Bodies took to the streets, protesting. Armed bodies surrounded Rushdie and his associates, guarding. Other armed bodies trained to kill. Bookstores were firebombed and books were torched. Rushdie's Italian translator was assaulted, his Japanese translator was stabbed to death, and Rushdie himself was reduced to the status of a hyper-proliferating image: an image without a body. The movements of these bodies drew out new spaces of interaction: exiled from his house, Rushdie was banished to a diffuse dwelling. Moving in and out of police cars, he was rushed to anonymous rooms in remote hotels around the world. Western diplomats were recalled from Iran and Iranian representatives were sent home. Deleuze and Guattari call the abstract machine behind the sum total of these intermingling bodies a 'machinic assemblage' (1987: 88).

The machinic assemblage constantly cuts in and out of another machine with an entirely different function: the 'collective assemblage of enunciation', whose task is the production of statements (Deleuze and Guattari, 1987: 88). The *fatwa* itself was a statement, a meaningful semantic structure, and like all statements it was above all an imperative, an order-word: 'I inform the proud Muslim people of the world'. But information had very little to do with it. The informational content of the *fatwa* merely refers to the divine line that connects the seer's vision to his God, but its performative function is necessarily commandmental: it is uttered in order to be obeyed. 'Language is made not to be believed but to be obeyed, and to compel obedience' (1987: 76). To give an order is not to inform someone about a command, but to effectuate an act. The *fatwa* transmitted a command – a divine sting – whose primary purpose was to be passed on and circulated.[5] Thus, Iranian revolutionary guards issued statements of devotion to Khomeini while Western politicians demanded its revocation in furious epistles. An enormous number of letters of support were sent to Rushdie, and an even greater number of essays diagnosed his predicament. Rushdie himself issued statements of apology, and later, retractions of those apologies. The validity of the *fatwa* as a theological imperative was both questioned and affirmed, depending on the political allegiances of the speaker. Each statement precipitated still others.

For Deleuze and Guattari, the machinic assemblage of bodies and the collective assemblage of enunciations are entirely independent of each other. This independence, however, does not amount to a lack of relation between them, or an impossibility of the intervention of one into the other. On the contrary, statements are constantly cutting across bodies, modifying and rearranging them, and bodies always interfere with statements, slowing down or speeding up their production. Every account or retelling of a state of things is already a modification of that state, since the relation between statements and bodies is distributive, rather than representational. 'A criminal action may be deterritorializing in relation to the existing regime of signs ... but the sign that expresses the act of condemnation may in turn be deterritorializing in relation to all actions and reactions' (1987: 87).

The intervention of each of these two assemblages into the other produces something absolutely new which falls outside the limits of both assemblages: this is what Deleuze and Guattari have called the 'event': an 'incorporeal transformation'. Unlike the bodies which move about in calculable times and measurable spaces, incorporeal transformations occur instantaneously, in thought: they spread out the filmy surface that simultaneously brings together and sets apart bodies and statements: 'they are the expressed of statements but are *attributed* to bodies' (1987: 86). This is precisely how the declaration of the *fatwa* was concurrent with the affective transformation of a vast number of places and people. With the transmission of Khomeini's brief statement, Rushdie suddenly became a fugitive, a martyr and a convict, all at once. Bookstores turned into health hazards. Iranian tourists mutated into potential hijackers. And the *fatwa* itself, which was issued as a death sentence, transformed into the international symbol of the violation of free speech.

But the enunciation of the *fatwa* was not merely 'concurrent' with the effectuation of these incorporeal transformations in a straightforward sense. By adopting a purely performative function,[6] Khomeini's decree managed to move in two opposing temporal directions: its structure was that of the 'future-past'. Unlike a *directive* ('kill him!'), which on the face of it anticipates a state of things, or an *assertive* ('he's dead!'), which presupposes that state, the *fatwa* was a *declarative* illocution ('he is sentenced to death!'): it effectuated a state of things by describing that state as already effectuated: 'He is sentenced to death', or in other words, 'he will have been dead'. A declarative statement folds a prospective command into the retrospective structure of an assertion.

The authority of an order-word such as this is not, on the face of it, a matter of course. It must be recognized. Declaratives, in other words, must pass through a process of selection before they can be articulated as transformative expressions. As Kierkegaard puts it, it remains the apostle's responsi- bility to produce the impression of authority, whether anybody bows before his authority or not (Kierkegaard 1962: 93–4). But the final recognition of this impression is neither the function of a particular individual or institution, nor of the totality of all individuals and institutions as a whole, but rather of the collective assemblages of enunciation in their vaguest sense. The judge who transforms the prisoner into a criminal, the priest who turns the fiancée into a wife, the hijacker who declares the passengers to be hostages, are all disposable and transient variables whose function is to actualize the expressive murmur of their respective assemblages. They occupy a paradoxical place as corporeal *semblances* of the abstract assemblage. The authority of their statements is not ultimately traceable to a set of transcendental institutions that corroborate their enunciations. Rather, the material content of the institutions (the bureaucrats, the hijackers) as well as the forms of their contents (courtroom-space, airplane-space) weave themselves into their expressions with the thread of these declarative illocutions. The order-word is, in the final analysis, a redundant statement: 'You will have been dead because I say so!'

This means that order-words are not context-sensitive in the analytic sense. The context that verifies their authority – and allows a declarative to be 'successful' – is not the corporeal and institutional assemblage that emits them, but rather the abstract assemblages of which those institutions are an expression. These assemblages are internal to language itself. 'Every particular slogan',

*A Thousand Plateaus* quotes Lenin, 'must be deduced from the totality of the specific features of a definite political situation' (Deleuze and Guattari, 1987: 83). But Deleuze and Guattari retort that these political features are aggregates immanent in language itself: 'politics works language from within, causing not only the vocabulary but also the structure and all of the phrasal elements to vary as the order-words change' (1987: 83). This is what Deleuze means when he says that the vision of the apostle or the seer 'no longer has to be justified' (Deleuze, 1989: 20). The ultimate support of the order-word is immanent in its very declaration.[7]

## Reduction and totalization

Woven as they are into the fabric of bodies and statements, it is impossible not to miss the moment at which incorporeal transformations unspool themselves into life. As a result, in the face of their obscure and ominous hazards, it becomes tempting to analyse them into their isomorphic corporeal counter-parts: to break down the event, which is incorporeal and infinitive, into subjective conjugations of words and individuated allocations of bodies, and thereby rob it of its essential productive feature: its generative anexactness. This is a temptation that has defined and permeated the strategies of Rushdie's supporters from the beginning: to translate the multiple and prolif-erating senses of the *fatwa* into the symmetrical rows and columns of a diplomatic crossword puzzle. Analysis, in other words, confuses the sense of the *fatwa*, whose function is always to be absent from its own place, with its signification, which, on the contrary, attaches itself to all of the various actual-izations of the *fatwa* as a sedentary point of anchorage.[8]

The various analyses of the *fatwa* have tended to operate according to the double strategy of reduction and totalization: first, reduce the multiplicity of your subject to a manageable number of distinct corporeal variables; then, totalize the specificity of these variables into general rules and statements designed to explain and solve the problem. For example, the *fatwa* is often diagnosed as the symptom of the megalomania of an archaic despot; the strategy assumes that Khomeini would remain an authoritarian leader even if he was abstracted from his God and his people. Once the *fatwa*'s collective assemblage of enunciation was reduced to the singular body of the leader, it became possible to target this body as the object of a general and totalizing formula: get rid of the leader, and your problem will be solved. 'The issue is whether or not a tyrant, or would-be tyrants, should be allowed to impose their views through death threats' (Taheri, 1990: 15).

This strategy quickly proves to be misdirected. Soon after the promulgation of the death threat, other members of the Iranian government, as well as various other Muslim leaders around the world, affirmed and applauded Khomeini's sentence. On 4 August 1990, the Nineteenth Islamic Foreign Ministers Conference adopted a mandatory resolution calling on all member states to take 'all necessary steps, including economic sanctions, against the publisher of the *Satanic Verses* and its holding company' (Bedford, 1993: 155). Rushdie's reaction to the *fatwa*'s social metastasis was another gesture of reduction: Islam, he wrote, had been taken over by a 'powerful tribe of clerics' and it was up to Western politicians to pressure these tyrants into submission to international laws. The opposition between a single archaic tyrant and a multiplicity of enlightened *cogitos* was thus replaced by another reductive face-off, between a pack of unruly thugs and international regulations codified in an effort to contain their dangerous drifts.

But the thugs kept multiplying, and the calls for their excision soon became a pretext for the elaboration of a fantasy about the organic unity of Western Culture. Three days after the imposition of the *fatwa*, the London *Times* ran a commentary by Robert Kilroy-Silk in its editorial page (1989). The piece is a good example of the dual operation of an imaginary identification with Muslim immigrants and a projective expurgation of the same group: 'We have been robbed of our confidence. We also lack the simple certainties and self-confidence enjoyed by the minorities', bemoaned the piece, presenting the 'confidence' of British immigrants as an ideal object which would lend coherence to the shattered Western body. Then, in a peculiar rejection of the notion of the immigrant as citizen, it insisted that 'if Muslim immigrants cannot and will not accept British values and laws then there is no reason at all why the British should feel any need, still less compulsion, to accommodate theirs. We are not supplicants in our own country' (Kilroy-Silk, 1989). We have no confidence, but we are not supplicants; the immigrants hold British passports, but they are false pretenders, sorry simulations, since they will not accept our National Values.

The invocation of an imaginary culture, a Britishness pristine in its wholeness and shared by the entire nation, was also at work in an open letter, published in the London *Times* soon after Rushdie's retreat into hiding, by the British Home Office Minister, John Patten. Citing as its aim 'the full participation in our society by Muslim and other ethnic minority groups', the letter was a how-to guide for becoming British. Among the essential axioms of Britishness that, in Patten's opinion, all the immigrants must embrace were 'a fluent command of English', and a 'knowledge of institutions, history and traditions' of England, as well as 'a clear understanding of British democratic processes, of its laws, the system of Government and the history that lies behind them, and indeed of their own rights and responsibilities' (Patten, 1989). It did not seem to occur to the Minister that his exhaustive prerequisites for Britishness would instantly rob the entire population of Britain of their prized national identity.

The *fatwa* had invented two fuzzy sets: the 'proud Muslim people of the world' who were to kill 'all involved' in the production of the *Satanic Verses*. Rather than resist the ideological power of these sets, Rushdie's supporters chose to adopt and utilize them in their polemics against Iran. By the time British playwright Tom Stoppard commemorated the third anniversary of the *fatwa*, the category of the 'Muslim fundamentalist' as a key player in the Rushdie Affair had turned into a commonplace. 'The eighteenth-century Enlightenment', wrote Stoppard, 'made the discovery that man was perfectible, that change was progress, that progress was good'. Then came the rub: 'We Westerners have moved with the times … Muslim fundamentalism has not. Is that what we are saying? Evidently so. Our entire culture is saying it. I believe it' (Stoppard, 1993: 118).

The trite exclusion of 'fundamentalism' from the Enlightened realm of the 'West' is a gesture which is as ordinary as it is hollow. It is also an ironic gesture, since it betrays an implicit acceptance of the *fatwa*'s declaration: Stoppard's 'fundamentalists' are none other than Khomeini's 'proud Muslims', that is, members of an imaginary and vague category which was invented anew by the *fatwa*. More surprising, and far more ironic, however, is Stoppard's presentation of the 'West' as a self-enclosed unity whose 'entire culture' embraces the values of eighteenth-century Enlightenment. Stoppard seems oblivious to the fact that in May 1989, 30,000 British citizens had called for Rushdie's death in a demonstration in London's Hyde Park, that seven months later, on the UK day of Muslim Solidarity as many as 300,000 British Muslims had taken part in shows of hand-raising in favour of the death-sentence on Rushdie, and that a majority of the British population, according to a Gallop Poll published in the *Daily Telegraph* in May 1990, had felt that Rushdie should apologize for writing the *Satanic Verses* (Bedford, 1993: 145, 149, 153).

The closing moments of Stoppard's text demonstrate the extent to which the tactics of reduction and totalization fail to capture the elusive force of the *fatwa*: 'We should not be busy standing up for the rights we have accorded ourselves: we should be busy questioning the rights assumed by Iran, beginning with the assumption that Islamic law prevails over all other law in all other countries' (Stoppard, 1993: 120). The assumption that the *fatwa* is the symptom of a 'nation', coupled with the further assumption that Khomeini, or Iranian clerics, or 'Iran', have assumed a particular 'right' to promulgate a death sentence, are precisely the sorts of reductive misrecognitions that have been undoing the fibres of the Rushdie campaign from the beginning.

## Neo-archaism

It becomes clear, then, that the primary function of 'fundamentalism', as a spectral, alien and regressive category, is to attribute a semblance of unity to the heterogeneity of the Western State-form. 'Fundamentalism' is Enlightenment's imaginary – a mirror to reflect a Whole Body, but only as a flat and alienated surface, presenting a copy without a model. The scapegoat-function is then utilized as a projection of this irreparable fracture: to become whole again, we must excise the tyrant, the tribe of clerics, the swarm of fundamentalists, and by logical extension, our very selves and our own citizens, since the Absolute State has no citizens, only axioms.

All these analyses – whether they trace Rushdie's predicament to an individuated body or to a particular statement – seem to say either too much or too little about the crisis. They are overcodified evaluations that fall short of the mark. Moreover, they utilize a massive and cumbersome discourse of cultural taxonomy in order to approach a micropolitical problem. What is missing in all of this is an acknowledgment that the discourse of the Enlightenment, the modern notion of the nation-state, and its corresponding formulations of rights and responsibilities, all fail to take into account the fundamentally mixed, transformative and diffuse distribution of state-signs (cf. Deleuze and Guattari, 1987: 125, 147). Regimes of signs are always mixed: they incessantly flow into one another, in so many movements of translation and transformation. An analysis of their differences cannot be content with defining the types and characteristics of each regime in opposition to other, adjacent forms. Rather, the question is one of charting the transformations of each pocket of signs into all the others. The East/West divide, whose bankruptcy is generally taken for granted, as well as the more recent discourse of the Diaspora versus the Nation, still haunt the political analyses of the *fatwa*: they are content with mapping differences and oppositions, a parade of 'I's against a trudge of 'Not-I's, even when the 'I' considers herself to be an 'Othered-I'. They are therefore inattentive to all the movements of becoming that fall in between.

Theories of regression, such as the one suggested by Stoppard, soothe a culture in crisis. They identify an aggressive force with a past trauma, in an effort to misconstrue its power and tame its uncanniness. Fundamentalism, according to this formula, signifies the return of the medieval. As such, it can be marginalized in the name of progress and of the future. But the formula will obviously implode at its limits once this phantasm of the past proves itself to be the future itself, misidentified as a relapse. To interpret the fundamentalists' God as the unfortunate resurrection, or the stubborn persistence, of an archaic force simply misconstrues its radical novelty.

It would be more feasible to acknowledge the organization of a *new* deity for the world after Nietzsche: call it the post-God God. This God does simulate the coordinates of the one whose death was announced by Nietzsche, and it invokes the same archaic laws, but its archaism must be understood as a creation, not a regress: 'What is really at stake is a different use of preexistent formulas of behaviour or representations, in order to construct *another* life-surface, or another affective space, laying out another existential territory' (Guattari, 1995: 23). Fundamentalism is a Neo-Archaism.

The construction of a new territory, as Guattari and Foucault have shown, does not take the form of a systematic and historical transformation, but expresses itself in sudden flashes of mutation and instantaneous incorporeal transformations: it is an 'aternal event'. Epistemological ruptures detonate the spontaneous combustion of an ancient regime – a hysterical mood-swing of global proportions at infinite speed. This fact appears to be the only variable

143

which can explain the untimely interference of postmodern coordinates in the matrix of fundamentalism: it is also the very notion that the political discourse of modernity, with its commitments to the themes of historical progress and dialectical development, refuses to acknowledge.

The story of the logical progress of modernity, whose every phase must be rigorously applied to the developing world, condemns this world to a permanent reactive position. It prescribes an unceasing pursuit of a model in motion, but it forgets that such a model, even if it did exist, would offer its breathless oriental pursuers nothing more glorious than the image of its backside, as it fades into the future. Meanwhile, the most radically anti-humanist aspects of Foucault's theories are finding their way to the required reading list of divinity students in Iran's holy city of Qom, where future clergy leaders of Iran are being trained; and President Rafsanjani himself is honouring a two-volume survey of poststructuralist philosophy as Iran's book of the year. Muslim fundamentalism is already imbued in postmodern coordinates, and the minoritarian strategies of political resistance in the West are referring to the same cynical convictions which the Iranian fundamentalists have been affirming from the beginning. The political struggles of anti-racism militants, radical environmentalists, and AIDS activists are distancing themselves further and further from the modern ideals of dialogue and consensus, and opting for various forms of direct action which would not, on principle, shy away from arson and bombing. Every strategy of flight from this line of abolition must, therefore, match its deadly novelty. Failing this, it will be the liberal intellectuals who, to their astonishment, will find themselves in the position of regression in the face of their neo-archaic executioners.

## Variation

Deleuze and Guattari have always insisted on the primacy of the lines of flight in the construction of all assemblages. 'Power', they write, 'seems to be a stratified dimension of the assemblage'. The stratifications of power, in other words, are not ubiquitous. 'The diagram and the abstract machine have lines of flight that are primary, which are not phenomena of resistance or counter-attack in an assemblage, but cutting edges of creation and deterritorialization' (Deleuze and Guattari, 1987: 531). The Rushdie Affair, and the question of fundamentalism in general, calls for a more specific formulation of this theory. The problem here is how to flee from flight itself; how to draw a line of creation out of a speeding line of annihilation.

Escaping Iranian fundamentalism is not, primarily, a matter of resisting a totalitarian state apparatus: such an apparatus does not exist in Iran. Rather, it is a matter of escaping from a religious war machine that has overcome the state apparatus: 'When fascism builds itself a totalitarian state, it is not in the sense of a state army taking power, but of a war machine taking over the state' (Deleuze and Guattari, 1987: 230). This formula explains the futility of every attempt to untangle the Rushdie knot on the scene of international politics: the shooings in and out of Iranian diplomats from their various embassies never intersect with the workings of the machine that records Rushdie's fate.

The failure of the dialogic strategy of point-for-point talk-back, whether in the guise of a 'noise-free communicative action', or in the more aggressive register of international sanctions and threats of military intervention have necessitated a search for other forms of flight. The task is no longer to resist or denounce an abomination, but to subvert its deadly force: to compel it, in other words, to misrecognize itself. This calls for a new strategy of simulation: not a rational discourse with the fundamentalist Other, but a sophistic and subterranean becoming-fundamentalist.

The oddest feature of Khomeini's *fatwa* was the fact that it was actually pronounced: why warn your victim before killing him? As a premeditated and public gesture, the *fatwa* not only called for Rushdie's death, but also warned him of it: 'We're coming after you: do something'. More than a death-sentence, whose execution would have been more efficient without a public statement, the *fatwa* was a message to flee: 'it would be oversimplifying to say that flight is a reaction against the order-word; rather, it is included in it, as its other face in a complex assemblage, its other component' (Deleuze and Guattari, 1987: 107). The *fatwa*'s function, therefore, was not only to convict, but to circulate. The gesture of warning, together with Rushdie's inevitable reaction, guaranteed this circulation.

The necessary fuzziness of the group of 'proud Muslims' who were ordered by Khomeini to murder Rushdie, as well as the aporiatic and diffuse avenues through which the *fatwa* had to pass in its proliferation, are open points within the structure of the *fatwa* through which so many movements of subversion can flow. The 'proud Muslim' has no model which would give itself over to rigorous imitation: resemblance, as Foucault joyfully recalls, can only take place in thought. It is rather similitude, the vague and approximate reproduction of one earthly and imperfect variable by another, that can ever be subjected to the trials of verification (cf. Foucault, 1983). This, precisely, is the source of the Power of the False, and the triumph of the False Pretender.[9] The objective is not to invoke, in various degrees of bad faith, the ossified tenets of humanism or essentialism in order to open up a field of resistance against the war machine, but rather to enter the already-open space of the war machine itself, and counter-actualize its events in new directions.

Similarly, the usual methods of supplication to the state and its bureaucrats, in the form of petitions and letters of protest, garnished by signatures like so many withering leaves of parsley on the corner of the despot's plate, seem supinely ineffective in the face of the disguised and anonymous packs emanating from the speeding war machine. In fact, any statement that traces its authority to the proper name of the particular subject who utters it or the sedentary place from which it is uttered is bound to be abolished by the deterritorializing movements of the war machine. Better, then, to depend on the facelessness of rumour and the homelessness of gossip and misquotation: to speak in the name of another.

The enduring force of the *fatwa*, long after its actual disappearance, depends on its revitalization and recirculation in the forking paths of mass media. These paths can either be clogged up and bogged down with non-starters about the freedom of expression, or they can be saturated with simulated reinterpretations that would implode the official meaning of all order-words from within. How does one escape an order-word? Through a weaving of lies and a creative forgetfulness: 'a kind of instantaneousness in the emission, perception and transmission ... a wide variability, and a power of forgetting permitting one to feel absolved of the order-words one has followed and then abandoned to welcome others' (Deleuze and Guattari, 1987: 84).[10]

It is not enough to regard these strategies as merely facetious. They present, rather, a rigorous frivolity. The irrevocability of the order-word, the paradox-ical structure of the event, and the incorporeal transformations that they cause, cannot be addressed, only subverted, replayed in an odd key. This neces-sarily precludes the utilization of a pre-established plan of attack to be traced step by step toward a predetermined goal. The conjunctions and disjunctions of events cannot be expressed in terms of 'brute causality' (Deleuze, 1990: 170). Rather, they must be made to resonate with other events, put into new and unexpected variations. New edicts must be issued, and they must emerge through the blinding glitter of simulation.

## Notes

1  What are here called 'spiralling' and, later, 'speeding' semiotics loosely correspond to Deleuze and Guattari's 'postsignifying semiotic' (1987). The 'spiralling semiotic' evokes the postsignifying regime in so far as this regime has reterritorialized the Cartesian subject into a post-despotic and post-imperialist function. Here it is the despot's throne, as the empty seat of democratic power, rather than the despot himself, which defines the moving centre of the spiral. On the other hand, the 'speeding' semiotic, which is also fused by a high coefficient of the despotic func-tion, evokes the prophetic and authoritarian aspects of the postsignifying regime, but remains essentially imperialist. It is important to note that the cogito of the spiralling semiotic, and the apostle of the speeding semiotic, retain certain features of the paranoid and imperialist despot.

2  Deleuze and Guattari, oddly, do not recognize the distinction between the despotic hermeneut and the passional seer. The seer, for them, is still a despotic bureaucrat: 'The interpretive priest, the seer, is one of despot-god's bureaucrats. A new aspect of deception arises, the deception of the priest: interpretation is carried to infinity and never encounters anything to interpret that is not already itself an interpretation' (1987: 114). However, the distinction between the content of an interpretation (which relies on deciphering a set of external codes) and the expres-sion of a vision (which is justified by nothing other than its own immanent and passional force) explains the alignment of the seer with the postsignifying regime.

3  On the power of the order-word to invent or extract a subset of people, see Deleuze and Guattari: '[Lenin's 1917 text, 'On Slogans'] constituted an incorporeal transformation that extracted from the masses a proletarian class as an assemblage

of enunciation before the conditions were present for the proletariat to exist as a body. A stroke of genius from the First Marxist International, which "invented" a new type of class: Workers of the world, unite!' (1987: 83).

4 For a discussion of the two bodies of the leader, and the political and ideological implications of this doubling, see the following texts: Kantorowicz (1959); Lefort (1988: 243–6); and Zizek (1991: 253–73).

5 For a discussion of the order-word as a 'sting' which can only be passed on, rather than dislodged, see Canetti (1978: 303–11).

6 On the difficulty of determining the performative purity of utterances, as well as the distinctions among directive, assertive and declarative utterances, see Austin (1962).

7 For an alternative argument against the context sensitivity of performatives, see Jacques Derrida's critique of J.L. Austin in 'Signature Event Context' (Derrida, 1982).

8 The *fatwa*, in other words, functions as the elusive 'object = x' that causes the two series of statements and bodies to resonate with each other. Deleuze elaborates on the concept of the 'object = x' or the 'empty square', as well as the distinction between sense and signification, in his *Logic of Sense* (Deleuze, 1990: especially 50–1).

9 On the Power of the False, see Deleuze (1989: 126–55); on the triumph of the False Pretender, see Deleuze (1990: 262).

10 For a powerful account of an active and wilful silence as a tool for resisting mono-logical power structures, see Baudrillard (1988: 207–19): 'And so the strategic resistance is that of the refusal of speech, or the hyper-conformist simulation of the very mechanisms of the system, which is another form of refusal by over-acceptance' (219).

# References

Austin, J.L. (1962) *How to Do Things with Words*, J.O. Urmson and Marina Sbis (eds), Cambridge, MA: Harvard University Press.

Baudrillard, Jean (1988) *Selected Writings*, Mark Poster (ed.), Stanford: Stanford University Press, 207–19.

Bedford, Carmel (1993) 'Fiction, Fact and the *Fatwa*', in MacDonogh, *The Rushdie Letters: Freedom to Speak, Freedom to Write*, Kerry: Brandon, 1993: 125–83.

Canetti, Elias (1978) *Crowds and Power*, trans. Carol Stewart, New York: Seabury.

Deleuze, Gilles (1989) *Cinema 2: The Time-Image*, trans. Hugh Tomlinson and Robert Galeta, Minneapolis: University of Minnesota Press.

—— (1990) *The Logic of Sense*, trans. Mark Lester, Constantin Boundas (ed.), New York: Columbia University Press.

Deleuze, Gilles, and Guattari, Félix (1987) *A Thousand Plateaus*, trans. Brian Massumi, Minneapolis: University of Minnesota Press.

Derrida, Jacques (1982) 'Signature Event Context', *Margins of Philosophy*, trans. Alan Bass, Chicago: University of Chicago Press, 307–30.

Foucault, Michel (1983) *This is Not a Pipe*, trans. James Harkness, Berkeley: University of California Press.

Guattari, Félix (1995) 'So What', trans. Chet Wiener, *Chaosophy*, Sylvière Lotringer (ed.), New York: Semiotext(e).

Kantorowicz, Ernst (1959) *The King's Two Bodies*, New Jersey: Princeton University Press.

Kierkegaard, Soren (1962) 'Of the Difference Between a Genius and an Apostle', *The Present Age*, trans. Alexander Dru, New York: Harper Torchbooks, 89–108.

Kilroy-Silk, Robert (1989) 'Defending Ethnic Majorities', *London Times*, 17 February: 14.

Lefort, Claude (1988) *Democracy and Political Theory*, trans. David Macey, Cambridge: Polity.

MacDonogh, Steve (ed.) (1993) *The Rushdie Letters: Freedom to Speak, Freedom to Write*, Kerry: Brandon.

Patten, John (1989) 'The Muslim Community in Britain', *London Times*, 5 July: 13

Rushdie, Salman (1988) 'India Bans a Book for Its Own Good', *New York Times*, 19 October: A27.

—— (1989) 'The Book Burning', *New York Review of Books*, 2 March: 26.

—— (1991) 'Why I Have Embraced Islam', *Imaginary Homelands: Essays and Criticism 1981–1991*, London: Granta, 430–2.

Stoppard, Tom (1993) 'On the Third Anniversary of the *fatwa*', in MacDonogh, *The Rushdie Letters: Freedom to Speak, Freedom to Write*, Kerry: Brandon, 1993: 117–20.

Taheri, Amir (1990) 'Reflections of an Invalid *fatwa*', *Index on Censorship*: 4: 14–16.

Zizek, Slavoj (1991) *For They Know Not What They Do: Enjoyment as a Political Factor*, New York: Verso.

# 11

# DIAGRAM, INSCRIPTION, SENSATION[1]

## Thomas Lamarre

The Heian court arose on the Japanese archipelago in the ninth century – a local precipitation from a larger nexus of states, commandaries, and courts that coalesced, fragmented, and dispersed across East Asia in the wake of the Han empire.[2] Prior to the Heian court, the idea of empire gathered various clans, by force and by alliance. Sometimes tentatively, sometimes violently, one clan, the Yamato clan, strove to organize the court around consistent genealogies, bureaucracies, and myths, yet the court's centre remained mobile. Across two to three centuries, the imperial centre continued its semi-nomadic movements, migrating from site to site at uneven intervals, for various reasons (genealogical conflicts, unpacified spirits, troubled ghosts or lands). With each successive removal, the structure of court – a grid-like city with avenues laid out in accordance with auspicious lines of force – emerged with greater precision and extension, ever closer to the dynastic ideal. The Heian court, in a sense, marked the culmination of the mobile series, for the court leaves off its nomadic style. It also marked the start of a new series of flows in and around the capital, the contours of which continued to waver.

### Paperscapes

The surface for inscription is not neutral. The papers used for Heian calligraphy begin with vegetal fibres of various types. Types of fibre result in papers that differ greatly in texture, that absorb ink differently, that affect the style and allure of brushwork. The fibres, teased from husks, barks, or other sources, are swollen and pulped, then water is removed in order to mat the fibres into a sheet. The result is a surface without horizontal or vertical orientations: fibres overlap any which way, twining and meshing wherever attractions spring up between teased-up microfibres. The sheet of paper may be square or rectangular, but there is no way to determine an up or down, a right or left, amid the entwined, matted fibres. This is a decidedly 'smooth space'.

There are a number of ways in which orientations are introduced to this smooth space. Often sheets join to form long scrolls of paper. In the absence of any marks or traces on the paper, however, this remains a rather vague

*Figure 11.1* The Yoshinobu Section from the Nishihonganji edition of 'The Collection of Thirty-Six Poets', Nishihonganji Temple

orientation, with only an anticipation of horizontal and vertical movements of inscription. In general, paper formats do not introduce much orientations to smooth space – they are contingent borders, not frames. To these smooth spaces, Heian art commonly introduces colours, patterns, or figures. At this level, two poles start to emerge. Some applications of colour and pattern tend to bring as much orientation or striation as possible to the smooth surface. At this extreme are those papers that bear vertical lines to create columns for characters. Many 'canonical texts' (such as Buddhist and Taoist sutra) adopt such measures to ensure in advance that writing follows and imparts a strict orientation. At the other extreme are those papers that amplify the random variations of smooth space. Flecks of gold or silver scatter, dyes seep and swirl, or papers of various colour are pieced together like a crazy-quilt with fluid-edged patches.

The papers used at the Heian court for poetic inscription – particularly for important occasions like contests, banquets, and ceremonies – typically deploy such techniques, and frequently deploy all of them at once, in order to amplify the smoothness of paper. The result is the fantastical 'paperscapes' that underlie Heian calligraphic poetics: trails of dark ink run over lavenders, greens, yellows, and reds that pool and stream, dotted with showers of gold and silver – all of which seems to anticipate or prefigure poems that sing of celestial and terrestrial movements: petals flutter, rivers flow, autumn leaves scatter, bugs chirp and susurrate, lovers meet and part, moons wax and wane.[3] But this resonance between the poetic 'naturescape' and the paperscape does not belong to the realm of representation: those scattered flecks of colour are only like petals, leaves, snowflakes in so far as they betray an analogous motility and play of variation. Likewise with the currents and eddies of dyes, or the layers and patches of papers: this is a manner of mimicry, not pictography or illustration. Consequently, it becomes difficult to determine whether paperscapes mimic naturescapes or the reverse; or maybe both emerge together, arising from some common source.

At the level of paper, there arise innumerable admixtures of smooth and striated space. Some papers apply patterns that replicate embroidered silk, imparting a sense of vertical–horizontal orientation, with emblems and motifs that echo the woof and warp of textile. There are also papers rubbed with distinctly oriented designs, or painted with grasses, trees, bugs, birds. Such figures are not as strictly striated as the vertical columns of, say, a sutra. And yet, they introduce less random variation than the swirling, fluctuating colours and lines of the paperscapes. In practice, there emerges a range of intersections of smooth and striated space. Nevertheless, it is the aesthetic will to smooth that comes to the fore in the almost delirious paperscapes of the renowned poetic anthologies of the Heian court.

Next come the movements of the brush as it unfurls a series of signs (characters) down the page. Typically, the onset of writing, whether pen or brush, has a particular hold on the modern imagination: the moment when brush or pen encounters the blank page is the moment of ultimate, originary creation – out of the void emerges order; on a field of possibilities arrives the mark, the sign, the word. Calligraphic papers – especially the fantastical paperscapes – defy the notion of an originary mark. Nuance and texture are central to calligraphic expression, and calligraphy and poetry together constitute a kind of crazy-quilt economy of the palimpsest: the inscriptions on previous papers could be partially erased by soaking away the inks, then covering them over with dyes; or the unused margins or scraps could be pieced together; or entire sheets could be shredded, repulped, and matted with other fibres. All of these practical ways to reuse paper continually return texts into texture, and the art of text emerges from an art of patchwork.

Patchwork also affords an excellent analogy to the art of poetic composition and compilation. The art of composition pieces together a song from various bits of other songs and poems. The art of compilation of poem anthologies adds another layer of composition, piecing together songs from various sources. Heian poetics is an art of patching together (composing or compiling) bits and pieces, with skill and style. As with the aesthetic will to smooth at the level of paper, skill in Heian poetics could be said to entail the ability to detect and enhance the texture of bits and pieces, by way of juxtapositions, overlays, inlays, complications, alternations that create new resonances. The emphasis falls not on creation or expression as a form of origination, but expression as a style of synthesis – of disjunctive synthesis that follows patterns of dissonance or diffraction that arise between, and cross through, striations.

*Figure 11.2* The Ise Section from 'The Collection of Thirty-Six Poets', Ishiyama-gire

## Heian, baroque, and the crisis of Europe

There are certain traits that would account for the specificity of the Heian, and for the possibility of stretching it beyond its historical limits – in the manner of Deleuze with the Baroque (Deleuze, 1993b: 34). The quest for historical specificity then would not be an attempt to reconstruct, surround, and imprison the Heian, but to stretch its styles into other Heians, into our contemporary Heian. After all, Deleuze closes his Baroque on the note, 'We are all still Leibnizian'(Deleuze, 1993b: 199). Similarly, is it not possible that we are all still Heian? Yet it is impossible to deny a moment of reaction to this historical extension: who exactly is 'we'?

Alain Badiou is surely correct to fill in 'we moderns' (1994: 51), and from the standpoint of modernity, it may be possible for 'us' to reply 'what does it matter who is speaking?' Such is modernity. Yet, if a certain trouble persists around Deleuze's 'we remain Leibnizian', it is because the moment of historical specificity for the Baroque sets the boundaries of Western Europe, while the moment of historical stretching potentially extends across the globe. The possibility of stretching the Baroque beyond its historical limits is also the

152

possibility of stretching Europe beyond its geopolitical limits. Deleuze is not unaware of this trouble, and in his repairs on Leibniz, one of his gestures is to shatter God and the best of all possible worlds. The modern world becomes the site of junctures of incompossibles.

Deleuze thus presents two ways of dealing with the 'Orient'. (Note that his Orient is largely consonant with the Anglo-American Orient of the post-war era: East Asia as *l'Extrême Orient*, usually centred on China and Japan.) One way involves historical delineation by way of the usual lines of filiation. In this respect, Deleuze's evocation and isolation of the Orient is entirely conventional: the Baroque line, for instance, differs from the Oriental line, in a manner at once spurious and ingenious. By way of Simon Hantaï, Deleuze says of the Oriental line,

> Painted and non painted surfaces are not divided as are form and content, but as the full and the void in a reciprocal becoming ... in one and zero, Leibniz acknowledges the full and void in Chinese fashion; but the Baroque Leibniz does not believe in the void ... For Leibniz, and in the Baroque, folds are always full.
>
> (Deleuze, 1993b: 36)

This is ingenious because it tells us a great deal about Leibniz; spurious because it presents little other than a yin-yang formula for the range of Chinese art, which then stands in for all of the Orient, undifferentiated all the way to Hantaï. All the familiar Eurocentric genealogies and ethnicities are brought to bear.

Deleuze's second way operates on those same boundaries and genealogies as sites of multiplicity, as fractal edges at once finite and infinite – in contrast to the orgiastic approach to the limit that characterizes a Hegelian notion of differentiation grounded in historical synthesis or sublation. Deleuze (especially with Guattari) adopts a style of conceptual exemplification that picks up Japanese and Chinese poems, states, and war machines, somewhat randomly and reductively, yet nonetheless with clear intent to practice a disjunctive synthesis that does not rely on sublation at their borders (and with the caveat that it is not the example so much as the concept that is in play). Thus, at the same time that he enables an instrumental usage of the Orient, Deleuze enjoins an openness to the tool that would transform the one who picks it up, profoundly. 'It may be that the Baroque will have to confront the Orient profoundly' (Deleuze, 1993b: 36). It may be that the Baroque must profoundy confront the Orient – not as an afterthought but as part of its very constitution.

The Heian would implicate two folds for us. First, the Heian hovers in an uncertain site in the aesthetic and conceptual realms of modern Japan: folded between exotic and classic, foreign and native. This vacillation follows from the Heian's uncertain and unfamiliar position with respect to ethnic, linguistic, and historical boundaries between Japan and China in particular, and among East Asian nations in general. This fold follows along the creases of another fold – with another relation of point, line, and space – one which implicates the actual history and geopolitics of the Heian court. One could characterize this second fold by the Heian court's emphasis on two styles, two courts, two capitals: Kara and Yamato; the Tang court at Chang-an and the Yamato court at Heian-kyô. Today these are often translated into China and Japan in a belated violence on the fold; an attempt to cut it into isolated fragments, to sever geopolitical implications and complications. What remains troubling and fascinating about the Heian is that it operates between poles (like Kara and Yamato) that function as attractors for the fields and currents of modern poles – such as Japan and China, Occident and Orient.

Make no mistake about the era or event. It implies a series of crises of Europe and the West. It purposely evokes the anxieties of thinkers like Husserl, Claudel, and Blanchot – that Europe is just a peninsula of Asia, and a point of inflection of the so-called New World. Deleuze tries to reconfigure such crises in the affirmative, partly with poles like smooth and striated that complicate easy binarisms and entrenched divides. There is no either/or, no full or void, no Europe or Asia. There is a nuance or texture that folds, unfolds, refolds in between, at different intervals and junctures. It is like the Baroque fold – or the Heian paperscapes – which do not introduce relations of full and void between coloured and uncoloured, marked and unmarked, inscribed or uninscribed; always a depth that rises to the surface; an incompossible universe of values.

## Diagrams

The moment of the brush brings with it imbricated registers of expression. Its signs are at once visual and vocal; its art is intensely manual and gestural. Commentators and translators typically overlook these registers, dismiss them as unimportant to the project of their linguistic science, in which the major task is the extraction of verbal expression. Without some account of the interaction of vocal, visual, and manual registers, however, it is impossible to account for how anyone enters into these texts. It is not exactly a question of production and reception, for these notions ultimately relate to a closed economy of communication (sender, message, receiver) that does not exactly obtain at the level of brushwork. With brushwork, it is a question of sensory interpellation – or rather, embodiment.

Brushwork conjoins the visual/vocal matrix of the sign or character with the manual machine of the brush. (Note that, at this level of analysis, 'vocal' is preferable to 'verbal', for the sounds associated with signs may or may not be articulated as words; and even when they are articulated as words, poetic and calligraphic treatises situate them close to natural sounds – sighs, chirps, cries, etc. Poetry is as much vocal or musical art as it is verbal; an art of vocal modulations.)

When the tip of the brush moves down the page, it traces a series of characters; vertical columns of characters unwind across the page from right to left. In this respect, writing always constitutes a striation of smooth space, for it introduces distinct orientations. Striation need not always proceed vertically; there are environments in which characters are written horizontally from right to left (such as temple gates). Still, regardless of right–left or horizontal–vertical variations, inscription tends to striate. In some instances, Heian poetics attempts even to smooth the striation of writing. Sometimes, the characters of a poem 'hide' or are dispersed into a pictorial matrix – three birds on the wing are read as 'green' (three *mi* + bird *tori* = green *mitori*) – in which case writing and reading scrambles the striations of vertical columns or linear sequences (Mostow, 1992: 338–9). Sometimes the characters sprout leaves, spread wings, or stretch legs, entwining with pictures that underlie the written columns – in which case the eyes move freely between lines of characters and traits of images in the zone where the brush blurs the edges of striated inscription. These examples serve to recall that Heian poetics, at some level, always introduces traits that undermine the striation of space. On the one hand, the brush traces a series of characters that winds down the page in columns, imparting an orientation; as if ineluctably, inscription tends to striation – whence the mythic status of writing as a bearer of order. On the other hand, the Heian brush introduces a great deal of nuance between the lines of inscription and the textures and figures of its environment, creating semi-autonomous zones of disruption, disorientation, departure.

Characters themselves seem to sustain a certain degree of organization and orientation. This is not due to properties inherent in characters, however. If there are specific operations that attend characters, it is because various usages have sedimented a characteristic constellation of operations around them. First, characters impart a sense of right–left and up–down, but this orientation is no more decisive than the format of the page (square, rectangular, scrolling, etc.). Even with such an orientation, one could read from character to character in any direction; only conventions limit one's direction – conventions that constitute a striation or organization of the reader's body and its world. Second, in addition to right–left and up–down, characters conjoin visual and vocal elements. This conjunction of 'seeing' and 'sounding' is also subject to convention. The important and difficult question is that of how to imagine this conjunction of seeing and sounding; and then, how to get at its conventionality as well as its zones of autonomy?

Around the time of the Eastern Han, scholars began to classify characters in accordance to six scripts. Hsu Shen, in the 'Postface' to *Shuo wen ch'ieh tzu*, presents the formulations and examples of the six scripts that became the basis for subsequent theories of writing. First among his formulations for characters are those that 'indicate things'. These are characters that visually diagram their intent (one, two, three, up, down). Second are characters that 'model shape', characters like sun, moon, mountain, tree, river. These verge on pictography. Third come the characters that combine 'shape and sound', in which one half of the character classifies it by 'shape', and the other half presents its sound. Characters for birds – dove, quail, chicken, etc. – use the bird 'shape' alongside its sound – and in many instances the sound mimics the call of the bird. Fourth are characters that 'join intents', in which the intents of two forms are combined: two trees make a forest, the sun behind a tree makes east. Fifth are characters with 'interchangeable glosses', in which two different characters derive similar shape and intent from a precursor. Sixth are those characters derived from 'loan and borrow', in which a character like that for 'wheat' is used for 'to come' because the two have the same sound (Wang, 1979: 1–10; Billeter, 1990: 6–20).

This classification evokes various intersections of shapes and sounds, and suddenly, other, more recent conceptions – pictography, logography, phonography, ideography – seem to be subsumed, and of distinctly limited use. Another question emerges: how arbitrary are the relations between sound and shape? How are visual and vocal elements linked? On the one hand, Hsu Shen seems to allow for arbitrary links. In his third instance, characters combine a sound with a kind of classificatory shape, in a seemingly arbitrary manner. But then, on the other hand, the classificatory shapes do not seem entirely arbitrary: key examples link sound with shape by way of mimicry. In fact, for the most part, his categories and examples evoke various modes of natural mimicry: shapes of things (sun, moon, tree), shapes of operations (one, two, up, down), combinatory shapes (east is sun behind a tree), combinatory operations (forest is two trees), and shapes of things with their 'natural' sounds. Overall, this theory of signs tends to relate sounds and shapes in a non-arbitrary fashion to natural forms.[4] And so, if we detect a certain degree of combinatory arbitrariness between sounds and shapes, that arbitrariness occurs at the level of representation: shapes do not show what the sounds voice.

In sum, the shapes and sounds of characters are fundamentally arbitrary at the level of representation, illustration, or narration; but there is a level at which their conjunction is not entirely arbitrary – a level that we could only describe as prior to or beneath representation – that of the figural. At this level, the shapes and sounds of characters are to echo, mimic, or figure traits of the phenomenal world. Chinese legend, for instance, places the source of characters in the tracks of birds on the sands. Tracks and traces, signs and signatures arise in the world, and humans follow, striving to trace a path among them. Naturally, a variety of ways (or Ways) arise, codifying and overcoding natural traces to different degrees, in various directions. From one perspective, the tracks of the brush lend themselves to such overcodings. Deleuze and Guattari for instance write of different major types of imperial line that rend the abstract line from smooth space, convert it and accord it values – the Chinese imperial line entails a 'superphenomenal encompassing' (Deleuze and Guattari, 1987: 497). From another perspective, the assemblage of the brush – inks, papers, animal hairs, liquefied hands, characters, etc. – brings into play a mediator that traverses codes, stages, ways, and Ways, in which instances writing entails diagrams of sensation rather than codes of inscription and signification.

Now, the simplest way to open these diagrams of sensation is to consider that the brush, profoundly manual, passes over and through characters, conjoining visual and vocal elements. It is as if the movements of the hand/brush could stitch together or clump different registers or potentials. Unfortunately, this aleatory aggregation of registers rarely enters into the scholarly imagination of the art of writing. Usually, the conclusion tends to be that the constellation of elements within characters amounts to an endless game of combinations. Jean-François Billeter, for instance, concludes, 'fundamentally, then, Chinese writing is a combinatory art permitting a virtually unlimited number of compounds to be drawn from a limited number of elements' (Billeter, 1990: 20). From this position, it is only possible to imagine the finite nature of Chinese writing in terms of codes and conventions – the dead hand of tradition establishes the laws and limits for combination and interpenetration of elements; and the players, oblivious or benighted (only finite), never question the rules (ever infinite).

There may be a way at once simpler and subtler to think about characters, hands, and brushes. Visual, vocal, and manual registers gather around the hand/brush assemblage, and yet because no one register is finally reducible to another, a gap or aperture passes through their midst. To borrow the terminology of traditional Chinese commentaries: this aperture is 'heart/mind' (*hsin*). This is how infinite possibilities and permutations fold into finite expressions (and vice versa). This is how the virtual is actualized – a mediator that somehow clumps percepts into sensory aggregates.

So it is that the logic of sensation allows insight into the actualization of the virtual, by addressing a common impasse of empirical analysis. It is possible to classify elements (or rather, subsets), but how do they hold together – and transform? How to explain the new properties that arise at other levels of organization? How to pass from one level of consistency to another? The question can only be understood locally and empirically, in actualization.

## The spatial hypothesis

Regardless of the style, the hand/brush imparts some manner of balance to each character. Style would always imply some manner of balance, and calligraphy abounds in corporeal qualities of expression. There is even an athletic potential about the brush (recall the photos of Chinese calligraphers' hands among Leni Riefenstahl's Olympic series; or the warrior's equivocation of sword and brush). The athleticism of the Heian brush, however, is not that of the athlete but that of the mime: a careful slip or precarious control that swoons, collapses, or tumbles artfully.

Initially, the idea of calligraphic balance conjures up an almost Cartesian grid: one often learns characters on papers folded or ruled to produce the outlines of a square bisected horizontally and vertically, and the character is to be centred around the centre of this square. Balance at this level is a question of weight: the top should not look heavier than the bottom, or vice versa. Likewise with right and left: they should not be disproportionate, nor should they drift too far apart or squeeze too closely together. Such considerations of weight comprise a sense of the thickness and density of traits as well as of the shape derived from components (that is, a pronounced triangular shape above should be met with an inverted triangle below). On this level, characters seem to do little more than surround a centre in accordance with a simple geometry of proportions and balance.

The actual centre of character, however, is not its geometrical 'coordinate' centre, nor even its centre of gravity. As the hand/brush centres the character, it induces a centre of motion. Not only must the character cohere and balance, but it must also avoid any impression that it sags or descends. It must float and hover. The dynamics of the hand/brush move the centre of the character upward, and in a sense, outward on the page. Thus arises a tension between the coordinate centre (dictated by the geometrical sense of proportion) and the centre of motion. The centre of motion and its tension with coordinate space offer a convenient way to differentiate calligraphy from other modes of inscription. This is why calligraphed characters frequently evoke a sense of animate motion: every animate creature has its signature; we recognize different people by their gait on the basis of the distinctive pattern of tensions around centre of motion and centre of gravity.

In contrast, modern typography tends to produce signs that lope along the horizontal, feet planted firmly, without differentiating the centre of motion from the centre of gravity or from the coordinate centre.

Now, the typographic effect is often associated with the alphabet – oddly, since moveable type enters Europe from China and Korea, and Europeans changed little but the number of characters, which quantitative diminishment often suggested a qualitative loss, a diminishment of visual and conceptual possibilities (Etiemble, 1988). Thus Leibniz's Theophilus suggests that Europeans could introduce a Universal Symbolism, a popular one, and better than that of Chinese, 'if in place of words we used little diagrams which represented visible things pictorially and invisible things by means of visible ones which go with them, also bringing in certain marks suitable for conveying inflections and particles'. Theophilus concludes that 'this way of writing would be of great service in enriching our imagination and giving us thoughts which were less blind and less verbal than our present ones' (Leibniz, 1981: 399).

It is possible to construe Leibniz's project of Universal Symbolism as part and parcel of a mathematical or philosophical neutralization of signs. When modern typography takes up its 'little diagrams' (characters, letters, whatever), it renders them immobile in a neutral white space, a void that diminishes any sense of forces, movements, or textures prior to inscription. It is possible, of course, to print handwritten characters, to mask the advent of arbitrary space.

In fact, Tokugawa Japan resisted moveable type, holding firmly to wood-block prints of handwritten texts (not to mention non-arbitrary spaces of neo-Confucian thought). With the type associated with modernity, however, whether the characters move horizontally or vertically, the printed page ensures that the relations between ink and paper are not of consequence, nor are the sensible or mobile qualities of, and linkages between, signs. Everything now concerns the production of intelligibility within an arbitrary space. This is one way to approach Derrida's critique of Leibniz's Chinese prejudice. 'For him', writes Derrida, 'what liberates Chinese script from the voice is also that which, arbitrarily and by the artifice of invention, wrenches it from history and gives it to philosophy' (Derrida, 1974: 76).

Yet Deleuze reminds us that there is no void for Leibniz; that seemingly neutral and arbitrary space is not void but full. One might then think of its historical nuance and texture in terms of a 'graphic unconscious', like that which Tom Conley (1992) finds operative beneath the typographics of early modern poems. Or, later, poets like Mallarmé and Claudel strove to transform the modern typographic relations of point, line and space. Of course, it is not for nothing that they evoke fans, folds, textures, signs of their 'Orient' – Claudel most obviously with his poems handwritten on paperscapes with character calligraphy to attend and support them, as in *Les cent phrases pour éventail* (1985). Above and beyond these modern insinuations of a graphic unconscious, the movements of Heian brushwork engage a possibility that typographic poetics could only gesture at with its gradual deconstruction of books, lines, phrases, words, and finally, the letter – a smoothing of space within the sign itself.

As the brush 'falls' down the page, it oscillates through characters in a way that makes each sign resist or forget its coordinates and its gravity. It flutters, wavers, hovers, flickers, turns around a centre of motion. The page then appears not as a neutral coordinate space but as a space shot through with forces. The sign emerges at the intersection of forces, and its actualized coherence comes of the nuances of specific intersections (Massumi, 1992: 33; Smith, 1996: 34). Such intersections of forces are not unconscious constellations; they are to some extent unpredictable, mysterious, even spiritual (in the manner of vague material essences); yet external, and to some extent, amenable to art's intervention. Brushwork – at least of the kind described here – has the potential to come close to the virtual; it strives toward that moment of inclusive disjunction. No longer is it a question of geometry but of geomancy – that is, of a geometry of forces.

The tension between the coordinate centre and the centre of motion not only reprises the poles of the striated and the smooth, but it also brings into play two modes of cartography or geography. The one would involve an act of centring based on measures and proportions – a Middle Kingdom of paddies, taxes, and tributary states that report to the centre in accordance with their weight and overall balance. The other would involve a strategy of centring based on celestial and terrestrial configurations of forces, a Middle Kingdom of diviners, of wanderers, like warriors or the 'recipe men' (*feng shih*, or analogously *onyôji*) who peddled their magic techniques from court to court.

Likewise, there would be two stylistic poles. The one would minimize the effects of the centre of motion, by appealing to the proportions of characters. It would take care that the sizes and columns of characters do not vary, in this way ensuring that the centre of motion does not wander too much or undermine striation, proportion, or coordination. The other would seek to maximize the centres of motion and the resonance between them, and the lines of the brush would summon a kind of nomadic line. The lines of brushwork would not be lines that follow the distance between two points. The centre of motion – a point – would be that which arises between so many lines, among strokes, slashes, daubs, and dashes of the hand/brush. The centre of motion would become a point of inflection.

Suddenly, at the nomadic pole, things become complicated, because the calligraphic smoothing of space crosses and coagulates various registers that striations and proportions strive to separate and organize. It calls attention to qualities of paper in relation to qualities of ink, to the speeds and intervals of traits, and to the differentiation and coordination of different centres of motion. Thus the disposition of point, line, and space in these mobile styles leads to 'the irreducibly synthetic character of sensation' (Deleuze, 1993a: 23).

## The sensorial/motorial hypothesis

Gestures can conjoin sounds and sights. Take the infant as it learns to reach for a noise or a colour, and then to associate the two qualities of an object, using the gesture as confirmation: what is seen and heard can be located with the hands. Other gestures conjoin sights and sounds, too. A noise from behind, the head turns to look. This gesture also must be learned; initially, a child does not much worry about sounds behind it. Are the gestures of the hand in brushwork not similar? They stitch together sounds and sights, albeit at a greater level of abstraction: phonemes and icons. Still, is it not possible to think of them in terms of intersensory development?

Theories of intersensory development carry with them certain debates about priority. For instance, the debate often continues over whether the senses are initially coordinated or differentiated: is subsequent development a process of coordination or differentiation? This transforms into a question about the one and the multiple: are the senses initially one or many? The answer seems easy enough – development is a process of both differentiation and coordination (Bushnell, 1981: 6) – but the implications are potentially profound, in so far as we cannot situate a prior site of sensory unity within the human body.

In structural terms, Richard Cytowic writes persuasively of synesthesia – 'union of the senses' – which takes place in the limbic system, which arises on a level prior to 'higher' cognitive functions (representation, reflection, cognition, correlation), and which therefore can never be codified. Nor can it emerge with the predictable intersections. Pointy blue, loud green, round warmth, brittle F#, and so forth are already individuated; there is no one language of associations (Cytowic, 1989: 43–45). This manner of synesthetic intentionality (so to speak) effectively collapses hierarchical models of the brain (if any more evidence were needed): true synesthetes demonstrate the prior composition or coagulation on which cognition operates – prior agglutination, contraction, or subtraction. Research on intersensory development can add another twist to this scenario, one that differs from arguments centred on structures, forms, and development, for the question arises of whether this structural synesthesia is actually a true union of the senses, the site of oneness (or even a common sense). That is, the question of the one and the multiple invariably returns, and as one reaches for the site of the one, the unified senses, one discovers that structural, formal synesthesia is a loose, disjointed affair, already differentiated and coordinated. That is, connections and conjunctions occur around an almost primordial 'inclusive disjunction' (primordial to the human, that is). To adopt a morphic analogy: one inevitably reaches outside the human body for the site of oneness, and yet that oneness disperses into multiplicity, as if sublimating, proliferating – and one arrives at Deleuze and Guattari's plane of consistency, for now 'it is a problem not of the One and Multiple but of a fusional multiplicity that effectively goes beyond any opposition between the one and the multiple' (Deleuze and Guattari, 1987: 154).

Deleuze and Guattari propose two planes, or two ways of conceptualizing the plane. One is 'as much a plan(e) of organization as of development: it is structural or genetic, and both at once, structure and genesis, the structural plan(e) of formed organizations with their developments, the genetic plan(e) of evolutionary developments with their organizations' (Deleuze and Guattari, 1987: 265). This plane is not given but hidden; it can only be inferred. The other is the plan(e) of consistency or composition, a plane of immanence and univocality – 'the plane of Nature, although nature has nothing to do with it, since on this plane there is no distinction between the natural and the artificial ... a plane of proliferation, peopling, contagion' (Deleuze and Guattari, 1987: 266–7).

With respect to calligraphic assemblage (hand, brush, posture, ink, paper, characters, etc.), there would then be two ways of following the sensory intersections mobilized around the human body – i.e., the tactile qualities of the hand/brush in conjunction with textures and viscosities; proprioceptive qualities of posture, respiration, articulation of joints; visual qualities of characters, papers, inks; and tonal, vocal, verbal resonances. One learns the art of the brush in specific ways, performing the gesture, uttering the sound, recalling the centres and balances – in accordance to specific lineages, masters, and schools that overcode the body with specific styles. The discipline of calligraphy acts on the sensory qualities associated with corporeal potentials; it induces a structure, a development, and an organization. It cuts continuities and traces over discontinuities; it inscribes a body and a subject (but not an individual or interior). It constitutes a radical mutilation and mutation of the body. In particular, there is an amputation of the hand in favour of a new prosthetic hand/brush that transforms modes of touching, feeling, grasping. 'People feel, grasp brushes', writes one renowned calligrapher of the early Heian (Kûkai, 1984: 5).

Heian tales like *The Tale of Genji* push this structure of feeling to its limits: countless moments of crisis in which the brush leaps into the hand as fast as a tear to the eye and the sleeve to the face. This is a novel assemblage of feeling in the way it picks up hands, eyes and mouth: on the one hand, the prosthetic hand/brush; on the other hand, the tear-drenched sleeve that covers the face. Yet the two are linked: the prosthetic hand/brush feels its way down the page, stumbling over sounds and figures, while the drenched sleeve over the face reassembles the face into patterns at once visual and verbal – a patchwork of eyes and mouth; one has only to imagine how tears make the colours of sleeve seep and run in order to understand how the textures of paper and the patterns of textiles become the connective tissue of the Heian body – how its vocal, visual, and manual articulations verge on proprioceptive articulations around Heian structures of feeling.

This is also at the limits of the plane of development, at the limits of the discipline that structures, organizes, mutilates, and constructs the body and the subject. The body is falling to pieces, and the subject is dispersing, while the plane of consistency is in the offing. That is, individuality and interiority are on the point of emergence. There is a liquefaction of the senses that discovers a singularity and autonomy not of the body or subject.

Heian tales often turn around disappearing women. Above all, it is the body of the court woman that is most intensely overcoded with the structure of feeling. Hobbled almost to immobility with layers of robes, she inhabits the cavernous dark under low eaves, behind screens, blinds, curtains – relations of alliance take her nearly out of circulation. There are but a couple of nodes of mobility: fabrication and distribution of silks that links her across Asia, and the rounds of poem-exchanges that stitch other circuits and paths through the capital. It is not surprising that the smoothing of space in calligraphy, poetry, textiles, scents, and so forth, is associated with this feminine space. Feminine space is organized and distributed to the point that the only line of flight is on liquefied hands. When she disappears (as she often does), in her wake trails a series of scattered poems, brushed in her hand – singular traces of an autonomous style. If we have the impression in Heian tales that the feminine world is a zone of autonomy, singularity, and interiority – despite the physical imposition of such limited circulation – it is not simply that women have a lot of time to brood and worry and write, it is largely because their crises result in disappearances through which a singular style emerges. A line is drawn to the vanishing point, a nomadic line that turns around a point of inflection on an invisible horizon.

Nonetheless it is important to insist: all the felicity of Heian tales – the singular and autonomous style of the feminine zone – hangs on barbarism. It is important to insist because, when we read about the body without organs, the allusions to Taoism – 'great Japanese compilation of Chinese Taoist treatises made in AD 982–8' (Deleuze and Guattari, 1987: 157; the reference is presumably to Tanba no Yasuyori's *Ishinpô*) – tend to pass over the violent possibilities of deformation and transformation in the Heian. Violence remains associated with the schizo body, the paranoid body, the masochist body, or even courtly love. The Tao offers but a brief glimpse of horror: 'Is the Tao masochistic? Is courtly love Taoist? These questions are largely meaningless. The field of immanence or plane of consistency must be constructed. This can take place in very different social formations through very different assemblages ... with different types of bodies without organs' (Deleuze and Guattari, 1987: 157).

Although their evocation of the *Ishinpô* greatly reduces its specificity (equally dubious are the binary filiations of Japan and China), nevertheless, even if haphazardly, Deleuze and Guattari's shift of analysis to the plane of consistency zeros in on otherwise inexplicable intersections. For instance, the author of *The Tale of Genji* probably consulted the *Ishinpô* to write her scenes of spirit possession and feminine vengeance. Courtly romance intersects 'Taoist' medical treatises, and corporeal flows intersect fluid brushwork. It is all a problem of making a body without organs, of constructing a plane of consistency. As Deleuze and Guattari suggest, it would be meaningless to parse medicine from romance from brushwork. Yet it is important to underscore the violence and terror, if only to keep us from exoticizing the Tao or the Heian, or from botching our own body without organs.

In sum, the two stylistic poles of calligraphy could be seen to recapitulate a plane of sensorial and motorial development and a plane of consistency. One style, associated in the Heian imaginary with the masculine, pacifies centres of motion, making them uniform from character to character, balancing the contractions and dilations of the heart aperture (the point of inclusive disjunction of the senses). In effect, the aperture is restrained from pulsing too violently; and yet, in terms of sensorial development, this pole proves most violent and barbaric in its institution. The other style seems to consist of a relaxation of the confines of the first; by shifts in speed of the brush, it allows each character's centre of motion the autonomy to wobble with respect to others. It seems to enable a kind of cursification and abbreviation of the first. It does not simply come after the first, however. Its hasty traits could be seen as a recuperation of the child's awkwardness with the unwieldy brush, or her impatience with complex characters. Ultimately, it neither follows from the first nor precedes it, even as it announces both the former and latter: the becoming-child and becoming-woman of masculine style afford singularity and interiority, but only outside the body and subject, in a synesthetic disjunction that disrupts their organization.

# The cosmological hypothesis

Rhythm borders on the abyss, catastrophe, chaos. It is through the diagram – 'the operative set of strokes and patches, lines and zones' (Deleuze, 1993a: 194) – that the modern painter confronts the abyss. Deleuze writes of two poles, two ways of dealing with the catastrophe in modern art (Deleuze, 1993a: 194–5). On the one hand, abstraction (Mondrian, Kandinsky) tends to an optical, cerebral mode that reduces the abyss to a minimum (a code). On the other hand, abstract expressionism (Pollock) tends to a manual mode in which the diagram merges with the whole, toward the maximum of chaos (a scrambling). Heian calligraphy can be said to operate between two analogous poles, already mentioned above.

On the one hand, the 'stiff' or 'regular' style (*k'ai-shu*) presents symmetrical, even geometrical characters of fairly uniform size, with even application of ink and measured rhythms. In effect, in its classic form, this style operates at three levels at least. Traits, strokes, or elements of characters follow precise styles of brush attack and closure, with a codification of angles and inflections. Characters show distinct symmetry, geometry, and balance. Their centres of motion and their distribution on the page present even, harmonious series. The 'current' or 'running' style (*hsing-shu*) should be seen as the companion to the stiff or regular style. Although it presents greater cursivity and celerity with respect to strokes, it balances, abstracts, and harmonizes in the same manner. Because the resultant works are easy to read, this style could be considered to tend toward greater intelligibility. This is true to some extent, and yet, on its own, the criterion of intelligibility might miss the essential: this is as much code as information, and it presents a machine for striation (even its papers are carefully ruled or oriented). As a code, this style uses abstraction in order to maximize the optical at the expense of the manual; it offers an asceticism, a spiritual salvation. It is not surprising then that it characterises Buddhist sutra in the era that precedes the Heian, when the emphasis fell on translation and dissemination of various Buddhisms in and around the mobile court (Hirayama, 1969: 26).

On the other hand, the 'grass' or 'cursive' style (*ts'ao-shu*) unfurls lines that the eye often can barely follow. Traits or elements are amplified or diminished, elongated or foreshortened; sizes of characters become variable, as is the relations between centres of motion. These are the 'gothic' or 'nomadic' lines that pass between points. Sometimes, the reader's hand must retrace the brush's contractions and accelerations in order to make the strokes of the character legible. In addition, characters entwine with figures and designs, spread into textures. Finally, paperscapes contribute to the smoothing of space, and to the ability to pass across registers of expression. This style, characteristic of court anthologies and many tales, becomes ever more prevalent in the late Heian period, a period often characterized by a sense of imminent catastrophe, mobilized by the notion that the world was entering the 'latter days of the law' (*mappô*) when even the teachings of the Buddha would be of no avail.

This second pole, however, does not go as far as the frenetic dance of

Pollock, in which 'the entire painting is expressed all at once by the diagram, that is, the optical catastrophe and the manual rhythm' (Deleuze, 1993a: 197). It is closer to Deleuze's formula for Bacon: figuratively pessimistic (the latter days are at hand, the court in disarray, the world gone dark), but figurally optimistic (the fissures of the abyss reveal textures, its shadows nuances, its depths intensities – geometry becomes sensible, sensations clear and durable).

'There would thus be a tempered use of the diagram', writes Deleuze, 'a kind of middle way in which the diagram is not reduced to the state of code, and yet does not overwhelm the entire painting. To avoid both the code and its scrambling… Must one then speak of wisdom or classicism?' (Deleuze, 1981: 73). Deleuze ultimately rescues Cézanne and Bacon from the fate of classicism, discovering a use of the diagram to constitute an analogical language – a language of relations, which consists of expressive movements, paralinguistic signs, breaths and screams, and so on – with modulation, never moderation. All this could be said of the Heian as well, of its sighs, thumps, and flutters, of its paralinguistic operations of pivots and puzzles; the operations of characters in its poetry seem to embody the notion of modulation. Why do we make a classicism of the Heian? Or has Deleuze restored classicism in another guise (the Baroque)?

Everything depends on chaos and the abyss. If Deleuze does not promote classicism, if he does not reinstate Leibniz's God and the best of all possible worlds, it is because he situates himself so close to the abyss, not in an attempt to locate its seeds of order but to sustain the minimum of function, form, and so forth – whence chaosmos. The Heian, like the Baroque, lends itself to such a programme (with the same dangers), precisely because it affords a multivalent alterity that scrambles the modern subject and its objects. Then, however, the Heian emerges with a cosmological order with distinctive notions of autonomy and individuality. If the Heian oscillates between two poles, it is part of an effort to consolidate territories; its middle way is an art of governance. Heian cosmologies accrue stability as they alternate between celestial and terrestrial realms (sedentary and nomadic), in order to link two economies (riziculture and craft). Disjunctive synthesis – alternations, juxtapositions, conjunctions with a kind of inclusive disjunction – deploys 'calligraphic diagrams of sensation' in the precipitation of the archaic state and its territory. For 'we moderns', however, this is precisely the site of the catastrophe, of aestheticized politics, of an apparatus pressed into the production of ritual values for the nation-state. Notions of the body, community, and cosmology that accrue around Heian diagrams of sensation demand careful attention.

Traditional calligraphic theory revolves around two notions (Hirayama, 1969: 286). First, writing shows the composition of things. Second, writing presents movements: it shows the movements of the heart/mind (and thus human character), and it shows the movements of the natural world (and thus the operations of things). These are, of course, guidelines as much as truths. Because writing shows the composition of things, one is to write in a way that makes manifest the composition of things; and likewise with motions and operations. Naturally, there are many ways – and Ways – to accomplish this, but integral to them is an alignment of the movements of the heart and the movements in the natural world. Part of the art of the brush then consists of diminishing the dissonance between world and heart, with respect to compositions, motions, operations.

At this level, the brush does not function as a tool of conscious expression but as a kind of seismograph, feeling the oscillations and vibrations of the world and of the heart, and signing these on paper, silk, bamboo splints, etc. If writing is a medium, it is a medium in the occult sense – it delivers signs from other realms through the human body, or rather, through its heart/mind. The mark of the sage will be that his expressions – whether calligraphy, poetry, philosophy – are initially attuned to natural configurations. The heart is an aperture made sensitive to natural movements; it dilates and contracts with them, and the hand/brush twitches in response. Thus the writer assembles the body into a series of transformers or exchangers that translate motion to motion, operation to operation, composition to composition. The heart truly is that which moves through the middle. It is an 'eccentric' – that is, a machine for translating lateral movement into cyclical movement, and vice versa. When force is applied to a point somewhat off centre, the wheel turns; or if a point on the turning wheel contacts an arm or lever, the lateral piece oscillates – from oscillation to rotation, or rotation to oscillation. The eccentric recalls not only the eccentricities of the sage (who moves from the centre) but also the turns of the celestial realm that become such an important part of Heian poetry and calligraphy. These arts attempt to transform rotations or cycles (annual, diurnal, romantic, etc.) into the oscillation and alternation of lines and columns of poetry and calligraphy. Just as the lines of calligraphy retain the motion of things in their oscillations around centres of motions, so the turns of poetry transmit celestial rhythms in the use of transformers called pivot-words: nouns transform into verbs, verbs into nouns, adjectives into verbs, nouns into adjectivals, and so forth.

'The first turn, the original structure of turning (which later slackens in a back and forth linear movement) is poetry', writes Blanchot. 'Hölderin said (according to Saint Clair and Bettina): "Everything is rhythm: the entire destiny of man is a single celestial rhythm, just as the work of art is a unique rhythm"' (Blanchot, 1993: 3).

If Blanchot is so much like Heian poetics, it is because the modern attempt to construct the body without organs always involves an 'archaicizing attachment' – to use Guattari's expression (Guattari, 1995: 4; translation modified). Is it even possible to differentiate the cosmologies intertwined within the archaicizing attachment: Buddhisms, Taoisms, Confucianisms of the Heian, and the Christianities, medieval knights errants (Blanchot)? It would be essential at least to become more programmatic than fantastic. If historical specificity will only go so far in such instances, it still serves in the capacity of programme, in the sense Deleuze and Guattari attribute to programme in the construction of the masochistic body (Deleuze and Guattari, 1987: 151) – like the art of dosages that sustains experiment without overdose. If Blanchot himself botches the body without organs, it is not because of its constitution via the celestial rhythm of the first turn, but because of what passes and does not pass over it – he ends up with Europe cringing in terror, the cultural cringe of the West in crisis. It all happens around the work of art, making art into the secular religion, investing aura in the work, yet all the while looking at it in terms of oracles, divinations, signs, and rhythms. The contemporary evocation of the Heian or the Baroque runs the same risk, whence the need for caution with dosages and experimentation, whence the necessity of the programme in the form of historical or cultural specificity (that in its turn runs the risk of becoming an ethnic and linguistic schema for national development, forsaking the plane of consistency altogether).

What is the Heian but a cosmological rhythm? The hand brushes a series of characters in rhythms that are not precisely those of vocal rhythms – there are interpenetrations of twos and threes with fives and sevens; and the eyes follow the resonation of centres of motion that traverse the smooth textures of paperscapes. Verbal rhythms put words in motion, making them pivot and weave; while verbal images hover within and between poems. There are then rhythms of compilation that reprise and extend alternations and resonations of hand/brush, voice, and eyes: cycles of seasons, congratulations, loves, departures, sorrows, names, styles. It becomes a tremendous counterpoint that summons a single celestial rhythm in its wake – not unlike Baroque music but a very different sense of (micro)tones, (pentatonic) scales, and dissonance. Thus the point of inflection – the first turn – sets up rhythms that slacken into linear movements, that support human movements, that allow poetics to conjure up diaries, travels, stories.

This recalls Deleuze's 'phenomenological' hypothesis for Francis Bacon, in a way related to the previous sensorial/motorial hypothesis: every level or domain would have a way to refer to the others; there would be an existential communication between colour, texture, viscosity, tone, gesture, verb, image – akin to a communication of each of the senses with the others. This kind of originary unity (of the senses) would be in direct contact with a vital power, a power that is rhythm, one more profound than seeing, feeling, hearing, and so forth (Deleuze, 1993a: 192). Yet different concerns crop up around community and cosmology. For instance, whereas one might say that the modern painter makes rhythm visible, that the modern composer makes rhythm audible, the Heian artist not only seems to work in several media at once, but she or he also enters into a vast signature. The Heian work of art does not invoke a metaphysical or practical separation of the senses; nor does it isolate the individual subject as signified. A poetry anthology conjoins a series of compilers, a series of poets, a series of calligraphers – not to mention the attention paid to papers and scroll spindles – and even though each imparts a style, there are no individual signatures. It is impossible to evoke an individual subjective expression apart from this conjunction of expressions – which does not mean there is no individuation. Likewise, it is impossible to speak of certain divisions of labour around the senses – painting is read and heard, writing is viewed and touched; speaking is felt and seen – which does not mean there is no differentiation. In terms of the relationship of rhythm and sensation, one might say that Heian art makes rhythm legible, whether legibility derives from drawing, singing, writing, dyeing, etc. A multisensible Figure appears legibly in the service of an eccentric, disjunctive cosmology.

'Even though eras shift and deeds pass, and delights and sorrows come and go, the written patterns (*moji*) of songs continue', writes Ki no Tsurayuki, renowned poet, calligrapher, and compiler of the Heian.

> Should they be retained as changeless as bird tracks and transmitted as long as rampant vines, just as the evergreen needles never scatter and vanish, just as the threads of green willow always trail, then people who know the designs of songs and obtain the heart of words will surely look up to the high ages and yearn for this day, just as we look to the moon in the great heavens.
>
> (*Kokinwakashū*, 1971: 56)

## Notes

1 I would like to thank Ian Buchanan, who hosted the Deleuze Symposium at which an earlier version of this paper was presented; and Brian Massumi for his suggestions and insights. I would also like to thank the Fonds pour la Formation de Chercheurs et l'Aide à la Recherche of Québec and the Social Sciences and Humanities Research Council of Canada.

2 Dean and Massumi, in *First and Last Emperors* (1992), provide a useful model for thinking about the ways in which the first dynasty of the Qin emperor attempted to reconcile antagonisms between smooth and striated space by evoking modes of warfare, exchange, and social hierarchy which accelerated and blurred the two tendencies (like the spokes of a wheel) within a state that could only implode and explode. This dynamics of imperial formation and dispersion informs subsequent dynasties, courts, commandaries, albeit in a muted, tempered form.

3 These 'paperscapes' can be seen in any number of Heian texts. In this instance, I have before me the examples from the volume *Heian Kamakura no sho: sampitsu sanseki* (Komatsu, 1980): the *Kumogamibon Wakanrôeishû* (46), the *Gen'eibon Kokinwakashû* (49), the *Oshikishi* (53) and the *Ishiyamagire* (55). See too the Heian and Kamakura volumes of *Shodô zenshû* (1969), which give not only a series of plates but a number of articles and commentaries as well. In this context, the article on paper ('Sôshôshi ni tsuite', vol. 14, 28–34) is of particular interest because it gives the details of the production of papers and paper designs. As for the poetry, my point of reference is first and foremost the *Kokinwakashû*, compiled around the year 905; because in many ways this poetic anthology stabilizes and standardizes the poetic styles that characterize the Heian period (roughly, 794–1183). There are two available translations of this anthology, as well as good of deal of secondary literature in English, not to mention the extensive commentaries and interpretations in Japanese. If I do not cite much of this literature

directly in this paper (though it is implicit in all the descriptions), it is because I wish to shift the ground of poetic analysis away from the now standard emphasis on ethnic and linguistic closure (to wit, Heian courtiers used poetry to establish a Japanese language and identity distinct from China, somehow replicating the orientalism and nationalism of modern Japan one thousand years earlier). Those who are interested in further references and these other debates around Heian culture might consult the bibliography and text of *Uncovering Heian Japan* (Lamarre, 2000).

4　It is important to differentiate this notion of mimicry (via Deleuze, and Benjamin, 1986) from pictography and from Pound and Fenellosa (see Fenellosa 1936). For Foucault, in *This Is Not a Pipe*, the calligram is effectively an expanded version of the pictogram, and he relates Chinese writing – 'the old ideogram' – to this pictographic mode of combining verbal signs and images (Foucault, 1983: 22). More explicitly in *The Order of Things*, he suggests that 'in our traditional imagery' of China, 'even its writing does not reproduce the fugitive flight of the voice in horizontal lines; it erects the motionless and still-recognizable images of things themselves in vertical columns' (Foucault, 1970: xix). It is important that Foucault recognizes, even in chimerical form, that there could be a Chinese order of things – in contrast to Roland Barthes who discovered in Japan and China an exhilarating lack of the Western emphasis of signification – and yet, for Foucault as well, this order of things is, in the end, devoid of Europe's modernity; it is completely other. Foucault's association of pictograms and ideograms thus is ultimately not of much use in the analysis of characters or calligraphy. On the topic of visual qualities of characters, the legacy of Ernest Fenellosa and Ezra Pound is of greater interest in so far as their theory of the ideogram allied it both with pictogram and with processes and energies – with mimicry as much as pictography (Fenellosa, 1936). Of course, if Pound and Fenellosa were able to decentre the pictographic myth, it is partly because they entered into Confucian ideas about signs, from two directions: by way of Leibniz and Emerson, and by way of Fenellosa's Japanese informant, Mori Kainan. Nevertheless, in Emerson and Pound as in Foucault, figural qualities of characters remain inordinately tied to a pictographic imagination. Deleuze's notion of modulation, in the chapter on analogy in the book on Francis Bacon (1981), presents a more persuasive way to think about the effects of mimicry in poetic language. Moreover, in its concern with senses and bodies, Deleuze's logic of sensation often resonates eerily with many of the traditional Japanese and Chinese treatises on calligraphy and poetry.

# References

Badiou, Alain (1994) 'Gilles Deleuze, The Fold: Leibniz and the Baroque', in *Gilles Deleuze and the Theater of Philosophy*, Constantin Boundas and Dorothea Olkowski (eds), New York: Routledge, 51–69.

Barthes, R. (1975) *Alors la Chine?* Paris: C. Bourgois.

—— (1982) *The Empire of Signs*, trans. Richard Howard, New York: Hill & Wang.

Benjamin, Walter (1986) 'On the Mimetic Faculty', *Reflections*, Peter Demetz (ed.), New York: Schocken, 333–6.

Billeter, Jean-François (1990) *The Chinese Art of Writing*, New York: Rizzoli International.

Blanchot, Maurice (1993) *The Infinite Conversation*, trans. Susan Hanson, Minneapolis: University of Minnesota Press.

Bushnell, Emily W. (1981) 'The Ontogeny of Intermodal Relations: Vision and Touch in Infancy', *Intersensory Perception and Sensory Integration*, Richard D. Walk and Herbert L. Pick (eds), New York and London: Plenum, 5–36.

Claudel, Paul (1985) *Cent phrases pour éventail*, Michel Truffet (ed.), Centre de recherches Jacques-Petit 42, Paris: Les Belles Lettres.

Conley, Tom (1992) *The Graphic Unconscious in Early Modern French Writing*, Cambridge: Cambridge University Press.

Cytowic, Richard (1989) *Synesthesia: A Union of the Senses*, New York: Springer-Verlag.

Dean, Kenneth and Massumi, Brian (1992) *First and Last Emperors: The Absolute State and the Body of the Despot*, New York: Autonomedia.

Deleuze, Gilles (1981) *Francis Bacon: La logique de la sensation*, Paris: Editions de la Différence.

—— (1993a) *The Deleuze Reader*, Constantin V. Boundas (ed.), New York: Columbia University Press.

—— (1993b) *The Fold: Leibniz and the Baroque*, trans. Tom Conley, Minneapolis: University of Minnesota Press.

—— (1994) *Difference and Repetition*, trans. Paul Patton, New York: Columbia University Press.

Deleuze, Gilles and Guattari, Félix (1987) *A Thousand Plateaus*, trans. Brian Massumi, Minneapolis: University of Minnesota Press.

Derrida, Jacques (1974) *Of Grammatology*, trans. Gayatri Chakravorty Spivak, Baltimore and London: Johns Hopkins University Press.

Etiemble (1988) *L'Europe chinoise*, 2 vols, Paris: Editions Gallimard.

Fenollosa, Ernest (1936) *The Chinese Written Character as a Medium for Poetry*, New York: Arrow Editions.

Foucault, Michel (1970) *The Order of Things: An Archaeology of the Human Sciences*, New York: Random House.

—— (1983) *This Is Not a Pipe*, trans. James Harkness, Berkeley: University of California Press.

Guattari, Félix (1995) *Chaosmosis: An Ethico-Aesthetic Paradigm*, trans. Paul Bains and Julian Pefanis, Bloomington/Sydney: University of Indiana Press/Power Publications.

Hirayama, Mitsuki (1969) *Eien no sho: Kûkai hen*, Tokyo: Yûhôdô.

*Kokinwakashû* (1971) Ozawa Masao (ed.), Nihon koten bungaku zenshû 7, Tokyo: Shôgakkan.

Komatsu Shigemi (ed.) (1980) *Heian Kamakura no sho: sampitsu sanseki*, Nihon geijutsu zenshû 8, Tokyo: Gakken.

Kûkai Kôbôdaishi (1984) 'Sangô shiiki', in Yamato Chikyô (ed.), *Kôbôdaishi Kûkai zenshû* 6, Tokyo: Chikuma shobô, 5–86.

Lamarre, Thomas (2000) *Uncovering Heian Japan: An Archaeology of Sensation and Inscription*, Durham: Duke University Press.

Leibniz, G. W. (1981) *New Essays on Human Understanding*, trans. and ed. Peter Remnant and Jonathan Bennett, Cambridge: Cambridge University Press.

Massumi, Brian (1992) *A User's Guide to Capitalism and Schizophrenia: Deviations from Deleuze and Guattari*, Cambridge, MA/London: MIT Press.

Mostow, Joshua (1992) 'Painted Poems, Forgotten Words: Poem-Pictures and Classical Japanese Literature', *Monumenta Nipponica* 47:3, 323–46.

*Shodô zenshû* (1969) 3rd edn, 28 vols, Tokyo: Heibonsha.

Smith, Daniel (1996) 'Deleuze's Theory of Sensation: Overcoming the Kantian Duality', in *Deleuze: A Critical Reader*, Paul Patton (ed.), London: Blackwell, 29–56.

Wang, David Kuo-Wei (1979) *Definitions and Classifications of the Six Scripts According to Hsu Shen (ca. AD 58–147) and Leading Ch'ing Scholars,* Diss., Georgetown University.

# 12

# SOUND IDEAS

## *Aden Evens*

*Perfect Sound Forever.*
   Sony advertising slogan at the introduction of the compact disc (CD)

## The absolute sound

*The Absolute Sound*[1] – whose name refers to an aesthetics as well as an editorial style[2] – makes it doctrinal: the only goal of reproduced music is to sound as much as possible like live music. Accuracy in reproduction, fidelity to the original sound, is the sole standard in judging recordings and the equipment used to play them. One hopes that the recordings are made as accurately as possible and then, in playback, 'the philosophic assumption in the listening sessions is that components, ideally, should duplicate exactly the signals they are fed. The only correct goal of high fidelity sound reproduction, in our estimation, is a perfect re-creation of the musical experience' (Pearson, 1996).

Sound perceived is a contraction. A perceptive body experiences variations in pressure, and contracts this 'air wave' into sound. The wave, a variation in pressure over time, has discrete characteristics, including frequency, amplitude, phase, shape. Each of these is a motion, a change over time. But, in perception, the wave is contracted, and the corresponding characteristics of the sound are a-durational, independent of time. Pitch, loudness, location, and timbre, though associated with an enduring sound, are in themselves independent of this endurance. Time is contracted into the quality, the character of the perceived sound. For example, the pitch of a sound is mostly a contraction of the frequency of the corresponding wave:[3] the speed at which pressure moves up and down over time is heard as the timeless character of pitch, how high or low a note is. One does not hear the motion of an up-and-down, but a singular quality of a note, high or low.

An E-string bowed on a violin vibrates at once the string, the body of the violin, the other strings, the body of the violinist, the air around the violin, the material of the room, and the bodies of the listeners. The vibration vibrates any other vibrations in the room, any other sounds, such as those of instruments, the creaking of chairs, even the constant movement of the air.[4]

171

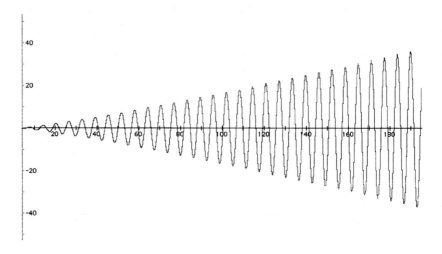

*Figure 12.1* A graph of an ideal sound wave

Notes:
y axis        pressure in the air, or the amplitude of the wave
x axis        time

Note that the wave is getting louder over time, but its frequency stays the same, i.e. its amplitude is increasing but it moves up and down at the same frequency as time goes by. It would sound like a pure tone getting louder.

Measured at some point in space, all of this vibration adds up to a single, continuous variation in pressure, a wave. Complex, irregular, and erratic, this wave changes constantly and so has no single frequency or amplitude. Nevertheless, it can be represented as the sum of a (possibly infinite) number of simple waves, sine waves, each of which has a specific frequency and amplitude.[5] Every wave is made of layers of such simple harmonic oscillations, pure tones, timbre-less notes of various volumes and pitches all sounding together. Hearing involves this further contraction of perception, the contraction of pure tones and the variation of their mixture into timbre, for what physics represents as the sum of sine waves is heard as the general character of a sound, the middle C of a Steinway and not a Bosendorfer, the bowing technique of Yo Yo Ma and no other. All of the richness, the distinctive quality of a sound is a matter of timbre, which contracts the complex layers of tone upon tone and the variation of this layering, from the clarity and strength of the primary frequency that determines the pitch of the note, to the infinite subtlety of the random fluctuations of the air that sound different in every room and at each event.

Given the complexity of the wave which reaches the body of the listener, it is not surprising that engineers are challenged to record and reproduce sound satisfactorily. One must capture a huge range of frequencies, as well as the most subtle changes of amplitude. And playback demands an extraordinary control over not only the production of sound, but also over the listening environment, to minimize distortions, which add to, subtract from, or otherwise modify the sound. Readers of *The Absolute Sound*, audiophiles, are convinced that the key to satisfactory sound reproduction lies in overcoming this engineering challenge. The implicit goal of sound reproduction is fidelity. There lurks here an epistemological bugaboo: fidelity to what? Although audiophiles are reluctant to reduce fidelity to physics, they offer no alternative to the engineers, who, in the absence of any other aesthetic analysis to guide their research, take good sound to be a question of accuracy: the recording and playback equipment should recreate the pressure wave as felt at some typical spot in the recording space, be it a concert hall or a recording studio. No gap exists between the wave and the sound; perception drops out of the picture.[6] The listener is a placeholder, an any-body, and the place which the body holds is defined by the physics of acoustics. Thus, fidelity in the reproduction of recorded music, and implicitly also the best sound, is achieved by the accurate recreation of the same pattern of sound waves at the listener's body (especially the ears) as would have occurred at the body of a listener who was present at the recording.[7]

Audiophiles believe themselves to be pursuing the 'best' sound by aiming for the most accurate reproduction of pressure waves. Fidelity, as a standard, is unquestioned, along with the epistemology of hearing. So, they are puzzled and disturbed by an evident lack of correspondence between high fidelity and musical involvement. Car stereos and transistor radios are notorious for providing that rare transcendent music listening experience.[8] And 'lo-fi' is not only the current buzz (!) in popular music production, but has been an integral part of the rock aesthetic. What might these 'lo-fi' listening experiences provide that higher fidelity does not? Audiophiles unwittingly undermine fidelity by attacking the objectivism which buoys it, and insisting that human ears are the only acceptable judges of the best sound reproduction.[9] Perhaps the contractions involved in perception exceed the capabilities of the mechanical. After all, music is a human practice, even if it incorporates the non-human, the incorporeal, the technical. To the extent that something moves in music, something which makes it more than a measurable aggregation of continuous sounds, but brings it together, relates it to its outside, to that extent, music is *expressive*. It is the expression in sound which cannot be measured, the expressive dimension that operates in conjunction with a person, a listener who also brings something to the sound. Where sound involves percepts and affects, where it presents a world, a world one could be in, there only a person can go.

The debate about the superiority of analogue versus digital media, specifically, the long player (LP) versus the compact disc (CD), focuses attention on the question of expression in the reproduction of sound. At the introduction of the CD, critical listeners had to learn to hear new kinds of problems in music reproduction, since digital's shortcomings were not the pops, hiss, and other familiar distortions associated with analogue media. The industry had to work 'toward a vocabulary that will help us "hear" [digital] distortions with greater celerity' (Pearson, 1996). Initially, many of the criticisms of the 'sound of digital' were inspired by a certain popular image of technology generally, and by the specific process of digital sampling. Digital sound, especially digitally reproduced music, is said to sound sterile, dry, or cold. It is claimed that CDs, by reducing music to a bunch of numbers, fail to capture its spirit, its feeling, its emotion. Says Neil Young, 'There's no challenge, there's no possibilities, there's no imagination. You're hearing a simulated music' (Young, 1992: 12). To others, who think perhaps of the process of sampling, digital sounds choppy, broken up, thin, or lacking detail. LPs are, by contrast, warm, full, rich, and expressive. A decade of engineering has overcome many of the problems which plagued early CD recording and playback, but still the primary complaint among digital's detractors is that CDs lack a certain pace, cohesion, integrity, musicality, wholeness. Though the right notes are all there in the right places, the music does not move, and so does not gather up the listener into its motion. In short, digital reproduction is accused of failing to express. Though these criticisms belie a misapprehension of digital sampling theory, they nevertheless note a genuine dissatisfaction with CD recordings. How does digital recording work, and where might it fail to reproduce the expressive elements of sound?

An analogue recording records an analogue of the original sound. A sound wave described by continuous variations of pressure over time is spread out in space onto a recording medium. Time is transformed into space and pressure variation is transformed into the variation of a specific property of the recording medium. The wave may be etched into the grooves of a vinyl record, or coated onto the surface of magnetic tape by varying the magnetic properties of the tape over its length in a pattern geometrically analogous to the original wave. In both cases, the recording must be played back – its variations allowed to modulate a loudspeaker thus producing an air pressure wave – to translate the variation in space on the recording medium back into a variation (of air pressure) over time.

Digital recording works by sampling, taking a measurement of the air pressure at regular intervals, and storing those measurements as numbers. It is like a movie camera, which opens and closes its shutter to take a series of snapshots. The snapshots, as they pass rapidly before our eyes, simulate the motion of the original scene. Likewise, the series of numbers which represent pressure measurements is used to recreate a wave of varying air pressure, which simulates the original sound. A single sample is a (binary) number which acts as an instruction to a volt-producing machine. Successive samples trigger a wave of voltages which is amplified and sent to a loudspeaker, whose driver moves in concert with the voltage variation, producing an approximation of the original wave. (Since the volt-producing machine must ramp up or down from one voltage value to the next, the signal is changed at that point from digital to analogue, from discrete values to a continuous wave.) Because sampling takes place at a regular interval, it is possible for some pressure variations to escape recording altogether: whatever variation occurs in the time between two samples will be missed. Higher sampling frequencies allow the sampler to capture shorter-term acoustic events; but since the length of an acoustic event is effectively a matter of its frequency, this means that faster samplers can record higher pitches.

The other primary factor which contributes to the theoretical accuracy of digital sampling is resolution. Resolution refers to the number of possible values which any one sample may have, or how fine a distinction can be made between adjacent pressure levels. A higher resolution means finer distinctions between values but also more information to store. CDs have a sixteen-bit resolution, so each sample can have one of $2^{16}$ or 65,536 values. When long-distance telephone signals are converted to digital (for example, to send them over a fibre-optic cable), they are converted using only about eight bits of resolution, or 256 possible values. Increasing the resolution of a system allows that system to capture more subtle variations, greater nuance. Just as the sampling frequency limits the recordable range of frequencies, so the sampling resolution limits the recordable range of nuance. Complex real world sounds almost always have components above the cut-off frequency of the CD (about 20 kHz),[10] and below the noise floor or maximum resolution of the CD. Sound varies faster and more subtly than CDs can capture. So why do we continue to have any faith that CDs store sounds the way we hear them? Engineers take solace in the conjunction of Fourier analysis and psycho-acoustics. Since every sound comprises a bunch of pure sine waves, it is supposed that the sine waves in any sound which have a frequency higher than the threshold of human hearing can be discarded or ignored in the recording and reproduction process, without affecting our overall perception of the sound. Thus, though a wave may have a great many big and small variations at high frequencies, these upper frequencies are chopped off without being recorded. In theory, this will not alter the way we hear the sound, as long as the missing frequencies are outside the range of human hearing, which is up to about 20 kHz. (High-frequency hearing range was the primary criterion for determining the CD sampling frequency.) If a sampler captures all the parts of a sound up to 20 kHz, then it is supposed that it captures all the parts of that sound which we hear. Moreover, clinical tests show that the resolution of most people's hearing is no better than the resolution of a CD. Even though the variations in air pressure are more subtle than what CDs can capture, we cannot hear them, so they need not be recorded.

Recent critics of the CD have argued that both the sampling frequency and resolution of that format are inadequate.[11] There is, in fact, some evidence that frequencies above 20 kHz affect human hearing, as our brains register activity under high-frequency stimuli, even if we are not consciously aware that we are hearing something. (Preliminary research is available on-line in Oohashi, 1991.) And audiophiles and other critical listeners have long contended that finer-than-CD resolution is audible as a smoothness or liquidity of the sound, even if it is undetectable under objective testing circumstances. There is still another technical complication of the CD, which, unlike those so far discussed, relates not to the principle of the recording/playback of digital sound, but to the pragmatics. Machines for recording and playback of digital signals rely on very precise timing mechanisms. The 'shutter' which opens and closes to take a sample of sound pressure, or reproduce that sample, must do so at exact regular intervals, for the dots (samples) which represent the wave form must be played back in their exact correct places. To shift a sample slightly too early or late is tantamount to adding a new low-level wave to the original waveform, a new frequency which was not in the original signal. The result of these timing errors is a kind of distortion called jitter, which is now blamed for most of the poor sound audiophiles have heard in CDs for the past ten years.

This analysis of the problems of the CD format only begin to suggest an explanation for the impaired expression that listeners hear in the CD. Undoubtedly, musical expression is a matter of some subtlety, as the difference between a great performer and a merely good one is not often primarily a question of technical proficiency, nor even of dynamics or pace, but rather a question of 'touch' or 'feeling', vague and subtle notions which point to something one cannot quite put one's finger on, but which make all the difference. Moreover, the singular sound of a particular violin in a particular performance hall on a particular day is distinguished not by some one analysable component of the sound wave, but only by the unique character of the entire sound, all the tones, all the variations of pressure, gross and fine. No doubt, we experience this singular sound not only in the consciousness of hearing but in the unconscious vibrations of our bodies, and expression is lived as much as recognized. Even the performer cannot assume conscious control over the fine details of the sound, but in the greatest performances, can almost stand back, letting her body, letting her instrument do the work, shaping the sound in its infinitely subtle variation, as she rejoices in the creation she feels lucky to be a part of (Sloboda refers to this experience as 'floating'; 1985: 96). The subtlety of expression will not show up when sound is dissected, since it is a coherence, a proper fit of the entire sound to its environment, to the audience, the room, the air, the other performers. Expression is the art of matching the notes to the room, of playing the audience as much as the score, of shaping the silent movement of air into sound.

## An ethics of intensity

One of the most impressive features of the CD was its increased signal-to-noise ratio, the nearly complete silence between notes which contrasted sharply with the crackles on the surface of an LP.

It is true that there is always a point at which the signal is masked by noise. Variations of a certain subtlety are so small as to be absorbed into the background of fluctuations of pressure, the constant movement of the air, the vibrations of the earth. What is this noise but cosmic vibration, the fused sum of all the vibrations to reach this point in time and space? Vibrations do not disappear, but dissipate, echoing all the while, for energy is conserved. Every vibration, every sound, hangs in the air, in the room, in bodies. Sounds spread out, they become less and less contracted, they fuse, but still they remain, their energy of vibration moving the air and the walls in the room, making a noise which still tickles the strings of a violin playing weeks later. Every sound masks an entire history of sound, a cacophony of silence. Even our bodies hum along with the noise of the universe.

In this complete history of sound, this cosmic echo which constitutes noise, sounds are not distinguished one from the next. Noise is the inarticulate, the confused mass of vibration, in which sound relaxes or dissipates. Perception requires a contraction, but noise is the uncontracted. Imperceptible, insensible, and sense-less, noise is the depth which gives to be contracted. It is the background, the substrate modulated by signal. Physicists have it backwards when they characterize the formal relationship as one where noise modulates signal. Though it is often the case that signal overwhelms noise, it is noise that binds the signal, that serves as a medium, a baseline, a plane of relief against which signal stands out. The background of noise means that the air which a sound vibrates is not still to begin with, and silence is never total. Every string plucked, every throat cleared, is vibrating a vibration, modifying an existing difference without dampening it or squelching it. Sound is a modulation of difference, a difference of difference. This eternal return of difference, noise, is what gives to be contracted, but is not in itself contracted. The contractions of frequency into pitch, of pitch into timbre and harmony, and the further contractions of melody, duration, rhythm, meter, are unproblematic, analytic; none of them can yet give sense to sound. Noise is the uncontracted, the depth from which these contractions of perception are drawn, and, though sense-less and insensible, it makes sense or gives sense to sound, by providing sound with its direction and by focusing sound to a point of clarity. Noise is the reservoir of sense, the depth in which sounds connect to each other, the background, the difference whose modulation is signal. Music and speech include many differences, not only between notes, words, or sounds, but within each sound, a wave of rising and falling pressure, whose difference gives sound its character. What rises and falls is already a field of difference, an entropy of difference, a noise which is the problematic substance of sound, the obscure reserve.

Noise is what gives to be contracted, or gives to be sensed. To be perceived, noise must be contracted to a point of focus, a clarity which distinguishes itself from the obscurity of the background. This is still not enough, for focus and clarity alone cannot give sense to sound; sounds only have sense when what is heard includes not only what is heard clearly, but includes also the implicated in what is heard. Before frequency is contracted as pitch, and pitch as timbre, noise is contracted as the implicated of sound. Sound implicates what it does not make clear. Explication only goes so far, and the contraction which draws clarity from noise drags along with it a residue of obscurity, lines of relaxation which anchor every sound to the noise it modulates. Sound implicates these obscure tethers, which connect sound to noise, thereby giving sound its sense. The implicated difference inholds an obscure reserve of sense.

Nor is the obscurity a problem of epistemological limitation, as though the difference which is not explicated were veiled, but still specific, as though noise contained sounds which were only too soft or too many. Only the explicated is specific, clear and distinct, a specific rhythm, a specific pitch, a specific loudness. The implicated is obscure by its nature, it withdraws from scrutiny. It provides the sense of sound only in being itself unhearable, the imperceptible of sound. The composer and the performer capture percept and affect in sound, implicating worlds of forces not yet unleashed, but whose reserve powers the music, driving it along. Personal histories, impersonal events, an intake of breath, a bloody battle. An entire history of music insists implicated in every note, every phrase, every contraction. A sonic history in every utterance, whose most contracted, whose clarity is the specificity of the sound, but not its sense. It is this contraction, the contraction of all sound, the contraction of all vibrations, which gives sense to sound, contracting clearly just *this* vibration, *this* sound wave, and letting the rest remain obscure, implicated in various degrees of relaxation. Implication pushes the music forward, by contracting noise again and again to a new clarity each time, and sound gets its sense in this movement. The implicated also moves itself, for the obscure is contracted along with the clear. Implicated difference makes the music move, but it is also what moves in the music, the equicentral force of contraction.[12]

We must be careful to distinguish the relative and casual sense of noise from its absolute, productive sense. In its relative sense, noise is just another signal, albeit a confused one: too many contractions which cancel each other, a babbling of many sounds at once. It is in this sense that one claims to hear noise, as static which interferes with FM radio reception, or the air conditioning fan which masks the soft passages in the concert hall. However, in its other, absolute sense, noise cannot be heard, it is the imperceptible, the uncontracted. Absolute noise, the very tendency to relax, to diffuse, is a different type altogether, not the same sort of thing as signal, nor as the relative noise which is a confused signal. It is a depth without dimension from which dimensions are drawn; noise is not a matter which gets formed but the matter of matter, not a vibration but the null space in which the vibration opens space. One can therefore hear only the effect of noise: one hears that there are sounds one does not hear. But noise's effect is not primarily negative. One hears also a positive effect of noise: to give force to music, to supply the implicated reserve of sense. Or, perhaps one only *feels* this effect, as the movement of music, as the contraction which makes music more than a sequence of unconnected sounds, and which draws together breath into words, phrases, meanings. The concert pianist draws on this noise, this background which she contracts in her playing, bringing certain frequencies, certain timbres, volumes, harmonies, melodies to the fore, while implicating the rest. To play music expressively is to demonstrate a sensitivity to this background, not only to read the audience, to hear the space around the instrument, but also to contract the silence between, beside, or behind notes, and to draw from this silence the appropriate contraction, just the right sounds. An instrument is a tool for shaping noise, contracting parts of it into perception, and a performer is always a sculptor, who works at once the contracted material and also the relaxed space around it. Noise is also perceived, but only as implicated.

Perhaps it would be better to say that noise contracts itself, for agency is particularly problematic in music and speech. Credit must be shared among composer and performers, but each performer owes his productivity to the others, so only a multiple subject can really take credit.[13] Moreover, what of the audience, the instruments, the instructors, the influences? What about the conductor, the bandleader, a previous recording? In speech, the subject of enunciation is not just the same as the speaker, for enunciations are machinic, the noise machine contracting meaningful speech from an intensive depth, which involves speaker and listener, as well as a context and culture. (Is this what Wittgenstein means by a 'form of life'?) From the imperceptible depth of noise, contractions pull or stretch into a new dimension which does not preexist them, creating a space whose poles are signal and noise in a relative opposition. The contraction articulates at least twice, separating the signal from the noise in amplitude, while articulating the signal in itself in the rise and fall of frequency and shape. These two articulations are distinct but interdependent, for it is only the molar variation in pressure, the up and down of a perceptible wave, that contracts this wave in itself and places it as foreground against the background of noise which retains within it the implicated. In this sense, the implicated remains as much in the signal as in the noise, as these are bound up in the same articulation. The implicated depth places both signal and noise in relief, it is the inarticulate matter in which they gather themselves. Thus, implication is both the force of contraction and is itself contracted in this contraction: the implicated comes into focus, or a part of it does, and this most focused aspect is a signal, rising out of the noise which is only then heard in the background.

Still no agent of contraction has come forward. Who selects what of the implicated is contracted? It is only the repetition of the contraction, the implicated implicating itself that makes this selection. The whole of sound is contracted each time, the contraction is always repeated, the implicated always implicates itself again, drawing its own skin inside of it, turning itself inside-out to show a new face each time. It is this repetition, this reimplication which moves sound forward, pushing the music along, as though squeezing it from a tube. Contracted sound immediately relaxes again, falling back into the noise it rose out of, and allowing other contractions to come to the fore. If sound is squeezed from a tube, then it is being squeezed back through its point of exit, in a dimensional paradox, a Klein bottle, whose unsatisfactory resolution is the paradoxical repetition which sets the implication in motion. The movement of the implicated is an involution, implicating itself again and again, and leaving melody, harmony, direction, and sense in its wake. Sound is this contracted repetition, which contracts the whole of sound differently each time, a seizure which writhes through the body of noise, turning it perpetually inside out like a salted slug.

What takes place in the movement from implication to explication? Which parts of sound are held back, and which parts contracted? Vertically, we contract the relations among pitches as harmony, so we do not so much hear several notes but a chord. Horizontally, we contract harmony as progression; chords are not heard alone, but as a motion, a progress. And this movement is not created by the chords, but produces them as its force, expressing itself through harmony. Chords do not make a progression, but are themselves created by a force which progresses in its headlong push. Noise is the reservoir of force which, in its repeated contractions, forces the flow of music through the musicians, the instruments, the audience. In the greatest performances, performers feel this flow when they 'float', when the sound sweeps through them, revealing that its sense, its movement comes not from within the musician, but from the unconscious implicated, the contraction of the noise of the room, the air, the bodies of the listeners. The performers are straits of contraction, where the flow of force is narrowed, focused, to the point of perception. Though the contracted pitches, rhythms, harmonies, even progressions are themselves explicit – available to consciousness, written on the page of composition – their coherence, their sense, what makes them pass is not explicit in the music, but heard only as this coherence, the drive of the music, the force of expression.[14] We *hear* the implicated as the sense of the music, including its drive, its resolution, its tension, the ominousness of a melody, the profound joy of a prolonged dissonance. Implication is what connects isolated elements to each other, in a creative synergy that produces more than it contracts: isolated pitches become timbre, isolated notes become chords, and isolated chords are perceived as movement, a harmonic progression. There is still a deeper instance, a greater contraction which gathers progression, harmony, rhythm, and timbre into the coherence of a piece. Creativity in music is always a matter of finding a force of movement, a new coherence, a world which produces or explicates an intensity, by drawing on its implicated. What of melody, itself a contraction that operates in a complex relation to the contractions of harmony and rhythm? What of dynamic variation, textural variation, stylistic variation which contracts musico-historical eras; Beethoven lurking in Hindemith, The Velvet Underground moves in Nirvana.

It must be emphasized that implication is not operating behind the scenes or after the fact, but is heard in perception. The contractions of melody, harmony, and rhythm are not just abstract, but are perceived: we hear chords, progressions, the motion of music. We do not construct this movement after the fact, or infer it from elements of the music. The music would never move but would remain a mere sequence of sounds, without a force which produces it as this movement. To hear a chord instead of isolated notes, to hear a progression instead of a bunch of chords, is to hear the implicated. Moreover, the implicated is already heard at the outset; we do not hear a chord progression and then understand it, but we hear its progress already at its beginning. (Hence, Meyer chooses in his earlier work the term 'expectation' instead of 'implication'. He stops using 'expectation' to avoid reference to the cognitive state of the listener, and also to mitigate the difficult idea of simultaneous contradictory expectations. See Meyer, 1973: 114–15 and note.) Expressive music gathers whole worlds into a single measure, and to hear a world in implication is to hear where the music is going. The feeling of tension before the resolution of a harmonic progression is neither an innate characteristic of human perception nor a learned response to patterns of Western music. The tension is real *in the music*, and not just in the listener, but it is implicated, so that the same progression performed without the appropriate expression will fail to induce the same tension in the listener. To bring implication to consciousness is to anticipate in the music, but implication is not the same as anticipation. Although we do form expectations on the basis of what is implicated in the music, it is not primarily what is to come that we hear in implication, but what is already there. 'The implications are inherent in the melody itself, by virtue of its structure; such implications may or may not be picked up by a listener and used to form expectancies on a given hearing' (Sloboda, 1985: 163). We hear an expression, a coherence, or a force, and if these produce expectations, then note that these expectations can always be radically incorrect without denying the implicated as heard. As obscure, the implicated is not conscious or explicit. It is a force which pushes the music forward without specifying where it must go.

This is not to say that musical form is arbitrary and purely conventional, as though the implicated were indifferent to the explicated. Consider, for example, the great role harmonic relations play in Western music: they not only determine the tone or mood, but also regulate the overall structure of many pieces. Melody too implicates what it does not make clear. A motif is a melodic line repeated, but differently each time; and this development calls for further development, another repetition. It is as though the implicated motion of the melody were unfinished, its momentum not yet exhausted. Nowhere is it more true than in music that repetition is never a repetition of the same but always of the different. Theme and variations are the rule. Rhythm and timbre are rich with implication, each masking characters whose exposition is the motion of the music, but is only accomplished in the change of timbre, the variation of rhythm. Even long sections of music, an entire movement perhaps, delimit what they implicate. Sonata form is based on these grand implications, which give rise to the expectations established and satisfied in the sonata.[15]

The notion of implication risks misunderstanding if it is thought in terms of expectation or other phenomena of consciousness. Though Meyer is quite correct that we already hear in the music what is not yet played, he construes this implication on the model of the clear and distinct. For Meyer, the implicated is just like the explicated – comprising all the specificity of melody, rhythm, and harmony – except that it exists only in the mind or expectations of the listener. On the contrary, the implicated is not contracted, or is not explicated in being contracted, and its vagueness or obscurity is not a matter of epistemological limitation. What is implicated is not an obscure version of the music yet to come, not a specific direction for the music to take, nor even a bunch of possible directions. Implication does not gather within it the specific vibrations which will be expressed as variations in air pressure. Rather, the implicated is obscure by its nature, incorporating not so much the clarity of sound waves as the singularity of events, historical events, musical events, masking within it affect apart from object and percept without subject. The implicated contracts noise, an entire history of sound, but the contracted events, percepts and affects, are still inarticulate, too relaxed to be clear. They are singular but not specific. Unlike expectation, implication does not specify the resolution, the harmonic progression, the melodic continuation, though it does establish the realm from which possibilities for these specifics can be drawn. In contracting noise to the point of clarity, implication brings close to the surface some of the depth of noise, powering the music while focusing the next contraction, the next repetition. If implication creates expectations, this is only so that the unexpected may also result.

When the relative clarity of a contraction rises out of the obscure implicated, the implicated changes its nature. The obscure is not just made clear, as though it had been clear in itself all along. Something must be lost for the obscure to become clear, and what is lost is the difference which the implicated holds within it and which gives force to the implicated. Implicated difference can only serve as the reservoir of sense while it is obscure; once it is crossed or cancelled in the contraction it loses its potential. Explication crosses this difference by moving from one air pressure to another, from high to low and back, which exhausts the difference that forces the sound forward. Difference expends its potential when the implicated is mapped into this linear motion, a two-dimensional function of pressure over time.[16] Only an exhausted difference is clear, for a difference still held within cannot be circumscribed, it cannot be perceived as a whole, but only obscurely, in bits and pieces, the whiff of a percept, the hint of an affect. Explication, which crosses or cancels difference in its movement, is the clarity of a pitch, the specificity of a meter, and the percepts and affects implicated in this clarity can never rise all the way to the surface.

The performer's challenge is to explicate just enough in order to implicate according to the demands of the music, as well as other demands of the audience, the room, the instrument. Performance requires a sensitivity to the whole situation, to the event of performance, to the entire history of sound implicated in noise, in order to coax from this noise just the right contractions. The performer plays her instrument, she plays the music, but in so doing she also plays the noise. She uses her instrument to play the noise, shaping it, contracting it as demanded by the musical material, but also by the noise itself. The implicative possibilities will always be specific to the venue, to the audience, to the event, and though performances of the same piece may elicit similar feelings, they never really implicate the same world, for each is singular. To explicate just enough means to leave just enough implicated, to draw the implicated to the verge of clarity, while letting it also extend back into the noise from which it is contracted. *Expression* is this ethics of implication, a question of finding the right balance, of explicating just enough, so as to tease the implicated depth into perception, to make the unhearable heard. 'The ethics of intensive quantities has only two principles: affirm even the lowest, do not explicate oneself (too much)' (Deleuze, 1994: 244).

The traditional aesthetics of performance locate the performer's challenge in the need to respect the composition as written, while playing it 'with feeling'. The musician must 'modulate' the score. It is not enough to play the correct notes; a great performance moulds something new out of the same old notes, choosing just the right passages of crescendo and diminuendo, ritardando and accelerando, legato and staccato, in order to implicate a different world, bringing as yet unheard percepts and affects to perception. Of course the subtleties of expression only really begin where the possibility of appropriate notation ends, so this musical terminology is too gross. Expression can only be expressed, but never made entirely clear, for it is precisely a matter of the correct balance of clear and obscure. Where a performance explicates too much, it sounds wooden, sterile, robotic. (Computers, which are at present mostly incapable of implication, generally make poor music, and, though digital sound synthesis has made a significant mark on modern music production, the current rage in electronic music is the revival of analogue synthesizers, with their quirky but 'full' sound. Modern digital synthesizers routinely attempt to reproduce the 'sound of analogue'.)[17] A performance which implicates too much allows the music to be overcome by the expression, so nothing becomes clear, and the audience hears nothing but a muddied implication, an obscure depth pierced by only the murkiest light. Too much implication doesn't draw the implicated into perception, but leaves the unhearable unheard, and so offers only confused percepts and inarticulate affects. Sometimes an overwhelming implication results in poor technical performance, and the clarity of the score is marred by mistakes. At its limit, the imbalance of implication brings the depths surging to the surface, but without exhausting their force of difference, so that musical performance

183

manifests the raw power of implication, the implicated history of sound brought to action, and the music crosses a threshold where it joins other revolutions, leaving its unique form and matter behind. In this case, the musicians may destroy their instruments, or the stage, the hall, or even themselves, for the implicated difference is a madness, and bringing it to perception always risks a loss of control, in which the implication gathers up even the performer in its violent expression of difference. Finally, music becomes revolution, and the musicians play the world as their instrument, contracting not just sound, but matter into new configurations, violently shaping not just percepts and affects, but also subjects and objects, bringing a world to life.

Given the subtle balance demanded by the ethics of implication, it is not surprising that the CD should lack some expressive potential. If noise contracted as implication is what holds a piece together, what gives it its force and pushes it forward, then the preservation of this noise is paramount in relaying expression. Or, at least, the right kind of noise must be recorded and played back, for expression demands that the noise and the sound suit each other. It is only the connection of the explicated to the implicated, the implication which repeats differently each time that provides a thread throughout the piece, a structure which weaves together any dissonance, no matter how fragile. But the subtleties of noise extend even to those highest frequencies which the CD does not capture. Indeed, the CD is designed not to capture noise, but to focus exclusively on signal, the explicated of sound, the clear and precise, so that the lowest resolution components of a signal, the noise which is modulated by the signal, are left out. Finally, the introduction of artefacts through jitter disrupts the underlying consistency of the noise, giving it a new character, 'digital' noise, which may not be suited to the music. If the performers are playing the noise, if expression is a matter of a sensitivity to the implicated, then a failure to preserve the character of this noise will necessarily also be a failure to capture the expression of the music. The result would sound like a loss of coherence, a lack of pace, a feeling that the musicians were disconnected; the music would no longer push forward, or would stop making sense. At its extreme, the loss of expression would sound sterile or cold. Implication – which the performer manipulates unconsciously, creating a sostenuto or a vibrato in response to or in concert with the sound in the hall on that day, choosing her contractions according to the ambient noise – this implication is specific to the event, and is easily lost in any reproduction, but especially one which doesn't heed noise. The CD may accurately reproduce an E♭ or a D#, but in a performance, the notes are not just E♭ but this particular E♭, which is contracted along with the implicated out of a depth whose singularity includes all the specificity of the hall, the audience, and even the stars. Musical expression is about capturing worlds, fitting together the intensive world of depth and the extended world of the performance, but the CD captures notes and durations, while ignoring the implicated difference to which these contractions are still connected.

184

This is enough to debunk the whole myth of the absolute sound, for expressive music is never the same thing twice. One should not ask of a recording that it recreate the experience of live music, but that it create new expressions, that it involve the listener in a new world. And this is only possible through an accord with the listening context, a sensitivity to the environment, including not just the space, but also the listening event. Some recordings and some equipment may demonstrate this sensitivity better than others, and perhaps the 'noise of analogue' meshes better with much music than does the 'noise of digital'. But there will still be contexts for any recording when it just does not sound right. Expression is a delicate balance between implication and explication, a mixture of the clear and the obscure. If the absolute sound is a matter of repetition, the repetition of the musical event, then we should look not so much to fidelity, which is only ever an objective standard, but to the implicated, which repeats entire events in expression. One climbs a mountain listening to Beethoven in one's living room, one is drunk to the point of sickness with Nick Cave. Though there are no sore legs or nasty mess to clean up afterwards, these events are real, if implicated. We *hear* them in the music, differently each time. The idea is to climb a new mountain, to find a new intoxication. The reproduction of sound is not a matter of physics, but of affect and percept. Expression exceeds fidelity, so hold on to your LPs.

## Notes

1 A journal for the critique and promotion of high-fidelity music reproduction and its associated equipment.

2 For example, 'We try to discourage our staff of reviewers from paying much (if any) heed to other publications since their work, lacking an absolute or any other editorial "philosophy", cannot be worth a close study' (Pearson, 1996).

3 Other characteristics of the wave also contribute, to a lesser degree, to the perception of pitch.

4 Technically, the process wherein one wave modifies another wave is called modulation.

5 If the original wave is described by a function, then a Fourier series – the specific series of sine waves of various amplitudes and frequencies corresponding to a given wave – can be generated mathematically. The Dirichelet condition qualifies this claim: the original wave must not be fractal, the amount of variation in any given interval of the wave must be below some finite limit.

6 Presumably, stereo equipment magazine writers believe unequivocally that trees *do* make noises when they fall in forests with no one around to hear them!

7 Reviewers sometimes describe the character of a recording or piece of equipment by pointing to a location in the hall: 'the sound of the Sigma 6 digital-audio converter was forward, placing the listener in row three'.

8 David Denby relates the story of being transfixed by an AM broadcast over a transistor radio of an old scratchy recording of Caruso's voice (Denby, 1996: 64). Some audiophiles have noted with surprise that music often sounds really good on the relatively poor stereos in their cars.

9 This anti-objectivism is prompted, in part, by the fear that the entire industry of audio equipment review could be supplanted by mechanical devices to judge

accuracy. The audiophile press is profoundly distrustful of equipment specifications and measurements.

10 CDs have a sampling frequency of 44.1 kHz. This means that in theory, they can record sounds up to 22 kHz, but to be safe, engineers generally filter out frequencies above 20 kHz.

11 Ironically, even the industry itself is now beginning to criticize the limitations of the CD, primarily to pave the way for the next music storage format, the DVD. One application of the increased storage capacity of DVD is to store sound recorded at a much higher sampling rate, and at a greater resolution. Consumers must be convinced that what they currently have is inadequate, if they are to buy the new format.

12 Equicentral, for contraction articulates or separates as much as it draws together.

13 Those who have experienced the best ensemble performance will recall how the band becomes one instrument, a music machine. Bill Evans's trio is noted for such a meld.

14 Leonard Meyer, who writes about the perception of music, recognizes that 'understanding implicative relationships is a complex and subtle cognitive activity. And it is an activity of our whole being, not just that artificial abstraction, the mind. The many facets of the human nervous system, physiological changes and adjustments, motor behaviour and the like, are all involved' (Meyer, 1973: 113).

15 Hindemith identifies compositional genius with the ability to envision a piece in its totality beforehand, or to provide an 'ultimate congruence', while noting that this vision of a complete musical form, 'illuminated in the mind's eye as if by a flash of lightning' has not the clarity of specific notes, but the obscurity of an implicated totality. (From Paul Hindemith, *A Composer's World: Horizons and Limitations*, qtd. in Sloboda, 1985: 120.)

16 There is a third diminished dimension, that of the difference between two listeners or between the two ears of one listener.

17 The 'lo-fi', pro-analogue phenomenon is so pervasive as to have taken over the rock music industry. The senior vice president of artists at Columbia Records notes, 'Tape hiss, guitar-amp noise, low-level garbage. Five years ago, we would have cleaned all that up. But today, the prevailing wisdom is to go lo-fi and let that noise become part of the music'. This is in the service of trying to 'capture a less digital sound' and goes hand-in-hand with embracing 'incidental noise and incorporat[ing] it into the mix to achieve a *heightened sense of reality*' (Chun, 1995: 36; my emphasis).

# References

Chun, René (1995) 'Fleeing Cold Perfection For Lovable Lo-Fi Sound', *New York Times*, 8 January: I: 33, 36.

Deleuze, Gilles (1994) *Difference and Repetition*, trans. Paul Patton, New York: Columbia University Press.

Denby, David (1996) 'My Problem with Perfection', *The New Yorker*, 26 August–2 September: 64–83.

Meyer, Leonard (1973) *Explaining Music: Essays and Explorations*, Chicago: University of Chicago Press.

Oohashi, Tsutomu, Emi Nishina, Norie Kawai, Yoshitaka Fuwamoto, and Hiroshi Imai (1991) 'High Frequency Sound Above the Audible Range Affects Brain Electric Activity and Sound Perception', presentation at the 91st AES Convention, New

York, Audio Engineering Society. Full text also available at <http://datura.cerl. uiuc.edu/sigsound/Msg1994-01-13-11-54-01.txt>

Pearson, Harry (1996) 'HP's Place', *The Absolute Sound*, at <http://www.absolute-sound.com/hpsplace.html> (This web site is now defunct, but the opinions quoted are strewn throughout the printed magazine itself.)

Sloboda, John (1985) *The Musical Mind: The Cognitive Psychology of Music*, New York: Oxford University Press.

Young, Neil (1992) 'Digital is a Huge Rip-Off', *The Absolute Sound* 17(81): 12. Originally appeared in *Guitar Player*.

# 13

# PUTTING THE VIRTUAL
# BACK INTO VR

*Andrew Murphie*

when the possible destroys the virtual, when substance smothers
the event, the role of a living art (or the art of life) is to reestab-
lish the equilibrium

(Lévy, 1998: 186)

## Navigating the world or the world as navigator?

I will suggest here that although there is now a common practice of associating virtual reality (VR) with the theatre as a form of representation with
stories, plots and characters, VR actually has more in common with performance (and here I mean performance art or ritual rather than the
conventional theatre), music and the visual arts. This is because what we could
call the 'classical' theatre establishes itself pretty much along conventional
lines, within pre-ordained forms of representation. It defers to the past. Performance art and ritual are about transformation and variation, about
investigating the unknown and producing the new.[1] Virtual reality's common-
ality with performance and art will therefore not be taken as its mimetic
qualities – its 'representation of an action',[2] so much as its qualities of modulation; its realization of the 'objectile', where an *object* is transformed into an
*event* of 'continuous variation' (Deleuze, 1993: 19). Virtual reality will be
discussed here in a way which is only slightly concerned with its current,
specific technological form (that is, for example, a helmet, glove, and a three-
dimensional, digitally produced, navigable world). I am more interested in VR
as a more general emergent series of cultural phenomena – a *machinic phylum*.
In this latter context, technological developments such as hypertext, the
Internet, and the World Wide Web can be seen as the first flowerings of a
'virtual age' (Stone, 1995: 17). The attempt here will be neither to valorize this
age, nor to condemn it.[3] Rather it is to seek out its characteristics and *the
modulation of the notion of modulation* it performs; the way in which, as a
concept, VR allows us to modulate our transformation of objects into objectiles, to shift the gears on the thresholds of perception, operation, and
expression more powerfully than ever before.

How then can we understand VR's expressions and modulations? The work of Deleuze and Guattari has provided one of the key tools of analysis in this area. For a start, as Stuart Moulthrop argues, in a summary of some of the more extreme of these analyses as regards hypertext, virtual media *can* offer a kind of dream of Deleuze–Guattarian 'smooth voyaging'[4] in a literalization of the 'sort of intertextual play [that] has been the preserve of poststructuralist critics like Hélène Cixous and Jacques Derrida, or postmodern novelists like Kathy Acker and Thomas Pynchon'.[5] In short, virtual media offer a kind of 'textual promiscuity' as a 'regular feature of ... cultural systems' (1994: 305). Moulthrop himself, however, sees little inherently liberating about all this, writing that it may be 'more delusion than Deleuzean' (306). In a much more precise reading of Deleuze and Guattari than those such as Nick Land (1992), Moulthrop warns against both 'technonarcissism' (1994: 309), and the 'misleading possibilities for multiple discourse' (308). Moulthrop further points out that, for Deleuze and Guattari, 'the dyad of smooth/striated represents not a dialectic but a continuum' (316).[6] From my own point of view, this means that it is not a matter of reconstituting Moulthrop's suspiciously contaminated smooth space. Instead, it is a matter of reinserting the play of smooth space into the inevitable 'continuum' of smooth and striated space. Only then can we approach the cautious optimism of Gregory Ulmer (1989), Pierre Lévy (1998), and others in regards to new media. Or even approach an ethics along the lines of Foucault's 'passion'; breaking up the system from within, and operating as an individual 'electric or magnetic field', not within 'persons or identities' (Deleuze, 1995: 93), or trademarks, that would totally striate such a field. In other words, it is a matter of evaluating actual and potential expressions in terms of operations, of the manner of living implied, rather than of the return of absolute values and properties to their owner, the subject.

With this in mind, then, an evaluation will be made of VR on the basis of its *operations* first – what it *does*, rather than whether it is inherently good or bad. In this, I am not so much interested in VR as a form of representation of reality as an *expression* of it. In any case, there is no doubt that VR, as yet, provides a very poor representation of reality and may, in the foreseeable future at least, not reach the degree of high-fidelity reproduction of reality that we already associate with older media such as television. Nevertheless, the high-fidelity reproduction of the world is not necessary to an expression of it, and there can be no doubt that VR, as with everything else in the world, expresses the world in a particular fashion.[7]

I have already begun to signal that this expression is complicated by the fact that VR as an expressing 'entity' can be considered in at least three different registers to be three different things. The first, and only the first, of these registers is that which is usually discussed – VR as a particular series of technologies. By and large, these occur in the form of a computer mediated space which combines various perceptual *mechanisms* and systems with operational *systems* (flight, weapons control, movement through VR space, etc.). The effect is both that one is immersed in a computer generated world, and that sometimes, through that immersion, one is able to operate more effectively in the world to which such technologies are linked. Such technologies include the now ubiquitous helmet-and-glove, Myron Krueger's 'Artificial Reality', in which the whole space is made interactive and the body itself is not so encumbered with technical apparatus, or, more generally, such technologies as flight simulators, computerized flight-control systems or video-guided missiles. All of these *express* a certain relation to the real, even if its representation is fuzzy or 'inaccurate'. In fact, often the fuzziness or inaccuracy is part of its expression of reality. The clearest example is the missile guidance system or cockpit which simplifies representational detail deliberately in order to express itself more effectively (and, at times, more maliciously) within the world. In these cases, less representational accuracy makes for more ballistic accuracy. Having discussed these technical aspects broadly, in what follows I will not cover the technical details any more than I need to.[8]

The second of the registers in which VR can be considered is a broadening of the first. This involves a consideration of the way in which, through a series of new media technologies, the line between the 'virtual' and the 'real' is generally blurred within communication systems (although, of course, it could be argued that the telephone has already accomplished this blurring). This occurs not just within the first register of what we could consider to be recognizably VR technology, which itself involves at the least a form of communication between body and machine, but in the broader arena of what Rebecca Coyle (1993: 162) has labelled 'meta-media', which would here include VR technology, the Internet, or cyberspace as a whole. These new meta-media, considered in themselves, are still only new *technical* systems, and neither the first nor the second register of Virtual Reality, in themselves, explain exactly why such technical systems or even larger arenas facilitated by these broader meta-media have arisen as they have and when they have.[9] As Heidegger has noted so famously, there is nothing technological about technology (1977: 4). Even considered *as* technologies, however, the meta-media seem to overwhelm our normal attempts to deal with them purely technologically. We are forced to *think* through them before we can make the next move. As Coyle notes, the 'reality' of the meta-media such as VR may well be determined 'philosophically rather than identified as a discrete area of communications practice'. She further notes the extreme importance of the 'ethical component of this philosophy' (1993: 162). This philosophical and ethical grasping is complicated by the way in which 'reality' and the virtual are so obviously blurred in VR. Coyle also quotes Brenda Laurel, who in 1991[10] said that, despite 'the word "virtual"' being 'okay ... the use of the word "reality" in the singular belies a certain cultural bias' (162–3).

In the following section I shall attempt to give the beginnings of a philosophy from a Deleuze–Guattarian perspective which describes how it is that the virtual is expressed in contemporary technological and cultural developments, and how this expression relates interactively to a reality which is certainly not singular. I shall argue that 'virtual' and 'reality' are not, as Laurel is cited by Coyle (1993: 162) as suggesting, 'oxymoronic' terms, but rather inter-active.[11] Furthermore, I shall argue that related areas such as metaphysics and physics are also – like the virtual and the actual – highly, mutually implicated. In this I shall write of a third register in which Virtual Reality can be discussed, one that encompasses the first and the second and, in fact, gives them their potential. This is, of course, the full Deleuze–Guattarian 'machinic', where machines are considered as separate from technologies and operate, autopoietically, as a series of 'diagrams' through both virtual tenden-cies and shifts in actual states of affairs.[12] I shall argue that VR technologies arise, and will continue to arise, in any number of previously *unthought* actual-izations. This is because there has been a profound series of shifts within the broader machinic which produces these 'technologies', 'us', and our thoughts about both. These shifts occur in both the virtual and actual, and are *shifts as regards the virtual itself*. To sum this up, because of these shifts in the machinic, perceptual, and operational, modulation is no longer a filter for a stable world but is applied to modulation itself, so that everything is taken up within this modulation of modulation. (For example, we used to watch television programmes. Now more and more we zap *between* channels, and this zapping forms a conscious activity in itself.[13] And all this is before one begins to consider various forms of more direct manipulations of screen content.) The threshold of perception, previously the unseen frame for a perceived 'stable' world, now frames itself, draws attention to itself as unstable and therefore as something that can be *operated* through like any other machine. Finally, the virtual flowers, not in its 'unreality' or transcendence, but in its immanent reality, also making it something through which we can operate.

In this I diverge slightly from the other major (seemingly[14]) Deleuze–Guattarian influenced assessment of the virtual that I am aware of, namely Pierre Lévy's extensive discussion in *Becoming Virtual* (1998). This is, perhaps, more a matter of bifurcation than disagreement. Lévy argues for an increased 'virtualization' (26–7) of the world, and gives extensive examples of this, from economics to the arts. Lévy, whose earlier work is used in Guattari's later formulations of the machinic (Guattari, 1995: 8), cautiously and optimistically welcomes what he sees as the potential consequence of the increased virtual-ization, attempting to 'follow some of my contemporaries in their attempt to live without fear and resentment' (Lévy, 1998: 184). He gives a clear account of the role of the virtual and the actual, although it is at times difficult to distinguish between the machinic and technological registers of these. He is also concerned, as quoted at the beginning of this article, with conserving the virtual against the reign of the possible. Although, of course, there is obviously much to agree with here, I am taking a different, though not necessarily incompatible path. Obviously, though I do not take technological advances as indicative of some disaster, neither do I take them as indicative of advance, particularly, in themselves, as an advance in the area of the virtual. This does not necessarily mean, of course, that *at times* they may not indicate such an 'advance', and arguments such as Lévy's can only increase the likelihood of more ethical uses of technology.[15] I, however, am arguing for a different flowering of the virtual, not in its *increase* or *evolution*, but in the passion and attention accorded to its simple shifting existence. I argue that it is not a 'virtualization' of the world that has increased, but our ability to operate the virtual. What is more, this increased ability to operate the virtual is by no means immediately ethically positive. It is not so until we answer the question, each time specifically, of what manner of living it implies, of what passions can break up the trademarks we increasingly live through every time we boot up.

## Virtual reality and the threshold of perception

> I might as well take the period that follows the mechanical age and call it the virtual age … virtual because the accustomed grounding of social interaction in the physical facticity of human bodies is changing.
>
> (Stone, 1995: 17)

Virtual reality expresses what might be called *the shock of the real immanence of the metaphysical*. We thought that the metaphysical lay 'beyond' us. Now we find it sticking to anything and everything and pushing us around. VR brings to an end the regimes of separation which would, through the operation of certain representations, deny the *interactive* reality of the virtual and actual in favour of a simple facticity of *stable* bodies and *fixed* states of affairs. Yet we are only at the beginning of the end of these regimes. No doubt VR still awaits its own Bazin or Kracauer who, as with their theorization of film, would attempt to describe not the 'bizarre' or 'unreal' nature of VR but the way in which the real is *expressed* within it in a distinct fashion.[16] Here I will be content merely with some introductory remarks, and with a use of Deleuze's discussion of the virtual in *The Fold* (1993) and *Difference and Repetition* (1994) to begin to discuss what it is that is expressed in VR. Again, I shall not extensively discuss VR as a form of representation except as a way of leading into the alternatives.

There can be no doubt that VR can be used to tell stories, to extend subjectivities, or to imitate an action, but none of these are operations exclusive to VR. Moreover, theoretically at least, like abstract painting or much modern music, VR could just present 'noise' without stories, or diagrams without beginnings, middles, and ends. In addition, there is certainly something suspicious about Capital's potential ability to use VR to extend human subjectification through the imitation of an action into areas such as home banking and shopping.[17] It comes as no surprise, for example, that William Gibson's version of cyberspace is ruled largely by banks and renegade cowboys. I have elsewhere criticized the treatment of technology on the basis of the imitation of an action (Murphie, 1996). Nevertheless, it should be reiterated here that even mimesis is never just representation according to Deleuze. It is always first and foremost a form of production. This productive aspect to representation is also clearly described in Michael Taussig's book, *Mimesis and Alterity* (1993). For Taussig mimesis always involves contact. It produces changes in relations, and is therefore a tool or weapon, used to gain control. Espen Aarseth points out, with regard to the context of the hypertext, that the main goal of designers such as Brenda Laurel, rather than transparent access, is to 'control what they call the plot' (Aarseth, 1994: 75). Here the system develops tight operational structures in which 'the situations and actions would be carefully orchestrated to fit its model of appropriate drama' (75). This is, in essence, as is Greek tragedy, not as far from a 'shoot-em-up and win' video game as one might like to think. It is certainly a long way from those systems that Aarseth calls 'indeterminate cybertexts'. Mimesis always involves some sort of control. When imposed by the system itself it always involves stratification and subjectification within that system as a form of control. As Aarseth writes of Laurel and similar theorists, 'it is hard not to see the potential for conflict between the user and this *deus in machina*' (75).

How can we then conceive of VR outside of mimesis? If it does not, despite the hype about representation, merely represent the real, or *even* represent it effectively,[18] what does it do? What does it create? What does it indicate? Does VR express a shift away from an interest in representation to *operation*, as I have suggested? If this is so, what are the consequences for any notion of 'real*ism*', if the real and the virtual are in co-extension, or when a fundamental assumption of new machines is that the virtual operates on the real, as in VR? To what 'unreal' would such a realism be opposed?

The last of these questions is no longer answerable. 'Everything is real', especially VR. Or real 'enough'. VR creates a totality which (potentially) both overwhelms present perceptive thresholds and creates, rather than represents, a 'total *enough* world' within the world(s) at large. VR has obviously real effects on those worlds with which it interacts. It presents humanity with the possibility of the modulations of the virtual, previously operating below the general threshold of perception, *being seen* to overtake and disrupt the more 'solid' notions of our social existence. In this, it instils a crisis in our normal, if false, dichotomy between reality and representation.

How then, again, can we approach VR? Firstly, it is necessary to take a machinic approach, as VR, as always, is a machine and the product of a machine *before* it is a technology.[19] As such it possesses a concept that traverses and *works* its plan(e). In this, it is important to remember that the 'concept is not defined by an attribute, but by predicates-as-events' (Deleuze, 1993: 42). I would suggest that the 'predicate-as-event' of VR is *the modulation of modulation*.

VR, however, also does possess a machinic phylum[20] or technological lineage, which I would define as *those machines which interact across different thresholds of perception* so as to, first, draw attention to them, and, second, allow participation with, or operation through, them. For example, in VR, territorial thresholds can be modulated by both the telecommunications system globally (one can operate at great distances – distance itself, large or small, is modulated), and the computer-body network locally (one can have access to the minute perceptions both of one's own body and of the computer in a manageable fashion). Information thresholds are crossed by the computer chip. Body/machine thresholds are crossed by augmented perceptual apparatuses, such as stereoscopic vision or even just the now common computer interface. Representation/'reality' thresholds are crossed by the affect and the percept operating in one joined represented/real space. In all these, VR provides a massive amplification of potentiality and variation in the realm of the modulation of modulation itself. The threshold of perception is itself subject to a massive broadening of its own limits. In short, we are now brought to the knowledge of the *power* of modulation.

## Extracting the world from the world

Of course, it is the amplification, control, and the self-reflexivity of the virtual in VR that is at issue here, not the question of its originality. The technologies involved here in some ways merely actualize, in a new formal series, an older virtual machine, which could be called the world. For Deleuze, following Leibniz, the world *is* virtual, has always been, and this virtuality includes the whole world (Deleuze, 1993: 51). The world is an infinite series (of folds or differentials) that permutates within extrinsic limits. For Deleuze, 'the word "virtual" … designates the unilateral character of inclusion' (1993: 52). This leads to the Leibnizian concept of an individual monad, each of which contains the whole world. This can be understood easily in reference to VR, where the technology itself is based upon an entire scientific understanding of extrinsic differentials of perception. VR is a matter of extracting the optimal degree of clear perception which effectuates the actual knowledge of a potential entire world (contained in cyberspace, the matrix, Internet … a simple disk or CD-ROM). The world of VR is virtual, then, in the sense that 'virtually', all the world is already there. Yet the individual in cyberspace has a perception which resonates with some of that world clearly, and other parts of that world less clearly. Some images in Gibson's novels of the 'matrix' give an adequate expression of this simultaneously clear and fuzzy perception of cyberspace. Gibson himself, as cited by Scott Bukatman, suggests that this may be because he acknowledges that cyberspace is as much about unconscious formations as conscious. Bukatman quotes Gibson and writes about 'what machines do with us, and how wholly unconscious this process has been, is, and will be' (Bukatman, 1993: 644).[21]

This is to question what humanity, consciously or unconsciously, is crucially able to *extract* from the machinic world by operating through a perception of it. Deleuze writes in this regard that 'inclusion is virtual, Leibniz specifies, because it has to be extracted, and because the predicate is included in the subject only "under a certain power"' (Deleuze, 1993: 52). The degree of perception, provided by the threshold between the clear and the 'fuzzy', is the *power* under which the virtual world can be extracted. On a simple level, the perceptive extraction of the world is a matter of practices, of ethics, and since it is about affording perception it is also about art – predicated upon the creation of percepts and affects. This predication is not 'an attribution' but an ' "execution", an act, a movement, a change, and not the state' (53). In other words it is an event.

Perception itself is not representation, nor is it even the more complex mimesis of an action. It is much closer to what we have come to separate from the classical theatre as performance art (with 'real' time, pain, pleasure, etc.) in its eventuality, as action, as event. For Deleuze, this event is the basis of conception. *Conceptions* of the world are also *per*ceptions of it and concurrently forms of *production* which execute the extraction of clear *relations* within it. There is a sense, for Deleuze, then, in which relations are events and events are relations (1993: 52). There are also relations within relations and events within events. For example, the world itself is a broad event/relation and all actions, perceptions within it are also events/relations within that broader event/relation. Therefore the 'world must be included in every subject as a basis from which each one extracts the manners that correspond to its point of view' (1993: 53).

Yet it is only the recent beginnings of the production of *concepts, affects* and *percepts* to do with this specific complexity that brings about the virtual age. Again it is VR that makes this perfectly clear, as a world of relations in which individuals may literally contain the whole world virtually (on disk or even in the simplest of interactive software, such as Netscape, for example) but must relate to it in different ways to extract any smaller event. This is not only a question of being able to tell stories well,[22] although it might be. It is also a question of which connections can be made, of the possibility *of* relation, of the possibility of allowing new events to occur and to interconnect with each other.

Once again, then, the aspect of VR that seems to characterize it as different from some other experiences is not the technology but its attitude to perception, not as a solid or stable representation but as a relation to an event. VR designers accept, with Deleuze, that:

> nothing authorizes to conclude in favor of the presence of a body that might be ours, or the existence of the body that would have happened to affect it. There exists only what is perceived.
>
> (Deleuze, 1993: 94)

It is the acceptance of the pre-eminence of this perception that characterizes the way in which VR opens up the world of the virtual to us. In short, by accepting the virtual as part of the real, the virtual can be *generally* perceived and one can participate in relations/events.

There are two aspects to this perception as conceptualized in *The Fold*. The first aspect is the above mentioned, that *perception is affective*. When one considers the materiality of sound vibrating the ear canal, the play of light on the retina, the movement of signals through the central nervous system, this is something which seems obvious. But there is more to it than this. Affect is not uni-directional. It is an exchange of deterritorialized quanta – an exchange that changes the entire continuum of vibrating matter that partici- pates in this exchange. Perception for Deleuze's Leibniz was not a matter of a subject 'perceiving' an object. Perception, instead, 'evokes a vibration gathered by a receptive organ' (Deleuze, 1993: 95). If we feel the pain of a needle dug into the flesh, perception 'does not represent the needle' but the awakening of tendencies in 'thousands of minute movements or throbs that irradiate in the flesh' (1993: 95). If there is a passage or movement as a signal here, this is a signal that both changes the fields through which it has passage, and a signal which in turn depends upon the field through which it moves. The signal as vibration and the field as vibration are inseparable. These perceptions are then 'objectiles', which were defined earlier in this essay as objects (now flows of or through matter) transformed into events of 'continuous variation' (1993: 19). A simple way of putting all this is that pleasure and pain, along with other perceptions, have an existence themselves, as modulating objectiles, which interact with the other objectiles that participate in the plane of variation such events create. For Deleuze's Leibniz this is an *interaction* of matter – a convergent series of vibrations that, as with any grouping of vibrations can make for a kind of harmony or disharmony. We might define harmony here as pleasure and disharmony as pain, although these two are also interactive. We are familiar with this both in the more obvious realm of the senses, and, as well as in the explorations of twentieth-century music. Pleasure and pain, harmony and disharmony are interactive themselves, and often fold over into each other. The broader point here is again that, as in the case of the pain experienced when a needle digs into the flesh, this 'pain resembles the move- ment of something pointed that would dig into my flesh in concentric circles' (1993: 95), an objectile or an event of continuous variation. Again, pain is not a 'thing' that resembles a specific object, such as a pin. Neither is it even simply a matter of a fluid representation to the 'thing' as apprehending subject. Perceptions such as pain, as objectiles, have their own existence. In short, pain, in our example:

> does not represent the pin in extension, but resembles molecular movements that it produces in matter. Along with perception, geometry plunges into obscurity. Above all it is the meaning of resemblance that entirely changes: resemblance is equated with what resembles, not with what is resembled. That the perceived resembles matter

means that matter is necessarily produced in conformity with this relation, and not that this relation conforms to a preexisting model.

(Deleuze, 1993: 96)

Perception as interactive process, as with the percept and affect of art, contains more complexity than a simple relation between an object and subject. This is crucial to an understanding of what is happening in VR. With VR, as with all interaction, it is a question of a *series* of interactions *between* that registers, with each affect being regarded as its own processual micro-ecosystem. To put this another way, a becoming resembles only itself. Mimesis, by virtue of its self-reflexivity, acts out its own becoming.

The second aspect of perception is that it has two levels, unconscious and conscious. Unconscious perception consists of minute perceptions, 'being-for the world'. In Spinozan terms this is *affect* on a miniature and immediate level. With every glance our eyes 'capture' millions of percepts. Conscious perception, like VR design, is based upon 'differential relations' (Deleuze, 1993: 94). Conscious perception, rather than perceiving every moment of an affect, every moment of folding, perceives the 'differential' which describes and produces the fold or affect. Our eyes survey thousands of details; we see a 'person'. This 'person' is the product of a 'differential' that operates through the miniature details.

## The virtual *is* difference

'Differential' here is both a mathematical and philosophical term. It refers in mathematics to differential calculus. Here, if $x$ represents a position on a horizontal axis and $y$ on a vertical axis, the figure $dy/dx$ can give the gradient of a curve predicated upon any change of position within these axes, no matter how large or small. The figure $dy/dx$ is thus also a way of describing infinitesimal differences mathematically.[23] This is not, however, quite the use Deleuze wishes to make of the term because this would refuse it 'any ontological ... value' (Deleuze, 1994: 170). For Deleuze, $dx$ is the philosophical mark of a broader differential, 'simultaneously undetermined, determinable and determination ... In short, $dx$ is the Idea ... the "problem" and its being' (171).

Here is the kernel of the theory of what Deleuze calls *different/ciation*. It explains how difference works through two series ($dy$ and $dx$), and how it is undetermined but determining. As Deleuze writes, this is because 'each term exists absolutely only in its relation to the other' (1994: 172). The differential is an expression of the in-between. Ideas are differentials, as is everything virtual (or dynamic). This is why thought always involves an *encounter* with an outside and, although difference is self-genetic, why thought's 'objects', its determinations (or actualizations), are not in themselves genetic. Rather 'the reciprocal synthesis of differential relations' is 'the *source* of the production of real objects' (1994: 173, emphasis added).

Deleuze also builds a theory of power into this notion of differential relations in that they are generative. For Deleuze, 'the differential is pure power, just as the differential relation is a pure element of potentiality' (1994: 175). What Deleuze values in the differential, then, is not that it describes infinitesimal changes that cannot be measured in any other way. Rather it is that it enables an escape from a primary consideration of relations *only through objects considered in their identity*, or through their negation if an identity cannot be found. The symbol $dx$ is therefore opposed to the 'not-A' (170) of philosophy.[24]

Philosophically, then, the differential gives us the beginning of an understanding of the in-itself of difference. This is carried further with the 'differenciator'. It gathers and works difference 'without any mediation whatsoever by the identical, the similar, the analogous or the opposed' (1994: 117). The 'differenciator' is a way of describing the internal dynamics of that process of folding itself. It is an expansion of the notion of the differential which provides a way of understanding the *coherence* of heterogeneous systems and the way in which this allows them to produce or express. All such systems are made dynamic by their relating to other such heterogeneous systems. This produces 'an internal resonance' – a kind of harmony or wave within the coupling – which leads to 'a *forced movement* the amplitude of which exceeds that of the basic series themselves' (1994: 117). Difference produces more difference. As I have noted, however, this difference is also coherent. The differenciator is, therefore, also a way of theorizing the coherence of interactive systems, especially as they produce difference rather than the 'same old story'.

In a subsequent attempt to give a more complete expression of the problematic of difference, Deleuze invents the term 'different/ciator'. The different/ciator exceeds the mathematical use of $dy/dx$ to express *some* of the specific coordinates of this problem at certain moments, of a specific expression of the moment of a gradient of a fold, for example. Deleuze uses the term 'different/ciator' to provide a broader means of understanding the virtual and the actual within a framework of difference as both productive and produced. Here differentiation determines 'the virtual content of an Idea' (1994: 207). Differenciation, on the other hand is 'the actualization of that virtuality into species and distinguished parts'. The latter is always related to the former, as giving so many solutions to a problem (Deleuze, 1994: 207).

The virtual is, then, the realm in which the totality of differential relations coexist. The latter are produced by particular problems set up by interactive sets of heterogeneous series.[25] The actual is the realm in which these are actualized through differenciation into particular differences. The differential comes into existence in the virtual. It operates in both the actual (through differenciation – the production of specific states of affairs) and the virtual (through interaction with other differentials, other heterogeneous series). What we have come, in the present, to call 'Virtual Reality', then, can be seen, at different moments, to present us with *both the virtual and the actual* in the way they have been described here. It is the specific differentials that remain crucial, however, in both the virtual and the actual, as it is the differentials that both produce and operate in the threshold between different virtuals on the one hand, and the virtual and the actualization of its specific cases[26] on the other. The operation of the differentials forms the two parts of difference, namely that of different*iation* and differen*ciation*. Deleuze suggests that to fully describe the 'integrality of the object we require the complex notion of different/*ciation*' (1994: 209). This means that 'every object is double' although it is not the case that the actual resembles the virtual or vice versa (1994: 209). The virtual, as a necessary part of the object, is therefore absolutely real, but this is in the sense of a reality which is constantly different/*c*iated and produced as different/*c*iated.

For an understanding of perception, different/*c*iation is crucial. It allows for a notion of perception based upon difference and change rather than upon identity and stasis. For example, as discussed, the differential creates a kind of threshold between molecular, unconscious perceptions and Molar, conscious perceptions. These two levels of perception, unconscious and conscious, though thoroughly interdependent, are quite different operations which form two heterogeneous series. Yet there are no absolutes. What might provide a heterogeneous series of minute perceptions for a cell of the body might provide a differential for a molecule in that cell. What provides a moment of perception for a muscle might be the result of a differential of many cells' heterogeneous, minute perceptions.

The implication of this is as follows. *That which we normally see as perception, perhaps of the 'same' or the 'identical' is in fact a differential operation at the threshold between macro- and micro-perceptions*, which extracts a 'clear zone of perception from minute, obscure perceptions' (Deleuze, 1993: 96). It is this very under-standing of perception which forms the basis of VR – namely that *one does not have to reproduce an exact representation of reality in order to make reality work, one just needs to provide the broader differential relations between heterogeneous series*. Beyond this, however, what Deleuze, through Leibniz, is suggesting here is that *all* perception is based upon this extraction of a clear zone of perception from fuzzy perceptions by a virtual differential. This whole operation itself is now able to be clearly perceived. We now know that we all already live in the virtual as well as the actual. As previously noted, in some ways all VR does is give us the shock of realizing how close the metaphysical is to us. It shows us that the metaphysical inheres within the relations of our bodies. At the deep levels of both virtual and actual, this shock indicates that we are increasingly aware of relations of differ-ence, of the way in which everything seems interconnected and interactive, and at the same time endlessly individuated because everything is a multiplicity.

## The differential relation does not exclude individuation

Individuation – as a process – is the specific series of actualizations of the different/*c*iations of the virtual. As Ideas are *active* – creative as well as created – they are formed between series in differentials as 'problematic or perplexed multiplicities' (Deleuze, 1994: 244). Actualizations are the multiple 'solutions' to these problematics. In other words, they are produced in the way that bodies interact to form new bodies. These bodies are intensifications of relations. In this, 'Intensity is the determinant in the process of actualization. It is intensity which dramatizes' (1994: 243).

The seat of this process is given another account in Deleuze's discussion of Leibniz's monads, although Deleuze (as shall be discussed shortly), at the end of *The Fold*, expresses a desire to turn Leibniz's 'monadology' into a 'nomadology' (1993: 137). For Deleuze's Leibniz, the construction of perception within itself (resemblance with what resembles) explains in part the ability of the monad to be both self-enclosed and to contain the entire world. The monad is like a house with two levels. The upper, the level of the '*soul*', is completely enclosed, and perceives only its own projections on its own interior folds. The lower, more closely identified with *bodies*, has windows, and in a sense opens out onto the world. There is of course, in Deleuze's account, intermingling of body and soul, and of the two levels. This reflects the way in which minute perceptions (of the body) and macro perceptions (of the soul) are dependent upon each other for definition. Here minute perceptions are 'distinct and obscure' while macro perceptions are 'clear and confused'. For Deleuze, in Leibniz's texts, for example the first, though obscure, are the directly expressed and relate to:

> the continuum of differential relations or the unconscious virtual Idea ... all the drops of water in the sea like so many genetic elements with the differential relations, the variations in these relations and the distinctive points they comprise.
>
> (Deleuze, 1994: 253)

If we are covered in insects, or out in the rain, our microperceptions are of hundreds of little bites or drops of rain. This is not what we consciously and clearly feel (panic at the insects? delight at the rain?). What comes to be the coherent 'expressor' of all these, panic or delight, or just the more general 'insects' or 'it is raining' occurs at the macro level. It only becomes clear by virtue of *confusing* the specificities of the micro, virtual or unconscious Idea in favour of a 'whole'. Deleuze relates this to the noise we hear when we hear 'the sea', which 'clearly expresses only certain relations or certain points by virtue of our bodies and a threshold of consciousness which they determine' (1994: 253). Of course, this distinct and obscure/clear and confused relation is very consciously operated on in many new technologies. I have previously noted this as regards VR, but it is equally true of the Internet.

There is, therefore, once again a threshold of perception between 'distinct and obscure' (micro-perception – the unconscious) and 'clear and confused' (macro-perception – the conscious). For Leibniz's monad this is realized in a severing of an inside and an outside, which, as with Baroque architecture, leads to the independence of the 'façade from the inside ... and the autonomy of the interior from the independence of the exterior, but in such conditions that each of the two terms thrusts the other forward' (Deleuze, 1993: 28), as in the differentiating relations of two heterogeneous systems.

Again VR literalizes this for us even in some of its trademarked forms of content and expression. There is a body and technologies, computers, levers, hands on triggers at the 'lower' level. There is a 'closed room' connected to it at an upper level, be that inside a VR helmet with computer-generated projections on its walls and sounds vibrating in its earphones, or the 'blacked out' cockpit of some of the more recent fighter planes.

What defines a monad in terms of perception is the clear zone of perception this whole machine gives it. Though the whole world is present within and available to the monad most of it is not clearly perceived. The remainder is noise. The minute perceptions are there but not dominated by a differential into consciousness. This is, in fact, the aim of, for example, the blacked-out cockpit, that is, to extract the necessary clear perceptions from a very high level of 'noise'. The more general problem in the modern world, one solved by VR, is not one only of perceiving the world accurately but of being able *not* to perceive the world's many perceptual bombardments, of defining an effective upper level to the 'monad'.

Each monad not only defines itself through, but draws its power from, its ability to actualize (in the soul) and realize (in the body) its own clear expression of the world. Another way this is put is that it finds accord or harmony, in the form of a differential, between different vibrations. A monad *expresses* this accord on a virtual *and* an actual level. Or alternatively, by applying a differential, the monad literally folds the world, and in a sense creates both soul and body as a particular fold of that world. Thus the degree to which the monad can realize and actualize itself through its ability to fold through the differential *is* its power. *The folding is the event that creates a form of power.* The body is the fold's realization and the soul its actualization.[27] However, as with the abstract machine and its effectuating machines, neither the soul nor the body should be considered to be the same as the event (Deleuze, 1993: 105).

Following on from this, pain can be considered to be a lack of harmony (the refusal of the differential or the grating of heterogeneous series without a differen*t/ci*ator) and the challenge is to bring harmony out of pain (the creation of acknowledgment of a satisfactory differential, such as, for example, a new concept). Harmony 'explains the correspondence between each soul and the material universe' (Deleuze, 1993: 106).

The more harmony there is, the larger (literally) the zone of clear expression, as harmony is another way of expressing a differential or fold. The ethical task is once again to increase harmony, to increase the clear zone of expression, the expressive power. This is so even in bringing discord into harmony, in producing a harmony of apparent discords. Territorialization on a Major such as the State or Capital, on the other hand, will reduce the clear zone of expression, the expressive power of what can be extracted from the virtual in all the power of its differentials. It can be seen that these ideas relate strongly to Deleuze and Guattari's other ideas about the machinic being interconnective and interactive, about the productive which increases connection and the antiproductive which limits the clear zone of expression or perception which may be extracted from the general noise. More especially, what becomes 'universal harmony' in *The Fold* relates very strongly to Spinoza's spiritual automaton, which can affect and be affected by more and more of the world because of the harmony between ideality and material objects.[28]

As I suggested in the beginning, an Aristotelian-style dramatic model will not necessarily give this ethical impetus. This is at least true of the model of *The Poetics*, with its neat beginnings, middles and ends, especially as interpreted by some theorists such as Laurel this century, who see the 'imitation of an action' as something that neatly separates representation and life, mimesis and production, the copy and the copied. This representative, dramatic model, as used by those such as Laurel, both underlies, and at the same time cannot come to grips with, a general cultural crisis about the status of representation as brought about by such technologies as VR.

What is proposed here is that performance models such as performance art and music – a bringing of harmony without sacrificing the difference inherent to disharmony – provide a much better method of understanding VR's machinic consistency and its potential productions. They enable us to counter-actualize the events and productions of VR.

John Cage, for example, attempted to expand harmony infinitely in his music, by making all 'noise' music simply by shifting the thresholds by which music was perceived. He often told the story of being told by Schoenberg that he had no feeling for harmony, and that he would reach a point in his creative life where he would come up against a wall that he would not be able to break through (Cage, 1990). He decided, since he had dedicated his life to music, that he would keep hitting his head against that wall. Eventually, he found himself thrown back away from that wall and considering the space that lay all around it (that is, around conventional, or even at the time nonconventional, harmony). Towards the end of his life[29] I heard him say that he finally felt that he was finding harmony in his work – something he had not expected since the meeting with Schoenberg. This was during a discussion accompanying the performances (in London) of his *Europeras 3 and 4*, in which 'harmony' consisted of two pianists playing operatic overtures, twelve old 78 rpm record players with operas playing, and several singers singing arias of their choice – all simultaneously, in combinations determined by chance operations! Cage's understanding of harmony here is a new concept of harmony – not the same as previous concepts, a new conglomeration of composites, the allowance of a different/ciator of great magnitude. His conceptions of silence,[30] of interpenetration and unimpededness and so on, enabled him to develop a new process of different/ciation. Going around that wall effectively tore the wall down for him. His new conception of harmony (the concept of silence) broadened his (and our) zone of clear expression immeasurably. And when it is said that he created new concepts, this is meant in precisely the manner described by Deleuze and Guattari by which concepts are created, quoting Leibniz as saying 'I thought I had reached the port; but … I seemed to be cast back again into the open sea' (Deleuze and Guattari, 1994: 22). A new concept throws one to the high seas and also enables walls to be torn down because it can expand the extension of the zone of clear expression so much. According to Deleuze and Guattari, this makes Cage a philosopher as well as an artist because whereas an artist creates percepts and affects (Deleuze and Guattari, 1994: 163), only philosophers can create a concept. To recapitulate, a concept here defines itself by the coherence of 'a finite number of heterogeneous components traversed by a point of absolute survey at infinite speed' (Deleuze and Guattari, 1994: 21). The concept then, like Cage's music, combines a number of components into a kind of philosophical machine which is actual (it is a point) but works at infinite speed like the differential in *The Fold*.

Once again we can conclude, as regards the interactivity of new technologies, that *an ethics of interaction is in interaction itself*. This ethics lies in pursuing interaction beyond its present limits, and sustaining new potentialities of interaction, building new machines, whether they are artistic or philosophical. This is a constant movement of expansion of interactive possibilities. Yet it is not a colonial expansion. It does not constantly search for new territory to submit to a despotic 'interpretation'. Rather it seeks more interactive involvement in the immanent – in the difference at hand. Whether or not VR imitates actions is somewhat inconsequential compared to the ways in which it too involves interaction, expands it, or limits it, what machines it connects with or disrupts. It may be, for example, that the telephone system, if it is more interactive, will always be more exciting than a 3-D narrative when it comes to how we define 'virtual reality'.

## How do we express expression?

Once again, we see that VR, even in the early forms by which we began to become conscious of it, such as elements of Leibniz's philosophy, indicates a *shift in our threshold of perception as regards the threshold of perception itself*. VR involves the sweep of new abstract machines through the world, even more than new technologies (machines of control perhaps but *also* machines leading to different, perhaps broader harmonies – the two are related), of new organizations, new differentials. VR is not there to tell new stories, or even to enhance communications.[31] It is an effectuation of a change in the nature of the perception of the threshold of perception. Understanding VR as *technology* is secondary to understanding its *machinic indices as regards perception*, and perhaps Rheingold (1991) is right to compare it to primitive performances in the Lascaux Caves.

We can take this a little further. Perhaps the reason that VR foregrounds the perception of the threshold of perception is that it expresses the obvious way in which the body and 'soul'[32] need each other *in order to express the world*. In terms of perception there are no differential or macro-perceptions without micro-perceptions. There is no perception inside a helmet or cockpit without the vibrations of the physical world, the hand touching the inside of the glove (or no point to a fighter's weapons if there are no bodies to destroy), or even the synapses and computer connecting in Gibson's novel. VR is not an escape from the body, any more than (probably less than) television. VR is merely reconfiguring the relations between micro- and macro-perceptions, bringing to light the possibility that these relations are subject to change, and that different social machines, different conceptual apparatus may make it possible to have different bodies, different souls, or different zones of clear expression without always having to submit them to a major reterritorialization.

There are at least two possible ways for these relations between macro- and micro-perceptions to be reconfigured which are of relevance to VR. The first is one in which *the body is deterritorialized* – for example its movement's significance is removed from its position in a small space and shifted to a virtual space of any 'size', which is largely perceived through the head (the eyes and the ears) and is therefore a kind of reterritorialization of the body on to the face (Deleuze and Guattari, 1987: 181). This often consists of an enhanced way of *seeing*, of determining *significations*. It is a stratified or 'striated' (479) approach. The second way in which the micro and macroperceptions can be reconfigured is in conceiving of virtual worlds not as enhanced representations in this way but as 'smooth spaces'. In this model, rather than the face, it is the haptic,[33] the use of the whole body which becomes the more important, and more nomadic, means of negotiating the space. It is here that we can, at last, valorize a conception of 'smooth space', not as the anything goes of 'textual promiscuity' but as a political and ethical specificity that engages with the striated by breaking it down. Here, smooth space is not one of organization, 'things' or fixed dimensions. It is:

> directional ... filled by events or haecceities ... a space of affects ... It is haptic rather than optical perception ... materials signal forces and serve as symptoms for them. It is intensive rather than extensive space ... smooth space is occupied by intensities ... The creaking of ice and the song of the sands. Striated space, on the contrary, is canopied by the sky as measure.
>
> (Deleuze and Guattari, 1987: 479)

Of course, both the haptic and the optical are combined at the moment in VR, but it may be that the *domination* of one over the other is a matter of how the politics of VR are configured within general politics of representation or nomadism. It is a choice between the measuring sky and the 'song of the sands'. This is, of course, a choice that must constantly be made and re-made. However, to qualify this, it is not always a matter of the *literal* haptic[34] or optical,[35] as the former can sometimes serve to striate space, while the optical can also reinstate the smooth, 'liberating light and modulating colour, restoring a kind of aerial haptic space' (Deleuze and Guattari, 1987: 479). It is a question of deciding whether smooth or striated space is *presupposed* in the use of the haptic or the optical; of whether the lines followed are abstract or nomadic lines (that Deleuze and Guattari equate with art) that pass 'between' and are 'positively motivated by the smooth space drawn'. (496–7) Or, on the other hand, whether the space of VR going to be subject to 'concrete lines', which are motivated by 'a feeling of anxiety that calls forth striation' (496–7).

The fact that VR is partially a representational technology enabling an 'image-ining' of a constructed world – even if this is in a quite remarkable way – is absolutely secondary to these considerations of the smooth and the striated in the formations of virtual space. On the other hand, to consider VR primarily as a representational technology is to summon up striation and anxiety, with little chance for the nomadic and the smooth. In all this, perhaps, an interaction between nomadism and anxiety will be forced upon us. For, as Deleuze writes when discussing Spinoza, imagination diminishes its own object over time – that is, what seems at first the magical assertion of the 'presence of its object' soon enters into a kind of 'vacillation' which will even-tually lead to the object's 'dissipation' (Deleuze, 1992: 295). In short, any magic to VR's representational illusions will soon disappear. Then the consid-erations of how it functions, what it *does*, will commence in earnest.

## The virtual, aesthetics and passion

This consideration of VR leads to a more general question regarding interac-tion. Is the body generally repressed within the new machinic by a new 'subjectifying soul' as much as it has been within previous machinic 'ages'?

More positively, how much can the 'new souls' of an ethical 'passion' be developed in order to express the percepts of a 'new body'. These souls, as the incorporeal expressions of individuation, arise from interactions between bodies in the first place, which in turn are produced by the events which inhere within them. As such, the body and the soul are, of course, interdepen-dent. Nevertheless, the body *appears* in the world of the 'soul' as an other – as the intrusion of the multitude of heterogeneous micro-perceptions in the harmony of macro-perceptions. If being bitten by hundreds of insects, for example, it is *perhaps* better to feel even panic than each bite! Yet this is liter-ally a movement away from our animality, as dangerous as that might be to feel. To feel the micro-perceptions clearly, not obscurely, is to feel the animal other that resides within the notion of the soul.

[A]nd first of all the little animals inseparable from the fluid parts of my body ... 'our body is a type of world full of an infinity of creatures that are also worthy of life'. The animals that I meet outdoors are nothing but an enlargement of the latter.

(Deleuze, 1993: 109)

Paradoxically to enable the expression of the complexity of a 'new soul' in new technologies to begin, it may be necessary to 'become-animal', and to understand now how what Deleuze and Guattari refer to in *A Thousand Plateaus* as 'becoming-animal' relates to other becomings-minor and becomings-molecular. All are attempting to broaden the extension of the clear zone of perception, the resonance with the world, and of *a world that starts with the micro-perceptions of the body*. One can see why German artist Joseph Beuys's animals were so important to him, why talking to a dead hare about art, considering the hare, the bee, and so on as perceptive, and resonating with them, could relate to his idea of 'social sculpture' as a broader interconnection of actions, a happening which must always involve a becoming-animal on the level of the percept. It is precisely away from transcendent 'truths' and unifying subjectivities to such becomings-animal that one must move in order to then become-molecular. One must become more and more specific in order to know the world – or rather to resonate with it. One can understand here the specificity of Cage's work, and why following nature 'in her manner of operations' (Cage, 1990) means introducing elements of chance which molecularize the whole aesthetic process, throw it open to the full specificity of the entire world, at that moment.

Once, purely by accident while visiting the Copenhagen Zoo, I stumbled across the back of the polar bear enclosure. There was a little barred window at which an enormous and seemingly bored polar bear sat, looking out, face right up to the bars. Of course, there was another set of bars between my face and the bear's, but we were close – less than a metre apart. It sniffed and sniffed and looked eye to eye with all comers. *It* would not be interpreted. *I* thought of it, given such a meeting in its own territory, preparing to attack and possibly eat us. Plainly this was a ludicrous, generalizing and somewhat pathetic thought in such sad circumstances. Yet when this thought evaporated what was left to think in the space of the insistent staring and sniffing of the bear? Could I follow such a becoming through and still think that I could leave the bear behind its bars? The world gapes at such moments and calls to us. How do we resolve such dissonances? VR, if designed only as a representational machine that reinforces the present State of our disharmonies, cannot.

Several years previously, in the same city, I went to the holographic museum, which had an early VR game. I persuaded a friend, neither of us having tried it before, to go into the virtual world with me. So we strapped on our belts and pulled our guns out of our holsters. At first, neither of us could navigate as the pteradactyls flew overhead, but I was lucky enough to find the paths and the stairs. I could see my friend's figure at the edge of a platform, facing into 'space', and therefore unable to figure out where she was. *As a friend* I called out to her to turn around in order to be able to see where she was going. But I'd played so many of these games before. I knew the story, and as she turned around I, *as an enemy*, shot her. It was, after all, only a game. She, of course, never having been interested in such games, could not believe it. How stratified can it get? How much more serious can these issues be when it is no longer just a matter of idly amusing oneself in Copenhagen, but of how we are constructed by and reconstruct the world at every moment?

Such questions are painful, and they reflect our pain in adaptation to a shift from a world of bears trapped in order to be representative to a world in which the biggest trap lies in not knowing how to manipulate the virtual controls without leading to further entrapments. I shall take a short digression to begin to discuss this pain, and attempt to understand the function of the pain that is famously prominent in performance art, and subsequently in our performative work of making and remaking the world. I have discussed performance as providing better guidelines than the classical theatre of representations for work with new technologies. The pain often involved is usually not masochistic (someone such as Australian artist Stelarc rightly denies any such psychoanalytic or mystical purpose to his various painful engagements such as suspensions from hooks, or the movement of his muscles by triggers sent over the Internet) or sensationalist but a way of clearly expressing and 'resolving dissonance' (Deleuze, 1993: 131). Once again this involves a broadening of the zone of clear perception, of the threshold of which pain is the signal and therefore entirely legitimate material for artistic practice when this is directed towards an extension of expression. State art simply refuses to cross or even approach its limit and instead demands the negative masochism of identity in confirmations of limits about which it pretends not to know, of clear separations between things such as representation and life, the copied and the copy. The classical theatre, for example, demands natural*ism*, but never the shifting *real*.

The artistic use of pain to *cross* limits in the work of artists such as Marina Abramovic and Ulay, where for example, in *Night Sea Crossing* (1983), they sat still facing each other for seven hours at a time on ninety (non-consecutive) days, is specifically differentiated from this kind of contractual Majoritarian masochism[36] because in masochism, according to Deleuze's account (Deleuze, 1991), the point seems to be to *reaffirm limits*, in fact, to contract them out to a 'third party' in order to have them reaffirmed. As opposed to this, an artistic use of pain is that which seeks to break the rules of the game. While it is important for masochism to *maintain* the fantasy against reality and against the danger of the return of the father, *the artist, on the other hand, uses pain to contact reality and to dismantle the father.* When pain is understood this way, both in performance, and in the crossing of the barrier of *conceptual* pain brought on by some new technologies, it can point the way to new contacts with the world, and to the dismantling of oppressive social contracts. For Deleuze the 'resolution of dissonance is tantamount to displacing pain, to searching for the major[37] accord with which it is consonant' (Deleuze, 1993: 131).

Harmony here, as opposed to the unities and identities which State art and masochism assume, is a harmony *between differences*. The harmonic different/ciator in nomad art practices describes the relations *between* series, the process of each remaining intact. It can provide a harmony *between* dissonances without always *resolving* them. Pleasure and pain are intrinsically related in testing this harmony's limits. In short, 'harmony has many formulas' (Deleuze, 1993: 132). According to the formula of *The Fold*, and in the promise of VR, such notions as the action, or even simple stories are like melodies which come after, not before, the creation of a harmonic plane of consistency. In other words, stories, like melodies, only have their uses later, when they interact with other harmonic elements. *The Fold* suggests, in fact, that at this point there can be a 'harmony between harmony and melody' (1993: 135). This in turn suggests a possible place for the mimesis of an action *within* broader considerations of *inter*actions. This is an action or melody conceived as the ongoing 'horizontal and collective extension' of harmony which Deleuze places at the limit of 'the material universe'. Some would think Bach, but the feedback on a guitar is as good an example of this extension of harmony through a melody. Here, in a kind of 'counterpoint', each melody is 'spilling over its frame and becoming the motif of another such that all of Nature becomes an immense melody and flow of bodies' (1993: 135). Melody (or story, or action) is a realization in 'extension' (135) of the intelligible (interactive harmony) to the sensible (vibrating bodies and matter). At this point it makes sense to talk about an action, or even mimesis, not as explaining or copying, *but as resonating, and expressing*.

Harmony and melody, interaction and action are confounded in technologies such as VR or work such as Cage's. The perceptual threshold is so thrown by the dynamic of the diagram's effectuation that it is hard to tell the difference between vertical harmonies and horizontal melodies. This is the point at which Deleuze says that our world differs from that of Leibniz, and new tonalities are required (such as Cage's, Glenn Branca's, or for that matter punk music or bands such as Sonic Youth's, to give just musical examples) which accept dissonance.

In this, our playing with the perception of the virtual is moving us all from 'monadology' to 'nomadology'. For the consequence of the Baroque's fragmentation of *the* world is that there is no longer a *single* world but 'several worlds'. It is these several worlds that the monad must contend with, and in doing so, Deleuze suggests the monad 'is kept half open as if by a pair of pliers'. This is a world now composed 'of divergent series (the chaosmos)' and 'it now opens on a trajectory or a spiral in expansion' (Deleuze, 1993: 137).

To sum up, by following Deleuze and Guattari's accounts of the virtual, the machine and technology, we can begin to assume that the 'Virtual Age' has only just begun. Until we begin to participate in its machining of the modulation of modulation itself more freely, and with less anxiety, we will not be able to convert our monadological lack of an outlook into a nomadological participation in the outside.

## Notes

1  Of course, here I am generalizing about two tendencies, both of which could be said to have existed within both the theatre and performance art *as practised*, that is, one towards re-presenting the already established, and the other towards producing something undetermined. While I would still argue that the 'classical theatre' tendency is still a common one amongst critics and practitioners this has not been the only tendency and I would not like to suggest that it has been. I am not alone, of course, in favouring the performative tendency, that which investigates the new rather than seeking to re-present the old. Critics such as Gregory Ulmer (1989), Sandy Stone (1995) and Espen Aarseth (1994) have all moved their discussions of new media technologies in this direction. Stone is also a performer herself. In addition to these critics, there is a host of artists and performers who have worked in this area, from Stelarc to VNS Matrix. I have discussed the general issue of performance art and new technologies in Murphie, 1990. Those interested in further writing on the issue of performance and new technologies should consult *Works and Days* 13.1/2 (1995) (<http://acorn.grove.iup.edu/en/work-days/wdhome.html>) or *The Journal of Computer Mediated Communication* 1.2 (1995) (<http://shum.huji.ac.il/jcmc/vol1/issue2/vol1no2.html>).

2  I have elsewhere given an explanation of the machine according to Deleuze and Guattari and further criticized some of Laurel (1991) and Rheingold's (1991) more theatrical approaches to Virtual Reality (Murphie, 1996).

3  Many critics do, however, valorize or condemn the virtual age. Landow (1994), Ulmer (1989), Lévy (1998) and Rheingold (1994) are among the best of those that seek to valorize the participatory or democratic pluralism of the virtual media themselves, while qualifying this with condemnation of some of the uses to which they may be put by unscrupulous or repressive powers. Their arguments should be taken seriously and in a sense one prefers such cautious optimism, which gives some hope of a plan for the future, to other critics such as Virilio (1995) or Baudrillard (1981) who are, of course, almost unendingly pessimistic.

4  The concept of the rhizome has had an enormous, if at times dubious, influence on the attempt to develop and conceptualize hypertext. Both Moulthrop (1994) and Rosenberg's (1994) essays attest to this, as does the *Rhizome* project itself in which Rosenberg was involved. As Moulthrop points out, '*A Thousand Plateaus* serves in this discussion as more than an example of proto-hypertext. It has also been a major influence on social theories and polemics that have had a strong bearing on the cultural integration of new media' (Moulthrop, 1994: 301). McKenzie Wark, in *Virtual Geography*, writes that the book was written in part as a working out of some notions of Deleuze and Guattari, specifically in a 'rewriting of the Deleuzo–Guattarian negative historicism of deterritorialization in terms of my own experience' (Wark, 1994: 225). A somewhat less sober (and perhaps more absurd) Deleuzean in this respect is Nick Land, who writes that 'our human camouflage is coming away, skin ripping off easily, revealing the glistening electronics. Information streams in from Cyberia; the basis of true revolution, hidden from terrestrial immuno-politics in the future. At the stroke of midnight we emerge from our lairs to take all security apart, integrating tomorrow' (Land,

1992: 219). This latter-day techno-poet-philosopher might do well to listen to the more coherent Deleuzean appropriations of Wark and Moulthrop, among others.

5 Landow (1992: 38–9) inadvertently gives a stunning example of how this interplay does not always work, at least in terms of ethics, appropriating the feminist writing of Hélène Cixous into the uneasy context where 'her own practice also antici- pates what has become an important mode in the hypertext document'. The simple mistake made here is the substitution of one highly interactive world for another, that of the hypertext medium for that of the written, with little consider- ations of the *other* interactions that surround and engage with these worlds, such as the worlds of specifically gendered bodies.

6 Moulthrop concludes that 'Hypertext – and its yet more distant cousins, virtual reality and cyberspace – will not produce anarchist enclaves or pirate utopias' (1994: 316). He makes the point that 'we who write theory tend to suffer from a surfeit of idealism and an antipathy to operational compromise' (315). Deleuze and Guattari, of course, were much more interested in operations than ideals.

7 Rebecca Coyle cites Krueger on this issue, who writes that 'artificial realities are a medium of expression and experience … Increasingly, people are products of arti- ficial experience. Vicarious experience through theater, novels, movies, and television represents a significant fraction of our lives. The addition of a radically new form of physically involving interactive experience is a major cultural event which may shape our consciousness as much as what has come before' (1993: 160). I would argue that this new medium is produced within a relation to changing consciousness. This will be discussed shortly.

8 These are discussed much more fully in Rheingold (1991), Coyle (1993), and Pryor and Scott (1993).

9 For a more specific discussion of the precise social situation of cyberspace see Hayward (1993).

10 At a talk given at The University of Technology, Sydney, 9 October 1991.

11 Or, as Cornwell puts it, 'The abstract idea of virtual reality can be frightening because it reminds us that all reality is illusory'. According to Cornwell, this leads to an anxiety, a 'fear of nothingness' which 'sometimes leads people to try to impose safe limits on what virtual reality can or cannot be. These rules make little sense, however, when placed in the context of the potentially $n$-dimensional nature of virtual reality' (Cornwell, 1992: 232).

12 I have discussed this at length in Murphie (1996). Nevertheless, the simplest example of a machine is found in Foucault's extremely well-known discussion of Jeremy Bentham's 'Panopticon'. This is a machine which is actualized in various forms, operates through various discourses the constitution of certain fields, and yet has a virtual form – is an event – which exceeds all these actualizations.

13 When we no longer find this zapping confusing, the postmodern age is over for us.

14 Lévy rarely mentions Deleuze, except as useful for a theory of the difference between the virtual and the possible. He also uses Guattari and Serres on occa- sions. On occasions he differs greatly from Deleuze and Guattari , for example, in arguing that the event can be actual and/or virtual (Lévy, 1998: 74).

15 I find the book confusing on this point. At times, it seems that computers and other new technologies have in themselves given the space to increased virtualiza- tion. At others, aware of the need for some caution in more utopian moments, Lévy notes that he does not 'deny that relations of power (*pouvoir*) and domination exist', but is merely interested in the fact that whether these are present or not, there is an increasing 'collective intelligence' (Lévy 1998: 151). He is critical of some forms of technological advance, for example arguing that the 'information superhighway' will 'reify the virtual'. Yet he can also, while acknowledging that

cyberspace and money are not incompatible, make statements such as 'in cyberspace we have no need of money' (160)! One can only hope that the virtual nature of such statements is actualized time and again!

16  Perhaps it is Lévy's work that begins this immense project. As a further note, this is not to imply that VR only, as Bazin (1975) can be seen to imply as regards film, contains a form of real*ism*. Once again I am interested in what is expressed in the virtual(actual)/reality interaction, not in what is represented.

17  In another context, Rheingold (1994: 10) writes 'I've been colonized; my sense of family at the most fundamental level has been virtualized'. Rheingold's books *Virtual Reality* (1991) and *Virtual Community* (1994) give perhaps the best coverage of the actual technological and social developments in this field. The second, *Virtual Community* is considerably less 'starry-eyed' than the first and one can only admire Rheingold's commitment to a true virtual community, as exemplified in his net defence of the independence of the Internet.

18  As Sally Pryor notes, 'current state-of-the-art VR worlds are not convincing enough to be seriously confused with the "real thing"'. More importantly, the representation of 'reality' in VR is actually a highly specific view of the world, a view which unthinkingly assumes a Western tradition and ideology (Pryor and Scott, 1993: 168).

19  Most of the technology for VR pre-existed it. VR as a technology is a specific multiplicity drawn together from previous technologies (such as stereoscopic vision, stereo sound, digital image processing, etc.) so it is actually quite hard to pinpoint what is actually 'new' about the technology *per se*.

20  Deleuze and Guattari write of a '*machinic phylum*, or technological lineage, wherever we find a *constellation of singularities, prolongable by certain operations, which converge, and make the operations converge, upon one or several assignable traits of expression*'. The example they give is of the 'iron sword, descended from the dagger' and the 'steel saber, descended from the knife' (Deleuze and Guattari, 1987: 406). The important point here is that each 'phylum has its own singularities and operations, its own qualities and traits, which determine the relation of desire to the technical element (the affects the saber 'has' are not the same as the sword)' (DeLanda, 1991: 406). Manuel De Landa differentiates two aspects of machinic phyla. First there is that of 'self-organization' which 'include all processes in which a group of previously disconnected elements suddenly reaches a critical point at which they begin to "cooperate" to form a higher level entity' (6–7). An example he gives is that of termites cooperating 'to build a nest' (7). Second, there are 'the particular assemblages in which the power of the processes may be integrated' (20).

21  Gibson is quoted here from the 'Author's Afterword' to the electronic edition of his cyberspace novels (Gibson, 1992).

22  Which stories for a start? – those narratives of increased performativity that Lyotard (1984) points to as informing so much of our culture, and which certainly seem to have invaded computer mythology and sales.

23  In this a 'system of difference must be constituted on the basis of two or more series, each series being defined by the differences between the terms which compose it' (Deleuze, 1994: 117). These differences between the two series are, in mathematics, the $dy$ and $dx$ as discussed, where $d$ stands for the difference which moves through possible positions of $x$ and $y$. To give a simple example relevant to the fold, the differenciator is the force that runs through a particular curved fold (in a curtain, in a body). This is not necessarily, of course, a regular folding.

24  Where identity is based upon assumptions such as 'A equals A', 'A does not equal B', etc.

25  For Deleuze, the virtual 'is opposed not to the real, but to the actual ... is fully real in so far as it is virtual ... "Real without being actual, ideal without being

abstract"; and symbolic without being fictional. Indeed the virtual must be defined as strictly a part of the real object – as though the object had one part of itself in the virtual into which it plunged as though into an objective dimension … far from being undetermined the virtual is completely determined. When it is claimed that works of art are immersed in a virtuality, what is being invoked is not some confused determination but the completely determined structure formed by its genetic differential elements, its "virtual" or "embryonic" elements' (Deleuze, 1994: 208–9). Here we again see evidence of a slippage of terms (Deleuze himself is here correcting his own previous opposition of the virtual and the real) in the discussion of the abstract which will later come to mean something quite similar to the virtual. The point remains clear, however. The virtual is not a confused realm, but a precise genetic realm.

26 Deleuze writes that 'the genesis takes place in time not between one actual term, however small, and another actual term, but between the virtual and its actualization – in other words, it goes from the structure to its incarnation, from the conditions of a problem to the cases of solution, from the differential elements and their ideal connections to actual terms and diverse real relations which constitute at each moment the actuality of time' (1994: 183).

27 Once again, the terms slide a little in Deleuze's work. He writes, 'there exists an actual that remains possible, and that is not forcibly real. The actual does not constitute the real; it must itself be realized, and the problem of the world's realization is added to that of its actualization. … The world is a viruality that is actualized in monads or souls, but also a possibility that must be realized in matter or in bodies' (1993: 104).

28 By 'spiritual automaton' Spinoza means the manner in which 'a true idea … shows how and why anything is or is made, and that its objective effects proceed in harmony with the formality of its object'. The soul, in other words, 'acts according to certain laws and resembles a spiritual automaton' (Spinoza, 1910: 255). This accord between true ideas or the soul and the body and its affects is the basis of the process whereby an increased understanding results from increased interaction.

29 Speaking in London in 1990.

30 For Cage, 'silence' was only silent when we chose not to hear it. For Cage, there was no part of the (often repressed, as in the spaces between the chosen musical notes of a composer's score) silence which could not become music if it was brought into a zone of clear expression.

31 More communications will not exist without increased thresholds of perception, differential mechanisms that will filter a harmony from them – a filter that is called the 'vinculum' in The Fold (Deleuze, 1993: 110–11).

32 By 'soul', here I mean the incorporeal component of our individuation. Put more crudely, it is that, which through both its coherence and its incoherence or ability to shift with consistency, enables us to have an idea of ourselves. Put differently, if our bodies are a series of actualizations, our souls are real as a series of virtualizations. I do not, of course, refer here to any inner residing spirit relating to a transcending beyond. In more Foucauldian terms, of course, this soul is socially and materially formed within political processes, like anything else.

33 This relates both to the sense of touch and to the body's interior sense of its own movement.

34 And what Deleuze and Guattari also call 'close vision' (Deleuze and Guattari, 1987: 496). Close vision is a way of determining the eye as more of a participant in the haptic than the representational. For example, in close vision, as when one sits too close to the screen in a cinema, 'perspective' is lost.

35 Also 'distant vision'.

36 I am indebted to my colleague Nick Mansfield for an understanding of masochism and culture, which he discusses in *Masochism: The Art of Power* (1997). This is not to say that he would be in agreement with these points.
37 Once again a slippage of terms. The 'major accord' here is one which can tolerate dissonance *as* harmony. Again the work of Cage is exemplary.

# References

Aarseth, Espen (1994) 'Nonlinearity and Literary Theory', in Landow, *Hyper/Text/Theory*, Baltimore: John Hopkins University Press, 1994: 51–86.

Baudrillard, Jean (1981) *Simulacres et simulation*, Paris: Galilée.

Bazin, André (1975) *Qu'est-ce que le cinéma*, Paris: Cerf.

Bukatman, Scott (1993) 'Gibson's Typewriter', *The South Atlantic Quarterly* 92(4): 627–45.

Cage, John (1990) *I Have Nothing to Say and I am Saying It*, video, Allan Miller (dir.), Allan Miller and Vivian Perlis (producers), The Music Project for Television, Inc. and American Masters.

Cornwell, Regina (1992) 'Interactive Art: Touching the "Body in the Mind"', *Discourse* 14(2): 203–33.

Coyle, Rebecca (1993) 'The Genesis of Virtual Reality', in Hayward and Wollen, *Future Visions: New Technologies of the Screen*, London: British Film Institute, 1993: 148–65.

De Landa, Manuel (1991) *War in the Age of Intelligent Machines*, New York: Zone.

Deleuze, Gilles (1991) 'Coldness and Cruelty', trans. Jean McNeil, in Gilles Deleuze and Leopold von Sacher-Masoch *Masochism*, New York: Zone. 9–138.

—— (1992) *Expressionism in Philosophy: Spinoza*, trans. M. Joughin, New York: Zone.

—— (1993) *The Fold: Leibniz and the Baroque*, trans. Tom Conley, Minneapolis: University of Minnesota Press.

—— (1994) *Difference and Repetition*, trans. Paul Patton, London: Athlone.

—— (1995) *Negotiations: 1972–1990*, trans. Martin Joughin, New York: Columbia University Press.

Deleuze, Gilles and Félix Guattari (1987) *A Thousand Plateaus: Capitalism and Schizophrenia*, trans. Brian Massumi, Minneapolis: University of Minnesota Press.

—— (1994) *What is Philosophy?*, trans. Graham Burchell and Hugh Tomlinson, London: Verso.

Guattari, Félix (1995) 'On Machines', trans. Vivian Constantinopoulos, *Journal of Philosophy and the Visual Arts*: Complexity: Architecture/Art/Philosophy 6: 8–12.

Gibson, William (1992) 'Author's Afterword', *Neuromancer*, New York: Electronic Editions, 541–2.

Haraway, Donna (1992) 'When Man[TM] Is on the Menu', *Incorporations*, Jonathan Crary and Sanford Kwinter (eds), New York: Zone, 39–43.

Hayward, Philip (1993) 'Situating Cyberspace: The Popularization of Virtual Reality', *Future Visions: New Technologies of the Screen*, Philip Hayward and Tana Wollen (eds) London: British Film Institute, 180–204.

Hayward, Philip and Tana Wollen (eds) (1993) *Future Visions: New Technologies of the Screen*, London: British Film Institute.

Heidegger, Martin (1977) 'The Question Concerning Technology', *The Question Concerning Technology and Other Essays*, trans. William Lovitt, New York: Harper Torchbooks, 3–35.

*The Journal of Computer Mediated Communication* (1995) 1(2) (<http://shum.huji.ac.il/jcmc /vol1 /issue2/vol1no2.html>).

Land, Nick (1992) 'Circuitries', *Pli: Warwick Journal of Philosophy*, 4(1–2): 217–35.

Landow, George (1992) *Hypertext: The Convergence of Contemporary Critical Theory and Technology*, Baltimore: John Hopkins University Press.

—— (ed.) (1994) *Hyper/Text/Theory*, Baltimore: John Hopkins University Press.

Laurel, Brenda (1991) *Computers as Theatre*, Reading, MA: Addison.

Lévy, Pierre (1998) *Becoming Virtual: Reality in the Digital Age*, trans. Robert Bononno, London: Plenum.

Lyotard, Jean-François (1984) *The Postmodern Condition: A Report on Knowledge*, trans. Brian Massumi and Geoff Bennington, Minneapolis: University of Minnesota Press.

Mansfield, Nick (1997) *Masochism: The Art of Power*, Westport, CN: Praeger.

Moulthrop, Stuart (1994) 'Rhizome and Resistance: Hypertext and the Dreams of a New Culture, in Landow, *Hyper/Text/Theory*, Baltimore: John Hopkins University Press, 1994: 299–319.

Murphie, Andrew (1990) 'Negotiating Presence: Performance and New Technologies', in *Culture, Technology and Creativity in the Late Twentieth Century*, Philip Hayward (ed.), London: John Libbey/Arts Council of Great Britain.

—— (1996) 'Computers are not Theatre: The Machine in the Ghost in Gilles Deleuze and Félix Guattari's Thought', *Convergence: The Journal of Research into New Media Technologies*, 2(2): 80–110.

Pryor, Sally and Scott, Jill (1993) 'Virtual Reality: Beyond Cartesian Space', in Hayward and Wollen, *Future Visions: New Technologies of the Screen*, London: British Film Institute, 1993: 166–79.

Rheingold, Howard (1991) *Virtual Reality: Exploring the Brave New Technologies of Artificial Experience and Interactive worlds from Cyberspace to Teledildonics*, London: Secker and Warburg.

—— (1994) *Virtual Community: Finding Connection in a Computerized World*, London: Secker and Warburg.

Rosenberg, Martin (1994) 'Physics and Hypertext: Liberation and Complicity in Art and Pedagogy', in Landow, *Hyper/Text/Theory*, Baltimore: John Hopkins University Press, 1994: 268–98.

Spinoza, Benedict (1910) 'Treatise on the Correction of the Understanding', *Spinoza's Ethics and De Intellectus Emendations*, trans. A. Boyle, London: Dent. 225–6.

Stone, Allucquère Rosanne (1995) *The War of Desire and Technology at the Close of the Mechanical Age*, Cambridge, MA: MIT Press.

Taussig, Michael (1993) *Mimesis and Alterity: A Particular History of the Senses*, New York: Routledge.

Ulmer, Gregory (1989) *Teletheory: Grammatology in the Age of Video*, New York: Routledge.

Virilio, Paul (1995) *The Art of the Motor*, trans. Julie Rose, Minneapolis: University of Minnesota Press.

Wark, McKenzie (1994) *Virtual Geography*, Bloomington: Indiana University Press.

*Works and Days*. (1995) 13(1/2) (<http://acorn.grove.iup.edu/en/workdays /wdhome. html>).

# 14

# TRANS-SUBJECTIVE TRANSFERENTIAL BORDERSPACE

*Bracha Lichtenberg Ettinger*

## In-outer screen of vision and artobject

The artist is a patient. This is the common-sense assumption: the artist loses her mind and spirit to the work, which the viewer analyses. The artist is a doctor. This is Deleuze's proposition: 'the writer as such is not a patient but rather a doctor, doctor of herself and of the world. The world is the whole set of symptoms in which sickness is confounded with humankind' (Deleuze, 1997: 3).[1] The therapy that the artist offers consists in inventing, through 'a new vision', a people that is lacking, inventing 'a possibility of life' hollowed out by a kind of foreign language within a language, by 'a becoming-other of language' (15) that opens 'an outside or flipside consisting of Visions and Hearings … These visions are not phantasies, but veritable Ideas constituted by the passage of life into language' (16). The Ideas are not phantasies, but they are analogous to them.

To these two possibilities add a third: the artist is *a doctor and a patient*, re-distributing a multiple-several and shared *sinthôme* [2] where the drive and desire meets a Thing on the screen of phantasy, or where the symptom and phantasy share a fate, offering this conjunction, diffracted and transformed, via artwork. We can establish an analogy between the subject's inner world of symptoms and its out-inner extimate *screen of phantasy* on the one hand, and on the other between the sphere of artistic Ideas and what I have called – establishing a supplementary analogy between Deleuze's 'writer' and a painter – the in-outer *screen of Vision* (Lichtenberg Ettinger, 1996a). The artwork is both the illness and the remedy, enacting otherwise impossible rapports and realizing the passage onto the screen of Vision of psychic traces from what is otherwise either absence (irremediably lost) or potentiality (not-yet-born).

The intrapsychic trans-subjective doctor-*and*-patient sphere with-in the artist is transported onto inter-psychic trans-individual relations between the artist and the viewer with/through the artwork, via a bordersphere captured in the artwork, where transgressive psychic real *things* are realized, hybrid objects are incarnated, and intrapsychic amnesia is transformed into conductible *sinthômes*. This doctor-*and*-patient borderspace finds its echoes in the viewer; its vibrations impregnate the viewer's psychic borderspace. It sheds light on an archaic trans-subjective rapport between *I* and *non-I* and on a possible transmission between different subjects and objects, beyond time and space, in a potential in-between zone of object-*and*-subject borne and yielded by painting. It sheds some light on the potentiality to engender/produce/invent and analyse transferential relations in psychoanalysis.

## Out–inner screen of phantasy and *objet a*

*According to Freud, a symptom is a disguised, repetitive substitute* for ideas connected to wishful childhood impulses that have been repressed. These ideas are sexual, if by sexuality we mean not the genital but rather the partial

*Figure 14.1* Bracha Lichtenberg Ettinger. From the series 'Eurydice' 1992–6
Source: Photograph by Jacques Faujour

pre-Oedipal dimension (Freud, 1916–7: 313–4, 323–9). A 'veil of amnesia' covers the early infantile sexual world and its libidinal development. 'Wherever there is a symptom there is also an amnesia, a gap in the memory' concerning traumatic *failure* in the infantile erotic world (Freud, 1910b: 27). Interpreting repetitions in transference and uncovering forgotten memory-traces by 'filling up this gap' imply 'the removal of the conditions which led to the production of the symptom' (Freud, 1910a: 20; 1910c: 41). Thus psycho-analysis aims at the transformation of repetition and/or amnesia into memory, by working-through regression and repression in the framework of transferential relations between the doctor and the patient.

The repressed ideas are connected with what Lacan describes as 'holes' in the Real, which are otherwise connected to art (Lacan, 1975–6). This is implied by the term *sinthôme*. 'It is the *sinthôme* we must deal with in the very rapport Freud maintained was natural – which doesn't mean a thing – the sexual rapport'. The *sinthôme* deals with the 'impossible' feminine sexual rapport. Sexuality is the domain in psychoanalysis where art may be articulated, since we enter the drive, *jouissance* and art via the same cavity, where they exchange affects, where art by accumulating potentiality shakes frontiers of sense into becoming thresholds, and infuses changes in culture. Art, says Lacan, is related to *jouissance* through the 'anatomy' of a cavity (vacuole). An inaccessible trace of a lacking part-object – *objet a* – 'tickles the Thing (*das Ding*) from within' and this is 'the essential quality of everything we call art' (Lacan, 1968–9).

An artwork attracts, shifts or originates a desire for an object that mysteriously embodies a space in that cavity. A desire, still saturated with the drive, awakens where an artobject joins forces as beauty and horror with an estimated (an outside captured within) gaze or *objet a*, by-passing repression and regression at the price of dangerously approaching the Thing, the primary source of the *Unheimlich* – of uncanny anxiety – which appeals to the viewer to follow it into a mysterious, invisible space beyond yet inside the visible, to abandon defences and to weave into the work its own invisible affect, phantasy, engagement, knowledge. The 'impossible' encounter between the drive and the aesthetic object in the in-outer screen of Vision is analogous, up to a point, to the impossible meeting between the drive and the mental object in the out-inner screen of phantasy.

The 'holes' hidden from the expanse of signification are the Thing, its vacuole and their originary repression (*Urverdrangung*), *jouissance* (sensual pleasure or pain) and its cavity, and *objet a* and its site. *Objet a* is a remnant of the split from the impulses, from 'bodily samplings' of my corpo-reality and from what I call the archaic m/Other.[3] The *objet a* indexes that a libidinal event linked to the *Thing* took place in the psychic space that is a hole. It is a mental trace issued in the course of a primary schism between the drive and its objects through which the subject itself emerges and is cleft. For Lacan, the unconscious reposes on this cleft.

# Feminine sex-difference in the poïetic and aesthetic space

We enter art and sex difference through the field of the Real spreading between trauma and phantasy. Trauma is saturated with traces of corporeal and sensorial events whose accompanied affects direct the flowing of the libido; phantasy draws the routes of the libido's flowing and derivation both when the trauma takes place and when the *I* later awakens, to search for lost part-objects. And since for Lacan the span of the Real evades the Symbolic, the libido can only be a participant in the hole, and this goes for all other modes through which the body and the Real are presented; 'it is obviously through this that I am trying to get back to the function of art' (Lacan, 1975–6). Part-objects are archaic mental samples of bits of me, of others and of the exterior world, to which we are or were once attached as particles 'by nature fragmentary and fragmented' (Deleuze and Guattari, 1983: 5). These do not compose a 'whole': milk, breast, penis (if you have one), but also voices without their masters, gazes without their owners. Whereas Lacan emphasizes the relevance of their loss to art, in the figure of the *objet a*, Deleuze and Guattari insist on their ever-renewed presence and their productivity by naming them 'desiring machines'. With the concept of desiring machines we are still bound to bodily organs, but the scope of the part-object's producing and desiring capacity opens up to embrace animalistic, industrial, sociological, ecological and historical organs. Things – crumbs of *the* Thing and/or elements producing 'cuts' in the Thing's fluid and undifferentiated existence – become part-objects if I establish erotic and affective non/pre-Oedipal relations to them which inscribe primary psychic archaic traces, or which echo for the post-Oedipal subject repressed archaic traces, by way of repetition and regression, thus temporarily breaking down genital-Oedipal identity to create new patterns for non-genital non-Oedipal libidinal flow. Deleuze and Guattari's equivalent for the Lacanian, Freudian and Kleinian Thing is the 'body without organs'. The relations between the desiring machines and the body without organs can be compared to those between the Thing and the part-objects in other psychoanalytical models. For Lacan 'there is an *Urverdrängung*, there is a repression that is never annulled. It is the very nature of the Symbolic to involve this hole; and I am aiming at this hole, which I recognize in the *Urverdrängung* itself' (Lacan, 1975–6). The symbolic subject is the flipside of the part-objects. It replaces their traces, and the originary repression of the Thing is forever inaccessible. Deleuze and Guattari also locate the originary repression at the level of the relations between Thing and part-objects, as the 'repulsion of desiring machines by the body without organs', which is inseparable from the genesis of those machines (Deleuze and Guattari, 1983: 9).

When from a psychoanalytic perspective we approach art via these 'holes' in the Real, art is not the effect of given part-objects, it is not produced by pre-existing part-objects, but rather produces them. The 'artistic machine', as Deleuze puts it, produces fragments without totality, cut-up particles, partitioned scenes analogous to part-objects, as well as resonances linked to Eros and Thanatos (Deleuze, 2000: 155–69)

*Objet a* is Lacan's term for the trace that the archaic part-object has left in my unconscious after I have separated from it or lost passionate contact with it. *Objet a* is no-more a part-object. It hides behind the screen of phantasy, exercising fascinating and horrifying power, threatening to burst into the present Real or to approach consciousness. Between the Thing and the object, it is a product of the archaic Real, a non-sense, a lack or an imprint of a split from the organ marking its loss in the passage into language via originary repression. *Objet a* is also not-yet a part-object, for it is a remnant retroactively created by discourse. The part-object itself, like originary repression, is never accessed by the symbolic subject. Rather, it is produced by the Symbolic *qua* lack, since there is no pre-discursive psychic reality. Thus, whereas the Lacanian subject *replaces* the *objet a*, Deleuze and Guattari's subject, 'with no fixed identity, wandering about over the body without organs', remains *beside* the part-objects (Deleuze and Guattari, 1983: 16).

The *objet a* with its beyond-appearance vibrations is structured by Lacanian theory in a phallic way through a split, inasmuch as primary inscription replaces production and is replaced by secondary – symbolic – inscription. For Deleuze and Guattari on the other hand the desiring machine remains an eternal source of production, a presence that motivates the connective synthesis. A part of the libidinal connective energy is transformed into a recording energy of inscription ('Numen') motivating the disjunctive synthesis. A part of the Numen transforms in turn into energy of consumption ('Voluptas') motivating the conjunctive synthesis. Here, production extends into inscription, whereas with Lacan inscription's price is production: the Real is sacrificed in the passage into culture. The difference between these two theories is that one erects and the other eradicates the Oedipal mechanism of castration. In both theories, however, psychoanalysis supplies a conceptual framework for dealing with the enigma of art in terms of the space opened between part-objects/desiring machines/*objet a* on the one hand, and on the other hand the Thing/body without organs. And in both the enigma of the poïetic process interlaces with that of the primary psychic relations designated by the term originary repression. In this space art, the aesthetic objects and the poïetic processes are fatally linked to lack, loss, and foreclosure for Lacan, and to presence, production, and the eternal return for Deleuze and Guattari. This is also, for me, precisely the space where the question of a non-phallic sex-difference arises. The matrixial object/*objet a* and link, as we shall see, are between presence and absence, negotiating both co-emergence and co-fading, the potentially present and the almost lost erotic aerials of the psyche, since they are produced for and shared by a particular kind of trans-subjective hybrid entity, a subjectivity that is feminine but is neither pre-Oedipal nor castrated, that operates within the partial dimension, designating a non-Oedipal, feminine sex-difference, produced/inscribed *already* in the passage between the Thing and the part-object, and therefore negotiating an aesthetic difference.

## The cleft phallic gaze

In the scopic sphere of vision, the *objet a* is the *gaze*, lacking and split forever from the passions of the eye, and dwelling in the Other. For Lacan, the eye and the gaze are forever cleft, secluding what is shown to the subject from what it desires to see. The Other doesn't look at me from where I look at him, nor from where I would like him to look at me, and 'what I look at is never what I wish to see' (Lacan, 1964: 103). When I look for the gaze it hides, and precisely for that reason the field of vision is relevant to the unconscious subject; the split in-forms the eye as erotic. A drive is concealed/revealed in the schism from the gaze: 'The eye and the gaze – this is for us the split in which the drive is manifested at the level of the scopic field' (1964: 72–3). Via the artwork, a lacking gaze accesses consciousness in the form of a 'strange contingency' revealed by an *Unheimlich* signalling that we are on the horizon of experience, namely approaching 'the lack that constitutes castration anxiety' (1964: 73). Thus the underlying threat is the 'appearance of the phallic ghost', for the *Unheimlich* reposes on castration complex (1964: 88).

Since the painter undertakes a dialogue with the gaze, something of the gaze is always contained in the tableau. The painter seduces the eye of the viewer and offers it some imaginary food, but the viewer is solicited by the tableau 'to lay down his gaze there as one lays down one's weapons' (Lacan, 1964: 101). Something that is fermented by this laying down of the gaze is granted to the subject's eyes of phantasy. The painter's stroke does not origi-nate in a decision, but concludes an internal stroke which also participates in regression, against which it now creates (as in a reversal of the course of time) a gaze, a product that is also a cause, to which the painter's actual stroke becomes a *response*. The gaze fascinates and horrifies the stroke, attracting it into becoming, from the site of the *Irreal*. In front of the amazing snare of the gaze on apparition's horizon, consciousness can only conclude the artist's act by ascribing images and thoughts to that which had none. The viewpoint of the gaze is the artist's blind spot linked to the Thing, incarnated in painting. When Lacan attributes substitutions of loss-as-a-split to this tacit gaze, it becomes a phallic-extimate relic, an archaic outside captivated within, whose schism is then embodied by the screen of phantasy: the gaze is cast upon the screen when the subject is suspended, and if the subject does rarely appear on the screen, it is as a *stain* in the picture, while the gaze disappears.

## Intersubjective gaze as want-in-being

A slightly different gaze, presented by Lacan in 1965, emphasizes the dimen-sion of intersubjectivity, but the cleft is even more clearly erected, since it is precisely the relations to the want-in-being (*manque à être*) that are being contrived here.

*Figure 14.2* Bracha Lichtenberg Ettinger. From the series 'Eurydice' 1992–6
Source: Photograph by Jacques Faujour

And remember what I said the *tableau* [painting] is, the *real tableau*. It is the gaze. It is the tableau that gazes at whomever is caught in its field, falls into its snare. The painter is he who makes the gaze fall before himself, from the other. [...T]he figure [is] projected before him [Signorelli],[4] the figure of he who no longer knows from whence he sees himself, who no longer knows the point from which he gazes upon himself. For the S of the schema which I have shown to be the constitutive site for primordial identification – the identification of the *unary stroke*, the identification of the I[maginary], the somewhere from which everything falls into position for the subject – this S, it must be emphasized, has no point, it is that *outside* which is the *point of birth*, the *point of emergence of some creation*, which may be on the order of a reflection, on the order of the secretly organized, of that which falls into position, of that which is instituted as *intersubjectivity*. With regard to this light – which appears suddenly on the very image of the one whose name is lost, of the one who is presented here as *lack* – Freud leaves the thing in suspense for us, leaves us kind of tongue-tied, so to speak. It is the *apparition of the point of emergence in the world* from the bursting forth point which, in language, can only be translated as the *want-in-being*

(Lacan, 1964–5)

It is in the no-place of the *Thing* in art that Lacan first detects, via the gaze, the uncanny 'phallic ghost' (1964). Via the tableau Lacan tracks something of the revelation of intersubjectivity as want-in-being (1964–5), in which the archaic Other as a point of emergence is outside and lacking. Later, in relation to literature (1975–6), Lacan hints at some revelation that passes via a 'feminine' sexual *rapport* (relationship) in the *sinthôme*, a rapport he considers impossible. If the gaze in art is an elevation of 'woman' to the level of the Thing (1968–9), then the *sinthôme* is a possibility of a revelation of 'woman' as incarnating an impossible rapport. Up until the end of his teaching Lacan repeatedly claimed that *there is no sexual rapport* (1973–4, 1975–6), that psychoanalysis itself testifies to this, that this lack of rapport is the basis of psychoanalytic discourse. But, if such a rapport existed, it would be feminine. With the *sinthôme* he enigmatically implies an incarnation of a 'supplementary' feminine site, stretched out from and retreating back into art, separated from psychosis by less than a whisper.

## Female swerve, feminine rapport and matrixial sex-difference

In discussing the gaze and art, Lacan (1964) referred to Freud's idea that the *Unheimlich* strangeness in aesthetic experience 'springs from its proximity to the *castration* complex'. But enigmatic *Unheimlichs* are also attached, according to Freud, to the unconscious infantile complex 'of intra-uterine existence' or '*womb*-fantasies' (Freud, 1919: 244, 248). These I have called matrixial. The two complexes, the phallic and the matrixial, to my mind indicate two different clusters of mechanisms, functions, and processes. The phallic structure accounts for an arena of non-rapport; the matrixial apparatus may hold for a space of border-linking.[5] 'Elevating' onto art matrixial sparkles that correspond to a channel induced by pre-birth incest has to do, in my view, with yet another phenomenon of the *Unheimlich*, in its relation to *transference*. Thinking these two concepts together conveys an underlying, dangerous female swerve and a feminine/pre-natal rapport that vibrate on the horizon of *with-in-visibility* in art.

*Swerve* and *borderlinking* are incidents in the Real at the basis of a feminine-matrixial sex-difference. The swerve as spacing, distancing-apart as well as deviation, digression, and deflection, relates to Merleau-Ponty's *écart* [gap] and *dehiscence*, which I transfer from the realm of perception to that of psychic affectation; borderlinking relates to his 'thinking on two'. Speaking of ontogenesis of the aesthetic universe, Merleau-Ponty articulates a space of bursting and dehiscence in the Real prior to the bifurcation into subject and object, where the *écart* between-two is a 'fragmentation of being' and a becoming or 'advent of the difference' in a 'virtual foyer' (Merleau-Ponty, 1968: 215–6).

Minimal affectation conditions the genesis of art-creation and of the painter-gaze (Lyotard, 1995). But where Merleau-Ponty (1968: 201) speaks of *perception* as *écart* in relation to a *level* (*niveau*), I am thinking of *affectation* as a *swerve* in relation to a *Thing*, and of an *affected originary borderlinking* which allows us to associate the *écart* 'between two', or between several, to the *pli* (fold: 'differentiation of the undifferentiated' [Deleuze]) and to the *Zwiefalt* (Heidegger). A '*pli-de-deux*' (two-fold), an '*entre-deux*', where 'it is difference which is differentiated' (Deleuze, 1993: 10).

Affected *swerve* and *borderlinking* inaugurate a psychic co-poïetic space[6] of transformation and differentiation in-between the several opened by the feminine, where a subjective web is linked to woman's corpo-real Thing. The difference of the feminine is inaugural of its own space and is originary; it is not deduced from the masculine or the male. The originary female swerve is not engaged during the split of the subject nor is it dissolved inside relations to the Other defined by Lacan as 'treasure of signifiers', yet it imprints psychic traces. The originary swerve, which concerns the female invisible corporeal specificity (womb) for both male and female infants, is captured in a feminine rapport of the *I* with the uncognized other. The affected swerve and rapport generate and engrave passages and means of transport through which traces of joint events, *jouissances*, and phantasies are channelled, means that do not converge on the process of castration. They are non-Oedipal; they account for a difference in a non-phallic apparatus and create supplementary feminine-Other-desire, transported, transformed and transferred within the matrixial borderspace, beyond metaphor and metonymy, by what I have termed in my remarks on painting *metramorphosis* (Lichtenberg Ettinger, 1993). A feminine borderlinking discloses art as a transferential borderspace.

Echoes of matrixial 'holes' and knots sprout through art and re(a)sonate meaning, since in the act of painting the schize between the gaze and the eye falls apart – yet not into absence by fusion or annihilation. These knots display themselves enigmatically, and it is up to us whether to contemplate them once the act is over. I have transported the vague ideas of *matrix* and *metramorphosis* from art into psychoanalysis in order to unveil through them (become concepts) a particular spectrum of opaque, trans-individual, shared-in-difference, affected mental events and phantasies bounded by traces of archaic rapport with the feminine-Other. In the matrixial apparatus and by metramorphic processes, this spectrum reaches *some* level of organization and we may perceive *something* of it when it arises, partially, in fits and starts, at the horizon of the space of transference.

## Withness-in-differentiation, transgression, and hybridity

Matrix is an unconscious borderspace of simultaneous co-emergence and co-fading of the *I* and an uncognized *non-I*, neither fused nor rejected, which share and transmit joint, hybrid and diffracted objects via conductible borderlinks.

The matrix is a model of a feminine/pre-natal rapport conceived of as a shared psychic borderspace in which *differentiation-in-co-emergence* and *distance-in-proximity* are continuously reattuned by a metramorphosis created by and further creating (interwoven by matrixial affects) *relations-without-relating* on the borders of presence and absence, subject and object, me and the stranger. The matrixial stratum or sphere, involved in the process of creating feminine-Other-desire and Other-sense, coexists and alternates with the phallic stratum. Metramorphosis is a process of inter-psychic trans-individual communication and transformation between/with-in several entities in a matrixial borderspace. It is the route of a passage through which matrixially affected events, materials, and modes infiltrate the Symbolic and diversify on its non-conscious margins through/by sub-symbolic webs. In a joint and multiple marginal trans-individual awareness, perceived boundaries are dissolved into becoming new boundaries; forms are transgressed; borderlines are surpassed and transformed into becoming thresholds; conductible borderlinks are conceived, transformed, and dissolved. Contingent transgressive borderlinks and a borderspace of swerve and encounter emerge as a sex-difference and a creative instance which engrave traces which may be revealed/invented in *withness*-in-differentiation.[7] In the matrix, relation-without-relating transforms the unknown other and me, and turns both of us into partial subjects – still unknown to each other – in subjectivity-as-encounter. Metramorphosis is a co-poïetic activity in an inter-psychic web that remembers, conducts, transfers, and inscribes feminine *jouissance*, swerve, and rapport. Via art the effects of the borderlink's activity are transmitted to the threshold of culture.

## *Thingnified Ça-voir,* [8] swerve and borderlinking

Something of the erotic antennae of the psyche transmits to and receives from the Other, through the phantasy mechanism, an echo of matrixial 'holes': resonances of an archaic *incestual rapport* with the becoming-mother and affective remnants from the female swerve and the hybrid *objet a*. Metramorphic *borderlink* diffracts and assembles traces in a trans-subjective web, disengaged from and unappropriated even retroactively by the phallus. And if art and sexuality come to play with each other through the mediation of partial drives, then elucidating the specificity of the matrix as sex-difference in the partial dimension leads to articulating a supplementary aesthetic-erotic zone. Conceptualizing a level of an-Other feminine difference and of a non-equivalence between the sexes[9] promoted by feminine *jouissance*, swerve, and borderlinking is possible only if whatever of it that escapes pre-established discourse is nonetheless unthinkingly known, and *not only ex-sists* with-in female corpo-reality but is traced by the artist, 'written' in/by art, becoming somewhat thinkable through the contemplation of art and its production, making some sense, finally articulated and shared in a transferential borderspace.

The knowledge of the Real is not a host of data awaiting decoding by

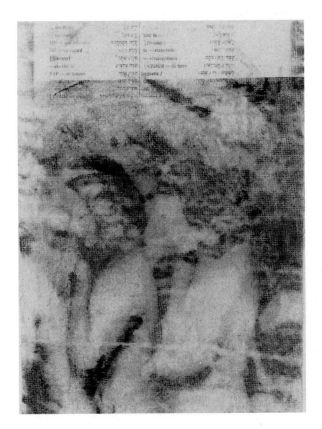

*Figure 14.3* Bracha Lichtenberg Ettinger. From the series 'Eurydice' 1992–6
Source: Photograph by Jacques Faujour

means of signification to produce signified knowledge (*savoir*) that will also constitute the subject as cleft, but is rather an 'invention' that happens 'in any first encounter with sexual rapport' (Lacan, 1973–4). Thus a metramorphic process of webbing-in-withness – exchanges of affects based on the conduction of/in shared (asymmetrically and not in the same way) trauma and phantasy, and transmissions-in-transformation of phantasy, beginning between a becoming-subject and a becoming-m/Other-to-be, but more generally between any *I* in co-emergence with an uncognized *non I*, in a *between* which initiates a plural-several, partial and diffracted 'woman' – can release knowledge from 'holes' in the Real and inscribe traces of a rapport in what a '*sinthôme*' would turn into if viewed from this feminine side: as an intersection that creates/invents/reveals/releases a potential desire from its dangerous (foreclosed in the phallus, but *between foreclosure and repression* in the matrix) archaic zone. In painting, metramorphosis knits *thingnified Ça-voir* and not *signified savoir.* The matrixial-other sex-difference treasures a dimension of potentiality and transgressivity in an inter-psychic, trans-individual, connectionist sub-symbolic web.[10]

## Severalized hole, floating eye, diffracted gaze

If a 'hole' may 'become two holes' according to Lacan (1961–2), who uses here somewhat embryological imagery, then it may also become several holes. And moving from the phallic to the matrixial perspective, the several holes stand for a *diffraction* of the eye-and-gaze between several – not infinite, not one – entities, a *sharing* of the eye-and-gaze by several individuals, a *composing* of the eye-and-gaze by several components, and a *dispersal* and *divergence* of 'grains' of subjectivity between several different individuals, by which some eye-and-gaze(s) become *borderlinks* between partial subjects along which a diffracted gaze is plaited within the multiple-several holes, with their floating eyes, without fusion or split. All of this takes place to begin with in relation to a female swerve, since it occurs with-in the becoming subject co-emerging in pre-birth incest together with the mother-to-be. (I emphasize that when I write of the partial subject-to-be in the womb I refer only to the last intra-uterine period when the infant is already 'post-mature' [Winnicott] and we assume that its phantasy life has begun. The feminine 'archaic origin' echoed by the 'matrix' doesn't indicate any limitation on women's rights over their bodies, quite to the contrary! This configuration supports woman's full co-response-ability for any event occurring with-in her own not-One corpo-reality and disqualifies phallic regulations of it.) The subject-to-be is a pre-subject in the desire and the discourse of the m/Other-to-be who transgresses her own individual psychic boundaries and shares the pre-subject's Real that stretches 'between trauma and phantasy'. The matrixial angle illuminates the borderspace between inside and outside in subjectivity-as-encounter, where a *continuity* rather than a *split* between inside and outside and eye and gaze comes to light. This continuity, connecting to a hybrid gaze and a floating eye, is sieve-like. It is a mark of difference whose advent is transformation, and which roves, since its elements are diffracted between several floating erotic points of vision that do not converge at a fixed emergence point.

Swerving the 'gaze', the 'tableau' and the '*sinthôme*' towards the matrix allows further articulation concerning art and its production. In art, by means of metramorphosis, something of the secret organization that begins with vagrancy and severality with no possible fixed point of vision rises to the surface as a shared, hybrid, and severalized gaze in relation with (and not split from) the severalized hole and its eroticized floating eye – just as something of the horror of castration emerges through the phallic gaze and its fixed/fixing eye. In the gaze, the Phallus carves intersubjectivity together with a point of emergence into what is want-in-being, so that the split of the eye from the gaze is constitutive of the subject. In the matrix, the gaze carves trans-subjectivity in co-emerging entities in a becoming-rapport, between presence and want-in-being in severality; for the gaze in the matrix rolls into several eyes, transforms the viewer's point of vision and returns through his/her eyes to the Other of culture transformed.

## Matrixial *Unheimlich*

In the experience of the matrixial *uncanny*, the gaze is not split and yet not fused with the eye, grasped as the *eroticized aerial of the psyche*. The gaze is saturated with primary distributions of energies that correspond to a rotating swerve, with traces of archaic *jouissance*,[11] and with intensities striving for apparition. These traces and intensities are unexpectedly incarnated in swerve and borderlinking in/by the act of painting beyond-as-inside the visible. In the act of painting, the gaze moves between several archaic as well as potential participants, creates/disjoints each subject (potential-viewer) as partial with-in subjectivity-as-encounter – the subject's view transformed in difference from other viewers' transformations. The gaze of the artist, having trespassed its eye, is vibrated by it, so as to awaken a new swerve or roll it up in a rapport. The matrixial gaze is re-diffracted by each affected eye onto a potentially joint-by-several erotic screen of Vision. Wallowing with-in a shared and moving eye, the gaze re-diffracts at the moment of its rolling-in. Something – but not-all – of this act and its affects is transported into and conducted via the artwork, thus transforming the point of view of the viewer in difference from, yet in relation to, the non-conscious swerves and links of the artist, who captures/produces/conducts Ideas and phantasies. The tableau connects the gaze of the viewer who happens to be touched by it with its own lost zone beyond-the-schize, via vibrations embedded in the tableau that mysteriously conduct *diffracted traces* (Lyotard, 1995) of the artist's act and gaze.

A severalized cavity opens, indexing a hidden female site which arises as originary feminine swerve, along with a borderlinks capturing the singularity of each pre-birth incest arising as transgression, as originary feminine difference. A non-conscious transferential channel is opened which offers the possibility of inscribing traces of inter-psychic non-fusional and non-split encounter with-in the Other, by weaving the matrixial web into an enlarged-Other, which would thereby contain sub-knowledge that is not conditioned by the repression of signifiers but rather by the emerging-, dispersing- and fading-in-transformation of the materials of the Real.[12] Such a relation with its swerve(s) is transferred via artwork from the artist to the viewer. It is also transferred from the artwork to both viewer and artist, transforming their own erotic point of emergence of vision – the eye-*with*-gaze in the scopic psychic dimension.

## Besidedness with-in-out a transferential borderspace

In terms of the unconscious art-coefficient and relations of transference, Duchamp suggests a kind of aesthetic osmosis between the artist and the viewer via the artwork (Duchamp, 1975: 188–9). I suggest that a transferential borderspace of inter-with-ness, besidedness,[13] and transgression embedded in relations of transference seeks ways to become known and thinkable via the screen of Vision. Psychoanalysis can discern, apprehend, and otherwise work-through an analogous borderspace embedded in a screen of phantasy stretched in transference/counter-transference relationships, in which an assembled and diffracted *trans-individual* doctor–patient entity can roll itself bit by bit into the Symbolic level.

It was Freud (1910) himself who qualified some transferential phenomena as *Unheimlich*, thus opening the route for Duchamp to deliver them to an aesthetic sphere and to make them intersect with aesthetic experience. 'Mysterious', even 'mystical' (Freud, 1910: 22), affective uncanny contingencies underlie the therapeutic potentiality of psychoanalysis, in terms of the patient's openness to inter-personal interaction, influence and suggestibility, or his/her 'tendency for transference' in the encounter with the doctor with-in the psychoanalytic process. This tendency for transference, since it reposes on 'sexuality, on the activity of the libido' (Freud, 1916–7: 446) enters our 'holes'.

Doctor and patient arrive at their transferential encounter with different phantasies and desires. Nevertheless, their phantasies and desires are somehow, mysteriously, temporarily and partially shared in a non-symmetrical yet reciprocal way, and are transformed in/by the encounter, and re-transmitted. Furthermore, phantasies and desires are created in the *transferential borderspace* as *already* conductible and shareable though in-difference, contrived specifically in/for each unexpected and unique psychoanalytic encounter. A matrixial borderspace for inscribing originary *besidedness with-in-out* is opened in the space of transference. This vagrancy of phantasy and desire is not a replacement of one's own phantasy and desire by that of an other. Beside a phallic transference/counter-transference an other one happens, where trans-individual subjectivity-as-encounter is created between an *I* and an unknown other, or between an *I* and the unknown zone of a known *non-I*. The *Unheimlich*, both allowing and accompanying the transference/counter-transference matrixial *rapport* between doctor and patient, signal to both that a common-in-difference event which equally-but-differently concerns each of them approaches the margins of shared awareness, surrounds the edges of its cavity and is about to appear. *Traces of a buried-alive trauma are about to be re-born from amnesia into co-emerging memory, and the potentiality of partially sharing it in the transferential borderspace is the condition for its appearance.*

Such *Unheimlichs* allow and accompany seeing with-in/through a work of art. That is how we may read Duchamp's *art coefficient* connected to *space of transference* : the artist and the viewer transform the artwork and are transformed by it in different times and places and to different degrees, in different-yet-connected ways. Each viewer gives the artwork new life, and what escapes the capture of the artist's awareness is the kernel of this process. Such *Unheimlichs* otherwise allow and accompany the borderlinking through psychoanalysis.

Affective phenomena like admiration, amazement, empathy, anxiety and awe which are hidden inside the patient's readiness for transference, as well as closely related phenomena like wonder, dread, compassion[14] and again empathy (and even telepathy), which are hidden in the doctor's *tendency for counter-transference*, also arise in viewing art, as if transferential object becomes a partial subject and communicates with us. Shared, exchanged and diffracted on the unconscious partial dimension, these affects attract and diffuse aesthetic matrixial threads and participate in the artwork's potentiality for hurting and healing.

## Co-poïesis inter-with the other

A matrixial phantasy bursts forth in each *individual in withness* within a composite subjectivity, testifying that the feminine/pre-natal archaic encounter does not retroactively melt away into an Oedipal 'castration' model and is not constructed, subjugated, or destroyed by the phallus, but rather opens a different channel beside it. The transferential encounter may involve a form of potential communication through which some materials and modes from the matrixial stratum may find expression, beyond art and psychosis, in psycho-analysis. And maybe that is where Lacan aims when, transporting the analyst from the status of a subject supposed to know (*sujet-supposé-savoir*) to the status of relics in the form of the *objet a*, he somewhat subversively remarks: 'I have said and done enough to stop anyone – at least anyone from my close circles – from daring, from risking, to advance that one can be the mother [as an analyst in a didactic analysis]. Yet this is precisely what this is all about' (Lacan, 1961–2, June).[15] Parallel to this passage from positioning the analyst as a *sujet-supposé-savoir* to positioning him/her as an *objet a* we note that there occurs a passage from a masculine to a feminine position, and a move from transference as repe-tition to transference as 'impossible' yet potential encounter between subjects and with their becoming-joint-through-sharing psychic part-objects.

Feminine *jouissance*, which 'does not wait for phallic organization to enter into play, will take on aspects of *revelation* which it will keep forever' (Lacan, 1961–2). This revelation emerges in the matrix from the singularity of each encounter as a unique *co-poïesis*. It inscribes a potentiality appearing as a series of unexpected revelations in the transferential space. Another kind of appear-ance, or rather apparition, consists of modes of revelation in/by art. Raising the phallic *objet a* as 'woman' in art to the level of the Thing in primordial extimacy does not designate a regressive step. And linking with an inter-with matrixial *sinthôme* via art does not indicate a return to the womb in the Real nor a psychotic disintegration or fusion, but rather a realization of unforeseen potentiality with-in-out, where 'original' and 'readymade' intersect in differ-ence. The enigma of femininity that touches upon the originary repression of the Thing – the *Urverdrängung*, the primordial unconscious as connected to sex and death beyond/before the separating line of castration, beyond/before the threshold of language – is foreclosed in the phallus but is emerging- and fading-by-transformation in the matrix. Something of those co-emergence and co-fading in the Real is delivered to the Symbolic's 'margins' via covenants hidden in art. Since a matrixial co-poïesis is also experienced in transference and counter-transference, I take psychoanalytic relations as always containing a dimension of uncanny borderline trans-subjectivity, and psycho-analytic theory as a laboratory for new concepts born in/by art.

Something is interwoven between several entities into a tissue whose connections may become accessible via art. Something, but not-All.[16] If for Lacan the 'woman' between jouis-presence and jouis-absence is Other even when she is in-between (1971–2), in the matrix she is a border-Other becoming-between in witness. A metramorphic dissolving is not a parting/cutting by either repression or foreclosure but rather a shared-in-difference *transformation*. Something of the impossible feminine position of *in-ter-with the Other* is interlaced in trans-subjectivity in relation-without-relating. Trans-subjectivity lies beside the One and the split subject.

## Re-in/di-fuse

Let us now consider some of the aesthetic potentialities of the matrixial gaze, at the moment of its emergence and its eclipsing, still saturated with *jouissance*, aroused by the libido, excited by the drive to pass from the artist to the art and back again, and from the art to the viewer and back again, via erotic tunnels. Let us consider poïetic subjectivity-as-encounter, still stretched between trauma and phantasy, creating/producing different yet connected desires in the artist and the viewer.

In the scopic sphere in the matrixial partial dimension, the gaze rolls with-in the eye without its collapsing, since the matrixial gaze is hybrid and diffracted and the eye is a floating, severalized and shared erotic conductible antenna with no fixed-and-one point of emergence, with-in subjectivity-as-encounter. Metramorphosis directly creates and covenants knots in a trans-individual non-conscious web, and touches upon the *sinthôme* from a feminine site in a joint borderspace. A matrixial place/space/side awakes in the act of painting when a schize is transformed into a link. Awareness of some sparkles from it in the transferential space does not necessarily indicate psychotic disintegration, schizophrenic multiplicity or *folie-à-deux*.[17]

This web-like subjectivity conducts and transmits a diffracted gaze, where we appear on the screen as a *with-in-visible* sieve. Each witness engenders its particular sieve in which, beyond the visible, a gaze that is the continuity of the inside outside and the outside with-in inspires and expires: inspirits us. Encounters, in the screen of phantasy as in the screen of Vision, attest that imprints are interwoven: that traces deviating from an unknown Other etch imprints in me unconsciously, that traces abandoning me still keep in touch via my unknown Others, and that an im-pure object is created inside trans-subjective heterogenesis.[18]

230

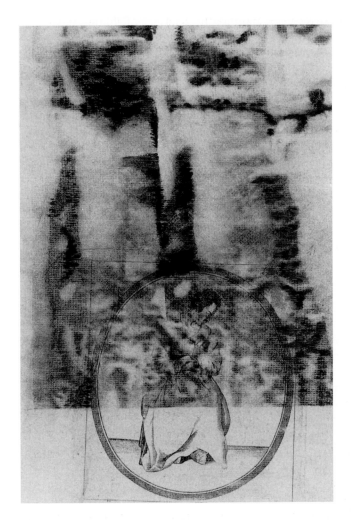

*Figure 14.4* Bracha Lichtenberg Ettinger. From the series 'Eurydice' 1992–6
Source: Photograph by Jacques Faujour

In the matrixial borderspace partial subject and partial-object intersect and transmit poïetic archaic traces upon each other and in a connectionist web, while a partial *non-I* co-emerges with them. The flowing of the experience is inscribed in metramorphosis as asymmetrical yet reciprocal relations that create erotic antennae, shared but possessing different re(a)sonating minimal sense for each partial subject, artist, and viewer. These aerials register what returns from the Other as traces, and transmit a centreless or several-centred gaze. The matrixial filter tears affected trans-subjective events out of foreclosure.[19] Metramorphosis transgresses the boundaries of the body-in-identity as male and female, and confers meaning to a variety of shifting traces of borderlinking beyond-as-before gender identifications. These traces do not converge into the confusion of One nor do they disintegrate into undifferentiation or total absence.

Even in the fading-by-transformation of the matrixial borderspace, diffracted gazes still twinkle in one another's eyes. Awareness of the impossibility of a total split and the *impossibility of not-sharing* implies certain modifications in the classic Lacanian understanding of the structure of the unconscious, continuing the very late Lacan in Deleuze and Guattari's anti-Oedipal direction.[20] This has ethical implications beyond aesthetics, concerning covenantal relations with *several strangers* who induce changes in me, and whom I sway, in recognition of the impossibility of being fully cognizant of or of total splitting from the Other.

The doctor *and* patient co-emerge in the transferential space, sharing-in-difference the screen of phantasy through floating sharing and floating attention. The artist and the viewer, as *doctor and patient*, co-emerge in diverse ways with the work and by the work, sharing-in-difference the screen of Vision through passage-to-action and floating viewing. A matrixial gaze floats to the edges of visibility when a floating eye traverses the screen. Artist and viewer are not in passive/active *contradiction* in relation to the screen, and yet neither do they amalgamate; they are not the *same*, and they are not symmetrical. They exchange and keep a distance in proximity that allows the artist a freedom to act and allows the viewer emphatic com-passion as well as the freedom to *re-in/di-fuse*: a possibility for re-diffusion *and* re-infusion of elements in the transferential borderspace where elements neither fuse nor refuse each other. Re-in/di-fusing with-in the matrix hollows a critical space of subversion and resistance which becomes indeed a *refusal* of/for the split subject inside the phallus with its 'woman' as absence.

## Com-passionate withnessing and transgressive potentiality

Of all of the kinds of contemporary means of production that compel the gaze of the viewer to meld with the gaze of the artist or the camera, hiding symbiotic gratification behind the offer of a controlling gaze, painting renews its critical relevancy as a vehicle for com-passionate yet critical distance, offering a grasp of floating time and space shared with the other while retuning distances-in-proximity.

The phallic gaze excites us while threatening to annihilate us in its emergence on the screen, giving us the illusion of a participation in mastery. The matrixial gaze thrills us while fragmenting, multiplying, scattering, and joining grains together. It turns us into what we may call *participatory witnesses* to traumatic events, at the price of diffracting us into grains. It threatens us with disintegration while allowing transgression towards a drama wider than that of our-individual-selves.

232

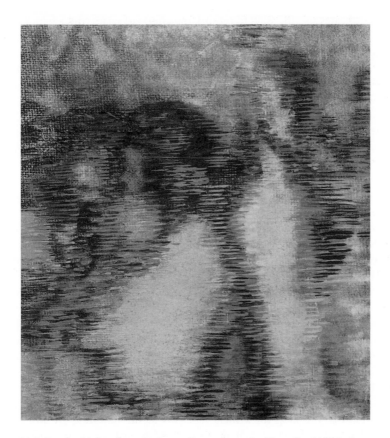

*Figure 14.5* Bracha Lichtenberg Ettinger. From the series 'Eurydice' 1992–6
Source: Photograph by Jacques Faujour

The matrixial perspective invites us to reassess the contemporary 'death' of painting, for its killing is the product of a phallic overdose. This reflex, like the total death of the subject, concerns the split subject only. In the matrixial border-space, there is never One-split subject nor its total want-in-being, but rather marginal and migratory severality. Painting ever-opens new aesthetic fields.

The matrixial gaze cannot be encompassed entirely by only-one subject, and cannot encompass it either. It was never a lost wholeness nor an endless multiplicity,[21] and it remains partial, allowing for com-passionate screening without identity, because while it breaks your imaginary wholeness it also conducts you to its (and your) margins and out of its (and your) own one-space. Different grains, spaced in a floating time, yet timed by a floating transferential borderspace in the artwork, will have no control over the gaze, nor will any grain suffer its total loss. The matrixial gaze reflects and creates libidinal metamorphic routes as it partly perishes and partly arises through its diffraction in the several, in its passing to several other grains and webs. Thus the matrix indicates specific ways to rethink the effects of series (Buci-Glucksmann, 1995), and of the transition from one period to another. Trauma is defined in the matrix as relational; it can therefore only be worked through in a new transformational relation. Likewise, I rethink the phenomenon of unconscious transmission between artists and over generations in terms other than those of copy versus original, influence, etc., and instead in terms of transgression, trans-subjective and trans-generational 'phylogenetic' memory,[22] and as an axis of potentiality for future realization of relational working-through.

The matrixial transferential borderspace carries contemporary art beyond the Duchampian era, in the sense that the binary contradiction between 'an original' and a 'ready-made' fades away; yet the two do not collide, but rather make each other swerve further with new exchanges. The matrix suggests a supplementary relief to the idea of transference that Duchamp transferred from psychoanalysis to art. The rapport between original and readymade in the matrixial sphere in painting creates a third zone of severality in the space of transference. Wandering, scattered and sprayed among floating eyes, it is impossible to re-gather the matrixial gaze's traces; but you may *join them* in a labyrinth woven in the course of creating the matrixial web in the screen of Vision.

The artist with-in his/her doctor-and-patient dimension is a *withness without event* [23] in com-passionate withnessing. The viewer is challenged by the artwork to join this matrixial borderspace. Beyond representation, s/he is carried by an event s/he did not necessarily experience, and through the matrixial web an unexpected transformation and reaction to that event arises. This, I believe, touches on an ethical aspect *already* carried inside aesthetics via affects attached to the *objet a* and to borderlinks. It was Lévinas who traced a radical path of thinking the ethical in terms of the feminine. In doing so he claimed, as I have said elsewhere, a space of sexual difference that unfolds directly in/from the feminine (Lévinas, 1993; 1997).

And nothing guides us in advance as to what withnessing the matrixial gaze will destine me or the Other, or as to which witness we will allocate the gaze.

Nothing foresees or prescribes the passage from a symptom to a *sinthôme*, neither in the phallus nor in the matrix.

Nothing paves the way for the passage onto an Irreal-Real in the form of an artwork. Nothing inscribes the artistic act in the painter's stroke.

Nothing guarantees the power of the artwork to give rise to a response in viewers nor indicates in advance what transformation will take place in the shared matrixial web. The matrixial gaze is an encounter, and it can be partially retrieved only in another encounter.

Nothing proscribes specific linking of out-inner knots in-to an in-outer trans-subjective web.

*Figure 14.6* Bracha Lichtenberg Ettinger. From the series 'Eurydice' 1992–6
Source: Photograph by Jacques Faujour

And nothing decides beforehand what would lead the viewer to produce his/her own threads-'cause'/*objet a*/borderlink with-in a particular transferential borderspace.

## Memory and amnesia: Conclusions

I suggest considering a matrixial transferential borderspace in artmaking and the artobject. This inaugurates a channel of co-emergence and co-fading where trauma, phantasy and desire join traces. It is a space of diffraction, severality, dispersal and partiality, shareability and hybridity, with-ness, conductivity, passability and transmission, a space of potentiality. It is opened in/by the act of painting through a transgression of the splits between eye and gaze and *I* and *non-I* which momentarily defies the unconscious. The act of painting perforates

235

a borderspace which is not conscious, but does not correspond to the structure of the unconscious as defined by a network of repressed signifiers worked through metaphors, etc. If amnesia plays a part here, it is double-edged. It looks toward a future in which whatever of it will transform into memory will have become a memory of that which was neither repressed nor forgotten, that which from the onset appears for the first time as a shared memory in the transferential borderspace, creating its veil of amnesia, hurting while healing. The act of painting looks to the past when it elevates the screen of phantasy into a screen of Vision, by way of Ideas, while suspending-without-removing the veil of amnesia, healing traumatic relations while hurting.

In the matrixial co-poïetic borderspace, *I* and an extimate − intimate-unknown − *non-I* share an ephemeral, unpredictable and singular alliance, in which each participant (as well as their hybrid *objet a*) is partial and relational in differentiating jointness. Partial subjects discern each other via conductible borderlinks, interlinking while transmitting affects and pathic information, addressing one another in a relation-without-relating that takes place in the course of alternations in distance-in-proximity in reciprocal non-cognition. Each partial-object is composite; each partial subject participates in several specific covenants. A 'woman' which is not confined to the contours of the one-body with its inside versus outside polarity interweaves a sex difference based not on an essence or a negation but on borderspacing links and on webbing links to a female swerve. 'Woman' is not a foreclosed Other, but a border-Other, a vacillating withness. The matrixial borderspace of co-birth in originary differentiation produces com-possible feminine-Other-desire which allows one to work, in art's transferential borderspace, with the idea of an assembled and partial *doctor-and-patient* trans-subjectivity.

The matrixial apparatus made itself available to me through the act of painting. Putting it 'in the service' of psychoanalysis means a temporary contraction of its fluid sense into a particular channel. Thus the function of art for psychoanalysis may be to enlarge the scope of the unconscious and to question sex difference through analogies to phantasmatic binding with the lost *objet a* and with partial-objects, through relational trauma and phantasy, through further cohering with imaginary representation, through further adhering with desire, and by opening new symbolic significance that incorporates transferential history. The function of psychoanalytic theory for art may be to lend its conceptual tools to exposing the existence in art of a site of yet unformulated knowledge about sexuality and subjectivity, to clarify this site as a source for ideas that are awaiting signification in language, and to articulate them. If the act of painting elevates the screen of phantasy into a screen of Vision, by way of Ideas, while suspending without removing the veil of amnesia, and if it creates with its veil of amnesia memory as a *future anterior*, psychoanalysis may use revelations from the screen of Vision to perforate the veil of amnesia in the transference/counter-transference relations and attain/produce memories of trauma that are otherwise inaccessible but without which healing is impossible.

The encounter between trauma, phantasy, and desire behind the veil of amnesia yet without lifting it, or while producing it, is what is proper to artwork. If painting enables me to articulate something via ideas issued by/in/from it, it is in an after-time, from a temporary artist-as-viewer site still saturated with *doctor-and-patient* affectations. If psychoanalytic discourse reposes on 'woman' as absence, on the impossibility of elaborating what is beyond the phallus, on the impossibility of feminine rapport and on the *othering* of 'woman' to the point of her foreclosure, in an analogy to a 'gaze' that is the forever schized so that a certain unconscious and a split subject can emerge, then art may be a site from which some light may be shed on an-other 'woman', for in the act of painting the schize between the gaze and the eye melts and is woven into swerved difference. This act of art is not accessible to 'therapy', but the doctor and the patient in *transference/counter-transference* relations may elaborate something from whatever is imprinted for the first time in the transferential borderspaces of art, in order to lift culture's veil of amnesia.

## Notes

1 Most quotations from French sources were translated by Joseph Simas and Bracha Lichtenberg Ettinger. Existing English translations have often been modified. References indicate the corresponding passage in the published English translation, where available.

2 '*Sinthôme*' is Lacan's return to an ancient term which he uses to describe the symptom, as transformed by the writer into a piece of literature. It plays on *saint homme* (saintly man) and the English *sin* (sinful man), and refers to psychosis.

3 The scope of this article does not allow me a detailed presentation of the *objet a*. For further explanations see Lacan (1964) and Lichtenberg Ettinger (1995a, 1995b).

4 Lacan is referring to Freud's patient.

5 I.e., they do not simply indicate two different organs, the female womb and the male penis. See Lichtenberg Ettinger (1992, 1996a and 1997).

6 I have coined the term 'co-poïesis' after Maturana and Varela's 'autopoïesis' (1980). I use co-poïesis to designate a reciprocal but different trans-psychic engendering of partial subjects by one another in the matrixial borderspace.

7 I define *withness*-in-differentiation as jointness that puts the *I* and the *non-I* in a witnessing and sharing (with) relations.

8 *Savoir* is French for 'knowledge'. *Ça* is the 'Id' (as well as 'this') and *voir* is 'to see'.

9 Non-equivalence (Lacan, 1975–6) in no way implies inequality of rights.

10 On connectionism and sub-symbols, see Smolensky (1988).

11 It was Lacan in his 1972–3 and 1975–6 seminars who spoke of a *feminine-supplementary jouissance*. But for him, this *jouissance* is entirely incomprehensive in principle for both men and women.

12 Freud differentiates between two uses of the term unconscious: one to designate a particular system, which for Lacan corresponds to the treasure of repressed signifiers, the other to designate a phenomenon. I use the term non-conscious to indicate this second possibility of unconscious phenomena outside the 'unconscious' as a system (Freud, 1916–7: 437).

13 I am re-introducing and subverting the meaning of a *beside* rejected by Freud, for he believed in the more phallic *replacement* of the patient's old ideas with new

ones. Freud considered the *beside* only in relation to hypnosis, and he rejected it altogether when he replaced hypnosis with transference (Freud, 1916–7: 437).

14 'Compassion' in Hebrew: matrixes or wombs: *rahamim*.

15 In the theoretical passage from positing the analyst as a subject *who is meant to know* in the transference to positing him as an *objet a*, there also occurs a certain devaluation of the father's position and a movement from the definition of transference as *regression* to its definition as a meeting of the subject with a remnant (*objet a*), realized for the patient in the figure of the analyst.

16 According to Lacan's repeated claim (1972–3), a 'woman' is *not-All* in the phallic function.

17 Moreover, psychosis in a woman may relate to a total foreclosure of the matrixial stratum or to its melting into the phallic stratum. I therefore claim a 'normal'-'neurotic' dimension of the matrix and not its foreclosure as psychosis (see Lichtenberg Ettinger, 1997).

18 I start from heterogenesis in the sense of Lévinas, Deleuze and Guattari, but continue it in a slightly different way in the matrix. For Lévinas, for example, the total otherness of the Other-'woman' is its condition, while in the matrix I emphasize difference-in-jointness where 'woman' is not a 'total' Other. In this account, subjectivity, trauma, phantasy, and Vision are far from being private non-historical entities that a certain perspective in art history presents them to be in order to establish itself as its opposite, as the ethical one.

19 This is a claim to *non-Oedipal matrixial sublimation*.

20 Modifications in general agreement with the direction taken by the British Independent group and the British/American Relational group working around the journal *Psychoanalytic Dialogues*.

21 My non-Oedipal position, close in some aspects to Deleuze and Guattari's *Anti-Oedipus* (1983), diverges from it on several major points, and this is one of them: severality versus multiplicity.

22 Freud refers to an archaic memory that passes from one generation to another as a phylogenetic memory (1939: 102).

23 I am referring to the idea of 'events without witnesses' (an expression of Dori Lawb's), which is in my view linked to the matrixial gaze (Felman and Lawb, 1992). These events can be carried in a matrixial space and transformed by a matrixial gaze.

# References

Buci-Glucksmann, Christine (1995) 'Inner space of Painting', in *Bracha Lichtenberg Ettinger, Halala – Autistwork* (catalogue), Aix en Provence/Jerusalem: Arfiac/Israel Museum, 43–68.

Deleuze, Gilles (1993) *The Fold: Leibniz and the Baroque*, trans. Tom Conley, Minneapolis: University of Minnesota Press.

—— (1997) *Essays Critical and Clinical*, trans. Daniel W. Smith and Michael A. Greco, Minneapolis: University of Minnesota Press.

—— (2000) *Proust and Signs: The Complete Text*, trans. Richard Howard, Minneapolis: University of Minnesota Press.

Deleuze, Gilles and Félix Guattari (1983) *Anti-Oedipus*, trans. R. Hurley, M. Seem and H. R. Lane, Minneapolis: University of Minnesota Press.

Duchamp, Marcel (1975) *Duchamp du signe*, Paris: Flammarion.

Felman, Shoshana and Lawb, Dori (1992) *Testimony: Crises of Witnessing in Literature, Psychoanalysis and History*, London: Routledge.

Freud, Signmund (1910a–c) 'First, Second, and Fourth Lectures', *Five Lectures on Psycho-analysis*, in *Standard Edition of the Works of Sigmund Freud*, vol. 11, London: Hogarth, 1957, 9–48.

—— (1916–7) 'General Theory of the Neuroses,' *Introductory Lectures on Psycho-analysis*, in *Standard Edition of the Works of Sigmund Freud*, vol. 16, London: Hogarth, 1963, 431 –47.

—— (1919) *The 'Uncanny'*, in *Standard Edition of the Works of Sigmund Freud*, vol. 17, London: Hogarth, 1955, 217–52.

—— (1939) *Moses and Monotheism*, in *Standard Edition of the Works of Sigmund Freud*, vol. 18, London: Hogarth, 1964, 7–37.

Lacan, Jacques (1961–2) *L'identification* (unpublished seminar), n. pag.

—— (1964) *The Four Fundamental Concepts of Psycho-Analysis* (seminar of 1964), trans. Alan Sheridan, New York: Norton, 1981.

—— (1964–5) *Les problèmes cruciaux de la psychanalyse* (unpublished seminar), n. pag.

—— (1968–9) *D'un autre à l'Autre* (unpublished seminar), n. pag.

—— (1971–2) *Ou pire* (unpublished seminar).n. pag.

—— (1972–3) *Le Séminaire de Jacques Lacan. Livre XX. Encore*. Jacques-Alain Miller (ed.), Paris: Seuil, 1975.

—— (1973–4) *Les non-dupes errent* (unpublished seminar), n.pag.

—— (1975–6) *Le sinthôme* (unpublished seminar). n. pag.

Lévinas, Emmanuel (1993) 'In conversation with Bracha Lichtenberg Ettinger', in *Time is the Breath of the Spirit*, Oxford: MoMA.

—— (1997) 'Que dirait Eurydice', *Barca!* 8: 213–4.

Lichtenberg Ettinger, Bracha (1992) 'Matrix and Metramorphosis', *Differences*, 4.3: 176–208.

—— (1993) *Matrix – Halal(a) – Lapsus, Notes on Painting. 1985 – 1992*, Oxford: MoMA.

—— (1995a) *The Matrixial Gaze*, Leeds: Feminist Arts and Histories Network (Leeds University)

—— (1995b) 'Woman as *Objet a* Between Phantasy and Art', *Journal of Philosophy and the Visual Arts*, special issue on *Complexity*, 6: 57–77.

—— (1996a) 'Metamorphic Borderlinks and Matrixial Borderspace', in *Rethinking Borders*, John Welchman (ed.), London/Minneapolis: Macmillan/University of Minnesota Press, 125–59.

—— (1996b) 'The With-In-Visible Screen', *Inside the Visible*, C. De Zegher (ed.), Cambridge, MA: MIT P, 89–113.

—— (1997) 'Feminine/Prenatal Weaving in Subjectivity-as-Encounter', *Psychoanalytic Dialogues* 7.3: 367–405.

Lyotard, Jean-François (1995) 'Diffracted Traces', in *Bracha Lichtenberg Ettinger, Halala – Autistwork* (catalogue), Aix en Provence/Jerusalem: Arfiac/Israel Museum, 5–31.

Maturana, Humberto and Varela, Francisco (1980) *Autopoiesis and Cognition: The Realization of the Living*, Boston Studies in the Philosophy of Science, vol. 42, Boston: D. Riedel.

Merleau-Ponty, Maurice (1968) *The Visible and the Invisible*, trans. Alphonso Lingis, Evanston, Ill.: Northwestern University Press.

Smolensky (1988) 'On the Proper Treatment of Connectionism', *Behavioural and Brain Sciences*, 11: 1–74.

# 15

# FROM TRANSFERENCE TO THE AESTHETIC PARADIGM

## A conversation with Félix Guattari

*Bracha Lichtenberg Ettinger*[1]

BLE: While studying the transcripts of the Jacques Lacan's seminars, I found a passage where you said something to this effect: When Lacan left the International Psychoanalytic Association and founded the Freudian School, breaking with a long tradition in the psychoanalytic movement, when he said '*I found; as always, alone*', he committed an act that weighs upon each and every one of us. He demanded of us a kind of return, in a certain avoidance of his responsibilities. Similarly, when he rebaptized something that had come down to us from the 'part-object' as '*objet petit a*', his act of denomination, his assumption of the paternity of a notional reclassification, placed all of us in a transferential relation toward his enacting of psychoanalysis after Freud. How are we to speak, after this act? It strikes me as having had an inhibiting effect. Most of us, certainly myself, have found it difficult to know how to proceed analytically in specific fields that are not exactly Lacan's, or that do not follow closely in his wake. We have a problem talking about our involvement in psycho-analysis. Or rather, our problem is that we don't want to talk about it in ways other than those signalled by Lacan.

To this, Melman retorted: 'It's hard for me to relate to that. I don't see the slightest problem, I don't sense the slightest shadow'. To which you replied, 'It's been going on for years'.

I had the impression that the idea of an enduring transference situation had been preoccupying you at the time, and that you were already ripe for a split. Since then, there has been a lot of water under the bridge. I don't want to take you back to May 1968, only to ask: are you still today, in some way, a 'Lacanian' analyst? Transference: what's left of it?

FG: I no longer define myself as Lacanian. You're right, there has been a lot of water under the bridge – a whole life's current. Today, I situate myself in a very different place. Whether the discourse is Lacanian, Jungian, or Adlerian, it matters little. Everything works. Everything is acceptable. I speak of '*discourses of reference productive of subjectivity*'. What matters to me is clarifying criteria for getting beyond the oppositions between the different kinds of discourse.

I do not believe that there exists a subjectivity that does not produce a narrative text. However, it is not the content of the text that is decisive. What is decisive is its repetition. There is also the repetition of the family romance, for example, or the repetition of phantasy. I don't make a distinction between Lacan's discourse and its practice, its social dimension. The unconscious, as Lacan formulates it or according to any other definition, is only a *model of production of subjectivity* that creates itself in and for a certain context, and is measured by its *existential function*. For me, individual, collective, and institutional mechanisms work in concert in the production of subjectivity.

BLE: In the context of the oscillation between theories of the drive and theories of object relations, how do you see emotional states that are generally interpreted as moments in a transferential process? In particular, what happens in a negative transference situation? You have been very sensitive to the negative effects of transference and the inhibitions they bring.

FG: In my work, I do not focus on transference. My role consists in helping the patient develop means of expression and processes of subjectification that would not exist without the analytic process. Often transference is nothing more than opposition to the analysis, which Lacanians tend to use manipulatively.

The patient's feelings result from the process. For me, they are signs of what is happening in the course of the analytic process itself, not of a primal libidinality. The La Borde clinic [where Guattari worked all of his professional life] provides any number of different paths toward subjectification. It does not encourage the creation of a classical transference situation. So to return to your question, 'what's left of transference?': there are transferential mechanisms that concern parts of the body, and there are also non-personal machines. But the mechanisms of transference touch the community of care-givers as much as that of the patients. They concern the whole gamut of activities through which the patients express themselves, which we as care-givers make possible and even encourage, and which contribute to the production of diverse nuclei of subjectification.

As for what is called 'negative transference', when resistance to analysis is produced, the analysis can in my opinion be stopped, at any point that it is not working. I do not agree with the myth that everything continues as usual during 'negative transference'. This is a myth analysts use to console themselves. Because it is a question of the production of new nuclei of expression, and not of the unmasking of pre-existent contents, I think of my active participation, and that of other personnel or communitarian elements, as *catalytic*. Either my work is effective, and I'm a good catalyser, or it is not, and I'm not, and in that case the process must be interrupted.

BLE: Yes, but when the analyst operates in the 'field', she is taking unforesee-able risks. Something directly connected to her active presence, to the fact that she cannot neutralize the surroundings, may emphatically not work with certain patients.

FG: In any case, even in a different therapeutic framework, an analysis that is not working after six months should cease. It's a pathogenic process.

BLE: Your critique of transference takes you in several directions. First, you decompose transference into numerous particles connected with indi-vidual, social, machinic, and even cosmic mechanisms. Then you disperse it among several sources. You even transfer its origin into the present, rather than conceiving of it as a return to the past. Not much remains of the concept as we have known it since Freud. But let us try to simplify, and to isolate, in the abstract, the caregiver/patient relation. On the one hand, you mean to abstain from 'Lacanian' transference, which you qualify as manipulative, and on the other you outright reject negative transfer-ence, or any interminable transference. In practice, when you are faced with a specific patient, what do you do?

FG: In practice, at the La Borde clinic, I participate in a great many ways. I involve myself on the social level of the patients' activities. It is therefore very difficult to talk about transference in isolation. The 'face to face' encounter takes place within a complex institutional system. It took me some time to shed the collective analytic superego. Analysts live in perpetual fear. They lose themselves in the gap between theoretical and practical discourse, and can't find the courage to take initiative.

BLE: That you involve yourself means that the patients are not the only ones who must be 'productive', and that you also must renew yourself and create. In transferential relations that I term *matrixial*, I see change in myself, the analyst, as a sign of progress in the treatment, occurring in a matrixial edge of relational space existing in-between the patient and myself, even if the patient has broken down temporarily. Thus there can be temporary situations where the patient does not progress, and even turns against me, and in spite of it all a productive development occurs. That is because the changes each of the participants undergo, in relation to each other and to their common borderspace, through their matrixial relation of *metramorphosis*, are not necessarily synchronous.

FG: But then you don't consider the process blocked. Neither do you attribute it to an *individual* libidinal drive projected onto you. And if you yourself progress, you don't interpret what is happening as 'resistance', and you don't use that kind of interpretation to justify a frozen situation of enduring hostility. And you don't hold someone else responsible for that situation. Isn't that right? Given that you assume the production and growth of a common subjective stratum of encounter, on the basis of a shareable prenatal/feminine stratum that your model theorizes as escaping

Oedipal phallocracy, wouldn't the very concept of transference have to be transformed accordingly?

BLE:  It's true, when you go from the phallic stratum to the matrixial stratum, even silence and perturbation are differently creative – as in painting. It becomes evident, through the processes of the painting's creation, that the painting is not an object. Perturbation as creation, interruption of transmission …

FG:  And silence. You can see it in your painting: the machinic partial-object participates in an accumulation of intensities as part of a creation of subjectivity. This is all the more so because you don't pile up objects in an 'installation'. Instead, everything gets tangled up in the painting, *intensities* pile up in it, beyond all intentionality. It's not that the human partial-object is perturbed by a machinic partial-object that supposedly accosts it. Rather, interference or perturbation themselves become a 'refrain', as does silence. In your painting, when the historical partial-object bursts into a process treating the human individual, or when the corporeal partial-object bursts forth during a process concerning an animal partial-object, these emergences at the same time disturb and produce the aesthetic experience, become-refrain.

Although I wouldn't equate art with therapy, anti-Oedipal schizoanalysis operates with a complexity that Freudian analysis does not take into account. It therefore leads to a different aesthetic analysis. It doesn't limit itself to the individual, or even to the human. Reflections on transference must take into account ethological elements, incorporeal elements, becomings-animal, becomings-plant, non-human machines, machines of cultural subjectification like the mass media, machines of ecology and the environment. That is because unconscious phantasy deals with machines of all sorts, not just those from the past. Transference, then, has to do with *processual complexity*, with possibilities that are constantly developing. The emphasis is not on the past. In the course of his work, the analyst reveals himself and reinvents himself and takes risks. Instead of interpreting transference, he concentrates on what will reveal itself to be a new *polyphonic nucleus* of subjectification, something that was not imagined in advance.

The analyst faces the flow of the present, and the future, emphasizing existential territories rather than the symbolic, linguistic signifier. So to return to your question, the analyst who gets involved may well fail, but 'negative transference' and 'resistance', based on the analysis of pre-existent structures, simply serves to protect the analyst's honour.

BLE:  The dominant theoretical approaches in France, which have developed out of structuralism, close ranks around the linguistic signifier, disregarding non-discursive resonances and the emotional pathways connected to them. They disregard what you call *non-verbal intensities* that blaze existential terrritories and 'pathic' routes.

FG: Right. The linguistic signifier in no way encloses all of the components combining to produce subjectivity. But more generally, I want to emphasize that analysis has passed *from a scientific paradigm to an aesthetic paradigm*. In my opinion, young people today who try to apply Lacanian concepts in practice are just crazy. It's absurd, it's impossible. On the other hand, someone like Françoise Dolto, who knew how to work without getting bogged down in therapeutic theory, was just fabulous.

BLE: What do you think of the divisions between analysts in France, of the proliferation of groups, of therapists and patients? It's a very particular model that is creating a new situation that will have influence abroad.

FG: Already in the days of the Freudian School, I used to say that annual schisms should be practised as a principle. In the Freudian School, each had her territory. There was an enormous amount of difference and openness. But toward the end of his life, Lacan, old and sick, was no longer master of his acts and thoughts. Jacques-Alain Miller, who took over responsibility for Lacan's writings, wanted all the power for himself, he wanted to lord it over everyone. In that kind of situation, divisions are a way of refinding difference and opening. But beyond that, I think we must aspire to a wider kind of opening, beyond the model of diverse little groupings. Analysis must go outside, become a process that calls into question all social structures, the family, the school, the community. If analysis really is a process of the production of subjectivity, then what I would like to see some day is teachers and schoolmasters who are analysts.

BLE: In that case, what would be the particular meaning of analysis?

FG: Its meaning would reside in its *processual direction*, in its processual openness, in the refrain, understood not as a signification, nor as a petrified eternal repetition, nor as a fixation, but in the existential sense of an auto-affirmation.

BLE: In your theoretical approach, analysis would take into account lines of virtuality that carry this direction of creation toward the future?

FG: Exactly. The refrain holds together partial components without abolishing their heterogeneity. Among these components are lines of virtuality that are born of the event itself and reveal themselves, at the very moment of their self-creation, in the mode of always having been, with time itself conceived as a nucleus of temporalization and mutation. Thus the refrain gives new meaning to therapeutic interpretation.

Translated by Brian Massumi

## Notes

1 Between 1986 and 1988, I translated into Hebrew some of Jacques Lacan's writings. I accompanied that translation with a series of articles on the development of his theory and the changes it had inspired in psychoanalytic associations in France, beginning in the 1950s. As a follow-up to this series of articles, I interviewed

several psychoanalysts about the state of psychoanalysis in France 'after Lacan'. Among them was Félix Guattari. I was particularly interested in learning something about what remained of the transference that the analysts had developed in relation to Lacan, in the specific and extraordinary context of the Paris scene, which seemed to me to be characterized by a peculiar kind of susceptibility, and even violence (more or less contained). This led me to think about the concept of transference in general, and what remained of it. The Israeli journal in which my series of articles and translations appeared in 1989–90 (Lichtenberg Ettinger, 1989–90) did not see fit to publish this interview with Guattari, conducted at his home in Paris on 20 June 1989. I subsequently submitted it to the journal of the Israeli Lacanian association, which also declined to publish it. I then produced the Hebrew text in my workshop in 1990, in seven signed and photocopied copies, under the title *Analysts Live in Perpetual Fear*. In 1994, I reprinted ten copies of the text in Hebrew and French under the title *Le transfert, ou ce qu'il en reste* (*Transference, or What's Left of It*).

# References

Lichtenberg Ettinger, Bracha (1989–90) 'Introduction to the Study of the Writings of Jacques Lacan, and to the Question "Who is the Analyst?"' in *Sihot – Dialogue: Israeli Review of Psychotherapy*, 3:2 (1989): 194–207; 3:3 (1989): 85–93; 4:1 (1989): 44–53; 4:2 (1990): 136–8; 4:3 (1990): 212–6.

# INDEX

Note: numbers in italics indicate illustrations.

*Irreducible to one another* (21)